SOFTWARE QUALITY: ANALYSIS AND GUIDELINES FOR SUCCESS

Capers Jones, Chairman
Software Productivity Research, Inc.
1 New England Executive Park
Burlington, MA 01803
Phone 617 273-0140
FAX 617 273-5176
E-mail capers@spr.com
CompuServe 75430,231
World Wide Web http://www.spr.com

ABSTRACT

Software quality has long been a key factor in business competition. The companies with the best software quality levels also tend to have the shortest times to market, and are most likely to be able to compete successfully.

These same companies are less likely to end up in court because of damages caused by poor software quality.

Many claims have been made about software quality and how to achieve it. Few of these claims are supported by empirical data. From surveys covering some 600 enterprises and almost 7000 projects, the tools and methods being used for software quality purposes have been reviewed. A total of more than 70 quality approaches are discussed here.

Some quality approaches such as inspections work very well and are supported by solid empirical data. Others approaches such as ISO 9001 certification seem to have little or no tangible impact. Two common quality metrics, "cost per defect" and "lines of code" or LOC have serious flaws and are hazardous for exploring software quality or software economics.

This book summarizes both average and "best in class" software quality approaches and provides quantified data on the defect levels and defect removal efficiency levels achieved by top software development groups.

Books are to be returned on or before
the last date below.

Software Quality

Analysis and Guidelines for Success

Capers Jones

LIVERPOOL
JOHN MOORES UNIVERSITY
AVRIL ROBARTS LRC
TITHEBARN STREET
LIVERPOOL L2 2ER
TEL. 0151 231 4022

LIVERPOOL JMU LIBRARY

3 1111 00768 2733

THOMSON
COMPUTER PRESS

International Thomson Computer Press
I(T)P® An International Thomson Publishing Company

London • Bonn • Boston • Johannesburg • Madrid • Melbourne • Mexico City • New York • Paris
Singapore • Tokyo • Toronto • Albany, NY • Belmont, CA • Cincinnati, OH • Detroit, MI

Copyright © 1997 Capers Jones, Chairman, SPR, Inc.

 International Thomson Computer Press is
A division of International Thomson Publishing Inc.
The ITP Logo is a trademark under license.

All rights reserved. No part of this work covered by the copyright hereon may be reproduced or used in any form or by any means—graphic, electronic, or mechanical, including photocopying, recording, taping, or information storage and retrieval systems—without the written permission of the publisher.

Products and services that are referred to in this book may be either trademarks and/or registered trademarks of their respective owners. The Publisher(s) and Author(s) make no claim to these trademarks.

While every precaution has been taken in the preparation of this book, the Publisher and the Author assume no responsibility for errors or omissions, or for damages resulting from the use of information contained herein. In no event shall the Publisher and the Author be liable for any loss of profit or any other commercial damage, including but not limited to special, incidental, consequential, or other damages.

For more information, contact:

International Thomson Computer Press
20 Park Plaza, 13th Floor
Boston, MA 02116
USA

International Thomson Publishing Europe
Berkshire House
168–173 High Holborn
London WCIV 7AA
England

Thomas Nelson Australia
102 Dodds Street
South Melbourne, 3205
Victoria
Australia

Nelson Canada
1120 Birchmount Road
Scarborough, Ontario
Canada M1K 5G4

International Thomson Publishing Southern Africa
Bldg. 19, Constantia Park
239 Old Pretoria Road, P.O. Box 2459
Halfway House, 1685 South Africa

International Thomson Publishing GmbH
Königswinterer Strasse 418
53227 Bonn
Germany

International Thomson Publishing Asia
221 Henderson Road #05-10
Henderson Building
Singapore 0315

International Thomson Publishing Japan
Hirakawacho Kyowa Building, 3F
2-2-1 Hirakawacho
Chiyoda-ku, 102 Tokyo
Japan

International Thomson Editores
Campos Eliseos 385, Piso 7
Col. Polanco
11560 Mexico D.F. Mexico

International Thomson Publishing France
1, rue st. Georges
75 009 Paris France

QEBFF 16 15 14 13 12 11 10 9 8 7 6 5 4 3 2
Library of Congress Cataloging-in-Publication Data

(available upon request)

ISBN: 1-85032-867-6

Publisher/Vice President: Jim DeWolf, ITCP/Boston
Project Director: Viv Toye, ITCP Boston
Manufacturing Manager: Sandra Sabathy Carr, ITCP/Boston

Production: Jo-Ann Campbell • mle design • 562 Milford Point Road • Milford, CT 06460

TABLE OF CONTENTS

FOREWORD

In the course of a lifetime most people usually encounter a few written works that change their perceptions of the world or are so powerful they actually shape their thinking. Works that come to mind are typically in the field of literature, great plays, and perhaps biographies. However, in my own professional career, a 25 page article appearing in Volume 17 Issue Number 1 of the *IBM Systems Journal* in 1978 clearly sticks out in my mind.

It was written by an IBM employee that had worked on special projects exploring the technologies of programming and the cost effectiveness of various programming methods. This person had joined IBM in 1967 as a programming writer and prior to joining IBM had worked as a programmer/analyst for Crane Corporation and for the U.S. Public Health Service in Washington D.C. This employee also received a B.A. in English in 1961. This employee was T. Capers Jones. The article was entitled *Measuring programming quality and productivity*.

In 1978, the state of the art of software quality was both summarized and advanced in those 25 pages. Today the state of the art, summarized by the same author, fills this volume. More importantly, an understanding of the content and context of this book is essential for today's software engineer.

The world of global software development and software competitiveness is upon us. Without software, all the hardware developments in processors, networks, and telecommunications are valueless. With adequate levels of quality, the software itself is rendered useless. Companies, and perhaps nations, incapable of producing quality software or recognizing the essential ingredients in quality software are doomed to fall behind competitively. Clearly a lot has changed technologically, politically, and competitively in the 18 years since that *IBM Systems Journal* appeared. However the need for an understanding of software quality and quality practices has not.

From a basic understanding of the primary factors impacting software quality to the quality issues impacting the Year 2000 software crisis, this book covers the quality landscape thoroughly and deeply. Particular attention should be paid by the reader to more than the metrics presented herein...social, political, and peopleware implications are included to.

LIVERPOOL
JOHN MOORES UNIVERSITY
AVRIL ROBARTS LRC
TITHEBARN STREET
LIVERPOOL L2 2ER
TEL. 0151 231 4022

This book also supplies a context for quality by connecting the many disjoint pieces that float around the literature and are spoken about at conferences. Development techniques, environments, and processes are tied together along with all important measures that must be woven into the fabric of software to ensure quality. From client/server to object to RAD, it's all covered and discussed. Best of all the data that you need to calibrate your own position and quality improvement velocity is there in terms of benchmark data.

The state of the art is moving constantly. This book is both a snapshot of the present and snapshot of the future for those that make the best use of it. Read it and learn, ideally faster than your competitors, from the accumulated wisdom of one of the most distinguished people in the field, T. Capers Jones.

Dr. Howard Rubin
Rubin Systems, Inc.

PREFACE

Many good books on software quality are available, but there is also a severe shortage of solid, quantitative data about quality and software defect rates. Further, there is a very severe shortage of data about how various quality control approaches such as inspections, ISO certification, or the many kinds of testing actually operate and what kinds of results they achieve in terms of improving quality, or not as the case may be. There is plenty of information about how to perform things like ISO certification, but little or nothing in print about what kind of quality results are being achieved afterwards.

A shortage of quantitative data has characterized the software industry since its beginning. The software quality community has also suffered from lack of firm empirical findings. One of the main reasons for the dearth of solid data has been long the use of the "lines of code" or LOC metric in the general software literature and the software quality literature as well.

Other widely used measurement approaches for quality are also suspect or known to be flawed. For example, the well-known "cost per defect" metric tends to penalize high quality and approach infinity as quality improves due to the impact of fixed costs. Even the "cost of quality" concept is not a good match for software projects and an expanded alternative is suggested later in the book.

In the mid-1970s Allan Albrecht and his colleagues within IBM developed the function point metric. Function point metrics are synthetic metrics derived from enumerating and weighing five external attributes of software applications: inputs, outputs, inquiries, logical files, and interfaces.

Function point metrics were placed in the public domain by IBM in October of 1979. Since that time, usage of function point metrics has expanded widely. The non-profit International Function Point Users Group (IFPUG) and its affiliates now constitute the largest software metrics association in the world. IFPUG and its affiliates are now the major software measurement associations in at least 20 countries.

Unlike lines of code metrics, function point metrics can be used to explore the quality and defect levels of non-coding deliverables. This means that it is now possible to analyze the relative contribution of errors which originate in requirements, in design, and in other non-code work products such as user manuals and training materials.

Much of the data in this book is expressed in terms of function point metrics. Version 4 of the IFPUG counting rules are assumed unless otherwise stated.

Although function point metrics are superior to metrics such as lines of code and cost per defect, even function points do not cover every topic of importance to the software quality community. For example, the emerging and very important subject of data quality is outside the current scope of functional metrics. It is hoped that perhaps a "data point" metric equivalent to the function point metric might be developed in the future.

This book attempts to place software quality on a firm, empirical basis using information derived from software assessment and benchmark studies coupled with function points for normalizing and comparing the results of different quality approaches.

The author is fortunate in having a substantial volume of data from software field studies. Since 1985 Software Productivity Research has worked performing assessment and benchmark studies with about 600 companies and gathered information on roughly 7000 software projects. Our management consulting group brings in new data at a rate of perhaps 50 projects per month, so the volume of information is increasing rapidly.

Although we have a quite lot of data, there are also biases and gaps in our data. Most of our clients are large corporations, so we have comparatively sparse data from enterprises whose software populations total to less than 50.

We're usually commissioned to study large software projects in the 1,000 to 100,000 function point range. This means that we have more data on software projects in excess of 1000 function points in size than we do small software projects of less than 100 function points in size.

We have data from more than 60 industries, including aerospace, automotive manufacturing, banking, brokerage, computer manufacturing, defense, federal government, energy and oil, entertainment, financial services, health care, hotel chains, insurance, outsource vendors, software companies, state governments, telecommunications manufacturing, telecommunications operations, retail store chains, and wholesale store chains, to give a representative sample.

However, we have never been commissioned to study software in the fast-growing computer game industry. Although we've worked with companies such as Microsoft that produce games, we were working with other groups and not with the game or entertainment portions.

We have not done very much research with universities, although universities build substantial amounts of their own software. We have also not worked very much with book, newspaper, and magazine publishers although the larger publishers have substantial portfolios of their own software.

There are about 220 industries that produce software judging by the standard industry classifications (SIC) used by the department of commerce for statistical analysis. I doubt if anyone has data from all 220 industries that produce software. Our knowledge base is fairly extensive, but no known software knowledge base is truly complete.

About 10% of our data, or roughly 700 projects out of almost 7,000, comes from overseas. Data from abroad is coming in at a rate of 10 to 15 projects a month so the volume is expanding. Here, too, there are gaps in our knowledge base. We've collected assessment and benchmark data in about 20 countries including Canada, most of Western Europe, the United Kingdom, Japan, South Korea, Australia, India, Israel, and Thailand.

However we have not done direct studies in China; we have also not studied much of the Pacific Rim, Eastern Europe (such as Russia and the Ukraine), Central and South America, and most of the Middle East. We have reviewed secondary data sources from throughout the world, but secondary data has to be used with caution in the software domain because measurement practices are so poor.

The point is that we have gaps in our data and it is not a perfect replica of the world at large. This statement is probably true for all other software research companies, too.

This book is intended for those who already have some knowledge of software quality assurance principles and practices. It is not a pure tutorial, although it does have explanatory material. What this book attempts to do is consolidate a growing body of quantified software quality assurance information. It then evaluates the information and points out which quality approaches have been highly effective.

What sets this book apart from many other books on software quality is the inclusion of current quantitative data on software quality levels and on the observed efficiency of defect removal by various kinds of reviews, inspections, and test activities.

There are many opinions about software quality, but opinions do not carry much weight unless there is quantitative data behind them. This book is an attempt to provide as much quantitative information about software quality and reliability as the current state of the art possesses. Some of the data has a high margin of error, but since numerical quality data of any kind is scarce, it is hoped that the publication will be an incentive to additional quantitative studies.

Software quality has many definitions, and some are ambiguous. Some definitions of quality are also difficult to measure. Indeed, the word "quality" is one of the most ambiguous terms in the English language and is particularly ambiguous when applied to software. In this book, the term "quality" will be used to mean software that has these six attributes:

1) Low levels of defects when deployed, ideally approaching zero defects.

2) High reliability, or the capability of running without crashes or strange results.

3) A majority of users expressing satisfaction with the software when surveyed.

4) A structure that minimizes "bad fixes" or insertion of new defects during repairs.

5) Effective customer support when problems do occur.

6) Rapid repairs for defects, especially for high-severity defects.

The limited definitions of quality used here have been selected because of hard, practical experience. The author and his colleagues at Software Productivity Research often serve as expert witnesses in litigation involving claims of poor quality in cases brought by disgruntled clients. The six quality factors discussed above in this book are the ones that tend to be important in the law suits by clients against software developers and contractors.

There is yet another reason for limiting the quality topics to the six shown. As this book is written, most software packages developed in the United States are not supported by explicit warranties. This practice must eventually be brought to an end if the software industry expects to become a true engineering discipline.

When formal warranties are issued in support of software packages, vendors will have be very thoughtful about just what is included in those warranties. It is reasonable and makes good business sense to warranty that a product will be free from serious defects and promise to repair those defects that might occur. Such a warranty provision has many precedents from other kinds of products ranging from automobiles to refrigerators.

Freedom from serious defects under field conditions is the most critical quality factor for warranty purposes. It is an interesting phenomenon, well supported by empirical data, that software projects which fail to achieve low levels of defects often fail under the other five quality definitions as well.

Software projects developed in such a way that defect levels are high at the time of release to customers are almost never capable of satisfying users in other ways. Further, there are also strong correlations between delivered defect levels and software reliability, measured using "mean time to failure" and "mean time between failures." This means that software packages with significant defect volumes still present at delivery have the highest probability of dissatisfied users and a higher possibility of ending up in court.

Conversely, software projects developed in such a way that defect levels are low at the time of release tend to have better than average levels of user satisfaction. Software reliability intervals are long as well for software with low defect levels.

Additionally, projects developed in such a way that initial defect levels are low tend to be structured well enough so that downstream maintenance operations are facilitated, too. Such projects also have a reduced probability of ending up in court under claims of breach of contract or consequential damages as a result of some harm that users have experienced from errors in the software.

Although freedom from overt defects is a major aspect of quality, the idea that quality means nothing more than error-free software is intellectually and emotionally unsatisfying. When we see other kinds of objects that impress us as being of high quality, there is also a sense of beauty, of fitness for purpose, and of elegance that goes far beyond the simple absence of overt flaws.

The aesthetic appeal of quality is hard to capture and hard to quantify. Examine a well made Japanese sword, a Stradivarius violin, a hand-crafted canoe, or a even an excellent dress or suit. All of these can be essentially flawless in terms of defects, but that aspect of quality is not what we find so attractive about objects produced by true craftsmen.

An additional aspect of quality is that the object is a perfect fit to the requirements for which it was constructed. But even this is not quite enough. The requirements themselves must be well formed and well defined so that we will know at once when we experience the object that the requirements have been met or even

LIVERPOOL JOHN MOORES UNIVERSITY
LEARNING SERVICES

exceeded. Indeed, a very subtle aspect of quality is that it sometimes excels far beyond the requirements, although this does not happen often.

The assertion that quality is a perfect response to well-formed requirements is troublesome for software. Unfortunately, many software projects have ambiguous requirements that are unstable and also difficult to understand.

For software, there is a deeper implication to the concept that "conformance to requirements" necessitates clear and well formed requirements. Software requirements historically have been a major source of errors and confusion for software projects.

For one thing, the observed rate of requirements change during the development cycle ranges from about 1% per month to more than 3% per month after the conclusion of the formal requirements phase. Second, when performing root-cause analysis on software defect origins, more than 15% of the defects found in the code can be traced back to ambiguities or errors in the requirements themselves. (Indeed the well-known "Year 2000 problem" is a prime example of a major requirements error.)

This means that to achieve good software quality levels there is yet another factor at play. The process of development must itself be analyzed, and the sources of ambiguity and error tracked down and eliminated—including errors in the requirements themselves.

An effective process that leads to high quality cannot start with testing. Testing occurs far too late in the process. Quality testing must encompass the entire life cycle, and it must begin with the requirements.

High quality software cannot really be achieved in response to ambiguous and conflicting sets of requirements. Every software deliverable and internal object needs to be carefully constructed in order to achieve high levels of overall quality.

Because software defect levels correlate so strongly with user satisfaction and other less tangible aspects of quality, two key aspects of software quality are measured by essentially all "best in class" software quality producers:

- The *defect potentials* of software applications.

- The *defect removal efficiency* of the operations used to remove defects.

The "defect potential" of a software application is defined in this book as the sum of errors or bugs found in five software artifacts:

1) Requirements

2) Design

3) Source code

4) User manuals

5) Bad fixes or secondary defects that are a byproduct of faulty defect repairs

The "defect removal efficiency" of a series of defect removal operations is calculated by enumerating all of the defects found during development and then comparing the resulting value to the total number of defects found after a fixed interval, usually one year, of production.

Incidentally, the term "defect" simply means a problem which, if not removed, would cause software either to stop running or to produce incorrect results. Defects can be as simple as branching to the wrong location, or so complex that weeks of analysis may be needed to detect them.

Direct measurement of defect removal efficiency is one of the most powerful metrics in the software industry. As discussed later in this book, current U.S. averages are only about 85%, but "best in class" software groups are averaging more than 95% in defect removal efficiency and achieving levels higher than 99% on their top projects.

Two other important kinds of defects or errors are also discussed in this book, but there is currently insufficient data available to explore defect removal efficiency levels against these two: data errors and test case errors.

For software used for data bases, repositories, data warehouses and other purposes where information is recorded, it is a known problem that the data is frequently incorrect. Indeed the author and some of his colleagues who are exploring data quality have hypothesized that there are many more data errors than software errors.

Since most of the data comes from the clients or users themselves rather than the software vendors, data quality has not been a topic under control of software quality assurance groups. Research in data quality is new and still somewhat experimental.

Errors in test plans and test cases have been explored intermittently since the 1960s and are known to be significant problems. A related topic of redundancy, or having multiple test cases for the same condition, is also a serious problem. Yet the topic of test case errors is severely under reported in the software quality literature.

Test case defects do not reach software clients, but errors in test cases often allow other errors in code to slip by. Therefore the topics of validating test plans and exploring test case errors are both important ones for software quality assurance.

Software quality is now a major issue for the success of companies, industries, and even countries. Software itself has become one of the most pervasive technologies of the 20th century. Within the past half century, software has spread from a small number of comparatively specialized applications to become a critical factor in almost all engineered products.

Software has also become a major factor in consumer goods and in corporate operations, military strategy, tactics, and weapons systems, and in government operations. Twenty to thirty years ago, poor software quality was often annoying, but today poor software quality can literally shut down a phone system, a weapons system, and even a company. Any reasonable prognosis makes software even more critical in the future, and hence software quality will become more critical as well.

I have been associated with software quality groups for much of his career. During the 1970s he worked at two of IBM's software quality assurance labs in San Jose and Palo Alto, California. He was later assistant director of programming at ITT and a member of the corporate software council.

In 1992, my company, Software Productivity Research (also known as SPR), was commissioned to explore several different aspects of software quality internationally. This survey has become a continuing annual practice and surveys were performed during 1993, 1994, 1995, and 1996. The research will continue into the future in 1997 and beyond.

SPR's consulting engagements include the collection of quality data from many software producers. (In any given month, SPR will be working with three to six corporations. The total number of companies where SPR has gathered data is now larger than 600, and growing continuously.) In addition, SPR assists organizations in starting software quality and productivity measurement programs. As a result, the author and his colleagues have amassed a substantial volume of "hard" software quality data.

The total volume of data on software quality now available is growing very rapidly. Indeed, there is now enough software quality information to merit a full encyclopedia of software quality.

Although this book is not exactly an encyclopedia, it uses the format of an encyclopedia. That is, software quality topics are presented in alphabetical order. The alphabetic format is useful for reference books, although it is not optimal for tutorial materials.

When the book was first envisioned, I had planned to discuss about 150 topics associated with software quality in alphabetical order. As the writing got underway, I quickly realized that discussing all of those topics in enough depth to deal with fundamental issues would have created a book of more than 1,000 pages.

I had originally planned to have separate discussions of various Department of Defense standards such as DoD 2167, DoD 2167A, DoD 498, and so forth. However, the set of DoD standards is both large and in flux due to the move to adopt civilian best practices. Therefore, I opted for a single discussion of military standards rather than separate sections. This same consolidation also occurred for IEEE and ISO standards and for several other topics.

The final result is a book that covers about 70 topics that affect software quality. The length of the discussions range from less than a page to more than 20 pages. The organization of the book is alphabetical by topic, which hopefully makes finding relevant topics easy.

It is both a good and bad feeling to have too much data available. The good side is that software quality is obviously growing in importance, and it is satisfying to realize this. The bad side is that an author wants to cover topics completely, and when there is so much information to choose from, some topics have to be left out or covered briefly.

The superabundance of articles and books on quality leads to a difficult decision. A full bibliographic discussion of the software quality literature would encompass more than 1,000 journal articles and 200 books. In this book, the references are restricted to only the books and journals that actually contributed to this book. These references are shown in the form of an annotated bibliography.

Much of the data in this book is not derived from the quality literature or from secondary sources. The bulk of the information comes directly from the studies which my company performs for clients. In other words, this book contains a high volume of primary research and comparatively low volume of secondary research.

Primary research is sometimes a trial and error affair. There is a high margin of error in some of the tables and data shown in this book. My main reason for publishing data that may later turn out to be incorrect is so that other researchers will have a starting point from which to improve the findings.

ACKNOWLEDGMENTS

As always many thanks to my wife, Eileen Jones, for making this book possible in many ways. She handles all of our publishing contracts and by now knows the details of these contracts as well as some attorneys. Thanks also for her patience when I get involved in writing and disappear into our computer room. Also thanks for her patience on holidays and vacations when I take my portable computer.

Great appreciation is due to my colleagues at Software Productivity Research for their aid in gathering the data, assisting our clients, building the tools that we use, and for making SPR an enjoyable environment. Thanks to Mahashad Bakhtyari, Ed Begley, Mark Beckley, Barbara Bloom, Julie Bonaiuto, William Bowen, Kristin Brooks, Sudip Chakraborty, Craig Chamberlin, Michael Cunnane, Charles Douglis (SPR's president), Dave Gustafson, Bill Harmon, Steve Hone, Rich Gazoorian, Jan Huffman, Peter Katsoulas, Donna O'Donnell, Mark Pinis, Jacob Okyne, Kevin Raum, Cres Smith, Richard Tang-Kong, and John Zimmerman.

Special thanks to the families and friends of the SPR staff, who have had to put up with lots of travel and far too much overtime.

Thanks also to former long-time colleagues who have now retired or changed jobs: Lynne Caramanica, Debbie Chapman, Carol Chiungos, Jane Greene, Wayne Hadlock, Shane Hartman, Heather McPhee, and Richard Ward. Thanks for both the years of help and the many long hours.

Many other colleagues work with us at SPR on special projects or as consultants. Special thanks to Allan Albrecht, the inventor of Function Points, for his invaluable contribution to the industry and for his outstanding work with SPR. Without Allan's pioneering work in function points, the ability to create accurate baselines and benchmarks would probably not exist.

Many thanks to Hisashi Tomino and his colleagues at Kozo Keikaku Engineering in Japan. Kozo has translated several of my prior books into Japanese. In addition, Kozo has been instrumental in the introduction of function point metrics to Japan by translating some of the relevant function point documents.

Appreciation is also due to the officers and employees of the International Function Point Users Group (IFPUG). This organization started about 12 years ago, and it has grown to become the largest software measurement association in the history of software. When the affiliates in other countries are included, the community of function point users is the largest measurement association in the world.

Thanks also to Joel Bragen, Michael Bragen, Dr. Bill Curtis, Rich Desjardins, Charlie Duczakowski, Ken Foster, Bob Kendall, John Mulcahy, John Piasecki, and Dr. Howard Rubin for the work they do with us from time to time.

Much appreciation is due to the client organizations whose interest in software assessments, benchmarks and baselines, measurement, and process improvements have let us work together. There are too many groups to name them all, but many thanks to our colleagues and clients at Amdahl, Andersen Consulting, AT&T, Bachman, Bellcore, Bell Northern Research, Bell Sygma, Bendix, British Air, CBIS, Charles Schwab, Church of the Latter Day Saints, Cincinnati Bell, CODEX, Credit Suisse, DEC, Dunn & Bradstreet, DuPont, EDS, Fidelity Investments, Finsiel, Ford Motors, Fortis Group, General Electric, General Motors, GTE, Hartford Insurance, Hewlett Packard, IBM, Informix, Inland Steel, Internal Revenue Service, ISSC, JC Penney, JP Morgan, Kozo Keikaku, Language Technology, Litton, Lotus, Mead Data Central, McKinsey Consulting, Microsoft, Motorola, Nippon Telegraph, NCR, Northern Telecom, NYNEX, Pacific Bell, Ralston Purina, Sapiens, Sears Roebuck, Siemens-Nixdorf, Software Publishing Corporation, SOGEI, Sun Life, Tandem, TRW, UNISYS, U.S. Air Force, U.S. Navy Surface Weapons groups, US West, Wang, Westinghouse, and many others.

Appreciation is due to many researchers and authors in the quality domain whose work preceded this book and has been useful to me. All of us who write on quality are grateful to the pioneering efforts of W. Edwards Deming, Joseph Juran, and Phil Crosby whose work at ITT overlapped mine for a brief period.

Thanks also to Dr. Victor Basili, Dick Bender, Boris Beizer, Dr. Barry Boehm, Dr. Norm Brown, Dr. Bill Curtis, Tom DeMarco, Robert Dunn (another ITT colleague), Mike Fagan, Dave Gelperin, Tom Gilb, Robert Glass, Bill Hetzel, Stephen Kan, Dr. Tom Love, Dr. John Marciniak, Dr. Tom McCabe, Dr. Ed Miller, Dr. Daniel Mosley, Dr. John Musa, Glenford Myers, Bill Perry, Dr. Larry Putnam, Dr. Howard Rubin, Paul Strassman, Dr. Gerald Weinberg, Ed Yourdon, and the late Dr. Harlan Mills for their own solid research and for the excellence and clarity with which they communicate ideas about software quality. The software industry is fortunate to have researchers and authors such as these.

INTRODUCTION

Suppose you were the chief executive of a mid-sized manufacturing company. Your approval is needed for expenses of more than $100,000 and you are asked to approve the costs of building a new order-entry software system.

Your chief information officer and the vice president of sales propose to build a new client/server order entry system to replace the current system which is aging and inadequate. They present you with a planned development budget of $100,000 and a development schedule of 18 months.

What will probably not be discussed when the proposal is put before you is the fact that the chance of actually finishing the project in 18 months for the estimated amount of $100,000 is less than 50%. Since you are not a software expert, you have to approve the plan more or less on faith.

What is likely to occur as the most common scenario is that the project will take 24 months and not 18 months. The development costs will be $150,000 and not $100,000.

Although it will probably not be reported to you, the portion of the development costs that goes to software bug repairs will be about $50,000 or one-third of the total development expense.

Once the software is installed and operational, you will probably spend another $25,000 in the first year to fix bugs that slipped through and were still in the project when it was put into operation.

Even worse, your new order entry system has occasionally lost orders so that both your customers and your sales personnel are highly dissatisfied and are considering moving to the competition.

In retrospect, you were asked to approve expenses of $100,000. Yet you have actually spent $150,000. Some $75,000 or three quarters of the initial proposal went for nothing more than finding and fixing bugs. Between the development costs and the first year operational costs, 50% of a total of $150,000 has gone to finding and fixing bugs.

Even worse, the software errors have probably cost another $200,000 in lost business. Is this the way you or any other executive really want to run a business? It is not. Almost every chief executive in the world is troubled by situations just like this one.

Yet software does not have to be the way it often is. There are some companies that could have built the same application in 16 months for less than $75,000 and spent only about $15,000 for defect removal expenses. What do these companies do that ordinary companies don't do? This book shows what methods and tools are used by companies that have software under control.

Software has become a vital component of business, government, and military operations. The importance of software makes software quality a major issue. In industrialized countries, computers, and software affect every aspect of people's lives and careers from the moment of birth until death, and indeed even afterwards due to computerized processing of inheritance and estate taxes. Potentially, software errors can affect the life and safety of every citizen, and software quality is an important but hidden factor that we tend to take for granted.

In the course of a typical day, an average U.S. white collar worker might be involved with computers and software more than 100 times, often without even realizing it. Early in the morning we might use a computer at home to check for e-mail or weather.

Some of our kitchen appliances also contain embedded computers and software, so we might start using a computer if we prepare breakfast before leaving for work. (A computer malfunction in one family's microwave oven burned out a wall of their home when the oven started spontaneously after they left for work. Software quality is becoming important even for home appliances.)

If we drive to work, our automobile fuel injection system is probably computerized, as are many other automotive components. Many traffic signals on public streets are now computer controlled. If we stop to buy gasoline on the way to work, we will probably use a credit card in a computerized gasoline pump. We may stop by an automatic teller machine enroute to work. Our bank is highly computerized and indeed could not operate without high software quality.

Upon reaching work, there may be a computerized security system that requires card access to enter the building. At work, we may use at least one computer as part of our job and some of us use several, such as both desktop and portable computers. We will probably use spreadsheets, word processors, data base programs, communication packages, and perhaps custom software directly related to our jobs.

We will certainly make use of telephones, FAX equipment, and perhaps e-mail or the Internet at work, and all of these require software. Many of our contacts with clients are now computerized for things such as purchase orders and checking order status.

If we go on a business trip or vacation, our travel and hotel arrangements will be handled by computers and software. When we fly, the airplane itself is highly computerized, as is air traffic control.

If we become ill and see a physician, many medical instruments and diagnostic procedures are now computerized, as are our medical histories, pharmaceutical records, and our billing and insurance records. Should we become seriously ill, many modern diagnostic techniques such as CAT scans could not be performed at all without computers and software.

Errors in any one of these countless computerized transactions can affect us personally in unpleasant and sometimes serious ways. Some kinds of errors, such as those involving medical procedures, automotive safety devices, aircraft instruments, or associated with air traffic control, can threaten our lives.

Twenty-five years ago software quality started to become important as computers moved into business and government operations. Today, software quality is a critical topic for every company and government agency in the industrialized world.

As we enter the 21st century, software quality is going to become a major factor of global business competition. Software quality is critical to a number of major business issues, including but not limited to:

- Reducing time to market for new products.

- Enhancing customer satisfaction with all products.

- Gaining market shares from direct competitors.

- Minimizing "scrap and rework" expenses for software products.

- Attracting and keeping "top-gun" personnel.

- Minimizing the risk of litigation under outsource agreements.

- Minimizing the risk of serious operational failures or delays such as those affecting the opening of the Denver Airport or the shutdown of America Online.

- Minimizing the risk of bankruptcy or business failure which may sometimes be attributed directly to poor quality or poor software quality.

In spite of the importance of quality, the software industry has had a great deal of trouble achieving satisfactory quality levels. The quality problems associated with software are partly attributable to the nature of software itself and partly to the way software is constructed. Also, the way software quality has been measured in the past using "lines of code" metrics has contributed to the problems of poor software quality.

Until software applications are finished and operational they have been difficult to validate or test. Once software is completed and undergoing testing, it is often too late for correction of deep problems associated with flaws in the fundamental architecture or design.

Obviously, for a software application to achieve high quality levels, it is necessary to begin upstream and ensure that the intermediate deliverables and work products are also of high quality levels. This means that the entire process of software development must itself be focused on quality.

Achieving high quality in the final end product of a software project requires attention to quality in every stage of development and in every deliverable and work product starting with the initial requirements themselves. High quality cannot really be achieved if the requirements themselves are ambiguous, filled with conflicting demands, and changing at rates in excess of 2% every month.

Lack of solid empirical quality data has led to a major misunderstanding regarding the economics of quality in a software context. High quality projects cost less and ship earlier than low-quality projects because most software schedule slips and cost overruns are associated with applications that have so many bugs they can't be released. This is why software quality is now becoming a competitive weapon in many industries.

THIRTY-SIX FACTORS AFFECTING SOFTWARE QUALITY

While this book uses the format of an encyclopedia and lists topics in alphabetic order, it is useful to preview the overall contents. This introduction highlights thirty-six key factors associated with software quality: Six aspects that constitute the meaning of software quality; six origin points for software errors; six root causes of software errors; six methods for minimizing errors and enhancing quality; six software size ranges and the quality levels associated with each; and six software subindustries and the quality methods typical in each.

There are of course more than thirty-six factors that influence software quality and indeed more than 70 factors are discussed in this book alone. However, illustrating six general quality sets which each contain six quality factors is enough to make the main point of this book: Software quality is a multifaceted topic. There is no simple, "silver bullet" solution that can improve quality all by itself. If you are interested in software quality improvement be prepared to deal with many different topics.

Six Software Quality Definitions

Almost every book on software quality, and many books on manufacturing quality, begins by pointing out that "quality" is a difficult topic to define. The concept of quality is somewhat like the concept of beauty. Each of us has a strong opinion about what constitutes beauty, and we recognize it at once when we see it. But when asked to explain exactly why we regard an object as beautiful, it is hard to put the factors into words. In this book, the meaning of quality will center around six key factors:

1) Low levels of defects when deployed, ideally approaching zero defects.

2) High reliability, or the capability of running without crashes or strange results.

3) A majority of clients with high user-satisfaction when surveyed.

4) A structure that can minimize "bad fixes" or insertion of new defects during repairs.

5) Effective customer support when problems do occur.

6) Rapid repairs for defects, especially for high-severity defects.

There is strong empirical evidence that unless software can achieve low levels of bugs or defects, customers or users are almost never happy with other aspects. Indeed, if defect levels are too high, usage will decline and sometimes the product and the company can go out of business.

These six quality categories tend to be important in another context. The author and his colleagues often serve as expert witnesses in court cases between clients and software contractors who are being sued because of alleged poor quality. High defect rates and short reliability intervals, coupled with lengthy repair cycles, constitute the major claims of many court cases. Therefore, software developers would be well advised to pay serious attention to software defect levels or risk expensive litigation.

Further, software must eventually become an industry that offers explicit warranties. The basis of almost all manufacturing warranties is freedom from overt or serious defects. If software expects to be taken seriously as an industry, or to become a true engineering discipline, then warranties will be part of the future of software companies. Therefore, defect levels and reliability intervals are steps on the path to professionalism in the software community.

Defect levels and reliability intervals have a strong correlation, so in order to achieve long-term execution without catastrophic failure or unexpected results, software needs to achieve low defect levels. Low defect levels result from a synergistic combination of defect prevention and defect removal strategies. Neither prevention nor removal, by itself, is fully sufficient. Both are needed to achieve exemplary quality levels.

User satisfaction is a complex topic covering multiple factors, including ease of learning, ease of use, usefulness of features, reliability, customer support, and defect repair intervals. Any software product aiming at high levels of user-satisfaction must achieve high quality levels.

Since both defect repairs and future enhancements are the norm for software once it goes into production, a minor but significant aspect of quality is thinking ahead about future updates. This means that the software should be well structured, include useful comments and module prologs, and have error messages that are clear and unambiguous.

When software problems do arise, vendors and development organizations need to meet two additional criteria in order for clients to be satisfied: 1) Customer support should be easy to access, courteous, and knowledgeable; and 2) Repairs for defects, and especially for high-severity defects, should be rapid.

Six Software Defect Origins

The next topic to be discussed is the sources of software errors or defects. The six main origin points for software errors are errors or problems deriving from:

1) Requirements

2) Design

3) Source code

4) User manuals or training material

5) "Bad fixes" or mistakes made during repairs

6) Flawed test cases used by the application

All six origin points for software defects have been measured by leading companies for more than 30 years. For example, IBM's quality assurance labs were exploring front-end quality issues as long ago as 1965. (Note that the author was employed by IBM from 1965 until 1978.)

IBM developed an automated software defect reporting system in the early 1960s that accumulated data on: 1) the numbers of software defects found; 2) the severity levels of reported defects; 3) whether the bugs were found by means of reviews, inspections, tests, or by customers; and 4) whether the defects entered the application from requirements, design, code, manuals, or whether they were secondary defects that were accidental byproducts of prior defect repairs.

The data available from IBM's defect reporting system was very sophisticated for the era of the 1960s and led to a number of important quality discoveries, including but not limited to the following:

*   Front-end requirements and design problems outnumber coding problems.

*   Coding errors in large systems tend to clump in "error-prone modules."

*   Formal inspections are more efficient than testing to find software bugs.

*   Secondary "bad fixes" can be very troublesome unless controlled.

*   Test cases and test libraries are often buggy themselves.

*   High quality leads to short schedules and low development costs.

*   Lines of code metrics don't work for cross-language comparisons.

*   Function point metrics are the best choice for software quality research.

*   Function point metrics can measure non-code software defect levels.

IBM is not the only company with a long history of software quality measurement. A number of other software-intensive corporations also deployed sophisticated quality measurements and reached similar conclusions: for example AT&T, Hewlett Packard, ITT, Motorola, Raytheon, and TRW were also early in exploring software quality and collecting software defect information.

The sixth defect origin point, faulty test cases used for testing the application, is studied less often and deserves a word of explanation. Test case errors do not reach software customers themselves, but gaps, omissions, and overt errors in software test cases tend to allow many serious defects to escape the net of defect removal operations and flow out into the field.

Therefore, it is a proper study for software quality assurance to investigate test case errors, redundancy, poor coverage, and other well-known testing problems. Unfortunately, the topic of test case errors is severely under reported in the quality and testing literature.

Six Root-Causes for Poor Software Quality

Root-cause analysis is a technique that works backwards from a particular problem and tries to ascertain what are the causative factors that led to the problem. For poor software quality, the six major root causes are the following, ranked in order of occurrence:

1) Inadequate training of managers and staff

2) Inadequate defect and cost measurement

3) Excessive schedule pressure

4) Insufficient defect removal

5) High complexity levels

6) Ambiguous and creeping requirements and designs

The first root-cause, or inadequate training of managers and staff, is endemic to the software domain. Many university software engineering curricula have no courses in software quality at all. Many other academic curricula have courses on testing, but none on inspections, quality measurement, or other topics. Academic training in quality for software managers is even worse.

Fortunately, in-house training in large corporations and commercial software education can partially fill the gaps left by poor academic curricula. However, from software assessment and benchmark studies performed by the author and his colleagues at Software Productivity Research, more than 50% of software technical staff and more than 70% of software managers are poorly trained in software quality control.

The second root-cause, poor measurement of quality and costs, leads to a kind of occupational blindness on the part of software project managers. In the absence of solid quality and cost data, many managers do not know how cost effective software quality control truly is. Conversely, software managers do not realize that failure to control quality early leads to a dangerous probability of schedule and cost overruns when testing begins.

The third root-cause, excessive schedule pressure, is a byproduct of the first two root causes, or poor training and no measurements. Since software managers lack understanding of the interrelationship of software quality control and software schedules, they tend to skimp on software quality approaches such as front-end inspections in the naive and erroneous belief that they are shortening their schedules. In reality, the schedules are heading toward major delays because the most common reason for schedule slippage is that the software does not work.

The fourth root-cause, inadequate defect removal, derives naturally from the first three root causes. Most software project managers and many technical software personnel are unqualified to plan an effective series of defect removal operations that can achieve high quality, short schedules, and low costs simultaneously.

The fifth root-cause, high complexity, is often attributable to excessive haste or to poor training and preparation. There are very powerful complexity analysis tools, and even code restructuring tools, on the commercial market, but many software personnel do not know about the availability of such tools.

The sixth root-cause, ambiguous user requirements and changing designs, are common phenomena for software projects. The observed rate at which software requirements change is roughly 1% to 3% each month after the requirements are initially determined. These changes obviously move downstream into the design. The design itself can evolve independently of the requirements. Indeed, a study at IBM in the 1970s found that "creeping improvements" introduced by software designers and programmers were almost as common as "creeping requirements" introduced by clients. The changes were well-intentioned, but sometimes extraneous to what the clients really needed.

A thoughtful analysis of modern commercial software packages such as spreadsheets, word processors, and operating systems indicates that software vendors appear to be in some kind of a heated "feature race."

Each time a vendor releases a new gimmick in a product, all other vendors do the same, and maybe add their own gimmicks as well. The result is massive suites of applications that take over 50,000,000 bytes of storage and contain features that may be used less than 1% of the time by less than 1% of the users.

The overall problem of frequent change is not so much with the changes in requirements and designs themselves, but with the fact that managers and technical personnel are not trained or equipped to deal with changes.

Rather than flexible architectures and design that envision future modifications, there is a tendency to attempt to build rigid software structures that are very difficult to modify later.

The other part of the root-cause, ambiguity, is a common problem for everything that requires understanding natural language. One of the deep problems of the software industry, far outside the scope of this book, is the need for better methods for visualizing and explaining software structures and features.

Six Software Defect Elimination Strategies

To eliminate or reduce software errors, six powerful strategies exist for achieving high levels of software quality, and all are important. These are methods and tools that lead to the achievement of:

1) Effective defect prevention

2) High levels of defect removal efficiency

3) Accurate defect prediction before the project begins

4) Accurate defect tracking during development

5) Useful quality measurements

6) Ensuring high levels of user-satisfaction

The topic of "defect prevention" refers to technologies that can minimize software errors and reduce the tendency of humans to make mistakes when performing complex intellectual tasks.

Examples of defect prevention approaches discussed in this book include joint application design (JAD), prototyping, quality function deployment (QFD), and (surprisingly) usage of software inspections. Inspections are not only the top-ranked defect removal method, but participants in formal inspections quickly learn to avoid mistakes noted during the inspections process so inspections are also among the most effective prevention activities.

The phrase "defect removal efficiency" refers to one of the most powerful of all quality metrics. The development team accumulates statistics on all bugs or defects found during development. When the software project is released, defect statistics are kept on user-reported bugs. After a fixed interval, such as one year of usage, defect removal efficiency can be calculated.

As an example of defect removal efficiency, suppose the development team found 90 bugs during development and the users of the application reported 10 bugs during the first year. In this simple example, it is obvious that the defect removal efficiency is 90% since the development team found 90 out of a total of 100 bugs.

Current industry averages for defect removal efficiency are only about 85% but "top gun" software vendors are averaging more than 95% and topping 99% on their best projects.

The topic of "defect prediction" refers to estimating the probable numbers of bugs or errors that are likely to be present. It also includes estimates of the defect removal efficiency levels of each review, inspection, and test, and then estimation of the cumulative defect removal efficiency of the entire series.

Although defect estimation is a difficult technology, there are commercial software estimation tools that can do a very good job of predicting both defect potentials and defect removal efficiency levels. There are also proprietary tools in the more sophisticated companies such as AT&T, IBM, Microsoft, and Motorola. The usage of defect estimation methods is one of the major distinguishing signs of a top-notch quality producer.

For many years, software defect tracking or keeping records about incoming defects and their repair status was a technology available only to large and sophisticated corporations who had built their own defect tracking systems.

However, starting in the early 1990s a number of commercial defect tracking tools have appeared. It is interesting that some of these tools are from start-up companies founded by ex-employees of sophisticated companies that had internal defect tracking capabilities.

An effective quality measurement program is one of the major signs of a truly sophisticated software producer. Quality measurement is so important that the overall business performance of companies with good quality measures is usually better than similar companies that lack quality measures.

The topic of "user-satisfaction" is a very specialized sub-domain within the overall field of software quality. Effective methods for achieving high levels of user-satisfaction include the use of cognitive psychologists, development and use of periodic user-satisfaction surveys, and special kinds of usability reviews and testing. Indeed, several major software vendors have built special usability laboratories that are fully instrumented and equipped with video cameras for watching typical usage patterns of software products.

Software Defects in Six Application Size Ranges

Finally, this book deals with the quality implications of six discrete software size ranges each one order of magnitude apart, since quality tends to decline as size goes up. Therefore, this book addresses software in the size range of:

1) 1 function point or 125 C statements

2) 10 function points or 1,250 C statements

3) 100 function points of 12,500 C statements

4) 1,000 function points or 125,000 C statements

5) 10,000 function points or 1,250,000 C statements

6) 100,000 function points or 12,500,000 C statements

An interesting general rule for predicting software defect potentials is to take the size of the application in function points and raise it to the 1.25 power. This simple algorithm will provide a rough estimate of the minimum sum of all problems or bugs in requirements, design, code, user manuals, and bad fixes.

Applying this algorithm to the six size ranges shown above quickly illustrates why quality control is progressively more important as overall software size gets larger: for a small application of 100 function points, the defect potential is only about 316 bugs; for a large system of 10,000 function points, the defect potential is an alarming 100,000.

Since U.S. companies only remove an average of about 85% of software defects prior to release of applications to users, it can easily be seen why careful quality control for large systems is a business and technical necessity.

Software Quality in Six Subindustries

Software quality methods tend to vary from company to company and from industry to industry. In this book, six major subindustries are discussed from a quality standpoint:

1) Systems software that controls physical devices.

2) Information systems that companies build for their own use.

3) Outsource or contract software built for clients.

4) Commercial software built by vendors for lease or sale.

5) Military software built following various military standards.

6) End-user software built for private use by computer literate workers or managers.

For quality purposes, the best industries are systems software, military software, and commercial software. Overall, systems software that controls complex physical devices has the most sophisticated quality measurements, quality assurance departments, defect removal operations, and overall quality levels.

Information systems software has been the worst in terms of quality control, and lags in measurements, pre-test defect removal, and testing sophistication.

Some of the best subindustries for software quality are computer manufacturers, telecommunication manufacturers, aerospace manufacturers, medical instrument manufacturers, commercial software companies that build operating systems, and defense manufacturers.

It is significant that these six subindustries have one important feature in common: All six support complex machines that require high-quality software in order to operate successfully.

As can be seen from this short discussion of these 36 factors, software quality is a wide-ranging topic with a host of issues and technologies involved. Let us now consider some of the specific topics associated with software quality.

ACHIEVING HIGH LEVELS OF SOFTWARE QUALITY

As software quality grows in importance, many companies are competing in the software quality domain: these include training companies, methodology consultants, test tool vendors, defect estimating and tracking tools, book publishers, among a host of others. All of these companies make claims that their goods or services will improve quality. There are a great many choices, and all claim quality improvements of significant proportions, usually without the benefit of empirical data.

For researchers, managers, and quality personnel exploring software quality, there is no standard taxonomy or schema for discussing the various and sometimes competing software quality approaches that are now available.

To provide a framework for discussing software quality, the following 10-part taxonomy was developed by the author:

1) Enterprise-wide Quality Programs

2) Quality Awareness and Training Methods

3) Quality Standards and Guidelines

4) Quality Analysis Methods

5) Quality Measurement Methods

6) Defect Prevention Methods

7) Non-test Defect Removal Methods

8) Testing Methods

9) User-satisfaction Methods

10) Post-release Quality Control

This taxonomy is not perfect, but it is at least a workable way of separating quality approaches into categories that can then be discussed and analyzed. Further, this taxonomy facilitates the selection of appropriate choices from the hundreds of available possibilities.

My colleagues and I have noted that "best in class" organizations in terms of quality tend to use methods from all 10 categories. Similar organizations with average to poor quality results tend to lack methods from several categories, such as having no enterprise-wide quality programs, failing to use non-test defect removal, or lacking any kind of quality analysis methods.

There are also interesting differences in quality approaches that vary with the size of the enterprise. Small companies with less than 50 total employees and only a few software personnel will utilize quite a different pattern from groups the size of IBM or Andersen with many thousands of software personnel and a whole complement of specialists.

Following are examples of software quality approaches noted within each of these 10 overall categories. Note that the topics are simply listed alphabetically within each major category.

Enterprise-wide Quality Programs

The quality approaches that address the entire enterprise cover many more topics than just software. They also deal with engineering, manufacturing, suppliers, support groups, and many other operational units as well as software. Because these enterprise approaches are so broad, software may even be overlooked in some of them.

The prime advantage of the enterprise-wide quality approaches is that when successful, they energize the company and create a climate where quality is appreciated and understood at all levels, from the chairman and the board down through every level of management and staff. Examples of enterprise-wide quality programs include:

- Baldrige Award preparation

- Benchmarking and "best in class" analysis

- Business Process Reengineering (BPR)

- Deming Prize preparation

- In-house quality award programs

- Quality assurance departments

- Quality goals and targets for executives

- Quality goals and targets for managers

- Quality goals and targets for technical staff

- Six-sigma quality programs

- Software Engineering Institute (SEI) Capability Maturity Model (CMM)

- Total quality management (TQM)

- Zero-defect programs

To be successful, the enterprise-wide programs need executive support from the top of the company, and they require energetic action. The well-known quality consultant W. Edwards Deming used to give his clients three years to succeed with his enterprise-wide program, and if they did not make visible progress, he would drop them as clients. This was an unusual but effective strategy which only a famous consultant could adopt.

Quality Awareness and Training Programs

This set of quality approaches is concerned with technology transfer, or disseminating information on quality-related topics throughout the enterprise.

There are many excellent conferences on quality and hundreds of books. However, these tend to attract people who already have some interest in and understanding of quality. The real problem of technology transfer in a quality context is that of reaching those who are not already predisposed to be interested in the topics associated with quality.

For top executives, the most effective way of gaining both their interest and support is to quantify the economic value that effective quality control brings to corporations. This is not an easy task, because software quality measurements have long been flawed by invalid measures such as "lines of code" and "cost per defect."

Many large corporations have in-house education and training curricula with excellent courses available on quality topics. Some have a whole range of courses running from 45-minute "executive briefings" for top management through intensive multi-day classes for in-depth training in topics such as inspections, testing, quality measurement, and other related topics. The quality awareness domain includes:

- Executive quality briefings
- External software quality seminars
- In-house software quality seminars
- Software quality professional associations
- Software quality conferences
- Software quality forums (Internet, CompuServe, etc.)
- Software quality journals, books, videos, and CD-ROMS

The quality awareness programs work very well indeed with those who are already interested in quality. The difficulty of such programs is twofold: 1) getting an audience with top executives who may not find quality a compelling topic; and 2) when top executives grant an audience, making a convincing case that quality has economic and business value.

Quality Standards and Guidelines

Many aspects of quality, including software quality, are covered by various international, national, and in-house standards. The well-known International Standards Organization (ISO) catapulted into prominence as Europe began to move toward creation of the European Union. It is a matter of sociological interest that the ISO 9000-9004 quality standards were among the first international standards to have real "clout" across national boundaries.

However, the ISO standards are not the only standards that deal with quality. In the United States, the impact of having a strong military organization has made military standards issued by the Department of Defense (DoD) a significant topic also. Indeed, since the U.S. military is regarded as the world technological leader for defense subjects, U.S. military standards are often adopted by many other countries. Therefore, among the military and defense community, the DoD standards are more pervasive than the ISO standards.

Every country has a standards organization. In addition, many industries and technologies also have standards bodies, such as the well-known standards published by the IEEE (Institute of Electrical and Electronic Engineers) and the European Computer Manufacturers Association (ECMA).

The various standards organizations are sometimes inconsistent, but in general the standards community has attempted to move toward commonality. Therefore considerable effort is being devoted to bringing various standards into concordance, or at least to eliminate major incompatibilities.

Many large corporations have in-house standards. Indeed, for software quality the internal standards used at companies such as AT&T, IBM, Hewlett Packard, Motorola, and many others are among the most effective in the world.

Sometimes these internal standards were built upon external standards such as those of the IEEE. In some cases, the in-house standards pioneered entirely new concepts such as Motorola's well known Six-Sigma quality standard.

A partial collection of various standards-issuing organizations include:

- Allied Quality Assurance Publications (AQAP) produced by NATO
- American National Standards Institute (ANSI)
- British Standards Institute (BSI)
- Department of Defense (DoD) in the United States
- Department of Defense (Def) in the United Kingdom
- Deutsches Institut fur Normung (DIN)
- European Computer Manufacturing (ECMA)
- European Space Agency (ESA)
- Federal Information Process Standards (FIPS)
- International Organization for Standards (ISO)
- Institution of Electrical Engineers (IEE)
- Institute of Electrical and Electronic Engineering (IEEE)
- Japanese Industrial Standards Committee (JISC)
- Japanese Union of Scientists and Engineers (JUSA)
- Software Publishers Association (SPA)
- Various in-house standards and guidelines by specific companies

On the whole, the software standards associated with quality have had only a marginal effect on quality. Many standards, such as those issued by the IEEE, have no provision for enforcement and can be taken or left at the discretion of whoever is using the standard.

The standards that have had some kind of mandate to ensure utilization, such as the Department of Defense (DoD) standards, tend to have more of an impact.

The new ISO 9000-9004 standards have a mandate but have not made much tangible improvement in quality as this book is written. This will be discussed later.

Unlike the standards for other occupations such as medicine and architecture, software standards seldom encapsulate proven best practices. Generally speaking, software standards are based on the subjective views of the standards committee, and seldom have even much solid empirical data behind them. I regard the gap between standards and best practices derived from empirical data as a problem which the software industry needs to address in order to become a recognized profession.

Quality Analysis Methods

Quality in products is derived from the processes used to build them. Therefore, quality analysis methods tend to explore the processes of development rather than examining the quality of the final products.

In recent years several new kinds of quality analysis or assessment methods have become prominent: Baldrige Award assessments, ISO 9000-9004 audits, and assessments using the methods of the Software Engineering Institute (SEI).

These various assessment approaches overlap to a significant degree. For example a company in serious preparation for a Baldrige Award assessment should have no particular difficulty with either an SEI or ISO assessment.

Two other analytic methods are also expanding in usage: benchmarks and baselines. In a business context the term "benchmark" refers to comparing one company's performance against another, or against a group of companies from the same industry.

The term "baseline" refers to the performance of an organization at a specific date or year, so that future progress can be measured against the initial results. Baselines and benchmarks tend to collect and use the same data, so they are often performed concurrently.

Included in the set of quality analytic methods are tools that can estimate software quality and reliability. It is a very significant achievement that it is now possible to have advanced warning about quality.

Some of these quality estimation tools will automatically adjust the results in response to various methods such as the presence or absence of inspections, programming languages, and other technologies such as prototypes, joint application design (JAD), and many other influential factors.

Significantly, that many of the various quality analysis approaches require trained specialists. Indeed, for several flavors of analysis, such as those dealing with the SEI assessments and those dealing with the ISO audits, the work needs to be done by those who are trained and have passed an examination on the materials in question. Some of the quality analysis methods are:

- Assessments
- Audits
- Baseline studies
- Benchmark comparative studies
- Cause-effect diagrams
- Defect tracking tools
- Error-prone module analysis
- Pareto analysis
- Project post-mortems
- Quality circles
- Quality estimation tools
- Quality measurement tools
- Risk analysis
- Root cause analysis

Some form of quality analysis is a necessary prerequisite to quality improvement. Most of the forms listed here have been effective when rigorously applied.

Quality Measurement Methods

The entire field of software quality has long been handicapped by the use of measurements that rank among the most imperfect and unreliable ever used. In particular, the use of "lines of code" as a normalizing metric essentially blinded the software community to the impact of bugs or errors in requirements, design, user manuals, and all other non-code deliverables.

The use of "cost per defect" measurements is just as bad since this metric cannot show the real economic differential between programming languages. Even worse, the cost per defect metric tends to penalize quality and grow higher as quality improves!

Normalizing quality data using function points as the base metric is now opening up major new avenues of research dealing with front-end quality matters in the requirements and specifications. Function point metrics are also starting to make some progress in exploring errors in test plans and test cases which seldom have been discussed in the quality literature.

A major quality topic that is not yet fully supported by metrics and measurement approaches as this book is written is that of data quality. There are no effective metrics to deal with the size of databases or data warehouses, with data quality, or to normalize the costs of repairing data defects. Quality measurements include:

- Complexity measurements

- Cost per defect measurements

- Cost of quality measurements

- Data quality measurements

- Defects per function point measurements

- Defects per KLOC measurements

- Defect distribution measurements

- Defect aging measurements

- Defect severity measurements

- Error-prone module measurements

For such an important topic, software quality is peculiarly sparse in measured data and convincing empirical studies. Part of this problem can be attributed to the flaws and errors associated with "cost per defect" and "lines of code" metrics as will be discussed later in this book.

Another reason for the lack of solid empirical data is the phenomenon that software originated as an offshoot of mathematical research. Neither mathematics nor research programs in general had a tradition of measuring topics such as productivity of the workers. Regardless of the fact that research depends upon accurate measures and metrics, those metrics are seldom turned on research itself.

Defect Prevention Methods

The class of defect prevention methods includes all approaches which can minimize the natural human tendency to make errors when performing complex tasks. Since most of the difficult problems associated with software originate in the requirements or in the design, the field of software defect prevention overlaps software specification approaches. The new research domain of "software visualization" is likely to prove fruitful in terms of defect prevention.

Measuring the effectiveness of defect prevention is much more difficult than measuring defect removal, although it is not impossible. In general, defect prevention approaches are evaluated by comparing a set of projects that use the method under investigation against a control group of similar projects that did not use the method. This is similar in principle to the way things like the effectiveness of vaccinations is explored in medical research.

Note that several defect prevention methods are also found under the heading of defect removal. In particular, participation in formal design inspections and formal code inspections ranks among the best forms of both defect prevention and defect removal. The removal aspects are more or less obvious and well-supported in the software quality literature.

The preventive aspects of inspections are not so well known, but they are equally efficacious. From observing the kinds of errors found in other people's work, participants in inspections spontaneously tend to avoid the same kinds of errors in their own work. Among the defect prevention methods may be found:

- Change-control boards
- Clean-room Development
- Code inspection participation
- Configuration control tools
- Design inspection participation

- Graphic design languages

- Joint Application Design (JAD)

- Mathematical modeling

- Model-based development

- Prototyping

- Quality function deployment (QFD)

- Reuse of certified components

- Risk analysis

- Software visualization methods

Defect prevention is similar to the concept of preventive medicine. Like preventive medicine, defect prevention can be very effective but is difficult to evaluate since it is hard to quantify problems that don't occur. Also, as preventive medicine has found, the human species tends to wait until problems occur before taking any kind of action whatsoever—whether they are dealing with their bodies or their software.

Non-Test Defect Removal Methods

The set of non-test defect removal methods happens to include several of the most effective approaches yet evaluated for software quality control: formal requirements inspections, formal design inspections, and formal code inspections. These methods are also effective in terms of defect prevention.

It is significant and supported by extensive empirical data that software quality control in "best in class" organizations depends heavily upon non-test methods prior to the start of testing.

One of the strongest abilities of the human mind is the ability to see correlations and to derive inferences from what might seem to be miscellaneous collections of facts. For complex issues involving potential software design problems or complex code structures, the human mind has not yet been challenged by automated tools.

Although the two domains are not equivalent, it is significant that human chess masters still tend to defeat expert-system chess programs. The complex range of issues that can occur when searching for potential software problems is far more difficult to master than chess, so it is not surprising that the human mind is still the most effective tool for dealing with the really tough problems of software quality control, especially for tough problems in design.

The set of non-test defect removal operations applied to software include:

- Code inspections

- Configuration audits

- Design inspections

- Editing of specifications, manuals

- Independent verification and validation (IV&V)

- Proofs of correctness

- Requirements inspections

- Risk analysis and reduction

- Syntax checkers

- Test plan inspections

- Test case inspections

- Usability reviews

Non-test defect removal remains among the most effective quality approaches ever conceived of for software projects. It is very significant that all "best in class" software quality producers make use of non-test design and code inspections.

Testing Methods

Testing is very effective in finding many kinds of "mechanical" problems with software such as overwriting the wrong memory location, branching to incorrect routines, or going through loops the wrong number of times. Testing is also effective in finding problem associated with timing or performance issues. However, for some kinds of deeper problems, testing is not very effective at all.

For errors which originate in the design and specifications of software, test cases have been noted to be ineffective. These test cases may not cover the topic at all because the design was incomplete. Even worse, if the design itself it wrong, then test cases might be constructed that confirm the error!

A classic example of testing confirming a major error is the existence of the "Year 2000" problem is millions of software applications all over the world. It is obvious that using two digits to store calendar year dates (i.e., storing 1997 as 97) would fail when 1999 rolled over to 2000 AD.

Yet all of the applications with two-digit dates were tested and the problem remains. This is because the 2-digit date field was both a business requirement and a design feature up until roughly 1994, when it became obvious that software was going to last longer than the century.

It is interesting and significant that "best in class" software houses tend to use a synergistic combination of non-test and testing activities. Prior to testing, formal design and code inspections cannot only find many errors in their own right, they also benefit the testing process by providing specifications which are more complete and have fewer errors.

It is also significant that "best in class" software groups tend to use trained testing specialists for the major kinds of testing that occurs after individual unit test by the programmers themselves; i.e., stress testing, regression testing, system testing, and the like.

The subject of testing includes these subtopics under that general heading:

- Acceptance testing
- Alpha testing
- Beta testing
- Black box testing
- Capacity testing
- Clean-room statistical testing
- Complexity testing
- Field testing
- Independent testing
- Integration testing
- Lab testing
- New function testing

- Platform testing

- Program debugging tools

- Regression testing

- Stress/performance testing

- System testing

- Test case generation

- Test coverage analysis

- Test library control tools

- Usability testing

- White box testing

Testing is a mainstream activity, but one which still needs extensive research and has gaps in the literature. Basic issues, such as the numbers of test cases needed, the ability to reuse test cases, and the automatic construction of test cases from specifications, remain open.

User-Satisfaction Methods

The topic of user-satisfaction is a multifaceted one. It is a well known fact that users are seldom satisfied with software that has a lot of bugs or overt defects. However, the mere absence of defects is not enough to ensure high levels of user-satisfaction.

It is easy enough to measure user-satisfaction once a software project is out and in the hands of users. But by then it is too late. The real goal of user-satisfaction research is to find effective ways of making users happy before the project is fully designed.

Since satisfaction is a sociological phenomenon, quite a bit of user-satisfaction research involves cognitive psychology. Indeed, some large software groups, such as IBM and Microsoft, employ psychologists and have rather well equipped "usability laboratories." These usability labs are instrumented facilities where users can try out software features under controlled conditions. Often, there will be video cameras recording user actions and even audio recordings of user comments.

Another sociological approach used for upfront needs assessment is that of "focus groups," where prospective users come together to evaluate potential features or control methods. Many commercial software vendors utilize such groups.

Also, most software packages with large user populations have some kind of user association form. These user groups serve the user community by sharing information and insights. They can also assist the product development organization by providing a channel both for requests for future improvements and for complaints about features that are not working very well. The major ways of ascertaining user-satisfaction levels include:

- Customer associations

- Customer satisfaction surveys

- Focus groups

- Human factors specialists

- Usability labs

- Usability testing

- User conferences

- User forums (Internet, CompuServe, etc.)

Achieving high levels of user-satisfaction requires dedication and quite a lot of solid effort. It also requires commitment from all levels of a company, and this is especially true at the executive level. One of the interesting byproducts of "the Internet Era" that we are entering is the ability for dissatisfied customers to organize and make their complaints known to other customers. Indeed, some customers have even established World Wide Web sites attacking companies they are dissatisfied with. User-satisfaction in a world of global nets will be a different story with than anything that has gone before.

Post-Release Quality Control Methods

Some software products have been in continuous usage for more than 20 years. For example, the Federal Aeronautics Administration (FAA) air-traffic control system was originally designed in the 1960s. The kernel of IBM's MVS operating system dates back to the original OS/360, which was also designed in the 1960s.

More recent examples include the continuing evolution of popular software packages for personal computers: Microsoft's office suite, the Lotus spreadsheet, WordPerfect, and many others are now more than 12 years old and still growing in terms of features and capabilities.

Many industries that are more than 50 years of age tend to have more people working to keep existing products running than to have people building new products. For example, in the United States there are far more mechanics who repair automobiles than there are workers in Detroit or Dearborn building new automobiles.

For software, the work of quality control does not stop with the first release. It will continue as long as there are any users at all.

The "best in class" software quality groups have efficient and extensive customer support organizations that deal with user-reported errors or questions. These customer support groups are also effective in eliciting suggestions for possible new features for future releases. The key topics associated with post-release quality include:

- Customer association support
- Customer support "hot lines"
- Defect removal efficiency calibration
- Defect tracking
- Error-prone module analysis
- Online customer support (Internet, CompuServe, etc.)
- Project post-mortems
- User-satisfaction surveys
- Warranties of software products

Quality and user-satisfaction issues do not stop with the first release. Indeed, a well designed customer support program is a major contributor to the client perception of the quality of both products and companies.

There is no "silver bullet" or a single approach that all by itself will create high-quality software. A serious pursuit of quality at the enterprise level requires selections from all 10 of the categories shown here.

Among the best companies that I have worked with, there is a significant finding that is hard to put into words. The best organizations try to do what is best, and if the best is not good enough, they try to develop something better. Innovation comes from an awareness that even the best current practices may be imperfect and need improvement.

Simply following a standard practice or even a "best current practice" may not be sufficient. The true leaders set today's standards and then try to improve them. This explains why the best in class organizations tend to develop some of their own tools, to use their own standards, and to perform their own in-house training. Often these approaches reach the outside world later, but many of them come from the pioneering work of top companies.

The best achievers in terms of quality do not follow "silver bullet" thinking or believe that quality will result from just one thing. The best organizations utilize approaches from all 10 of the categories discussed here, assuming that the companies are large ones with from 100 to many thousand software personnel.

Combinations of Software Quality Methods Noted in "Best in Class" Enterprises

Following are my observations and those of my colleagues on the quality practices that are found in industry-leading organizations that SPR's data indicates are among the top 5% of all our clients in defect prevention, defect removal, and user-satisfaction.

Note that this listing is an aggregate based on observations of about 30 organizations. No single organization utilizes all of these approaches concurrently, but most of the top 30 utilize several topics from every category.

Since there are rather notable differences in the pattern of usage associated with the size or number of software personnel, Table 1 shows three size plateaus: Large, Medium, and Small. In this context, "large" means more than 1,000 professional software personnel. The term "medium" means from 101 to 999 professional software personnel. The term "small" means less than 100 software personnel.

Table 1   Patterns of Software Quality Approaches in "Best in Class" Enterprises

	Large Enterprises	Medium Enterprises	Small Enterprises
Enterprise quality programs			
Baldrige awards	Maybe	Maybe	No
Quality assurance departments	Yes	Maybe	No
Executive quality goals	Yes	Yes	Maybe
Management quality goals	Yes	Yes	Yes
SEI CMM level 3, 4, or 5	Yes	Maybe	No

(continued)

Table 1   *(continued)*

	Large Enterprises	Medium Enterprises	Small Enterprises
Quality awareness and training			
In-house seminars	Yes	Maybe	No
Public seminars	Yes	Yes	Yes
Online quality forums	Yes	Yes	Yes
Risk-analysis training	Yes	Maybe	No
Quality standards and guidelines			
In-house standards	Yes	Maybe	No
IEEE standards	Maybe	Maybe	Maybe
ISO standards	Yes	Yes	Maybe
Quality analysis methods			
Assessments	Yes	Yes	Maybe
Baseline studies	Yes	Yes	Maybe
Benchmark comparisons	Yes	Yes	Maybe
Risk-analysis	Yes	Yes	Maybe
Quality measurement methods			
Function point normalization	Yes	Yes	Yes
Defect aging measures	Yes	Yes	Yes
Defect distribution measures	Yes	Yes	Yes
Defect severity measures	Yes	Yes	Yes
Root-cause analysis	Yes	Maybe	Maybe
Defect prevention methods			
Configuration control tools	Yes	Yes	Yes
Change control boards	Yes	Maybe	No
Design inspections	Yes	Maybe	Yes
Code inspections	Yes	Yes	Yes
Graphical specification methods	Yes	Yes	Yes
Prototyping	Yes	Yes	Yes
Risk-analysis	Yes	Maybe	Maybe
Quality function deployment (QFD)	Maybe	Maybe	No
Certified reusable materials	Yes	Maybe	Maybe

(continued)

Table 1   *(continued)*

	Large Enterprises	Medium Enterprises	Small Enterprises
Non-test defect removal methods			
Design inspections	Yes	Yes	Yes
Code inspections	Yes	Yes	Yes
Usability reviews	Yes	Maybe	Maybe
Testing methods			
Unit test by programmers	Yes	Yes	Yes
Complexity analysis	Yes	Yes	Maybe
Regression test by specialists	Yes	Maybe	No
Performance test by specialists	Yes	Maybe	No
System test by specialists	Yes	Maybe	No
Field test by clients or customers	Yes	Yes	Yes
Test coverage analysis	Yes	Yes	Yes
Test library control tools	Yes	Yes	Yes
Test case reviews	Maybe	Maybe	Maybe
Test script automation	Yes	Yes	Yes
User-satisfaction methods			
Usability laboratories	Yes	No	No
User focus groups	Yes	Maybe	Maybe
User-satisfaction surveys	Yes	Maybe	Maybe
Post-release quality methods			
Automated defect tracking	Yes	Yes	Yes
Customer support specialists	Yes	Yes	Maybe
Online defect reporting	Yes	Yes	Yes

Software quality is not a "one size fits all" kind of situation. There are major differences in the patterns deployed by large, medium, and small organizations. The goals are identical, but the methods of achieving the goals must be tailored to the size of the enterprise.

While most of the quality approaches listed for best in class organizations are understandable and intuitive, the list does contain some interesting phenomena that I found surprising.

For example, while "best in class" organizations may utilize international standards such as IEEE or ISO standards, they often have proprietary in-house standards that are much more rigorous and effective than any of the international quality standards.

Some "best in class" companies are openly hostile to the ISO 9000-9004 standard set and regard them as a step backwards compared to their own quality standards.

Note that the most extensive "best in class" patterns are those observed within large corporations such as Andersen, AT&T, Hewlett Packard, IBM, Microsoft, Motorola, Nippon Telegraph, Siemens-Nixdorf, and the like.

For a variety of reasons, large companies tend to produce the highest-quality software. (There are exceptions, and small teams or individuals of exceptional skill can produce excellent quality without much intervention or use of formal defect removal operations.)

These companies have thousands of software personnel including many specialists in the areas of testing and quality assurance. These large organizations also build very large systems in the 100,000 function point size range (such as IBM's MVS operating system and Microsoft's Windows NT operating system).

Smaller companies can achieve high quality more easily because they only build small applications. However, smaller companies may not have the staff or the funding for some of the more expensive approaches such as usability laboratories or even formal quality assurance groups.

For small companies with less than 100 software personnel, the topics of defect prevention, non-test defect removal, and testing are the key elements. A synergistic combination of prototyping, design reviews, code inspections, and user-satisfaction surveys can achieve very respectable quality levels for applications of less than 1,000 function points in size.

Perhaps the most difficult domain for software quality are mid-sized organizations whose software staffs are between 100 and 1,000 people in total size. Organizations of this size are large enough to tackle large software systems well in excess of 10,000 function points. However, many mid-sized organizations tend to be understaffed and underequipped for quality purposes.

Also, unlike really large enterprises, mid-size organizations tend to use the "generalist" principle where there are few if any specialists for things like quality assurance, testing, human factors analysis, or quality analysis and measurement. This means that the available skill levels in terms of software quality are often marginal within mid-sized organizations.

Further, the mid-sized companies are more likely to have "token" quality assurance groups than are the large corporations. That is, the mid-sized companies may have a manager or director of software quality, but the staffing level of the SQA function can be less than 1% of the overall software staff size.

Some mid-sized organizations do produce high-quality software. These typically use synergistic combinations of defect prevention, non-test defect removal, testing, quality analysis, and also utilization of quality measurements. The mid-size companies that produce high-quality software are also likely to have quality targets for software managers and executives.

In general, the mid-size companies that do a good job with software quality also do a good job with the quality of other kinds of products, such as engineered or manufactured products.

It often happens that the mid-sized companies with the best quality results happen to have executives who understand and support software quality. Without executive understanding, software quality is not as likely to occur because of the need for approaches that are effective but counter-intuitive.

ACTIVE, PASSIVE, AND TOKEN QUALITY ASSURANCE ORGANIZATIONS

The author and his colleagues at Software Productivity Research (SPR) have visited about 600 companies and some government agencies and military groups in performing various kinds of software assessment and benchmark consulting studies.

These on-site studies provide a convenient way of observing the software quality practices of cross-sections of major companies in many industries. The studies are continuous, and we visit from two to perhaps six companies or government groups each month.

Only a minority of the companies that are visited have any software quality assurance groups at all. Of the ones that do, it is apparent that they operate in three distinct "styles" which I have named "active quality assurance," "passive quality assurance," and "token quality assurance."

The approximate distribution among SPR clients in terms of the frequency of these disparate styles is:

No quality assurance	60%
Token quality assurance	20%
Passive quality assurance	15%
Active quality assurance	5%

Organizations Without Formal Quality Assurance

There is very little to say about the set of companies that have no quality assurance. If these organizations are of significant size, that is, having more than 50 software personnel employed, then the lack of quality assurance is often a sign of future troubles for their products.

Such companies are usually big enough to tackle applications of significant size, say up to 5,000 function points. However, organizations that lack quality assurance support are seldom successful in building large software projects.

When we encounter a medium to large software organization that is totally devoid of quality assurance groups, we usually suggest that they either establish a software quality assurance function or consider giving up on software completely and turning the work over to a more qualified outsource contractor.

There is an interesting exception where lack of formal quality assurance is not necessarily disadvantageous. Very small software organizations with less than 10 software personnel almost never have formal quality assurance groups because they are too small and often only marginally funded.

This size range is typical of start-up companies in their first year of business who are engaged in bringing out the first release of their initial product. Since small groups can usually only build software applications of less than 1,000 function points, where defect levels are often moderate, the lack of formal quality assurance may not automatically reflect poor quality.

If indeed the application is small, and the developers themselves are both capable and sensitive to quality issues, sometimes an excellent software product can be produced. Of course sometimes a product is developed with so many bugs that it has to be withdrawn or cannot be released.

Note that in this book the phrase "quality assurance" does not mean "testing." The concept of quality assurance is that of an independent opinion by a certified or experienced quality group (or individual for small projects) that a software project will meet relevant corporate, national, and international quality standards and targets.

Organizations With Token Quality Assurance Groups

The phrase "token quality assurance" refers to companies that have established at least a manager whose title has something to do with quality assurance. Unfortunately, there may be no quality assurance staff members at all. Or there may be a few quality assurance personnel, but not enough to be effective. For example, the ratio of quality assurance personnel to software development personnel is in the range of 1 to 100 in the companies with token QA organizations. That is the population of software QA personnel is less than 1% of the total software population.

In general, the companies with token QA groups recognize that quality is significant, but don't really know how to achieve it. The main function of the token QA groups seems to be threefold: 1) they answer quality-related questions put by senior executives; 2) they meet and discuss quality-related topics with customers who have questions or concerns; and 3) they allow the company to assert that there is a quality assurance organization when queried by potential clients, shareholders, the press, or anyone else who might ask.

Almost without exception the personnel who are employed in token QA organizations are bothered by the fact that they are being used under what appears to be false pretenses. The QA staff know that their numbers are insufficient to do a thorough job of software quality assurance, and when interviewed during assessment and benchmark studies they usually a need for more support.

Another aspect of the token QA functions is that they are usually are not staffed sufficiently to perform effective measurement of quality or to participate in formal design and code inspections.

On the whole, the token QA organizations are symptomatic of a lack of understanding about the business and technical significance of quality. Organizations with token QA groups are seldom found in the top 10% of their industry in terms of either quality, productivity, or time to market aspects.

Also, when companies with token QA organizations utilize the Software Engineering Institute (SEI) capability maturity model (CMM) they are usually found to have Level 1 status, which is the unhealthy end of the CMM spectrum.

Organizations With Passive Quality Assurance Groups

The phrase "passive quality assurance" refers to situations in companies that have established a formal quality assurance organization whose size is in the range of 1% to 2% of the software development community. That is, there is an approximate ratio of one QA staff member to about every 50 development personnel.

The work of the passive QA groups is primarily observational. They watch to be sure that quality standards are followed, they may participate as spectators in design reviews or code inspections, and they observe the results of testing. The primary output of a passive QA group is a report that summarizes their observations.

The boundary between the token and passive quality assurance groups is often blurred. They both share the common characteristics that they are too small to be very effective. However, by concentrating their resources on critical projects, sometimes the passive QA organizations can at least have a tangible effect.

From interviews with the personnel employed in passive QA organizations, they usually express frustration that quality control is not supported more fully.

Although companies with passive QA groups are seldom found among the "best in class" top 10% of companies in their industry in terms of quality, costs, productivity, or schedules, they can be found in the upper 50% very often. In situations where many companies have no QA focus at all, the passive QA organizations are at least capable of making visible contributions.

Organizations With Active Quality Assurance Groups

The phrase "active quality assurance" refers to well-staffed software QA groups with a ratio of about 1 to 20 in terms of the overall software population; i.e., roughly 5% of the software community is in the QA function. The work of the active QA groups starts early and is very hands-on oriented. The functions of an active QA group include the following.

The active quality assurance groups typically have their own chain of command reporting to a corporate vice president or executive vice president of quality. There may also be a vice president or director of software quality in companies which produce hardware as well as software.

The separate chain of command is important to ensure the independence and objectivity of the quality assurance function. If QA personnel are subordinate to the managers and executives of the projects they are working on, there would be possibilities for conflict of interest.

The roles or activities noted within active QA organizations include:

- Examining usability and human factors as well as defect levels
- Moderating software design and code inspections
- Performing research into advanced topics such as quality function deployment (QFD)
- Performing software complexity analysis
- Performing software defect estimation
- Performing software reliability modeling
- Performing software defect data collection
- Reporting on software quality results
- Reviewing development test plans
- Inspecting samples of test cases for redundancy and errors
- Reviewing test library controls
- Performing subsets of testing
- Developing courses on software quality topics
- Teaching courses on software quality topics
- Contracting with external quality consultants as needed
- Bringing in "big name" quality speakers for conferences and seminars

Although the active quality assurance form is the most expensive, it is also the most effective. This form is usually associated with "best in class" quality results and is found in groups such as AT&T, Hewlett Packard, and Motorola that typically do achieve good to excellent quality results in many of their projects.

Two very significant features are often noted when doing assessments and benchmark studies of companies that have active QA organizations:

- Software quality metrics and data collection are often at "state of the art" levels.

- Many new and improved QA approaches originate in the quality research labs which are only found in companies with active QA organizations.

As examples of software quality innovation coming out of the active mode of quality assurance, the IBM quality assurance research group in Kingston, New York pioneered formal design and code inspections in the 1960s and also defect removal efficiency measures; the IBM quality assurance research group in Gaithersburg, Maryland pioneered "clean-room" development in the 1970s; the IBM quality assurance group in San Jose, California developed IBM's first automated software defect estimation tools in the 1970s; and the IBM quality assurance group in Hawthorne, New York developed the new "orthogonal" defect categorization system in the 1990s, which is described later in this book.

Many more examples and many other companies could be cited, but the fundamental point is that active and well-supported software QA groups are proactive. Quality research labs in large companies are the source of many useful advances in quality assurance technology.

The existence of quality assurance research labs in large high-technology corporations is one of the main reasons the quality levels of large enterprises is often better than the quality levels of mid-sized enterprises. Not only do the large companies tend to utilize "best in class" methods, they also have a critical mass of quality research talent that is capable of advancing quality technologies to new levels.

It should be noted that the role of an active QA group is not to "police" the work of developers. It happens that software quality is a complicated technical topic, and the active QA organization tries to make a positive and professional contribution to the projects that they support.

It is an interesting observation that the QA personnel learn the products they are involved with so carefully and thoroughly that they may be asked to join the development group for the next release.

When I worked in IBM's software QA group, it was interesting that the software development personnel, maintenance personnel, and software QA personnel received the same training and had the same compensation plans and position levels. This meant that lateral transfers back and forth between development, maintenance, and quality assurance were easy to accomplish if the incumbents desired to move.

See also the section on Quality Assurance Organizations for information on the placement of the software QA function in an organizational context.

AGING OF REPORTED DEFECTS

Two topics of great significance to software quality (and manufactured quality also) are those of:

1) How long a bug or defect can exist before it is found?

2) When a bug or defect is reported, how long does it take to fix it?

As a general rule, the longer problems or bugs exist the more difficult it is to deal with them. The worst examples would be requirements problems that are not discovered until testing begins, sometimes more than 24 months downstream.

Among our clients about 450 out of 600 organizations have some kind of formal or semi-formal reporting methods for keeping track of bugs. The best 60 or so companies start their defect tracking early, during requirements and design. Companies that are construed as "average" start defect tracking during testing. Companies that are somewhat behind or lagging track only customer-reported defects. Companies that don't have a clue about quality don't track defects at all.

Several approaches have been developed that can minimize the delay between when software defects originate and when they are discovered.

When significant bugs or defects are found, the quality measurement program should attempt to identify the origin point; i.e., the bug originated in requirements, in design, in the code itself, or in some other work product. (IBM's software quality measurement program even attempted to explore the origin of customer-reported defects after the products were released.)

Formal inspections of major work products such as requirements and specifications are highly effective in finding bugs early and keeping them from cascading downstream. (See the section on inspections later in this book.)

The clean-room software development method features early discovery of software defects and utilizes its own kind of inspections to keep bugs from moving into later deliverables. (See the section on Clean Room Development later in this book.)

Here are some general guidelines for evaluating the defect aging process of software projects, using SPR's five-point evaluation scale:

Delay Between Defect Origin and Discovery	Status	Interpretation
1 Most defects found in less than one day	Excellent:	State of the art
2 Most defects found in less than one week	Good:	Better than average
3 Most defects found in less than one month	Average:	Improvement needed
4 Many defects found after 3 months	Poor:	Inspections needed
5 Many defects found after 6 months	Very Poor:	Serious QA flaws

An analysis of software defect aging patterns is one of the most effective tools for improving software development processes. Any software producer with a lag of more than six months between defect origination and defect discovery points is in need of a major process "tune up."

Once software defects are noted, it is important to explore how long it takes before the problems are repaired and a new version of the application is in the hands of users. The following table shows typical repair times by severity level for turning around software defects.

Note that achieving defect reaction times of less than one hour implies a number of concatenated factors, including: 1) direct communication between clients and vendors by e-mail or network; 2) around the clock availability of software maintenance programmers; 3) automated defect tracking; and 4) automated configuration control.

Table 1   Defect Repair Intervals for Fixing Bugs of Varying Severity Levels

	Severity 1 (Serious)	Severity 2	Severity 3	Severity 4 (Minor)
< 1 hour	10%	5%	0%	0%
< 1 day	20%	10%	5%	1%
< 1 week	65%	55%	25%	15%
< 1 month	5%	25%	45%	50%
< 3 months	0%	5%	25%	34%
TOTAL	100%	100%	100%	100%

Most commercial software houses use formal defect tracking systems that also record when bugs were reported and their current status. These tracking systems usually have some kind of warning that will alert managers when reported bugs have been in the queue for more than a predetermined period, such as a week or a month, without having been repaired.

One of the more common reasons for lengthy repair intervals has to do with bugs that the repair group can't replicate. This situation is often triggered by some unique combination of software packages on the client's system that are interacting to cause the problem.

One of the most effective ways of shortening the length of time needed to report defects and to achieve repairs or "work around" information is for vendors to utilize a major software network such as (in alphabetic order) America Online, CompuServe, the Internet, or Microsoft Network.

For example, the vendor forums on CompuServe can have literally hundreds of users all logged on simultaneously. When someone reports a problem via one of these forums, it is usually available for all to see. Often, some other user has experienced the same problem in the past and now knows of a solution or work around. It can even happen that another user will solve the problem before the vendor's own maintenance team!

The networks are so effective for defect reporting purposes that Microsoft and other software vendors have found that it takes many fewer customer support personnel to monitor network e-mail messages than it does to man "hot line" telephone support centers.

The author was once part of an international study team within IBM that explored delays in defect repair cycles. We found some interesting situations and even a few totally unexpected phenomena.

One common but surprising problem was routing defect reports to the wrong repair center, which tends to occur in large companies with many software packages and multiple maintenance centers. For example, one defect report bounced around to no fewer than four maintenance teams in Europe and the United States before it finally reached the right destination. That particular bug was in transit for more than three weeks before it reached the right place.

The most unusual situation, which was not easy to correct, was the discovery that shipments of software maintenance releases to some countries were being delayed by customs inspectors. Although the problem was eventually minimized by careful preparation of customs forms, it indicates that some customer support problems can be very complex indeed.

BAD FIXES

The term "bad fix" refers to a secondary defect accidentally inserted into a software product as an unanticipated byproduct of fixing a previous bug or defect. Bad fixes are surprisingly common. However, measurement of quality with sufficient precision to find bad fixes is comparatively rare.

Among our clients, bad fixes are essentially universal at the company level since 100% of our 600 or so clients experience at least some bad fixes. However, the range of bad fixes at the project level is from 0% (very rare) to over 20% (also very rare).

Data collected on IBM's MVS operating system indicated that on average, about 9% of defect repairs might introduce secondary errors unless rigorous steps were taken to prevent them from occurring. However, formal inspections of major defect repairs and careful regression testing could bring the incidence of bad fixes down to close to 0% on critical projects and the corporate average down to less than 2%. Fortunately the bad fix problem is solvable once software developers and managers realize how significant it is.

More recent data derived from other high-technology companies shows a bad fix injection rate which ranges from less than 2% to more than 20%, with modern averages in the 1990s running to about 7%.

Some software projects are much worse than average, and bad fix ratios in excess of 20% have been observed on some troublesome software projects. The probability of bad fixes tends to rise with complexity, so one of the more effective technologies to minimize bad fix injection rates is to analyze software complexity using metrics such as cyclomatic and essential complexity. Following are rough correlations between bad fix potentials and cyclomatic complexity levels.

Table 1   Relationship Between Cyclomatic Complexity and Bad Fix Probability

Cyclomatic Complexity	Bad Fix Percentage
1	2%
< 5	5%
5 - 10	7%
10 - 20	10%
> 20	15%
> 30	20%

An associated technology, also useful in minimizing bad fixes, is that of automated code restructuring. These tools parse source code and produce a graph of the control structure of the application. Then, using graph-theoretic methods, the initial graph is simplified. The source code is reconstructed using the simplified graph.

Code restructuring tools can reduce cyclomatic and essential complexity levels down to 1 if desired, or some other cut-off point can be established. However, code restructuring tools are available only for a few common languages such as COBOL, PL/I, FORTRAN, and C. These tools are not available for many newer languages such as Visual Basic, Realizer, or for Object-Oriented languages such as SMALLTALK.

Other control methods that are effective against bad fix injection include formal build and configuration control procedures which prevent casual changes to software without inspections or formal testing. Also, defect measurement tools that allow "bad fixes" to be identified are strongly recommended.

BAD TEST CASES

When formal inspections are applied to test plans and to test cases themselves, they reveal a hidden but important quality problem. The error density in software test cases is often higher than the error density in the software product that the test cases have been written for. Sometimes more than 15% of the total number of test cases created can have errors themselves.

From discussions with both SPR clients and with some of the local software development personnel in the Boston area in commercial software companies who are building new software products that also require the creation of new test cases, it may happen that almost 50% of the effort associated with defect repairs early in testing go to repairing the test cases and not the product during the first two months of testing. This is a very significant amount of effort to go more or less unreported in the quality literature.

Among our clients, the number of enterprises that have at least some bad test cases is approximately 100%. However, the number of clients that measure test-case quality is much smaller: only about 20 enterprises out of 600 or so.

The fact that a substantial amount of effort may be devoted to dealing with flawed test cases indicates three distinct threads of problems, all of which need to be examined and eliminated:

- Software root-cause analysis needs to be expanded so that the kinds of errors that occur in software test cases and test libraries are explored.

- Software cost and resource tracking needs a finer activity breakdown so that the effort and costs of running and later fixing bad test cases are captured. For example, the "cost of quality" approach does not include measures of defects in test cases themselves.

- Software defect reporting and tracking systems need a minor extension so that test-case errors can be recorded and later statistically analyzed.

Since running test cases that are flawed or in error is of no value in terms of quality and also expensive, there is an implied need for greater rigor in building and validating test cases and test libraries.

Some of the common problems observed with bad test cases include: 1) testing limits and ranges where those included in the test-case are themselves incorrect; 2) testing for numeric values where the test data contains wrong data; and 3) test cases derived from specifications or user requirements which contained undetected errors that were accidentally passed on to the test cases.

Another problem associated with test cases and test libraries is that of accidental redundancy, or having multiple test cases that look for the same condition. This is very common when multiple programmers or test personnel contribute to the same test library.

Some years ago, one of the IBM software quality assurance labs did an analysis of the contents of the regression test libraries for products developed at the site and found that almost 30% of the total volume of test cases duplicated others and could be eliminated without any reduction in coverage.

Yet another problem with testing is that of gaps, or portions of the application for which no test cases exist. Although 100% coverage is desirable, in actuality, coverage may be less than 70% unless special care is taken. Here at least tools and automation are available that can monitor the coverage of test cases when they are executed and point out paths or segments that have escaped testing.

One interesting phenomenon in gap analysis was noted in a study of why testing gaps occurred. The source materials used to construct test cases are the specifications for the software. Many gaps in test coverage reflect gaps in the specifications. (See the section on design defects for a discussion of specification incompleteness.)

Often specifications stop being updated long before the product stops evolving. That is, new features are frequently added to the software fairly late in development (such as in response to creeping requirements). It often occurs that these late features are not reflected in updated or revised specifications. When this happens, whole segments of the software may have no test cases at all because the test personnel are unaware of the existence of the new code. Even "black box" testing is impossible if the specifications do not describe significant features of the product.

Formal inspections of design and specifications not only eliminate a class of very significant errors but have a surprisingly strong impact on subsequent testing. IBM noted that test coverage and testing defect removal efficiency of products which used design inspections averaged at least 10% higher than for similar products where design inspections were not utilized.

Formal inspections of test plans and test cases are very effective in eliminating bad test cases, although this method is only used by a very small number of companies and projects. When IBM first developed the formal inspection process in the mid-1960s, inspections were tried for test plans and test cases and revealed that the testing process itself was seriously in need of greater rigor and quality controls.

As of 1996, no widespread and fully effective approaches have been developed to minimize or control the problem of bad test cases or redundant test cases. However, formal test-case library controls and performing sampling studies of test-case structure and validity appear to be advantageous. One of the most important gaps in the entire software quality literature, and in software quality tool sets as well, deals with flaws, errors, and redundancy in test-case libraries.

The following table reflects my observations with commercial software packages. This data is very unreliable and has a high margin of error. This is due in part to the fact that test-case quality control and reporting on test-case errors is almost nonexistent in the software industry. For some reason, errors in test cases have not attracted much coverage in the software quality literature. However, once the costs and negative implications of test-case errors come to be realized, it can be hoped that this issue will receive more research in the future.

Table 1   Numbers of Redundant and Defective Test Cases by Testing Stage

Test Step	Test cases created per function point	Percent redundant test cases	Percent of test cases with errors
Unit test	0.30	5%	15%
New function test	0.35	10%	11%
Regression test	0.30	15%	10%
Integration test	0.45	20%	7%
System test	0.40	30%	6%
AVERAGE	0.36	16%	10%

It is interesting to note that the chance of redundancy and the chance of errors in test cases seem to move in opposite directions. Test cases created by the programmers themselves have the lowest probability of being duplicated, but the highest probability of containing errors or bugs.

Test cases created later by test or quality assurance personnel have the greatest probability of redundancy but lower probability of containing errors. The high probability of redundancy is because test libraries are not the work of a single individual. Sometimes test cases are contributed by many people, and for regression testing, over a period of many years.

One again, the data on test-case redundancy and test care error density is provisional and has a high margin of error. It is included primarily to attract attention to a topic that is poorly covered in the software quality literature.

BALDRIGE AWARDS

The Baldrige Award was created by an act of Congress in 1987, after more than five years of background discussion and research. The award itself is named for the late Malcolm Baldrige, who was Secretary of Commerce in the Reagan administration until he was killed in a rodeo accident. The Malcolm Baldrige Quality Improvement Act was signed by President Ronald Reagan in August of 1987.

Although the Baldrige Award is aimed at all kinds of industries and companies and is not a software award at all, those companies who have won the Baldrige Award tend to have much better than average software methods.

As a class, Baldrige Award winners such as AT&T, IBM Rochester, and Motorola are much better in a number of quality control respects than most companies. It is interesting that even though the Baldrige Awards were not won for software quality, the Baldrige-winning corporations tend to be much better than most organizations in software quality too.

Also interesting is that quality control among Baldrige Award winners is often superior to software quality control among ISO 9000 certified companies. This appears to be due to the fact that applying for the Baldrige Award is a highly motivational event that stirs up a lot of enthusiasm for quality among all levels of a company from top executives downward. By contrast, ISO 9000 certification is essentially mandated and is often regarded as just another irritating and sometimes irrelevant obstacle to international business.

Further, Baldrige Award winners also tend to be superior in software quality to companies that espouse total quality management (TQM) but have not applied for a Baldrige Award. Unfortunately, some companies that say they are adopting TQM do not actually do much more than put up a few wall posters and have some publicity materials produced. This is not enough to win a Baldrige. To have a good chance at a Baldrige, a company must work hard, work smart, and can't fake any of the claims.

Baldrige Award winners also tend to be superior in software quality to organizations that are up to about level 3 on the Software Engineering Institute (SEI) capability maturity model (CMM). Here too, it is possible to learn how to answer the SEI CMM questions so that the scores are favorable. It is a bit tougher to get through the Baldrige criteria and the varieties of on-site analysis associated with successful Baldrige winners.

Of course, some companies go after all of these quality topics and others besides. Indeed, any company that is in serious contention for a Baldrige Award can sail through the ISO 9000 certification process, can be very effective in total quality management (TQM), and achieve at least level 3 status on the SEI CMM without much effort.

The Baldrige Award has a number of salient features, but perhaps the most striking feature is that the Baldrige Award is based on multiple criteria that cover a very broad range of topics.

The Baldrige is not a "silver bullet" that many executives are so fond of, where changing one factor is presumed to lead to enormous benefits. If a company is going to have a good chance of winning a Baldrige Award, it will have to get very serious about quality and you will have to make a lot of changes in a great many things.

There are seven major topics evaluated in order to win a Baldrige Award, and each contributes to part of the overall results.

Table 1   Seven Key Baldrige Award Criteria and Their Impact

Topic	Percent Contribution to Baldrige Awards
Leadership	9%
Information and Analysis	8%
Strategic Quality Planning	6%
Human Resource Development and Management	15%
Management of Process Quality	14%
Quality and Operational Results	18%
Customer Focus and Satisfaction	30%
TOTAL	100%

The most striking difference between Baldrige-class corporations and others is the use of software quality metrics and sophisticated quality measurement systems. Baldrige Award winners start quality measurements early in the life cycle and continue all the way through development and out into the field. Baldrige winners measure user-satisfaction, defect quantities, defect severity levels, defect origins, and defect removal efficiencies.

Not only do Baldrige winners, as a class, have better quality measurements than most companies, they use the data very effectively. Compared to similar companies that have not applied for Baldrige awards, the Baldrige winners are running more than 10% higher in defect removal efficiency levels and also are on the low side within their industries in terms of defect potentials.

More than any other group of enterprises surveyed, Baldrige winners tend to measure "defect removal efficiency" or the total percentage of bugs or errors removed prior to delivery of software. From a knowledge of this key metric, Baldrige winners are able to plan an optimal series of reviews, inspections, and test steps that in some cases removes more than 99% of software errors.

Although it is a subjective and anecdotal observation, I enjoy consulting with Baldrige-winning companies more than any other kind of company. In every company you can find people who are interested in and knowledgeable about quality, but seldom can such people be found in large numbers or in executive positions. In Baldrige-winning companies, the proportion of people who seem interested in quality is very high, and knowledge about quality among executive ranks is both noticeable and refreshing.

Also refreshing is the lack of "silver bullet" thinking among executives in Baldrige-winning organizations. That is, many executives are looking for a quick, cheap, and simple solution to very complicated technical problems. The executives in Baldrige-class companies seem to have a better grasp of the fact that topics like achieving high quality levels are not trivial, issues that can be solved with a few wall-posters and a kick-off meeting.

The Baldrige Awards have recently been questioned for various reasons, such as possible political maneuvering or the fact that several Baldrige winners have experienced poor financial performance within a year or two after winning the award. (The incidence of financial problems among Baldrige winners appears roughly equivalent to other companies within similar industries.) Nonetheless, the Baldrige Award seems to do more good for the culture of quality, and lead to better results, than almost anything else attempted.

Paul Strassman has criticized the Baldrige Award process as being primarily a very expensive kind of marketing ploy that does not seem to contribute much in terms of new jobs or benefit corporate operations in any significant way. His observations are thought-provoking, but other research comparing the financial results of Baldrige winners to similar companies has reached different conclusions. The Baldrige Award is only one issue, and corporate success and financial results are obviously based on many other factors besides the Baldrige process.

A number of companies such as IBM, Motorola, U.S. Sprint, and the like have internal awards that are derived from the Baldrige Award and utilize the same criteria. These internal awards are also beneficial to software quality and are an excellent precursor to applying for the actual Baldrige Award. However, these internal awards do not have the same status or prestige with clients and the outside world.

From 1990 through 1995, several Baldrige Award winners declared bankruptcy, leading many journalists to the conclusion that applying for a Baldrige and achieving high quality was a causative factor in business failure.

As far as can be determined, the years 1990 through 1995 were simply tough business years for many companies. The incidence of bankruptcy among Baldrige winners appears to be marginally better than among similar companies that have not applied.

For more information on the Baldrige Award or a copy of the Baldrige criteria, contact the National Institute of Technology, Route 270 and Quince Orchard Road, Room A537, Gaithersburg, MD 20809. The phone number is 301-975-2036 and the fax is 301-948-3716.

See also the citation on the Deming Prize, which is a prize for quality offered by the Japanese government. The Deming Prize is somewhat older than the Baldrige Award, and has an equal or even higher level of prestige but a different theme and different criteria.

BARRIERS TO SOFTWARE QUALITY MEASUREMENT

Historically, software quality was measured in terms of "defects found per 1,000 source code statements" (normally abbreviated to KLOC, where K stands for 1,000 and LOC stands for lines of code). Unfortunately, usage of "lines of code" as a normalizing metric is one of the chronic problems of the software industry. This metric does not measure either economic productivity or quality, and it tends to conceal true improvements in both domains.

Also flawed and invalid from the standpoint of economic understanding, software defect repair costs have often been measured using "cost per defect" metrics.

Unfortunately cost per defect metrics can actually move backwards and penalize high quality, due to the impact of fixed costs.

Neither KLOC metrics nor cost per defect metrics actually show the real economic benefits of higher quality and reduced defect levels. The situation with these metrics is so far from standard economics that their use might be regarded as being professional malpractice for some types of research. That is, the hazards of KLOC have been published long enough (since 1978) and widely enough (hundreds of articles; many book) so that they should be known and understood by every software professional.

Under the normal concept of professional malpractice, if KLOC and cost per defect metrics are used and the results are damaging, the practitioner should be liable for any damage that accrues. Unfortunately, the KLOC metric contains a built-in paradox which causes it to give erroneous results when used with newer and more powerful programming languages, such as Ada, object-oriented languages, or program generators.

The main problem with the KLOC metric is that this metric conceals, rather than reveals, important quality data. For example, suppose a company has been measuring quality in terms of "Defects per KLOC" which has been a common practice. A project coded in FORTRAN might require 10,000 lines of code, and might contain 200 bugs, for a total of 20 defects per KLOC.

Now suppose the same project could be created using a more powerful language such as C++, which required only 2,000 lines of code and contained only 40 bugs. Here, too, there are 20 defects per KLOC, but the total number of bugs is actually reduced by 80%.

In the FORTRAN and C++ examples shown above, both versions provided the same functions to end users, and so both contain the same number of Function Points. Assume both versions contain 100 Function Points.

When the newer metric "Defects per Function Point" is used, the FORTRAN version contains 2.00 defects per Function Point, but the C++ version contains only 0.40 defects per Function Point. With the Function Point metric, the substantial quality gains associated with more powerful high-level languages can now be made clearly visible.

Note that when the data is summarized, neither the "lines of code" metrics nor the "cost per defect" metric actually show the real economic difference associated with an 80% reduction in total defects. However, the "defects per function point" metric and the "defect cost per function point" metric both match the real economic picture exactly.

Table 1 Defect Totals and Repairs for Two Versions of the Same Program

	FORTRAN Version	C++ Version	Difference
Size in Lines of Code	10,000	2,000	-8,000
Size in Function Points	100	100	0
Software Defects Found	200	40	-160
Defects Found per KLOC	20	20	0
Defects Found per Function Point	2.0	0.40	-1.60
Defect Repair Costs	$25,000	$5,000	-$20,000
Cost per Defect	$125	$125	0
Defect Repairs per KLOC	$2,500	$2,500	0
Defect Repairs per Function Point	$250	$50	-$200

Note that between the FORTRAN and C++ versions of the same program, there were significant differences in source code volumes, defects found, and defect repair expenses. Both "lines of code" and the associated "cost per KLOC" fail to show the 80% reduction in overall repair costs.

The "cost per defect" metric does not show any difference at all, even though the total costs of repairing defects in the C++ version was $20,000 less than in the FORTRAN version.

Unfortunately, there is an even worse situation where cost per defect metrics actually move backwards and conceal real economic progress as quality improves.

This situation is the worst one imaginable for quality research. Cost per defect penalizes high quality and gets larger as software defect levels decline. Although this problem is a normal situation when fixed costs are part of the equation, most software quality researchers do not seem to realize that it occurs. The probable reason is the general lack of data for projects of similar sizes and attributes, but varying quality levels that range from very bad up to excellent or even zero-defect status.

The following example demonstrates this trend of cost per defect to penalize improved quality. The example shows two versions of the same project:

- A high-defect version developed in a careless, unstructured fashion where 50 bugs were found during testing.

- A low-defect version developed in a formal, structured fashion where only five bugs were found during testing.

Assume that both versions are the same size: 5,000 statements in the C programming language, or 40 function points in overall size.

Table 2   Comparison of Cost per Defect Metric for High- and Low-Defect Levels

	High-Defect Version	Low-Defect Version	Difference
Defects found	50	5	-45
Test case preparation	$1000	$1000	0
Test case execution	$3000	$1000	-$2000
Defect repairs	$5000	$500	-$4500
TESTING COST	$9000	$2500	-$6500
Cost per Defect	$180	$500	$320
Cost per Function Point	$225	$62.50	-$162.50

Clearly, when defects or bugs are reduced, the cost per defect goes up and this metric does not show the true cost savings. This trend of cost per defect to penalize quality is a general one. Cost per defect tends to rise as defect volumes decline. Even for zero-defect software it is necessary to create and execute test cases so there will be some expenses. For zero-defect software, the "cost per defect" would be infinity.

Note that when function points are used as normalizing metrics, the quality gains and the reduced costs associated with overall testing and defect repairs match the real economic picture perfectly.

The hazards of lines of code metrics can easily be seen when defects are graphed using both lines of code and function point metrics. The following graph shows data for several programming languages. Note how the lines of code metric penalizes high-level languages and makes low-level languages artificially better.

The reason for this problem is because the data in the graph also includes errors in requirements, specifications, and user manuals. These categories of errors are independent of coding errors and stay more or less constant regardless of choice of programming language. The high-level programming languages have fewer coding defects and reduced volumes of code to implement the same functions.

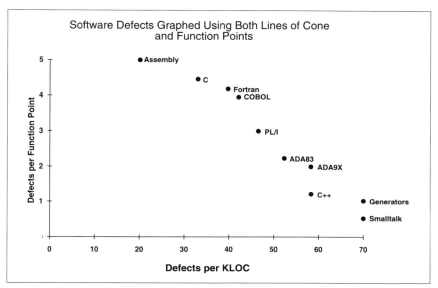

Figure 1 Software Defects Graphed Using both Lines of Code and Function Points

The "lines of code" axis uses the common abbreviation "KLOC" where "K" stands for increments of 1024 source statements.

My view that both "lines of code" and "cost per defect" are flawed metrics is counter to the views of many other authors. The simple examples shown here illustrate the basic mathematical flaws that also occurs in real life.

Although I don't recommend using lines of code or cost per defect, it is not because I lack data expressed in these metrics. Software Productivity Research has data from roughly 7,000 software projects, and this number is increasing at a rate of perhaps 50 projects every month.

Our data includes lines of code metrics, cost per defect metrics, and also function point metrics. Because we have so much data available and utilize so many metrics concurrently, the problems have become visible to us.

In fact, the key problems with lines of code metrics are usually not visible until a critical mass of projects has been carefully measured and the results analyzed. It was not until I had data on almost 500 software projects, written in 50 languages, that I saw why lines of code had serious flaws for economic analysis.

Early Studies on Software Metric Problems

It may be of interest to summarize how it was first discovered that both lines of code metrics and cost per defect metrics had serious problems. When first starting work in measurement and estimation in the 1960s I began my own research using both lines of code and cost per defect metrics. Indeed, function points had not been invented, and there were no other common metrics discussed in the software literature.

The first projects analyzed were IBM's systems software applications written in assembly language. For a single language the problems of lines of code are not readily visible. Only later when the data grew and began to include projects in PL/I, APL, FORTRAN, RPG, COBOL, and other languages did the paradox associated with lines of code metrics become visible.

When our quality research began, the first samples of software projects explored were fairly buggy. Here too, the sample was insufficient to note the problems associated with cost per defect metrics.

When IBM began a serious quality push on key software products such as the IMS database product, compilers, and other systems software applications, I began to get data on projects with very high quality, including one that achieved zero-defect status in the first year of production.

To my considerable surprise, the cost per defect metric got more expensive as quality improved. The real shock, however, was the realization that the cost per defect metric had no relevance at all for zero-defect software.

We had still used formal inspections and had written and run many test cases. We also had trained maintenance personnel, and some of them had been assigned to maintenance roles for several months until it became clear that no customer-reported defects were coming in.

Our quality control expenses for this project were not zero, even though defects in the application were. How could this situation of exploring the economics of zero-defect software be measured?

Fortunately I had the opportunity of hearing Allan Albrecht speak on function points at the joint IBM/SHARE/GUIDE conference in Monterey, California in October of 1979. This happened to be the first public speech on function point metrics, and it made a strong impression.

When I tried retrofitting function point metrics to the quality and productivity data I had been analyzing, it was immediately obvious that software had a powerful new research tool which it had long lacked.

Function point metrics correlated perfectly with the improvements in economic productivity brought about by high-level languages.

For quality, the metrics "defects per function point" and "defect removal costs per function point" gave a perfect match to the cost of quality improvements and to the reductions in overall defects encountered when using more powerful programming languages.

For the first time in software history, it became possible to explore software economics and software quality using metrics that did not conceal important findings. This is not to say that function point metrics are perfect and have no errors at all. However, function point metrics do correlate better with economic productivity and with software quality than any known rival metric.

It is a surprising sociological observation that many of today's strongest defenders of lines of code and cost per defect metrics don't actually use either metric in daily life and have essentially no data at all.

The most common defense of these two metrics is an ad hominem argument that the metrics must be valid because so many people have written articles and books using them. There is an implied belief that authors, or at least famous authors, are all-knowing and would not use a metric that was incorrect. As an author myself, I certainly know the flaws in this line of reasoning.

From the first public speech about function points in 1979, use of this metric expanded rapidly as other researchers made the same observations that I did: function point metrics offer insights and information that were previously unavailable.

BEST IN CLASS QUALITY RESULTS

The best software projects within the organizations that constitute roughly the upper 5% of the groups that SPR has assessed have achieved remarkably good quality levels. The data shown here is derived from the top 5% of the projects in the top 30 organizations SPR has analyzed out of a total of 600. Here are quality targets derived from "best in class" software projects and organizations:

- Average less than 2.5 defects per function point in potential defects. (Sum of defects found in requirements, design, code, user documents, and bad fixes.)

- Achieve defect potentials of less than 1 defect per function point on best projects. (Sum of defects found in requirements, design, code, user documents, and bad fixes.)

- Maximum defect potential never exceeds 3.5 defects per function point. (Sum of defects found in requirements, design, code, user documents, and bad fixes.)

- Cumulative defect removal efficiency averages higher than 95%. (All defects found during development, compared to first year's customer-reported defects.)

- Peak defect removal efficiency higher than 99% on mission-critical projects. (All defects found during development, compared to first year's customer-reported defects.)

- Average less than 0.025 user-reported defects per function point in first year. (Measured against valid, unique defects.)

- Best projects receive less than 0.002 user-reported defects per function point in first year. (Measured against valid, unique defects.)

- Average gap between defect origination and defect discovery is less than 10 working days.

- Achieve 90% "excellent" ratings from user-satisfaction surveys. (Measured on topics of product quality and service.)

- Allow zero error-prone modules in released software. (Modules receiving more than 0.8 defects per function point per year.)

- Improve software quality via defect prevention and defect removal at more than 40% per year. (Baseline is the current year's volume of customer-reported defects.)

There are thousands of ways to fail when building software applications, and only a very few ways to succeed. It is an interesting phenomenon that the "best in class" companies in terms of quality all use essentially similar approaches in achieving their excellent results.

Some of the attributes of the "best in class" quality organizations include:

1) Quality measurements.

2) Defect prevention (i.e., JAD, QFD, etc.).

3) Defect and quality estimation automation.

4) Defect tracking automation.

5) Complexity analysis tools.

6) Test coverage analysis tools.

7) Formal inspections.

8) Formal testing by test specialists.

9) Formal quality assurance group.

10) Executive and managerial understanding of quality.

The similarity of approaches among companies such as AT&T, Bellcore, IBM, Microsoft, Hewlett Packard, etc., is quite striking when side-by-side benchmark comparisons are performed.

CASE STUDY OF SOFTWARE QUALITY IMPROVEMENT

If you are dissatisfied with software quality in your company or enterprise and want to improve it, how would you go about it? This is not an easy question to answer. However, enough companies have improved software quality to put together a composite case study of how they accomplished it. Even the approximate costs and the timing of various activities can be sketched out.

Software quality is amenable to fairly rapid improvement, with a compound gain of more than 40% per year. There are two key components to software quality gains:

1) Reductions in total defect potentials using methods of defect prevention.

2) Improvements in cumulative defect removal efficiency levels.

Both components are necessary, and neither by itself, is sufficient. However, the combination is synergistic, and both components meld together very well. Of the two, improving defect removal efficiency is the easier to get started and typically improves the fastest. Defect prevention is more difficult to begin, requires more training and preparation, requires a longer time before results are seen, and also is harder to measure directly.

The following table shows the best software quality improvement rates which I have observed to date for a five-year period: Since the data is assembled from multiple companies over multiple years, the dates from 1996 to 2000 have been used as calendar headings simply to indicate annual progress.

Table 1   Maximum Software Quality Improvement Over a Five-Year Period

	1996	1997	1998	1999	2000	Average
Defect Potential	6.00	5.76	5.18	4.51	3.61	5.01
Removal Efficiency	88.00%	93.00%	96.00%	98.00%	99.00%	94.80%
Delivered Defeats	0.72	0.40	0.21	0.09	0.04	0.29
Annual Improvement	0.00%	44.00%	48.57%	56.50%	60.00%	41.81%
Customer Satisfaction	Poor	Poor	Fair	Good	Excellent	Good

This table shows a composite picture derived from some of SPR's clients whose software quality was initially marginal, and who wished to advance to state-of-the-art software status.

Also included are observations from other companies, such as IBM and ITT, where I was part of the corporate software quality measurement group and hence close enough to the improvements to observe the impact of various changes.

Some of the oldest data came from IBM's former Systems Development Division which mounted a concerted quality improvement program under J.H. Frame, the director of programming. This program included the software laboratories of Boulder, Hursley, San Jose, and Palo Alto.

While the IBM effort took place in the 1970s, it remains significant because it was one of the first major quality improvement programs in the software industry where both software productivity and quality measurements were in place so that the "before" and "after" conditions could be quantified, as well as the rate of change during a five-year period.

Other companies and other situations have been melded together in order to produce an overall composite picture of a successful software quality improvement program. It is perhaps useful to illustrate progress via a case study approach. The case study will simplify a number of factors, since the purpose is to illustrate typical problems and the responses to those problems that have been observed to work effectively.

Initial Conditions of a Software Quality Improvement Case Study

Assume that a division of a computer manufacturing company has received customer complaints about poor quality and reliability for some of its software products. It also has a significant annual volume of bugs reported from customers. Therefore division management, with the urging of senior corporate management who have become aware of the complaints, has decided to make a concerted effort to move toward "best in class" software quality control.

Assume a total staff of 500 software personnel with an average burdened annual compensation of $70,000 or $5,833 per month. The set of products already in the field is 25, and the total volume of function points supported is 150,000.

Assuming that the programming languages in which the packages are written include the procedural languages of assembly, C, and PL/S. The average expansion rate from function points to "lines of code" across this mixture is equal to an average of 110 source statements per function point. Therefore the total of 150,000 function points is roughly equal to a total of 16,500,000 source code statements or "lines of code" for the purpose of expressing some of the data in the common but unreliable "defects per KLOC" metric.

About 7,500 bugs per year from customers are being reported. However, there is a decidedly unequal distribution to the reported defects. The worst products, which have received the most customer complaints and have the highest levels of incoming defects, were only recently transferred into the division and are achieving bug reports that exceed the best products by several hundred percent. Here are the initial conditions of the division:

Table 2   Initial Conditions of a Software Quality Improvement Program

Occupation Groups	Number	Percent
Software development personnel	155	31%
Software maintenance and support personnel	125	25%
Software test personnel	75	15%
Administrative and support personnel	75	15%
Software management	60	12%
Software quality assurance personnel	10	2%
TOTAL SOFTWARE PERSONNEL	500	100%
Total Annual Expenses		
Annual Personnel Expenses	$35,000,000	
Annual cost per function point	$65.33	
Annual cost per KLOC	$2,121.21	
Software Supported		
Number of software packages supported	25	
Function points supported	150,000	
Number of KLOC supported	16,500	
Number of new products/enhancements	5	
Function points under development	20,000	
KLOC under development	2,200	
Software Defects and Expenses Repair Costs		
Bugs found during development per year	90,000	
Customer-reported bugs per year	7,500	
TOTAL BUGS FOUND PER YEAR	97,500	
Annual pre-release defect repair costs	$8,000,000	
Annual customer-reported repair costs	$9,000,000	
TOTAL ANNUAL DEFECT REPAIRS	$17,000,000	
Pre-release repairs per function point	$400	
Pre-release repairs per KLOC	$3,636.36	
Pre-release repairs per defect	$80.89	
Pre-release monthly defect repair rate	12	

(continued)

Table 2   *(continued)*

Software Defects and Expenses Repair Costs	Number	Percent
Post-release repairs per function points	$60.00	
Post-release repairs per KLOC	$545.46	
Post-release repairs per defect	$1,200.00	
Post-release monthly defect repair rate	7	
Best Product Annual Defect Reports		
Customer-reported bugs per function point	0.15	
Customer-reported bugs per KLOC	1.36	
Cost per function point	$75	
Cost per KLOC	$950	
Cost per defect	$2,200	
Average Product Annual Defect Reports		
Customer-reported bugs per function point	0.30	
Customer-reported bugs per KLOC	2.72	
Cost per function point	$175	
Cost per KLOC	$1,350	
Cost per defect	$1,200	
Worst Product Annual Defect Reports		
Customer-reported bugs per function point	0.85	
Customer-reported bugs per KLOC	7.27	
Cost per function point	$275	
Cost per KLOC	$1,950	
Cost per defect	$520	

An interesting aspect of this case study is that out of a total annual budget of $35,000,000 per year, some $17,000,000 or more than 48% of the costs are associated with either pre-release or post-release defect repairs.

This high ratio of defect repair costs is not unusual among commercial software houses, but what is unusual is a software measurement system accurate enough to highlight it. One of the main problems with software quality research has been the sparseness of the available empirical data, either due to no measurements at all or to measurements that were not granular enough to highlight major expense patterns.

Activities Performed in the First Year

Upon returning from a meeting with corporate management at headquarters, the division director convenes a meeting with software development managers and the local quality assurance managers and states that due to customer complaints at a recent shareholders meeting, he has been directed to make a major improvement in software quality. He then poses the following questions:

- "What steps should we take?"

- "Why does it take so long to turn around bug repairs?"

- "Why do so many bug repairs add new bugs?"

- "How long will it take to improve the quality of our key products?"

- "What will the quality improvement program cost?"

- "What will be the long-range impact of the quality improvement program?"

All six of these are important and valid questions when first commencing a major quality improvement push. The answers to the questions were not immediately obvious, so a second meeting was convened several days later to discuss the topics again.

Between the first and second meetings, some substantial analysis was performed of both local data and comparative data from other groups and locations. The overall picture that emerged was as follows.

Both software quality and user-satisfaction for the entire set of divisional products ranged from very good to embarrassingly poor. Three products could be singled out as needing immediate improvement, and another half-dozen would also benefit from quality and usability enhancement However, more than half of the division's products were receiving few if any defect reports and had generally high levels of user-satisfaction.

The QA manager noted that while testing had long been fairly effective within the division, the software products with the best quality and user-satisfaction levels both within the division and elsewhere also used formal pre-test inspections at the design and coding levels. However, the products with the most severe quality problems had been devoid of pre-test inspections or design reviews.

It was also noted by means of interviews with maintenance personnel that many of the most troublesome defects were introduced late in the development cycle in response to last-minute changes in the design or the product. It was suspected that test coverage of these late arrivals was sparse. To minimize such problems, a combination of formal inspections and formal change management procedures were suggested. The formal change management procedures would be linked to the testing process to ensure that proper test cases were created for features added late in the development cycle.

Further, for the software products that had severe quality problems, it had been noted elsewhere that errors tended to clump in a small number of places termed "error-prone" modules. Empirical data indicates that error-prone modules often tend to be higher in complexity than normal modules.

Also, many of the "bad fixes" or secondary bugs accidentally added to the products due to fixing prior bugs were associated with error-prone modules. The local average for bad fixes was ranged from 5% to about 8%, but against error-prone modules the bad fix injection rates were topping 20%.

The QA manager suggested an immediate analysis of local products to determine whether such modules were present, since the available quality data stopped at the level of the products and was not granular enough to determine the presence or absence of error-prone modules.

The question dealing with the length of time required to turn around defect repairs was not immediately answerable, since the route of defect reports was lengthy and included both the sales division and field-service division for some incoming reports. Further, for international clients, some of the outgoing updates had to be dispatched internationally and required customs clearances prior to being delivered. The inter-division defect repair intervals were known and were not unusually lengthy, but the defect reporting route and the update shipment route added time that was outside local control.

After additional discussion and contact with software quality assurance researchers elsewhere, it was decided to pursue two action plans, one for existing products that were already in the field and one for new products that were under development. Both were important, but the products in the field needed immediate improvement.

Initial Action Plan for Software Products Currently in the Field

- Analyze all existing products for error-prone modules.
- Determine what corrective actions were needed for error-prone modules discovered.

- Convene a cross-division study of defect reporting channels and durations.

- Expand the defect tracking system to support module-level recording.

- Analyze all existing products for complexity levels.

- Introduce test coverage analysis to ensure no testing gaps.

- Assign quality improvement targets to the responsible project managers.

Initial Action Plan for Software Products Under Development

- Ensure that state-of-the-art design methods were used.

- Ensure that state-of-the-art structured development methods were used.

- Introduce formal design and code inspections.

- Establish formal quality targets for project managers of new applications.

- Utilize complexity analysis during development.

- Utilize formal change management procedures during development.

- Ensure that quality measurements captured pre-release defects.

From a sociological viewpoint, the most interesting aspect of the software quality improvement program was its origin. The local software quality assurance manager had been recommending various quality improvement steps for several years without receiving much more than marginal funding. Although the development managers supported quality with words, their actions did not always indicate that they understood the relationships between quality, costs, and schedules.

Customers who were concerned about software quality were also significant shareholders in the corporation and raised the quality issue to corporate management during an annual shareholders' meeting. This triggered the software quality improvement program.

However, once started the software quality improvement program turned out to be self-sustaining. Indeed, since it produced shorter development schedules as well as higher quality levels and better customer satisfaction, aspects of the program moved rapidly to other divisions. Following are short discussions of the impact of some of the interesting components of the software quality improvement program.

The analysis of error-prone modules in key products was surprisingly effective. The initial analysis took about two calendar weeks and involved more than 50 software development personnel on a part-time basis. The study required about 15 staff months. At $5,800 per staff month, the cost was roughly about $87,000. A total of about 30 error-prone modules were identified in 10 products. The error-prone modules comprised less than 3% of the total volume of code, but the modules were receiving more than 45% of annual customer-reported defects across the entire division.

Repairing the error-prone modules was more difficult and required more than four calendar months. A total of 10 staff members were involved, but some of them worked overtime. It took about 45 staff months of effort to reprogram the error-prone modules. At a cost of $5,800 per staff month, the expense was about $261,000.

The total cost of error-prone module removal was about $350,000. However, the annual savings from reduced maintenance expenses totaled to more than $2,500,000 over about a two-year period. The savings started within six calendar months from the commencement of the error-prone module elimination program. Thus error-prone module removal generated a return of about $7.00 for every $1.00 invested in less than two and a half years. This is a very good return on investment, and elimination of error-prone modules is now a standard activity among many leading software producers.

As a byproduct of eliminating error-prone modules plus using inspections, the "bad fix" injection rate declined to about 2% for the division. The prior range had been in the 5% to 9% range, but for error-prone modules about 1 out of 5 repairs introduced fresh bugs.

The most difficult problem to eliminate was the long time period to turn around defect repairs. An interdivisional task force was convened and mapped every step of the defect reporting and repair process. This task force made some surprising discoveries and was eventually successful in reducing the average defect repair intervals from more than three months to less than two weeks.

The most surprising finding of the task force was that the actual repair of a software defect usually only required three days or less on average. The monthly defect repair rates for the maintenance teams were in the range of 3 to 9 defects repaired per staff month and averaged about 7 over long periods.

However, in some cases it took more than a month for the programming team to receive notification of incoming defect reports. This was because defects were not reported directly to the programming team, rather, they were filtered and analyzed by field service personnel, customer support personnel, or even by sales personnel who were sometimes the initial recipients of the defect reports.

Further, once the defect was repaired, it could take as long as six months before the repair reached the field in a new release of the product since both repairs and new features were being lumped together in semi-annual releases. Even worse, for international clients outside the United States, the new releases of the software sometimes required special paperwork in order to clear customs. While this was not a problem for many countries, for some countries the customs policies were either ambiguous or subject to individual interpretation. Therefore, from time to time shipments were delayed for as long as a month before customs cleared the material for eventual release.

The defect turnaround problem was multi-divisional so most of the expenses were not borne by the software development division, which contributed three systems analysts for a four-month period. The eventual solutions to the problem of lengthy delays included centralization of customer support, direct online defect reporting, electronic routing of defect reports to the repair centers, and immediate release of key defect repairs which could be down-loaded and deployed immediately.

The introduction of formal design and code inspections was another step with sociological interest. Formal inspections have two known features that are in direct conflict: 1) they have the highest defect removal efficiency level of any known removal activity; and 2) they are among the toughest technologies to get started because few people are comfortable with the idea of a close, personal scrutiny of their work.

One way inspections have been successfully introduced, including among the groups cited in this case study, is to start them on an experimental basis. The division director convened a general meeting about quality and asked for voluntary participation in a three-month trial period. Formal inspections would be used experimentally for three months, and then the development teams themselves would decide whether or not to continue. Further, the data on defects found during the inspection trial period would not be used for personnel appraisals or for any punitive actions.

This approach eliminates some of the initial apprehension about using formal inspections. Once started, the experimental inspections are almost always self-sustaining. When we see first-hand how many problems we have accidentally overlooked that are found during formal inspections of our work, most professionals wish to continue using the inspection process.

In the context of this case study, the initial training in inspections comprised two-day workshops for a total of 300 technical and managerial personnel over a three-month period. At $5,800 per staff month, the cost of the inspection tutorials was about $175,000.

The inspection sessions themselves average two hours in preparation before the inspection and each inspection averages two hours in duration. An average of five participants are part of every inspection. Therefore a typical inspection for the case study group would cost about $150 per staff member or $750 in total for every two-hour inspection session. Of course many hundreds of these sessions would be held on an annual basis.

Both design and code inspections tend to average more than 60% in defect removal efficiency, which is higher than any other form of defect removal. Further, inspections raise testing efficiency by more than 10% since inspected specifications are more complete and understandable than "raw" or uninspected specifications. Another byproduct of code inspections is that they help to lower the "bad fix" injection rates. It is also easier to test inspected code than uninspected code. Finally, inspections also serve as a defect prevention mechanism, since participants will avoid problems in their own work that they noted during inspection sessions.

The overall annual costs of holding design and code inspections for the case study division was about $600,000 per year, which indicates that more than 100 staff months per year were utilized during the formal inspection sessions.

Defect repairs are carried out separately from the inspections. The annual effort for repairing design and code defects noted during the inspection process amounted to about $400,000 and was roughly evenly split between design repairs and code repairs.

Some of the coding errors would have been found during testing, but very few of the design problems found by inspection would have surfaced during the testing process. Therefore most of these rather serious bugs would have probably gone out into the field, to be found by customers after deployment.

The inspections and associated defect repairs cost about $1,000,000 per year once they were introduced. However, the direct savings attributable to inspections from earlier defect removal and higher levels of defect removal efficiency were calculated to run about $3,500,000 per year, so the immediate return on investment was about $3.50 for every $1.00 expended in the first year of use. In addition, development schedules were shortened significantly and customer satisfaction improved, so there were other aspects of value besides direct savings associated with reduced defect repair costs. Once started, the inspection process quickly becomes self-sustaining.

The fact that formal design and code inspections reduce development schedules tends to make inspections self-sustaining once they are deployed. For the case study division, development software development schedules had been averaging about 21 calendar months. After inspections were introduced, the overall average schedules dropped to 18.5 months even though the inspections themselves added about three months to typical schedules. However, inspected software products zipped through integration and testing in less than half the previous time, as can be seen from the following table.

Table 3   Impact of Formal Design and Code Inspections on Software Development Schedules

(Schedule duration shown in calendar months)	Former Schedule	Revised Schedule	Difference
Requirements	2.00	2.00	0.00
Design	4.00	4.00	0.00
Design Inspections	0.00	1.50	1.50
Coding	6.00	5.00	-1.00
Code Inspections	0.00	2.00	2.00
Unit testing	2.00	1.00	-1.00
Integration	2.00	1.00	-1.00
Integration testing	2.00	1.00	-1.00
System testing	3.00	1.00	-2.00
TOTAL	21.00	18.50	-2.50

So far as can be determined from empirical studies and collected data, the human mind is still the top-ranked tool for improving software quality. In the more than 30 years of experience since inspections were first developed, nothing else has proved to generate consistently better results in terms of both defect removal and defect prevention.

As a historical footnote, the inventor of formal inspections (Michael Fagan of IBM Kingston) received an IBM outstanding contribution award for proving that inspections could improve software quality, costs, and schedules simultaneously.

Another aspect of the quality improvement program with very significant socio-logical overtones is the establishment of tangible software quality targets. Setting targets for software improvement has three key components, and all three need to be considered very carefully.

1) Who should be responsible for achieving the targets?

2) What rewards or penalties should be associated with the targets?

3) What should the targets actually be in quantitative terms?

It is obvious that assigning targets to personnel who lack the authority or "clout" to make changes happen is not going to be effective. Therefore the software quality targets were assigned to executives at the levels of the division director and the senior software managers. These levels have funding authority and the ability to introduce tools, training, and other process improvements so it is appropriate for the targets to be assigned to them.

The topic of rewards and penalties associated with targets is also a delicate one. For the case study division, it was determined that a portion of the annual executive bonuses would be based on tangible quality targets. This seems to be a fair if not per-fect solution, since bonuses are usually based on some form of performance criteria.

The case study division also had a well-funded award program for which all employees were eligible. The awards ranged from small "dinner for two" awards with a cash value of perhaps $100 up to major outstanding contribution awards that could be as much as $50,000.

As part of the quality improvement program, quality was added to the set of crite-ria for which awards were given. The smaller awards could be given by department managers at any time. For the larger outstanding contribution awards, nominations could come from department managers, but the award criteria were evaluated by an award committee. The major awards were given out at annual achievement banquets and were therefore visible to all employees.

Note an interesting sociological phenomenon:

- For top software executives, achieving the quality targets brought rewards in the form of increased bonus possibilities, while missing the targets reduced their bonus prospects, which can be considered a kind of "penalty."

- For technical employees, achieving the quality targets opened up a new possi-bility of rewards under the award system, but there was no penalty for not achieving the targets.

It seems appropriate to offer potential rewards for both executives and technical staff workers for achieving quality targets. However, if a company is introducing some kind of penalty for missing the target, then the penalty should only be aimed at those who have sufficient authority and responsibility to make change happen; i.e., executives and management.

The last topic associated with improvement targets is determining what the target itself should be. Targets should not ever be based on abstract goals such as "improve quality by 10 to 1" without any definition of what the starting value is. Setting an abstract target without knowing either the starting or ending value is so amateurish that anyone who does it would become subject to ridicule.

After serious deliberation and research by the Quality Assurance staff, the case study division director decided that the quality targets should be based on the actual performance of the best 10% of the company's software products. Note that the targets were based on all software within the whole corporation, and not just on local or divisional results.

The immediate target for the first year was based on achieving a low-level of customer-reported defects. At the time the target was set, the average for the division was an annual receipt of about 0.3 bugs per function point and the best products were receiving about 0.15 bugs per function point. However, the quality target was set at 0.1 bugs per function point, which was about three times better than division norms.

The "bad fix" injection target was set at 2% which also coincided with the better products in the company, and here, too, the target was roughly three times better than local goals.

As might be expected, several executives asserted that the targets were unachievable. However, by basing the target on real software products developed elsewhere within the corporation, it was possible to refute this line of argument.

Although the quantitative quality targets were initially greeted with some skepticism and complaints by the executives who were going to have to achieve them, the targets actually were achieved within the division within a three year period.

Somewhat surprisingly, one of the executives who had initially challenged the validity of the targets was the first to exceed them. Not only did his team exceed the targets, but he himself became a recognized authority on software quality and published several papers on the technology of software quality improvement.

From a sociological viewpoint, the establishment of a tangible software quality target for executives smoothed the way to the introduction of many software quality approaches and tools, such as formal inspections, complexity analysis, test coverage analysis, and the like.

When it was noted that schedules and costs were being reduced at the same time that quality and user-satisfaction were going up, the results of the divisional quality improvement program became very visible to corporate management. Indeed, the division director and the Quality Assurance manager were asked to put on a "road show" to explain the methods they used to other divisions and groups elsewhere in the corporation. There were also a number of technical articles, papers, and conference presentations given at external conferences and customer association meetings.

Follow-On Activities After the First Year of the Quality Improvement Program

Although the intense effort carried out in the first year solved the problems of poor quality in products already deployed, the quality improvement efforts did not slack for several more years. After the first year, the key emphasis was on the technologies of defect prevention and on methods that could benefit new products that were starting to be developed.

The divisional software quality assurance department was expanded by about 50% to meet the demand for more detailed quality measurements, participating as moderators in design and code inspections and other related activities.

One interesting aspect of the QA expansion was the creation of a small quality research team to acquire or develop advanced tools and methods for quality improvement. One of the practical byproducts of this QA research group was the development of a very powerful software quality and reliability estimating tool that could model the effects of any combination of design reviews, code inspections, and testing stages.

Another interesting predictive tool was a long-range planning model that included development and maintenance personnel, quality levels, size of the portfolio of applications, and size of the backlog of applications awaiting development.

When this model was run with the assumption that future quality levels would be equivalent to past quality levels while both the backlog and portfolio continued to grow, it predicted that the number of software personnel would double every 10 years and that two-thirds of them would be permanently locked in maintenance, enhancement, and defect removal of aging software with increasing entropy.

When the assumptions of the model were changed to include the planned improvements of both new projects under development and the geriatric program, it predicted a short-term increase in personnel of about 25% over three years, followed by a gradual reduction based on normal attrition. After 10 years, the software population would be back to approximately the size of the current staff; the portfolio the staff supported would be more than twice as large due to enhanced productivity. Even with a larger volume of software being maintained, the ratio of maintenance personnel and defect removal costs would drop below 25%. Further, the library of reusable components would allow any new application to contain more than 50% reusable designs, code, user information, and test materials by volume.

Another follow-on activity was the exploration of the division's regression test library and the discovery of both redundant test cases and defective test cases which contained errors themselves.

The fact that more bugs or defects originated in requirements and design than in code triggered a large-scale study of software design methodologies that evaluated some 150 specification and design approaches in order to determine the methods that might be most suitable for the division's software.

Although formal design and code inspections are extremely effective, their very success tends to create a long-range problem. After a year or two of using inspections, the defect prevention aspects of inspections becomes so effective that very few bugs are actually found during inspection sessions. This can lead to a false reaction by cost-conscious managers who want to eliminate the inspection process on the grounds that it no longer finds enough bugs to be cost effective.

However, elimination of inspections tends to cause a severe quality regression so that within a matter of months quality slips badly. Since testing cannot find major design flaws, the elimination of design inspections will quickly degrade testing efficiency.

These facts were discovered experimentally as part of the follow-on research performed in the few years after the initial quality push.

A very interesting long-range aspect of formal inspections is that inspected materials are more easily reusable than uninspected materials. Therefore a valuable byproduct of the introduction of inspections was a significant increase in the ability to reuse both design and code segments in other products in the second and following years after the quality push started. The relationship of formal inspections and software reuse is not widely reported in the quality literature, but it is very significant indeed.

Successful reuse of software components demands zero-defect quality levels. Reusing materials that are filled with bugs would generate a host of expensive recalls and degrade the economics of reuse to marginal or unprofitable levels. Since formal inspections coupled with professional testing activities come closer to achieving zero-defect quality levels than any other known technology, formal inspections are on the critical path for successful reuse.

Indeed, inspections are so effective as precursors for reusability that a special flavor of inspection tends to be created which focuses on factors that affect reuse potentials, as well as on conventional defects.

The success of the case study division in improving software quality, schedules, and costs simultaneously did not go unnoticed by the company, the company's clients, nor by competitors.

Migration of the Quality Team to Other Companies

An unexpected although predictable result of the division's success was the departure of several key executives who were recruited by other companies. The division director, as the most prominent executive who "led the charge" to quality improvement, was recruited by several other companies and presently became vice president of software for another major international corporation.

More than a dozen managers and quality personnel were recruited by the same company as was the director. The company was a major client that wanted to replicate the quality program in its entirety. This situation created another interesting sociological problem which also had business ramifications. When one of your 10 top customers recruits so many of your key personnel, what is the appropriate response?

It was finally decided that having so many "friendly" managers in key positions would probably be advantageous. However, there were top-level conversations between the chairmen of the two companies to discuss the desirability of slowing down the recruitment of key personnel.

Several other senior development managers and a number of technical employees were also recruited and left within four years after the quality improvement program commenced. In addition, several of the quality assurance managers and QA researchers were also recruited and left the company, with all of them receiving significant promotions elsewhere.

Within five years, at least 50 of the top managers and technical personnel of the division had moved to other companies as a direct result of the visibility of the quality improvement push. Approximately 30 were recruited by clients, and the other 20 went to competitors of various kinds.

However, the technologies that had improved quality and productivity within the division continued to be used and results remained better than corporate averages for all five years covered by this case study.

There is a strong lesson here for companies that want to improve software quality and productivity. If your company succeeds in making really impressive gains, then the managers and technical personnel responsible for those gains will find themselves in great demand by other companies. This situation is not completely unexpected, since "top gun" performers are always recruited heavily within every industry.

The case study companies were not ungrateful for the results of the quality improvement program. Indeed, salary increases and promotions for managers and personnel within the division were somewhat accelerated as a result of the quality and schedule gains. However, readers should recall a basic fact of business: for "top gun" personnel, changing companies often leads to faster career growth than can be achieved by staying within the same company.

If your company becomes "best in class" in terms of software quality, schedules, costs, or other aspects of the somewhat troublesome software domain then your company will also become a prime recruiting ground for other companies that have the problems you have already solved.

The overall conclusion of the case study is that software quality can be improved rapidly, and that the improvements will also benefit schedules and costs. However, quality improvement itself is not inexpensive. The first-year costs can exceed $1,000 per capita for the entire software community. Fortunately, the returned value will be at least three to four times that expense level in terms of direct savings due to reductions in defect repairs, with still more significant but less tangible value accruing from greater customer satisfaction and quicker time to market.

However, once state-of-the-art quality, schedule, and cost control for your company's software products has been achieved, you will find that your key managers, quality assurance personnel, and technical staff members are hot commodities on the software job market. Even if your personnel are rewarded very well, there will probably be some losses, since changing companies tends to bring better compensation packages and quicker career growth than staying within a company.

Long-Range Impact of the Software Quality Improvement Program

As a codicil to the quality improvement case study, it has been interesting to observe the long-range impact of the quality improvement program at five-year and 10-year intervals after the initial quality push.

Although about 50 of the original executives, managers, technical staff, and SQA personnel had changed companies within 18 months, the basic technologies that were introduced (i.e., inspections, complexity analysis, quality measures, etc.) continued to be utilized and division quality results stayed better than both corporate and national averages.

Indeed, more than 10 years after the original quality push the division received a corporate quality award similar in requirements and preparation to a Baldrige Award, with the software quality program as a major factor being cited.

The indications are, that high quality benefits so many other business activities that once it is achieved, there is a tendency for many aspects of the quality program to remain self-sustaining over long periods.

Of the personnel who had been part of the original quality improvement program, many utilized the results and valuable information gained to further their own careers. Several became senior managers, division directors, or vice presidents in other companies, and at least half a dozen new companies (including mine) were formed.

For those who stayed in the division itself, promotions and advancement tended to be somewhat better than average, which is not unexpected when an organization garners a reputation for doing work well.

From a distance of more than 10 years, it can be observed that the original quality improvement program benefited those who participated in it, as well as the sponsoring corporation. Further, since a number of the original personnel were recruited elsewhere specifically to replicate some of the same approaches, the quality improvement program tended to spread to other organizations as well.

A final interesting point about the quality push is that one of the products whose quality had been bad enough to trigger the program in the first place was improved so markedly that it became a top-seller in its class and continues to be marketed with high-levels of customer satisfaction and low defect levels more than 10 years later. Since the original product was so buggy that users hated it and modification was a nightmare, the elimination of error-prone modules and the restructuring of complex modules converted a significant software liability into a very profitable long-range asset.

A successful quality improvement program will benefit employees, clients, and business goals. However, a successful quality improvement program will also open up unexpected career changes for some of the participants.

CATEGORIES OF SOFTWARE DEFECTS

A careful review of the software quality literature reveals that the overall ambiguity in defining what "quality" means has carried over into the definition of software defects. There seems to be no effective and generally agreed to taxonomy of software defect categories.

This book attempts to follow the lead of other industries which have explicit warranties for their products (unlike software which usually is not warrantied). Assuming that software will eventually begin to issue warranties, this book concentrates on exploring the kinds of defects that are likely to trigger warranty repairs if they reach customers. For warranty purposes, there are four general categories of software defects that are of concern because they tend to be significant in product liability litigation:

- Errors of commission, where something is done that is wrong. A classic example at the code level would be going through a loop one time too many or branching to the wrong address. An example of this kind of error at the specification level was noted in an IBM software specification where the data format for information being transmitted was different from the format expected by the receive function of the same application. An example of this kind of problem in user manuals is frequently found in usage instructions, where the command sequence in the user manual differs from what the software really uses. Many applications are shipped with "READ ME" files which explain last-minute changes that were noted after printing of manuals occurred.

- Errors of omission, where something was left out by accident. A minor but common example for code would be omitting one of the parentheses in nested expressions. In requirements and specifications, another common error of omission is to leave out discussions of opposites. For example, a specification might say "users must enter a valid personal security code to access the system" but fail to say what occurs if the user enters an invalid code or none at all. A very serious design omission which turned into a code omission as well was forgetting to include calculations for February 29th, leap year, in the calendar routine for a software security program. All users were locked out at midnight on February 28th since the 29th was not recognized as a valid date.

- Errors of clarity and ambiguity, where two people reach different interpretations of what is meant. This kind of error is common with all natural language requirements and specification documents and user manuals, too. This error can occur with code also, and especially for languages such as APL that are difficult to sight read. A trivial example of natural language ambiguity is the expression "time flies like an arrow." The obvious meaning is about the rapid passage of time. However, a legitimate alternative meaning would be that creatures called "time flies" are fond of arrows.

- Errors of speed or capacity where the application works, but not fast enough. A classic example of this kind of error was noted during testing of an ITT telephone switching system, where performance was adequate for a few calls, but degraded to unacceptable levels as the number of simultaneous calls climbed above 20. A more recent example is that of the driver's license query system developed for the State of New Jersey, where the response time to query the status of a driver's license sometimes ran to more than 60 minutes when simultaneous queries were being made. The anticipated time for queries was less than 30 seconds.

Software defects can be found in any of hundreds of documents and work products including very serious ones in cost estimates and development plans. However, there are seven major classes of software work products where bugs or defects have a strong probability of triggering some kind of request for warranty repair if they reach the field.

The seven categories which follow are the major origin points of problems which have a strong impact on clients' ability to use the software once it is deployed:

1) Errors in Requirements

2) Errors in Design

3) Errors in Source Code

4) Errors in User Documentation

5) Errors due to "Bad Fixes"

6) Errors in Data and Tables

7) Errors in Test Cases

There are hundreds of possible kinds of errors overall with no easy or tidy way of summarizing the most troublesome subtypes. The best that can be done is to consider examples of the more common kinds of defects in each origin point.

Requirements Defects

All four categories of defect are found in requirements, although the two most common problems are errors of omission and errors of clarity and ambiguity. A significant and important aspect of requirements errors is that if they are not prevented or removed, they usually flow downstream into design, code, and user manuals. Historically, errors which originate in requirements tend to be the most expensive and troublesome to eliminate later. Therefore every effort should be devoted to minimizing requirements problems. For reducing requirements defects, prevention is usually more effective than defect removal.

Errors of omission are the most common form of requirements defects. For example, a user requirement for a software estimating tool might state "the application shall perform software cost estimates." In reality, what was intended would be something more like "the application shall perform sizing predictions for specifications, source code, and user manuals; software staffing predictions for technical employees and management; software schedule predictions from requirements through delivery; and software cost estimates for the activities of requirements, analysis, design, coding, quality assurance, testing, technical writing, and project management."

Since this book is written near the end of the 20th century, it is appropriate to mention that the requirement that software applications store dates in two-digit format is about to become one of the most expensive problems in human history. To conserve storage, many applications record the year as a two-digit number; i.e., 1996 is recorded as 96. For government software at least, this two-digit format was a formal requirement, and also a terrible mistake. When the calendar reaches the end of 1999 and moves to 2000, many applications will fail or start to produce irrational results. Although the Year 2000 problem originated in requirements, it also permeates the design and code of many thousands of software applications.

The Year 2000 problem also illustrates that defining quality as "conformance to requirements" is a hazardous practice since requirements themselves are the source of the most expensive and troublesome errors that software systems contain.

It is an interesting question as to whether requirements for large systems can ever be complete, given the observed rate of creeping requirements during the development cycle. Since requirements grow at rates between 1% and 3% per month during development, the initial requirements often describe less than 50% of the features that end up in the final version when it is delivered. Once deployed, applications continue to change at rates that approximate 5% to 8% new features every year, and perhaps 10% modification to existing features.

The second most common kind of requirements defect is the clarity and ambiguity defect. The following paragraph is from an actual software requirement and illustrates how poor natural language is for expressing software concepts: "The GPSS assembler is a two-pass program consisting of the DAG03 and DAG03 modules. Two intermediate data sets are employed between passes to retain original card images for listing purposes and partially processed card images which are used as input to the second pass. This method of operation enables the program to handle any size module and to be limited by memory size only for the number of symbols which may be retained and not by the number of input records."

The main problem with this paragraph is the use of "and" to create very long pairs of compound conditions. This construction puts a severe burden on human temporary memory capacity, which is limited to roughly seven words per topic.

All natural languages (i.e., English, French, German, Japanese, etc.) are ambiguous and prone to misinterpretation. However, natural language is the dominant method for expressing software requirements.

Thoughtful researchers such as Tom DeMarco have noted that requirements based on natural language will always be troublesome. Several formal requirements methods have been developed such as DeMarco's structured English with a well defined vocabulary and syntax, IBM's HIPO diagrams (Hierarchy plus Input, Processing, Output), the Problems Statement Language (PSL), Warnier-Orr Diagrams, the Structured Analysis and Design (SADT) technique and quite a few more. However, all of these more formal approaches make demands that the clients of software learn the method; hence they are not widely used.

Requirements can also contain errors of commission, or things that are just plain wrong or mutually contradictory. For example, a state motor vehicle registration processing system contained two conflicting requirements: 1) proof of valid insurance must be input to issue the registration; and 2) in another place the requirement called for inputting registration information prior to issuing a proof of insurance. In other words, the requirement contained a deadlock that would have prevented both the registration and the insurance proof from being issued since each required that the other come first.

Here too, having a contradictory deadlock in a software requirement statement illustrates the folly of defining quality as "conformance to requirements." It is necessary to have well-formed and unambiguous requirements before conformance is technically feasible. This means that it is necessary to have validation approaches and defect measurements that apply to requirements themselves.

Requirements can sometimes contain performance defects, too. The usual flavor of a performance problem in a requirement is to call for processing speeds that exceed the capacity of any known hardware/software combination.

Design Defects

All four categories of defects are found in software design and specifications, as might be expected.

The most common forms of design defects are errors omission where things are left out, and of commission, where something is stated that later turns out to be wrong. Errors of clarity and ambiguity are also common, and many performance-related problems originate in the design process as well. Overall, design ranks next to requirements as a source of very troublesome, and very expensive errors.

Here, too, a combination of defect prevention and defect removal is needed for success. However, formal design inspections are used by "best in class" software producers for major software applications. Formal design inspections are one of the most powerful and successful software quality approaches of all time, with a 30-year track record of success and one of the best returns on investment (ROI) of any known software engineering technology.

As an example of an error of commission, an early suite of office support tools (i.e., word processing, spreadsheet, database, graphics, etc.) was obviously designed by different teams, since the key specified for "HELP" in one portion of the application was specified as the "DELETE" key in another portion of the application.

Not only was this anomaly in the design, but the code was actually implemented with the same key alternating between HELP and DELETE functions based on which application was in use. External Beta testers usually found this problem when they accidentally deleted all of their work when they thought they were asking for help. The design was revised, and indeed the problem helped to trigger the more or less standard definition of using F1 as a help key in many applications.

The second common category of design defect are errors of omission. In fairness, it is not clear if it is technically possible to specify all of the features and functions in a large software system. If a system the size of Microsoft Windows 95 or IBM's MVS in the 90,000 function point size range were in fact fully specified, the volume of specifications would approach or even exceed the lifetime reading speed of a single individual. The total volume of specifications could exceed 500,000 pages.

Some years ago, I did a research study on design completeness within IBM. The results were surprising. For applications between 10 function points and 1,000 function points in size, the number of pages per function point increased more or less in proportion to the size of the software itself.

However, above 1,000 function points in size, the total volume of pages continued to ascend, but the number of pages produced per function point declined. Since I knew that large systems were even more complex and had even greater functional richness, that led me to conclude that the completeness of software specifications declined as system size increased.

To validate that hypothesis, I began to work backwards from listing of software code to explore what percentage of the code was actually defined in the set of functional and logic specifications which IBM guidelines called for. As I had suspected, the completeness of the specification set for large systems was well below 50%. That is, less than half of the functions in the code itself had any written citations in the formal specifications produced for the system.

Two graphs illustrate the original data on specification volumes and on specification completeness. The first graph shows the number of pages per function point for IBM software projects of various sizes.

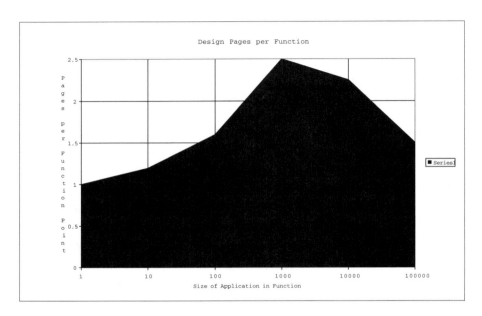

Figure 1: Software Design Volumes in Pages and Software Size in Function Points

As can easily be seen, specification volumes tended to peak sharply for software systems that were roughly 1,000 function points in size. Although the total page count in the design for larger systems continued to grow, the normalized number of pages per function point began to decline.

Since neither complexity nor richness of the feature sets declined, and indeed they usually increased with size, this phenomenon raised a very interesting question about how complete the specifications were for large systems. I worked backwards from samples of source code and attempted to quantify the percentage of the code whose features were actually present in the formal written specifications.

Figure 2 shows the completeness that I observed by working backwards from the source code. Small applications were specified fairly completely, but as the overall size of the applications grew, the percentage of features discussed in the specifications declined abruptly.

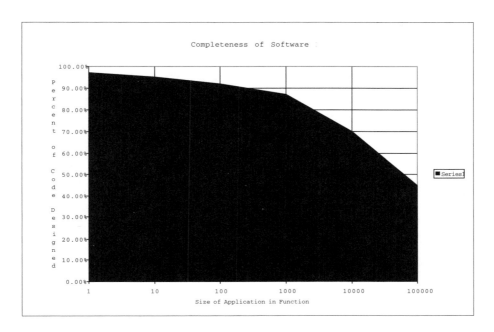

Figure 2: Percentage of Coded Features Defined in Software Specifications

This line of research raised an important question. How is it possible to build large systems when the specifications and designs are so incomplete? The answer is that human beings build systems, and we are able to compensate for partial designs by means of meetings, conferences, phone calls, memos, and other methods of communication. I hypothesize that if written specifications were the only channel of communication, large software systems would probably be impossible.

This line of research led to one other hypothesis. I attempted to estimate the volume of specifications that might be necessary to fully specify really large systems in the range of 10,000 to 100,000 function points.

The specifications for a 10,000 function point application would probably exceed 42,000 pages of text and graphics or more than four pages per function point. For an application of 100,000 function points, a complete written specification with no major omissions would probably exceed 525,000 pages or more than five pages per function point.

Since the observed volumes of specifications for systems in the 10,000 to 100,000 function point range may sometimes drop below one page per function point and seldom exceeds three pages per function point for civilian projects, it appears to be a logical conclusion that large systems are incompletely specified.

Figure 3 shows the difference between the observed volumes of specifications produced within IBM and the probable volume that would be needed to fully specify truly large applications in excess of 10,000 function points in size.

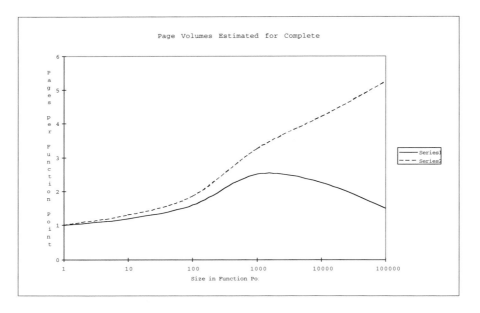

Figure 3: Difference Between Actual and "Complete" Specification Volumes

As far as I know, no human mind could encompass the volume of information needed to fully specify a really large system. Indeed, at a technical reading speed of 50 pages per day, it would take 840 business days for one person to read the specifications for a 10,000 function point system, which is almost four business years.

Reading the specifications for a 100,000 function point application would take 10,500 business days, or roughly 48 business years. This would exceed the total length of many careers from the first day of employment until retirement.

The study of software design found some other interesting topics. For example, the minimum set of specifications for an IBM software product discussed seven fundamental topics, and eight important but secondary topics. Errors in both the fundamental and secondary design topics are useful to consider.

Errors in Seven Fundamental Design Topics

1) Functions Performed

Errors in descriptions of functions the application will perform, are often errors of omission, where a particular function is accidentally omitted. Often the omitted ones are implied functions rather than those explicitly demanded by users. For example, if a software cost estimating program is designed to perform long-range maintenance estimates that may span five years or more, there is an implied need to include inflation rate adjustments over the same time periods. Implied functions such as the need for inflation rate adjustments often are forgotten in both requirements and design.

2) Function Installation, Invocation, Control, and Termination

Errors in how features, or even entire applications, should be installed are surprisingly common. At a lower level, information on how to start-up a feature, control its behavior, and safely turn off the feature when finished are also common for both commercial and in-house software. Numerically, errors of this class constitute almost 50% of the problems reported to commercial software vendors by users.

3) Data Elements

Errors in describing the data used by the application are a major source of problems downstream during coding and testing. A minor example of errors due to inadequate design of data elements can be seen in many programs that record addresses and telephone numbers. Often, insufficient space is reserved for names, or topics such as dealing with e-mail addresses as well as phone numbers are omitted.

4) Data Relationships

Errors in describing data relationships are very common and a source of much trouble later. A major problem involving data relationships actually occurred in a government agency when payroll and income tax calculations were first automated. Because of a design problem that did not ensure correct linkage of employee names with mailing addresses, every W2 tax form prepared by the agency's new software was mailed to the address of the person whose name was next in alphabetic sequence.

5) Structure of the Application

It is a well-known phenomenon that complex software structures with convoluted control flow tend to have high error rates. Poor structural design has been fairly common, and is often due to haste or to poor training and preparation. Many commercial tools can measure the cyclomatic and essential complexity of programs or systems. The problem is that once the systems are developed in a complex fashion, it may be too late. There are also commercial tools that can analyze complexity and restructure and simplify it. Although such tools are effective, prevention is often better than attempting a cure after the fact.

6) Sequences or Concurrency of Execution

Many errors of speed and capacity have their origin in failing to design for optimum performance. The most common reasons for poor performance are things like complex control flow and excessive branching, or too many sequential operations when parallel processing would lead to faster throughput. Also, minimizing external operations such as getting and putting data during performance-sensitive operations is significant.

7) Interfaces

Interface errors between human users and software, and between related software packages, are a chronic problem for software designers and developers. One example of interface errors is sending and receiving applications with incompatible data formats.

Errors in Eight Secondary Design Topics

The seven fundamental design issues actually describe the application itself. Therefore errors or defects affect what the software actually does.

The eight secondary topics describe various targets and goals, plus the hardware and software context of the application. Errors in the secondary topics are often errors or omission, although the other classes of errors are plentiful, too.

1) Security

As hackers and viruses become trickier and more common, every application that deals with business information needs to have security features designed into it. Errors in software security can result in viral invasion or easy penetration by malicious hackers.

2) Reliability

This section of software specifications defines the mean time to failure and mean time between failures targeted for the application. For contract software, reliability requirements should be stated explicitly. There is a strong correlation between reliability and software defect volumes and severity levels, so reliability targets lead directly to the need for effective defect prevention and defect removal operations. In some software development contracts, explicit targets for defect removal efficiency and post-release quality levels are now included.

3) Maintainability

This section of specifications discusses the assumptions of how software defects will be reported and handled, plus any built-in features of the application to facilitate later maintenance activity. Topics such as maintenance release intervals are also discussed.

4) Performance

This section discusses the throughput, transaction rates, and other targets for performance that the application is intended to achieve. Performance targets originate with requirements, but how they will be achieved is a major topic of the design process. Errors in performance design can lead to severe problems, including cancellation of the project or litigation for breach of contract.

5) Human Factors

This section discusses the need for training and tutorial information to ease users into full understanding of how the application operates. The human factors section also discusses screen layouts, buttons, pull-down menus, and other aspects of modern graphical user interfaces. Errors in this section can lead to notable complaints from users and low levels of user-satisfaction.

6) Hardware Dependencies

This section discusses the platforms on which the application will operate, and any special hardware drivers of devices that may also be necessary. Errors in this section may trigger substantial rework to add new hardware capabilities.

7) Software Dependencies

This section discusses other software packages that may be necessary in order for the application to operate. Errors in this section can lead to reduced functionality. A byproduct of listing specific software dependencies is the ability to explore interfaces in a thorough manner.

8) Packaging

This section, used primarily by commercial software vendors, discusses how the software will be packaged and delivered; i.e., CD-ROM, disk, down-loaded from a host, etc. Errors here may affect user-satisfaction and market shares. Also, the initial packaging decision will probably affect how subsequent maintenance releases and defect repairs are distributed to users also. For example, starting in about 1993 many major software vendors began to use commercial networks such as America Online, CompuServe, and the Internet as a channel for receiving customer queries and defect reports and also as a channel for down-loading updates, new releases, and defect repairs.

Coding Defects

All four categories of defects can be found in source code, with errors of commission being dominant while code is actually under development. Perhaps the most surprising aspect of coding defects when they are studied carefully is that more than 50% of the serious bugs or errors found in the source code did not truly originate in the source code. A majority of so-called programming errors are really due to the programmer not understanding the design or the design not correctly interpreting a requirement. Given the previous discussion of design errors, this is not a surprising situation. Software is one of the most difficult products in human history to visualize prior to having to build it, although complex electronic circuits have the same characteristic.

Indeed, the built-in syntax checkers and editors associated with modern programming languages can find many "true" programming errors such as missed parentheses or looping problems almost as soon as the programmer finishes the keystrokes. Even poor structure and excessive branching can now be measured and corrected automatically. The kinds of errors that are not easily found are deeper problems in algorithms or those associated with misinterpretation of design.

At least 500 different programming languages are in use, and the characteristics of the languages themselves interact with factors such as human attention spans and the capacities of temporary memory. This means that each language, or family of languages, tends to have common patterns of defects but the patterns are not the same from language-to-language.

Languages with highly complex syntax and arcane symbology tend to accumulate errors based on lapses in programmer attention spans or saturation of human temporary memory. Some older languages, such as assembly language, did not have much in the way of programming environments with built-in syntax checkers, code editors, and the like. Therefore the mechanical problems caused by typographical errors that were troublesome for some older languages are not really a problem with modern languages and their environments.

Programming in any language is a complex, intellectual challenge with a high probability of making mistakes from time to time. To make an analogy, most of us see occasional typographical errors when reading daily newspapers. Any major software application will have more source code statements than a daily newspaper has English words. The probability of making errors is higher with source code than with English text. The methods for finding errors are not as effective as proof reading text documents. Therefore software applications are likely to contain errors unless extraordinary approaches are used to eliminate them.

Defects in Low-level Procedural Languages

In any programming language there can be errors based on misinterpretation of design issues or poorly designed algorithms. These errors are not really caused by programming languages, but rather are caused by upstream problems in requirements, design, prototyping, or what the programmer does before coding commences.

For languages such as assembly language, C, FORTRAN, and COBOL syntactic errors are common. Also common are errors equivalent to typographical errors such as omitting a parenthesis, or inverting logical symbols (i.e., using ">" when "<" was intended).

Since low-level languages often manipulate registers and require that programmers set up their own loop controls, common errors involve failure to initialize registers or going through loops the wrong number of times.

Other common problems with low-level procedural languages involve allocating space or ensuring that data or subroutines do not accidentally overlay portions of programs. Also, embedded constants or data values can be troublesome.

For languages that are weakly-typed, which is to say have no built-in safeguards for ensuring that numbers and text are not accidentally mixed together when performing calculations, errors involving mismatched data types are common.

It is interesting that there is no solid empirical data that strongly-typed languages have lower defect rates than weakly-typed languages, although there is no counter evidence either.

Of course for all programming languages, branching errors are endemic. That is, branching to the wrong location for execution of the next code segment.

Defects in High-Level Non-Procedural Languages

Many higher-level languages, such as Ada and Modula were designed to minimize certain common kinds of errors, such as mixing data types or looping an incorrect number of times. Of course, typographical and syntactic errors can still occur, but the more troublesome errors have to do with logic problems or incorrect algorithms.

A common form of error with both non-procedural and procedural languages has to do with retrieving, storing, and validating data. It may sometimes happen that the wrong data is requested, or only part of the data.

The major problems noted in high-level non-procedural languages are those that originated upstream but find their way into the code: poorly designed algorithms, misinterpretation of design, and ambiguous requirements that do not become clear until the client sees the screen and the way the software operates.

Defects in Object-Oriented Programming Languages

Object-oriented (OO) programming languages such as SMALLTALK and Objective-C can contain syntactical errors. Errors also can be inherited due to nature of the object-oriented paradigm. However, the programming environments associated with many object-oriented programming languages are fairly effective in finding "mechanical" errors such as simple typographical errors.

With OO programming languages, the more difficult problems are those that originated upstream, such as poorly designed algorithms. Indeed, since OO analysis and design has a steep learning curve and is difficult to absorb, some OO projects suffer from worse than average quality levels due to problems originating in the design.

Additionally, some OO languages have problems for developing high-performance applications, such as those needed in weapons control systems or in-flight aircraft controls.

User Documentation Defects

User documentation in the form of both manuals and online information can contain errors of omission and errors of commission, but the most common kind of problem is that of errors of clarity and ambiguity. Performance-related errors are seldom encountered in user information.

The most troublesome problems in user manuals are found in examples and instructions for invoking or controlling certain features, such as installing the software, using it, and shutting it down. About five years ago, many newspapers, including the *Boston Globe*, ran a short article about error in a release of the WordPerfect text processing application. According to the *Boston Globe,* an error in the instructions for installing the release of this very popular word processing package led to more than 10,000 simultaneous phone calls to the vendor which temporarily saturated and shut down the phone system in the State of Utah.

Bad Fix Defects

The software quality literature has not discussed bad fix problems to the level indicated by the seriousness of the topic. The phrase "bad fixes" refers to attempts to repair an error which, although the original error may be fixed, introduce a new secondary bug into the application. Bad fixes are usually errors of commission, and they are found in every major deliverable although most troublesome for requirements, design, and source code.

Bad fixes are very common and can be both annoying and serious. From limited surveys of commercial software programming personnel, from about 5% to more than 20% of attempts to repair bugs may create a new secondary bug.

For code repairs, bad fixes correlate strongly with high complexity levels, as might be expected. This means that repairs to aging legacy applications where the code is poorly structured and resembles a "spaghetti bowl" in terms of loops and control flows tend to achieve higher than average bad fix injection rates.

Examples of common kinds of bad fixes include the following: 1) when attempting to correct a loop problem such as going through the loop one time too often, the repair goes through the loop one time short of the correct amount; and 2) when correcting a branching problem that goes to the wrong subroutine, the repair goes to a different wrong subroutine.

Often bad fixes are the result of haste or schedule pressures which cause the developers to skimp on things like inspecting or testing the repairs. Failure to validate repairs is a hazardous practice for software.

Data Defects

The topic of data quality and data defects is usually outside the domain of software quality assurance since most data is not an integral part of the software, but is added later by users once the software is deployed and in use. This is true for database packages such as Access, Paradox, IBM's Information Management System (IMS), Oracle, Alpha IV, and many others.

Since one of the most common business uses of computers is specifically to hold databases, repositories, and data warehouses the topic of data quality is becoming a major issue.

Data errors can be very serious and they also interact with software errors to create many expensive and troublesome problems. Consider the implications of data errors in credit history files, where a consumer is given a bad credit rating due to a mix up with someone who has a similar name.

Many of the most frustrating problems that human beings note with computerized applications can be traced back to data problems. Errors in utility bills, financial statements, tax errors, motor vehicle registrations, and a host of others are often data errors.

Some years ago, I remember reading a humorous but somewhat alarming short story that centered around data errors. The story was about a concatenation of data errors that started when a library book was overdue: the book was "Kidnapped" by Robert Lewis Stephenson. Because the library's computer was connected to other municipal computer systems, the reader was eventually arrested for kidnapping a victim named Robert Lewis Stephenson and brought to trial. As I recall, the unfortunate reader was finally convicted and sentenced to death, since the victim could not be found and was presumed to have been murdered.

As a real life example of a common kind of data error involved a trivial but typical situation. After a college racquetball tournament, there was a mistake in the records involving a dozen or so racquets checked out from the athletic department. Although the racquets were returned, there was a notice from the athletic department saying that they were billing $200 for the cost of athletic equipment since "their records showed that the racquets were not returned."

Upon investigation, one of the administrative people at the athletic department said that their records could not be wrong since they were computerized. Fortunately each racquet had an individual serial number. It was possible to show that although the athletic department failed to record the fact that the racquets were returned, their own computerized records showed some of the same "missing" racquets being checked out several times since the day of the tournament when they were supposed to have been lost.

The athletic department agreed to drop the charges for the racquets that had been checked out, but planned to continue charging for the racquets that had not been subsequently checked out.

This led to a request for an inventory check. Indeed, the missing racquets were all in place on the shelves within twenty-five feet of the spot where the discussion took place. This little scenario is a minor example of some major data problems:

- There was no chronological check to see if serial numbers reported as "missing" continued to show up in future transactions.

- The administrative personnel had a greater reliance on computerized records than on their own eyes or on common sense.

- When the database indicated something was missing, no one had bothered to check the inventory at all, even though the "missing" items were coming in and out every day.

Another common data error is that of duplication of information because of variations in the way information is sorted or the keys used. For example, my full name is "Thomas Capers Jones." Every week I tend to receive from two up to half a dozen copies of the same ads, catalogs, and magazines with these variations of the name on the address labels: Thomas Capers Jones, Thomas C Jones, TC Jones, Capers Jones, and C Jones.

Since sales of commercial mailing lists are very common and I've noted that about 15% of the non-personal items that reach me by public mail are duplicates that are based on some variation of my name. Expressed another way, I throw away more than two pounds of paper every week that reaches me by mail in duplicate form.

Multiplying my experience by the number of people who show up on commercial mailing lists, you may conclude that the U.S. mail moves about 1,560,000,000 pounds of duplicate material every year. To me personally, duplicate receipts may be only a minor annoyance, but the cumulative effect of this is a significant waste of energy, natural resources, and business expense, as well as an addition to the work load of the post office for no good reason.

Unfortunately, this kind of data error is very hard to eliminate. It might be possible to apply some kind of artificial intelligence or neural net reasoning to mailing list software that could eliminate such redundancies but this almost never occurs. Since each instance of a duplication is insignificant by itself and no one knows the total numbers of such instances, there is not enough visibility of this class of data error for companies to work out the economic impact of the problem.

A somewhat more serious kind of data error occurred to a mortgage company. Somewhat surprisingly a town's government *lowered* property tax rates for the 1996 year. A few weeks later notices were sent out from several mortgage companies that they were increasing payments because they assumed taxes had been *increased* which had occurred in past years. It has been very difficult to get the mortgage companies to fix this problem or even to understand that reductions in taxes occasionally happen. These are the kinds of data errors which plague industrialized and computerized nations.

A special category of data error can occur that is very difficult to eliminate. Data that is perfectly correct on a given date can change to become incorrect because the outside world which the data models has changed.

For example, the address of almost every U.S. citizen is stored in a host of databases owned by government agencies, magazine publishers, stores, service groups such as doctors and dentists, and many others.

If we move or change addresses, every single instance in every database that contains our old address will suddenly be incorrect. Since Americans tend to move fairly often, most of us know the procedures for updating our address files with the companies and government agencies that are important to us.

This is a minor example of a major kind of data error. Whenever a database stores ephemeral information that is likely to change, data errors will occur spontaneously without any change in the records themselves. Other examples of transient facts which are subject to change without notice include: marital status, number of dependents, employer, job titles, salary level, and for unmarried females who decide to change their names after marriage, names.

The most visible of all data errors based on the transient phenomena is the approaching "Year 2000" problem when many software applications will fail in the space of a single minute between December 31, 1999 and January 1, 2000 due to the common technique of storing years in two-digit form.

As computers and software become the dominant tools for storing business, personal, legal, and military information the topic of data quality, data errors, and data security are going to grow in importance in the 21st century.

Test Case Defects

The literature on software quality seriously understates quality problems with both test plans and test cases themselves. Some exploratory research carried out by IBM's software quality assurance group on regression test libraries noted some disturbing findings:

- About 30% of the regression test cases were duplicates that could be removed without reducing testing effectiveness.

- About 12% of the regression test cases contained errors of some kind.

- Coverage of the regression test library ranged between about 40% and 70% of the code; i.e., there were notable gaps which none of the regression test cases managed to reach.

Among the common kinds of errors noted for test cases were: 1) failure of the test-case to check for limits or boundary conditions; 2) errors in data that is part of the test-case; and 3) omission of certain conditions that should be tested, such as testing only three out of four possible outcomes.

Some concrete examples of errors noted over the years in test cases include things such as failing to test that enough space had been reserved for printing overtime payment reports. It happened that when monthly overtime exceeded $999.99 the high-order digit disappeared.

An interesting error in testing Microsoft Excel was noted while writing this section. Note that for the three tables in this section, the text for the Y axis is printed vertically. This is not done for aesthetic reasons, but because Excel truncates some of the characters when the label text is rotated 90 degrees. In the first table the phrase "Pages per Function Point" becomes "Pages per Function Poi" with the last characters missing when printed at right angles to the page.

Errors in test-case construction, like many coding errors, can be traced back to misunderstanding or ambiguities in the specifications and even the requirements.

The fundamental root cause is that software is a very difficult intellectual occupation. It is theoretically possible to envision better ways of visualizing software requirements and designs that might lead to the ability to generate test cases automatically. However, so long as ordinary natural language text is a dominant part of software design, we can expect errors of commission, omission, and ambiguity to remain common and troublesome.

CERTIFICATION OF SOFTWARE QUALITY PERSONNEL

The topic of certification of software quality personnel is somewhat confused and chaotic at present. Hopefully certification can be simplified in the future, but the situation will probably grow worse before it grows better.

Although SPR has been formally commissioned to perform only one large-scale study of certification, I have noted that about 125 enterprises of SPR's total client set of roughly 600 have at least a sprinkling of technical staff members who are certified in one or more software topics. The three most common forms of software certification among our clients are: 1) certified function point counter; 2) certified quality auditor; and 3) certified quality analyst.

The problem is that multiple organizations and certification groups are involved in various aspects of quality, and hence multiple certification exams might be necessary. In order to cover all of the bases, consider the following. A basic software quality analyst might want to become a Certified Quality Auditor (CQA) which is administered by the American Society of Quality Control (ASQC).

However, you might also become a Certified Quality Analyst (CQA) by taking a certification examination offered by the Quality Assurance Institute (QAI). Note that QAI and ASQC are not connected, and their certification requirements are different enough so that both kinds might be of interest.

You might also wish to become an ISO 9000-9004 auditor and you may need certification by the International Standards Organization (ISO) or an affiliate. You might also wish to become a Certified Computing Professional (CCP) in which case passing a certification examination given by the Institute for Certification of Computing Professionals (ICCP) is necessary.

If your quality data involves normalization using function point metrics, you might also wish to become a certified function point counter, and here the examination is administered by the International Function Point Users Group (IFPUG). Other organizations such as the DPMA, IEEE, ACM, SEI, and many others are also part of the certification loop.

As this report is written, the ASQC is extending and modernizing the certification exam for quality assurance personnel. There is a strong push in many non-profit associations to increase the rigor of the certification process, so that certification actually has a stamp of professionalism.

The National Software Council (NSC) is addressing both certification and also the prospect of some kind of licensing of various software specialties, perhaps along the lines of medical licensing and medical specialization.

Unfortunately, a deep problem exists with almost every aspect of certification in the software quality domain. As this is written, there is no solid, empirical evidence that correlates software quality levels with the presence or absence of certified quality analysts.

Empirical evidence shows that formal software quality assurance groups can benefit quality, but whether those groups are staffed by certified personnel or uncertified personnel remains ambiguous in terms of defect potentials, defect removal efficiency levels, user-satisfaction levels, or other tangible aspects of software quality.

The only controlled studies involving performance of certified versus uncertified technical tasks are some studies on the accuracy of counting function points where certified counters varied by only about 9% while uncertified counters varied by more than 100%.

A fundamental issue in the domain of software certification is the need to establish pragmatic evidence that certification increases job performance in some kind of measurable way.

CLEAN ROOM DEVELOPMENT

The concept of "clean-room development" is based on the work of the late Dr. Harlan Mills of IBM Gaithersburg and a number of his colleagues, including the well-known Rick Linger, who has become a prominent spokesman for the clean-room concept.

LIVERPOOL JOHN MOORES UNIVERSITY
LEARNING SERVICES

Among SPR's clients, some of the IBM labs and a few other groups in other companies have utilized the clean-room method. However, since SPR's data is too sparse for real statistical analysis, the data in this section is derived from secondary reports.

Clean-room software engineering, or CSE as Dr. Mills called it, is based on several related ideas:

- Defect prevention is more effective than defect removal, so care and structure are needed during analysis, design, and coding.

- Use formal specifications coupled with specification validation to prevent defects from moving downstream into code.

- Use a pipeline approach of incremental development of small components, with each one being validated as completed. This is termed "block-structured development."

- Use statistical-based testing, as opposed to more common forms of testing. The clean-room idea of statistical testing is based on anticipated usage patterns of the software.

- The usage patterns are hypothesized and included in the specifications themselves. Testing is performed by a separate test group with no testing (other than very private unit testing) by the developers themselves.

Dr. Harlan Mills and Rick Linger of IBM's Gaithersburg facility were the pioneers of this approach, and other industry analysts, such as Dr. Gerald Weinberg, have also espoused the clean-room development methodology.

Several successful experiments using the clean-room approach have been published by organizations such as the NASA Goddard Software Engineering Laboratory and U.S. Army's Piscatinny Arsenal. These experiments describe the use of clean-room approaches with systems software projects having a fairly stable set of requirements and generally less than 1000 function points in size.

However, other software quality and testing specialists, such as Dr. Boris Beizer, have taken violent exception to the clean-room concepts. Indeed, in a 1995 speech at the Pacific Northwest Quality Conference, Dr. Beizer compared the clean-room approach to the well-known children's tale of the Emperor's new clothes. (Two tailors tricked an Emperor by telling him they were making clothes out of a cloth so fine that only he could see it, leading to the Emperor making a public appearance without any clothes on at all.)

Unfortunately the Beizer statement was unilateral and made in a speech rather than in a panel session or debate, so there was no immediate opportunity for his observations to be challenged or rebutted by those who support clean-room concepts. Further, since Beizer is a consultant on testing and quality approaches that are competitive with the clean-room model, he is not a totally impartial observer.

The data on clean-room development published by Dr. Mills and Linger is favorable, but unfortunately it is ambiguous. The projects which have been developed using clean-room methods and protocols do achieve very high quality levels. However, the projects from which the data was developed had some special characteristics that may not have been recognized.

In the data presented by Linger at the International Function Point conference in 1994, the sizes of the clean-room projects ranged from 422 function points to about 1,600 function points. The average size was roughly 1,000 function points, as determined by "backfiring" or converting Dr. Linger's "lines of code" report into function point form.

These sizes coincide with the zone of software projects where software specifications tend to be rather complete. (Refer to the discussion of design completeness versus software size in the section on Categories of Software Defects earlier in this book.)

The types of software projects reported to date that have used clean-room methods have been those of systems software, telecommunications software, and military software. These three kinds of software happen to have a long history of formal specifications and are also the classes that are most experienced with approaches such as usage of formal design inspections and separate testing groups.

Some of SPR's clients in the telecommunications, systems software, and military software domains have achieved results similar or even superior to those reported for clean-room projects without using clean-room concepts. Companies such as AT&T, Bellcore, Motorola, the Navy's Surface Weapons group, and even other IBM laboratories have used alternative forms of defect prevention plus formal inspections and have had results at least equal, and occasionally better, than those reported for clean-room projects. (They also have much better defect reporting methods than anything yet seen from the clean-room domain.)

Unfortunately, most of the published data on clean-room methods is flawed to the point of uselessness. For one thing, the data is expressed in terms of either cost per defect, lines of code, or KLOC metrics, all of which are proven to be seriously flawed. (Refer to the section on Barriers to Software Measurement earlier in this book.) This means that the clean-room data itself is suspect, and the "industry" data to which it is being compared is essentially worthless.

Another problem with the published data on clean-room projects is that it has no granular structure. That is defects found in requirements, design, and coding have not been shown separately, nor has there been any discussion at all of errors found in user manuals and tutorial materials. Finally, since bad test cases or errors in test materials themselves is a major problem for the software industry, no solid data on the error density of clean-room test cases is available. (There is not very much data on errors in any other kind of test cases either.)

Since the sum of non-coding errors associated with software projects is usually larger than pure coding errors, the failure of the clean-room literature to present a full picture of software defect volumes in major software deliverables is unfortunate although typical.

Moreover, the clean-room data to date has been published without any serious attempt to quantify defect removal efficiency levels, or the percentage of bugs removed prior to deployment as determined on the first anniversary of shipment. This means that the entire literature associated with the clean-room concept is insufficient, anecdotal, and inadequate to either prove or disprove the clean-room claims.

To balance the equation, the counter-claims by clean-room opponents such as Dr. Beizer have not been based on firm, empirical results supported by accurate measures and metrics either.

From discussions with SPR clients who build applications of the sizes and kinds where clean-room methods have been used most often (i.e., systems software projects averaging about 1,000 function points in size) I have been able to construct a hypothetical model of how the clean-room method compares to system-software averages and to "best in class" results. I have assumed that the C programming language is used in all three cases, since C has been a common language for systems software.

The following table shows potential defects for "average" systems software projects of 1,000 function points, for clean-room projects of the same size, and for projects developed using conventional but careful structured design methods, formal inspections, and pre-test inspections. In all three cases, testing is assumed to be performed by teams of well-trained testing specialists. However, the "best in class" results reflect the utilization of formal pre-test inspections.

Table 1   Average, Clean-Room, and Best Practice Comparison of Defect Potentials for 1000 Function Point Systems Software in the C Language

(Data Expressed in Terms of Defects per Function Point)

	Average Project Defect Potential	Clean-Room Defect Potential	Best Standard Practices Defect Potential
Requirements	1.25	1.15	1.20
Design	1.25	0.75	1.00
Code	1.75	1.25	1.50
User Documents	1.00	0.75	0.75
Bad Fixes	0.25	0.05	0.10
TOTAL	5.50	3.95	4.55
Defect Removal Efficiency	90%	95%	97%
Delivered Defects	0.55	0.20	0.14

The formal block structure and pipeline approach of the clean-room method appears to be rather effective as a defect prevention method for requirements and design bugs. Reduction in front-end bugs and clear specification usually results in reduced levels of coding bugs, and slight reductions in user documentation bugs as well. Well-structured code leads to reductions in bad fix defects or secondary bugs inserted as a result of repairs to prior defects.

However, the standard "best in class" approach using formal pre-test inspections combined with formal testing by trained specialists has a long history of achieving high defect removal efficiency levels in excess of 99% against coding bugs. The overall result of 97% reflects the inclusion of other defect categories (i.e., requirements, user documents) where defect removal is more difficult.

Whether the data shown in the table is right or wrong (and note that it is based on very limited samples and has a high margin of error) it illustrates the kinds of information which the clean-room enthusiasts should collect if they want to make a solid case that clean-room development is effective. Using flawed "cost per defect" and "KLOC" data weakens the claims and makes the clean-room concept ambiguous.

It is not yet clear how the clean-room idea will mesh with approaches such as object-oriented analysis and design or client/server applications. It is also unclear how the clean-room method would work with the many MIS software projects that have highly volatile requirements where the rate of change in the fundamental requirements for the project exceeds 2% per month.

Further, for very large systems in excess of 10,000 function points, the observed completeness of the formal specifications hovers around 50%. This problem poses a severe challenge for the clean-room concept. Indeed, it is not even clear as of 1997 whether complete specifications are technically achievable for a complex system in the 10,000 to 100,000 function point size range.

How the clean-room concept would operate for a 100,000 function point system whose specifications exceed half a million pages and the time required simply to read the specifications approaches 50 working years is currently unknown.

Attempts are currently underway to broaden the clean-room concept and apply it to MIS applications with rapidly changing requirements. It is too soon to know whether the results will be favorable, but I suspect they will be only marginal at best. It is difficult to reconcile the clean-room concept with applications whose requirements grow and change at more than 2% per month during design and coding.

The current picture of clean-room development is unclear. There are also a number of interesting questions that should be answered. Here are a few samples of questions where more empirical data would be welcome:

- Does the clean-room approach reduce cyclomatic and/or essential complexity?

- Does the clean-room approach elevate user-satisfaction scores in a tangible way?

- What are function point defect potentials using the clean-room approach?

- What defect removal efficiency levels are found with the clean-room approach?

- What is clean-room productivity measured with function points?

- Are there classes of projects for which the clean-room approach is unsuitable?

- How many clean-room test cases are produced per function point?

- What is the error density of test-case defects when using clean-room testing?

- Are clean-room artifacts capable of effective reuse in subsequent applications?

When it works, the results of the clean-room approach are good, but for many projects with amorphous or rapidly changing user needs, clean-room concepts may not be appropriate or effective.

Further, for very large systems greater than 10,000 function points, there is no empirical data yet available and the probability of the clean-room approach working well above 10,000 function points is questionable. There are no known uses of the clean-room approach for applications in the 100,000 function point size range, so the empirical data on how clean-room concepts might support the upper range of software project sizes is essentially null.

From other studies, including those carried out by my colleagues and myself at Software Productivity Research, some of the fundamental tenets of the clean-room approach do appear to be sound.

Defect prevention is effective, and front-end defects in requirements and specifications should be eliminated prior to coding. Structure applied to design is always beneficial. Incremental development of discrete functional blocks is often beneficial too. Further, statistical testing that simulates usage patterns is known to be effective and is a beneficial adjunct to "standard" black box and white box test stages, even if it is not a full replacement. (See the section on Testing later in this book.)

Interestingly, statisticians at IBM's San Jose Programming Laboratory performed an analysis of computer utilization during testing at about the same time that Dr. Mills and his colleagues were developing the clean-room concept in the IBM Gaithersburg Programming Laboratory.

The San Jose study concluded that to approach 100% in defect removal efficiency using testing as the primary mechanism would require a number of machine cycles that approximated the sum of available computers of all of IBM's major customers. In other words, fully testing IBM's major software products would need computer resources beyond even that available to IBM, which is not a trivial amount of computer capacity.

So far as can be determined, this line of study has not yet been carried over to the clean-room statistical testing concept. In other words, there is not yet a theoretical model of the number of test cases, test runs, and machine capacity required to use clean-room testing on systems in the 10,000 to 100,000 function point range.

While systems that approach 100,000 function points are comparatively rare, they are also typically very important and have the greatest need for really effective quality control. Both IBM's MVS operating system and Microsoft's Windows 95 operating systems are just under 100,000 function points in size, for example.

Testing by separate test teams has also been measured and is known to be more effective than casual testing by the developers themselves, achieving defect removal efficiency levels more than 10% higher than casual testing by developers.

However, the clean-room concept that even unit testing be performed by professional testers cannot yet be considered validated. For this area, the available clean-room data is still incomplete, and the data from non-clean-room unit tests even more incomplete.

Unfortunately, the clean-room approach is sometimes being touted as a "silver bullet" that can cure all software problems. Here a possible analogy to medicine might be in order. Penicillin has been an effective medicine against a wide variety of bacterial infections. It has no impact at all against viral infections. Further, for patients allergic to penicillin, it can cause a potentially fatal side-effect known as anaphylactic shock. Used judiciously for the right condition, penicillin has long been successful. Used for the wrong conditions, penicillin can either be irrelevant or possibly fatal.

For the right kind of software, say mid-size systems applications whose requirements and specifications are stable, clean-room development appears to be an effective therapy. For other kinds of software, such as those with volatile and unstable requirements or those in excess of 10,000 function points, the efficacy of the clean-room method is currently unknown.

CLIENT/SERVER QUALITY

As client/server software applications become more pervasive, there is an urgent need to explore the quality levels, inspection approaches, testing methods, and other topics of significance.

Among SPR clients, more than 70% (around 395 enterprises out of about 600) have built or are building client/server applications. It is interesting to note that the incidence of missed schedules and cost overruns for first-time client/server projects exceeds 50% of those larger than 1,000 function points.

In our original survey performed in 1992, there was insufficient data available to discuss client/server quality levels at all. There was still a shortage of data in 1994 and 1995, but by 1996 there was no longer a total shortage. Indeed a growing library of somewhat alarming information on client/server quality has started to appear, with stories of poor quality and high maintenance costs beginning to occur in the major journals and even in some new books.

Unfortunately, the majority of client/server applications reviewed by myself and my colleagues during assessment and benchmark studies have been somewhat careless of quality control approaches. From very preliminary and partial data, the defect levels of client/server applications do not appear to be any lower than the U.S. norm for mainframe software of about 5 bugs or errors per function point, and indeed are often higher.

The defect removal efficiency levels against client/server applications appear to lag behind those of mainframe software. None of the preliminary results indicate defect removal efficiencies higher than 90%, and many are below 80%. This is based on a sample of just over 300 client server projects whose size ranged from less than 100 function points to more than 2,500 function points.

Client/server projects seldom use inspections or much in the way of rigorous development approaches. These findings, if they continue without improvement, can mean three things in the future:

- Dissatisfied client/server users.

- Low reliability levels of client/server applications.

- High maintenance costs when client/server applications themselves become legacy systems.

The following table shows a typical defect pattern for monolithic COBOL mainframe applications, using the metric "defects per function point" for normalizing the data. For the distributed client/server version, the programming language in the example is C++, although any of 30 to 50 other languages might also be used. Note that although this table is derived from observations of actual projects, the data is synthetic and rounded to show approximate results.

Table 1 Software Defect Pattern for Monolithic Mainframe Applications and Distributed Client/Server Applications

Defect Origins	Monolithic Main-Frame (COBOL)*	Distributed Client/Server (C++)*	Difference*
Requirements	1.00	1.00	0.00
Design	1.25	1.75	0.75
Code	1.75	2.00	0.25
User documents	0.60	0.50	0.10
Bad Fixes	0.40	0.65	0.25
TOTAL	5.00	5.90	1.00

* Measuring unit: metric defects per function point

The contrast between the monolithic and client/server versions shows the general effect of carelessness during development, which is often typical of client/server projects. The number of requirements problems is approximately equal between the two domains. However, due to increased the complexity levels associated with distributed software, design and coding defect rates are typically more numerous.

Also more numerous is the category of "bad fixes" which are secondary defects or bugs accidentally introduced into software while fixing previous bugs. The category of bad fixes is somewhat ominous since it has an impact on the long-range maintenance costs of client/server applications.

There is a minor difference in documentation errors between the client/server and monolithic forms, since client/server projects are often easier to explain to users due to the improved graphical user interfaces (GUI) which are a main virtue of the client/server approach.

Even more troublesome than the elevated defect potentials associated with client/server software are somewhat lower defect removal efficiency rates. Defect removal efficiency reflects the combined effectiveness of all reviews, inspections, and tests carried out on software before delivery. For example, if a total of 90 bugs are found during the development of a software project and the users find and report 10 bugs, then the defect removal efficiency for this project is 90% since 9 out of 10 bugs were found before release.

The average defect removal efficiency for typical monolithic mainframe applications has been about 85%. (Note that "best in class" companies average above 95%.) To date, the equivalent results within the client/server domain have been less than 80%, although the data on this topic is very sparse and has a high margin of error.

When the mainframe defect potentials of about 5 bugs per function point are reduced by 85%, the approximate quantity of delivered defects can be seen to average about 0.75 defects per function point.

For distributed client/server applications, the higher defect potential of 5.9 bugs per function point interacts in an alarming way with the reduced removal efficiency of 80%. The results indicate a defect delivery level of about 1.18 defects per function point, which is uncomfortably close to twice the typical amounts latent in mainframe software.

The delivery of software with high defect levels obviously implies three possible outcomes: 1) dissatisfaction among the user community; 2) higher down-stream maintenance costs for defects reported by users; and 3) a greater chance of litigation for projects produced under contract.

Preliminary observations indicate that some of these three things are already occurring. For example, the average volume of monolithic COBOL software that one person can maintain and keep running usually ranges from 750 to about 1,500 function points. For distributed client/server applications, the current range is from about 350 function points to 800 function points for maintenance assignment scopes. The post-release bug repair rate of monolithic COBOL applications ranges from about 7 to 15 bugs repaired per staff month with an average approaching 10.

For client/server projects, the monthly defect repair rate after delivery is only 4 to 10 bugs repaired per staff month and the average approaches 6. This is suspected to be due to the higher complexity levels associated with client/server architectures and hardware configurations.

Speaking of complexity, there is a need for more extensive analysis of the cyclomatic and essential complexity levels of client/server software. Very preliminary data indicates that average cyclomatic complexity levels may be substantially greater for client/server applications than for monolithic mainframe applications, although the client/server samples are too small to be sure. (See the following section on Complexity Analysis for additional information on cyclomatic complexity.)

Although client/server quality is often suspect today, that does not mean that it will stay bad indefinitely. The same kinds of methods, tools, and approaches that have been used successfully by "best in class" software producers for many years can also be used with client/server applications. These approaches can be summarized in terms of defect prevention methods, defect removal methods, and quality tools.

Among the kinds of defect prevention approaches that work with client/server applications, the concept of joint application design or JAD can be very useful. The JAD approach calls for joint requirements development between the client organization and the software group. The overall impact of the JAD method is to reduce the rate of unplanned creeping requirements and to reduce the number of defects in the requirements themselves.

Also occasionally effective in the defect prevention domain are methods such as rapid application development or RAD (when used properly and supported by formal RAD quality approaches), prototyping, reusable components, some aspects of information engineering (IE), and a variety of rigorous specification approaches such as the Warnier-Orr method, the Yourdon methods, and many others.

Structured programming and coding approaches are also helpful. Another very effective defect prevention approach, although one that takes several years to reach full power, is a quality measurement program.

In terms of defect removal, testing alone has never been sufficient to ensure high quality levels. All of the "best in class" software producers utilize both pre-test design reviews and formal code inspections. Design reviews and code inspections can both be used with client/server applications and should make notable improvements in defect removal efficiency.

In terms of tools that can benefit client/server quality, any or all of the following tools have a useful place:

1) Quality and defect estimating tools

2) Defect tracking and measurement tools

3) Complexity analysis tools

4) Design and code inspection support tools

5) Prototyping tools

6) Code restructuring tools

7) Configuration control tools

8) Record/playback test support tools

9) Test coverage analysis tools

10) Test library control tools

Client/server projects are growing in number, size, and business importance. Unfortunately, the results of attempting to build major client/server projects indicates a significant failure rate, major quality problems, and an increase in long-range maintenance expenses of major proportions. Hopefully the growing number of client/server quality vendors and tools can rectify these problems before the situation becomes catastrophic.

COMPENSATION LEVELS OF SOFTWARE QUALITY PERSONNEL

In 1995 Software Productivity Research was commissioned by AT&T to perform a multi-company benchmark study of software specialization within large companies. Some of the companies and government groups who participated directly in this study included IBM, Texas Instruments, and the U.S. Air Force. Other groups who were contacted by phone but not visited on-site included Andersen, EDS, Citicorp, Hewlett Packard, Microsoft, and Motorola.

The study was aimed at identifying how many different types of specialists were employed, how they were identified, how they were recruited, trained, and compensated. Another aspect of the study explored career opportunities for emerging kinds of specialists. Software compensation data was also collected from a variety of sources. The study was an attempt to focus on how many kinds of software occupations are currently present in the software industry and to speculate on what kinds of new occupations might occur as the 20th century winds down.

In an industry such as software that pays rather well, compensation for quality assurance specialists is not as high as compensation for many other occupations. Following are the approximate 1995 averages for various software positions with those related to software quality highlighted:

Table 1 Approximate 1995 U.S. Software Compensation

Occupation	Annual Salary	Bonus	Total	Equity
President of a software company	$185,000	$31,450	$216,450	Yes
Chief Scientist (software)	$150,000	$18,750	$168,750	Yes
VP - Software Engineering	$112,500	$16,875	$129,375	Yes
Chief Information Officer (CIO)	$105,000	$15,750	$120,750	Yes
Software research fellow	$100,000	$15,000	$115,000	No
VP - Information Systems	$95,000	$14,250	$109,250	Yes
VP - Software Quality Assurance	**$90,000**	**$11,250**	**$101,250**	No
Director of networks	$90,000	$11,250	$101,250	No

(continued)

Table 1   *(continued)*

Occupation	Annual Salary	Bonus	Total	Equity
Director of systems development	$87,000	$13,050	$100,050	Yes
Software business unit manager	$87,000	$13,050	$100,050	Yes
Director of software testing	**$85,000**	**$10,625**	**$95,625**	No
Director of Operations	$85,000	$10,625	$95,625	No
Director of Customer Support	$85,000	$10,625	$95,625	No
Director of software quality assurance	**$83,000**	**$9,960**	**$92,960**	No
Software project manager	$75,000	$9,000	$84,000	No
Director of Data Administration	$75,000	$9,000	$84,000	No
Software architect	$77,000	$5,775	$82,775	No
Senior systems programmer	$75,000	$7,500	$82,500	No
Senior systems analyst	$67,000	$6,700	$73,700	No
Systems programmer	$60,000	$3,000	$63,000	No
Systems analyst	$55,000	$2,750	$57,750	No
Computer operations manager	$55,000	$1,925	$56,925	No
Network administrator	$50,000	$5,000	$55,000	No
Database analyst	$52,000	$2,600	$54,600	No
Data security analyst	$52,000	$2,600	$54,600	No
Programmer/analyst	$50,000	$2,500	$52,500	No
LAN manager	$47,000	$4,700	$51,700	No
Quality assurance specialist	**$49,000**	**$2,450**	**$51,450**	No
Testing specialist	**$49,000**	**$2,450**	**$51,450**	No
Software planning specialist	$50,000	$1,250	$51,250	No
Software metrics specialist	$50,000	$1,250	$51,250	No
Software estimating specialist	$50,000	$1,250	$51,250	No
Database administrator	$50,000	$1,250	$51,250	No
Manager of software publications	$47,000	$1,175	$48,175	No
Programmer/Analyst	$42,000	$2,100	$44,100	No
Application programmer	$42,000	$2,100	$44,100	No
Business analyst	$40,000	$2,000	$42,000	No
Software technical writer	$40,000	$1,000	$41,000	No

(continued)

Table 1   *(continued)*

Occupation	Annual Salary	Bonus	Total	Equity
Customer support specialist	$37,000	$1,850	$38,850	No
PC technical support	$35,000	$1,750	$36,750	No
Computer operator	$30,000	$1,500	$31,500	No
Average (arithmetic mean)	$69,280	$7,047	$76,328	
Weighted average	$51,889	$3,201	$55,090	
Quality Position Averages	$61,142	$5,762	$66,904	No

The arithmetic mean is not very accurate, but the fact that the overall compensation for quality-related positions is roughly $10,000 below the overall average for all software positions is a tentative sign that quality-related positions are tolerated more than they are cherished. The fact that bonuses and equity arrangements for QA personnel are no more than "average" is also a sign that QA is regarded as perhaps a necessary evil rather than a valuable asset.

Another sign that quality personnel are tolerated rather than cherished by companies is the fact that QA personnel are often let go in significant numbers during downsizing operations. That is, the percentage of QA jobs eliminated is often higher than the percentage of direct development or line jobs.

COMPLEXITY ANALYSIS AND MEASUREMENT

The topic of "complexity" is a very ambiguous one. Researchers have not been able to agree on an exact definition of this term. Two other ambiguous terms in this set that are discussed elsewhere in the book are "data" and "quality."

When we speak of complexity in a software context, we can be discussing the difficulty of the problem that the software application will attempt to implement, the structure of the code, or the relationships among the data items that will be used by the application. In other words, the term "complexity" can be used in a general way to discuss problem complexity, code complexity, and data complexity.

Among SPR's clients, approximately 325 enterprises out of 600 utilize some form of complexity measurement tools for their software projects. The use of complexity measurement tools is common among systems and military software (> 50% of projects), and less common among management information systems, outsourced software, and commercial software (< 25% of projects). For end-user software complexity measurement tools seldom occur although are used from time to time: probably around 1% or so.

What is interesting about the usage of complexity measurement tools is the seemingly random patterns with which usage occurs. After two nearly identical projects occur in the same company where one may have utilized complexity analysis tools and the other, for no particular reason, did not.

The scientific and engineering literature encompasses no fewer than 30 different flavors of complexity some or all of which may be found to be relevant for software applications. Some of the varieties of complexity encountered in the scientific literature that show up in a software context include:

Algorithmic complexity concerns the length and structure of the algorithms for computable problems. Software applications with long and convoluted algorithms are difficult to design, to inspect, to code, to prove, to debug, and to test.

Code complexity concerns the subjective view of development and maintenance personnel about whether the code for which they are responsible is complex or not. Interviewing software personnel and collecting their subjective opinions is an important step in calibrating more formal complexity metrics such as cyclomatic and essential complexity. Unless real software people who have to work with the code assert that a cyclomatic complexity of 20 is tougher than a cyclomatic complexity of 10, it may not matter.

Combinatorial complexity concerns the numbers of subsets and sets that can be constructed out of N components. This concept sometimes shows up in the way modules and components of software applications might be structured.

Computational complexity concerns the amount of machine time and the number of iterations required to execute an algorithm. Some problems are so high in computational complexity that they are considered "non computable." Other problems are solvable but require enormous quantities of machine time, such as cryptanalysis or meteorological analysis of weather patterns.

Cyclomatic complexity is derived from graph theory and was made popular for software by Dr. Tom McCabe. Cyclomatic complexity is a measure of the control flow of a graph of the structure of a piece of software. The general formula for calculating cyclomatic complexity of a control flow graph is "edges minus nodes plus unconnected parts times two." Cyclomatic complexity is often used as a warning indicator for potential quality problems.

Software with no branches has a cyclomatic complexity level of 1. As branches increase in number, cyclomatic complexity levels also rise. Above a cyclomatic complexity level of 20 path flow testing becomes difficult, and for higher levels, probably impossible.

Data complexity deals with the number of attributes associated with entities. For example, some of the attributes that might be associated with a human being in a typical medical office database of patient records could include date of birth, sex, marital status, children, brothers and sisters, height, weight, missing limbs, and many others. Data complexity is a key factor in dealing with data quality.

Diagnostic complexity is derived from medical practice, where it deals with the combinations of symptoms (temperature, blood pressure, lesions, etc.) needed to identify an illness unambiguously. For example, for many years it was not easy to tell whether a patient had tuberculosis or histoplasmosis since the superficial symptoms were essentially the same. For software, diagnostic complexity becomes a factor when customers report defects and the vendor tries to isolate the relevant symptoms and figure out what is really wrong.

Entropic complexity is the state of disorder of the component parts of a system. Entropy is an important concept because all known systems have an increase in entropy over time. That is, disorder gradually increases. This phenomenon has been observed to occur with software projects, since many small changes over time gradually erode the original structure. Long-range studies of software projects in maintenance mode attempt to measure the rate at which entropy increases, and whether it can be reversed by approaches such as code restructuring.

Essential complexity is also derived from graph theory and was made popular by Dr. Tom McCabe. The essential complexity of a piece of software is derived from cyclomatic complexity after the graph of the application has been simplified by removing redundant paths. Essential complexity is often used as a warning indicator for potential quality problems. As with cyclomatic complexity, a module with no branches at all has an essential complexity level of 1. As unique branching sequences increase in number, both cyclomatic and essential complexity levels rise.

Fan complexity refers to the number of times a software module is called (termed "fan in") or the number of modules which it calls (termed "fan out"). Modules with a

LIVERPOOL
JOHN MOORES UNIVERSITY
AVRIL ROBARTS LRC
TITHEBARN STREET
LIVERPOOL L2 2ER

large fan in number are obviously critical in terms of software quality, since they are called by many other modules. However, modules with a large fan out number are also important, and are hard to debug because they depend upon so many extraneous modules. Fan complexity is relevant to exploration of reuse potentials.

Flow complexity is a major topic in the studies of fluid dynamics and meteorology. It deals with turbulence of fluids moving through channels and across obstacles. A new sub-domain of mathematical physics called "chaos theory" has elevated the importance of flow complexity for dealing with physical problems. Many of the concepts, including chaos theory itself, appear relevant to software and are starting to be explored.

Function point complexity refers to the set of adjustment factors needed to calculate the final adjusted function point total of a software project. Standard U.S. function points as defined by the International Function Point Users Group (IFPUG) have 14 complexity adjustment factors. The British Mark II function point uses 19 complexity adjustment factors. The SPR function point and feature point metrics use 3 complexity adjustment factors.

Graph complexity is derived from graph theory and deals with the numbers of edges and nodes on a graph created for various purposes. The concept is significant for software because it is part of the analysis of cyclomatic and essential complexity and also part of the operation of several source code restructuring tools.

Halstead complexity is derived from the "software science" research carried out by the late Dr. Maurice Halstead and his colleagues and students at Purdue University. The Halstead software science treatment of complexity is based on four units: 1) number of unique operators (i.e., verbs); 2) number of unique operands (i.e., nouns); 3) instances of operator occurrences; and 4) instances of operand occurrences. The Halstead work overlaps linguistic research, as it seeks to enumerate concepts such as the vocabulary of a software project.

Information complexity is concerned with the numbers of entities and the relationships between them that might be found in a database, repository, or data warehouse. Informational complexity is also associated with research on data quality.

Logical complexity is important for both software and circuit designs. It is based upon the combinations of AND, OR, NOR, and NAND logic conditions that are concatenated together. This form of complexity is significant for expressing algorithms and for proofs of correctness.

Mnemonic complexity is derived from cognitive psychology and deals with the ease or difficulty of memorization. It is well known that the human mind has both a temporary and permanent memory. Some kinds of information (i.e., names, telephone numbers) is held in temporary memory and requires conscious effort to move it into permanent memory. Other kinds of information (i.e., smells, faces) go directly to permanent memory. This topic is important for software debugging and during design and code inspections. Many procedural programming languages have symbolic conventions that are very difficult either to scan or to debug because they over-saturate human temporary memories. Things such as nested loops that use multiple levels of parentheses, i.e., "(((. . .)))" tend to swamp human temporary memory capacity.

Organizational complexity deals with the way human beings in corporations arrange themselves into hierarchical groups or matrix organizations. This topic might be assumed to have only an indirect bearing on software, except for the fact that many large software projects are decomposed into components that fit the current organization structure. For example, many large projects are decomposed into segments that can be handled by eight-person departments whether or not that approach meets the needs of the system's architecture.

Perceptional complexity is derived from cognitive psychology and deals with the arrangements of edges and surfaces that appear simple or complex to a human observers. For example, regular patterns appear simple while random arrangements appear complex. This topic is important for studies of visualization, software design methods, and evaluation of screen readability.

Problem complexity concerns the subjective views of the people asked to solve them about the difficulty of various kinds of problems. Psychologists know that increasing the numbers of variables and the length of the chain of deductive reasoning usually brings about an increase in the subjective view that the problem is complex. Inductive reasoning also adds to the perception of complexity. In a software context, problem complexity is concerned with the algorithms that will become part of a program or system. Determining the subjective opinions of real people is a necessary step in calibrating more objective complexity measures.

Process complexity is mathematically related to flow complexity, but in day to day software work it is concerned with the flow of materials through a software development cycle. This aspect of complexity is often dealt with in a practical way by project management tools which can calculate critical paths and PERT diagrams (Program Evaluation and Review Technique) of software development processes.

Semantic complexity is derived from the study of linguistics and is concerned with ambiguities in the definitions of terms. Already cited in this book are the very ambiguous terms "quality," "data," and "complexity." This topic is relevant to software for a surprising reason: many law suits between software developers and their clients can be traced back to the semantic complexity of the contract, where both sides claim different interpretations of the same clauses.

Syntactic complexity is also derived from linguistics and deals with the grammatical structure and lengths of prose sections such as sentences and paragraphs. A variety of commercial software tools are available for measuring syntactic complexity using metrics such as the FOG index. (Unfortunately, these tools are seldom applied to software specifications although they would appear valuable for that purpose.)

Topologic complexity deals with rotations and folding patterns. This topic is often explored by mathematicians, but it also has relevance for software. For example, topological complexity is a factor in some of the commercial source code restructuring tools.

As can be seen from the variety of subjects included under the blanket term "complexity," this is not an easy topic to deal with. From the standpoint of software quality, six flavors of complexity stand out as being particularly significant:

- Code complexity (determined by interviews)
- Cyclomatic complexity
- Data complexity
- Information complexity
- Process complexity
- Problem complexity (determined by interviews)

If these six aspects of complexity are high, based on either the subjective opinions of the technical staff who are building the software or on objective metrics, then quality, schedules, and costs are all likely to be troublesome for the project in question. Conversely, if these six aspects of complexity are low, then the software project is not likely to prove troublesome.

Unfortunately, complexity and size usually go hand in hand for software so the low-complexity projects tend to be those of less than 100 function points in size, while many of the projects larger than 1,000 function points in size, and almost all software projects above 10,000 function points in size, are rather high in terms of the six complexity factors that are most troublesome for software.

Most forms of complexity have two independent root causes for why they occur in software projects:

- Software development is a very difficult and challenging intellectual exercise, and some of the problems are just plain hard no matter what kind of complexity is being considered.

- Software development practices are lax enough so that sometimes complexity in terms of poor code structure or questionable design practices appears to be an accidental byproduct of poor training or excessive haste.

Although the two root causes are independent variables, they can and often do occur together. When very hard problems are coupled with lax, careless, or poorly trained developers the project seldom has a happy ending and may not get finished at all.

It has been known for many years that complexity of various forms tends to have a strong correlation with elevated defect levels, reduced levels of defect removal efficiency, and elevated maintenance costs.

The correlation between complexity and quality are not perfect but are strong enough so that "best in class" companies utilize automated tools for measuring the complexity of source code.

The two most common metrics for software complexity analysis that are supported by commercial tools are "cyclomatic complexity" and "essential complexity" which were both made popular by Dr. Tom McCabe, the chairman of McCabe Associates.

Cyclomatic complexity measures the control flow of applications. It is derived from graph theory and is based on the numbers of edges and nodes of a graph of the control flow of the application. The overall formula is number of edges minus number of nodes plus two. The following example illustrates the case of minimum cyclomatic complexity, or a straight linear sequence of execution without any branches at all.

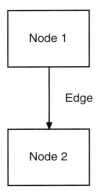

Cyclomatic Complexity = 1

Figure 1: The Minimum Cyclomatic Complexity With No Branching

Recall that the formula for calculating cyclomatic complexity is "edges − nodes + 2." Applying this formula to the simple graph yields: (1 edge − 2 nodes) + 2 = 1.

Essential complexity is derived from cyclomatic complexity, after redundant or duplicate code sections are eliminated. In the case of the simple graph shown here, cyclomatic and essential complexity are both one. However, for more complex programs the cyclomatic complexity number is often much larger than the essential complexity number.

Both metrics generate a scale that is normally expressed in integer form. A perfectly structured application will have both a cyclomatic and essential complexity level of 1, since there are no branches, and control flow is a straight path.

As complexity rises, the chance or probability of errors also tends to rise, although the data on the correlations between complexity and defect rates has some exceptions. In general, modules or applications with a cyclomatic complexity of less than 10 are considered to be well-structured. As the cyclomatic complexity levels begin to rise above 20, above 30, and above 50, defect levels and maintenance costs tend to go up accordingly.

Another aspect of an increase in cyclomatic complexity is a need for more and more test cases to cover all paths and permutations of paths. Indeed, full coverage testing is difficult for cyclomatic complexities above 10 and probably impossible for cyclomatic complexities higher than 20.

Many companies sell tools that can measure cyclomatic and essential complexity. McCabe & Associates is the dominant supplier in the United States, but there are also shareware and even freeware tools that can do such measurements. Most programming languages can be analyzed for complexity, and the standard mode of operation for the complexity analysis tools is to parse the source code directly.

Complexity analysis is an intermediate stage of another quality approach, too. Most of the commercial code restructuring tools begin with a complexity analysis, and then automatically simplify the graph of the application and rearrange the code so that cyclomatic and essential complexity are reduced.

Dr. Eric Bush, the former chairman of Language Technology in Salem, Massachusetts, was the pioneer for this approach. Dr. Bush later moved to IBM, and Language Technology was acquired by KnowledgeWare. The tool that Dr. Bush designed and several others like it continue to be marketed.

Although complexity analysis itself works on a wide variety of programming languages, the code restructuring tools were originally limited to COBOL. In recent years, C and FORTRAN have been added but there are many hundreds of languages for which automatic restructuring is not possible.

Complexity analysis plays a part in "backfiring" or direct conversion from lines of code (LOC) metrics to function point metrics. Because the volume of source code needed to encode one function point is partly determined by complexity, it is at useful to have cyclomatic and essential complexity data available when doing backfiring. In principle, the complexity analysis tools could generate the equivalent function point totals automatically, and some vendors are starting to do this.

Much of the literature on software complexity concentrates only on code, and sometimes only on the control flow or branching sequences. While code complexity is an important subject and worthy of research, it is not the only topic that needs to be explored.

Software Productivity Research uses multiple-choice questions to elicit information from software development personnel about their subjective views of several kinds of complexity. We normally interview half a dozen technical personnel for each project and question their perceptions of the factors which influenced the project, using several hundred multiple-choice questions.

It is relevant to show how perceived complexity increases with some tangible examples. Following are five plateaus for problem complexity, code complexity, and data complexity to illustrate examples of factors at play in the ranges between simple and highly complex in these three domains.

Problem Complexity

1) Simple algorithms and simple calculations:

- All problem elements well understood

- Logic is primarily well understood

- Mathematics primarily addition and subtraction

2) Majority of simple algorithms and simple calculations:

- Most problem elements well understood

- Logic is primarily deductive from simple rules

- Mathematics primarily addition and subtraction with few complex operations

3) Algorithms and calculations of average complexity:

- Some problem elements are "fuzzy" and uncertain

- Logic is primarily deductive, but may use compound rules with IF, AND, OR, or CASE conditions

- Mathematics may include statistical operations, calculus, or higher math

4) Some difficult and complex calculations:

- Many problem elements are "fuzzy" and uncertain

- Logic is primarily deductive, but may use compound rules with IF, AND, OR, or CASE conditions; some inductive logic or dynamic rules may be included; some recursion may be included

- Mathematics may include advanced statistical operations, calculus, simultaneous equations, and non-linear equations

5) Many difficult and complex calculations:

- Most problem elements are "fuzzy" and uncertain

- Logic may be inductive as well as deductive. Deductive logic may use compound, multi-level rules involving IF, AND, OR, or CASE conditions; recursion is significant

- Mathematics includes significant amounts of advanced statistical operations, calculus, simultaneous equations, non-linear equations, and non-commutative equations

Code Complexity

1) Nonprocedural (generated, database, spreadsheet):

- Simple spreadsheet formulas or elementary queries
- Small modules with straight-through control flow
- Branching logic close to zero

2) Built with program skeletons and reusable modules:

- Program or system of a well-understood standard type
- Reusable modules or object-oriented methods
- Minimal branching logic

3) Well structured (small modules and simple paths):

- Standard IF/THEN/ELSE/CASE structures used consistently
- Branching logic follows structured methods

4) Fair structure, but some complex paths or modules:

- Partial use of IF/THEN/ELSE/CASE structures
- Some complicated branching logic
- Memory or timing constraints may degrade structure

5) Poor structure, with many complex modules, paths:

- Random or no use of IF/THEN/ELSE/CASE structures
- Branching logic convoluted and confusing
- Severe memory or timing constraints degrade structure

Data Complexity

1) Simple data, few variables, and little complexity:

- Single file of basic alphanumeric information
- Few calculated values
- Minimal need for validation

2) Several data elements, but simple data relationships:

- Single file of primarily alphanumeric information
- Some calculated values
- Some interdependencies among records and data
- Some need for validation

3) Multiple files, switches, and data interactions:

- Several files of primarily alphanumeric information
- Some calculated or synthesized values
- Substantial need for validation
- Some data may be distributed among various hosts

4) Complex data elements and complex data interactions:

- Multiple files structures
- Some data may be distributed among various hosts
- Some data may not be alphanumeric (i.e., images. graphics)
- Many calculated or synthesized values
- Substantial need for validation
- Substantial interdependencies among data elements

5) Very complex data elements and complex data interactions:

- Multiple and sometimes incompatible files structures
- Data distributed among various and incompatible hosts
- Data may not be alphanumeric (i.e., images. graphics)
- Many calculated or synthesized values
- Substantial need for validation
- Substantial interdependencies among data elements

Over the years my colleagues at SPR and I have interviewed thousands of software development personnel using this form of complexity questionnaire, and they have also collected quantitative data on defect levels and defect removal efficiency levels.

As might be suspected, software projects where the answers are on the high side of the scale (4s and 5s) for problem, code, and data complexity tend to have much larger defect rates and much lower defect removal efficiency levels than projects on the lower end of the scale (1s and 2s).

Some interesting exceptions to this rule have been observed. From time to time highly complex applications have achieved remarkably good quality results with few defects and high levels of defect removal efficiency. Conversely, some simple projects have approached disastrous levels of defects and achieved only marginal levels of defect removal efficiency.

The general reason for this anomaly is that software project managers tend to assign the toughest projects to the most experienced and capable technical staff, while simple projects are often assigned to novices or those with low levels of experience.

Complexity is a very important topic for software. Indeed, the complexity of some software applications appears to be as great as almost any kind of product constructed by the human species.

Much more research is needed on all forms of software complexity, and particularly on complexity associated with algorithms, visualization, software requirements, specifications, test cases, and data complexity.

CONFIGURATION CONTROL

One of the key components of an effective software quality program is the combination of formal methods plus automated tools for dealing with changes in software deliverables. Changes can be due to changes in requirements, to changes in business conditions, to changes in laws or policies, changes in technology or platforms, or changes associated with the need to fix bugs.

Among our clients, more than 350 companies out of roughly 600 utilize some form of configuration control automation. However, only about 75 companies have really powerful configuration control suites which can deal with changes in requirements, specifications, source code, test cases, planning documents, and user manuals concurrently.

Approximately 275 additional companies have source code configuration control but lack automated capabilities for relating the source code to specifications, test cases, and other key software artifacts. What is somewhat alarming is the fact that approximately 250 companies use informal and only partially automated approaches to what is a very complicated and technically challenging kind of work.

Software projects change as rapidly as any product ever conceived by the human mind. Therefore one of the major challenges of the software industry has been to manage change as efficiently as possible.

This challenge was poorly met for many years. The primary change-management tools for source code were standalone file-based version control systems that supported source code only. Change management for text specifications and planning documents, cost estimates, test libraries, graphics and illustrations, and the inventories of bugs reported against software projects were all performed using only rudimentary standalone tools that often did not communicate or coordinate across domains.

In recent years, since about 1990, it has been recognized that source code is not the only deliverable that changes. In fact, for many projects source code is not even the major item that changes. For large software projects, many more words are created than source code and the words change more rapidly! There are also large volumes of bug reports, which need constant surveillance and monitoring during software development and maintenance.

Therefore, modern change management tools, or "configuration control" tools as they are commonly called, must be capable of dealing with every kind of software deliverable and artifact:

- Changing requirements
- Changing project plans
- Changing project cost estimates
- Changing contracts
- Changing design
- Changing source code
- Changing user documents

- Changing illustrations and graphics
- Changing test materials
- Changing volumes of bug reports

In order to discuss the rate at which software deliverables change, it is necessary to know at least approximately how big they are under normal conditions.

Table 1 below, shows the nominal sizes associated with a generic systems software project of 1,000 function points in size. This example project can be assumed to use the C programming language and is about 125,000 logical statements or 125 KLOC in size.

Table 1   Average Deliverable Sizes for a 1,000 Function Point System Software Application

Deliverable	Size per Function Point	Basic Size	Monthly Change Rate
Requirements	0.3 (pages)	300 pages	2%
Plans/estimates	0.2 (pages)	200 pages	10%
Design	1.5 (pages)	1500 pages	5%
Source code	125.0 (source lines)	125,000 LOC	7%
Test cases	5.0 (test cases)	5,000 cases	10%
User manuals	0.6 (pages)	600 pages	5%
Defects (bug reports)	5.0 (bugs)	5,000 reports	15%

Because non-code material such as text and graphics actually comprise the bulk of software deliverables, it is of interest to include some information on the approximate volumes of these two items.

Table 2 shows the approximate volumes of the major paper deliverables associated with software. Of course many more ephemeral documents are produced, such as letters, memos, presentations, progress reports, and the like. (A total of about 50 kinds of paper documentation can occur for large software projects.) However these ephemeral documents may not come under configuration control, while the basic specifications, contracts, plans, estimates, and user documents often do.

Table 2   Volume of Text and Words Produced for a Generic System Software Project of 1,000 Function Points

Deliverable	Basic Size in Pages	English Words	English Words per Function Point
Requirements	300	120,000	120
Plans/estimates	100	40,000	40
Design	1500	600,000	400
User manuals	600	240,000	240
Bug reports	5,000	1,350,000	1,350
Total	7,500	2,350,000	2,350

Since the volume of source code in this example is 125,000 logical statements, it can be seen that more than 184 words are created for every source code statement. (Had this been a military project, the total would have been more than 400 English words per source code statement.)

Both the large volume of information associated with bug reports, and the significance of this topic, implies a need for very strong defect tracking capabilities as part of configuration control tool suites.

COST ESTIMATING AND SOFTWARE QUALITY

The commercial software estimating business started in the early 1970s circa 1973. The first four commercial software cost estimating tools did not support quality estimates in their earliest form. PRICES-S, COCOMO, SLIM®, and ESTIMACS™ appeared between the years 1979 and 1983 and were the pioneers of today's software estimating business. However in their modern form these tools, and many newer estimating tools, do support quality estimation.

Among our clients, about 275 companies out 600 utilize at least one commercial estimating tool (or proprietary automated estimating tool). The other 325 companies do estimating using manual or "seat of the pants" approaches.

However, among our top clients that have the best overall results, the usage of multiple cost estimating tools may occur. For example, CHECKPOINT, SLIM, or PRICE-S and SEER or ESTIMACS and Bridge Modeler might be used concurrently to look for convergence or divergence.

The COCOMO estimating method was not originally a software tool at all, but rather a set of estimating equations described in Dr. Barry Boehm's 1981 book *Software Engineering Economics* (Prentice Hall). Since the equations were in the public domain, at least half a dozen software estimating tools were soon developed using the COCOMO "engine" as the base.

My own interest in software cost estimating started in the 1970s, too, when Dr. Charles Turk and I developed IBM's first software estimating tool for systems software. This was a proprietary estimating tool rather than a commercial product. For 1973 it was rather sophisticated and included software quality and defect removal estimates. However, the tool only supported the kinds of software inspections and testing steps used within IBM's systems development labs.

After leaving IBM, I joined ITT, which was a very diverse conglomerate. At its peak ITT owned more than 200 companies, more than 100 of which produced software. As a conglomerate, there was no consistency whatsoever in the methods, tools, and programming languages used for software development. I counted more than 50 programming languages and more than 15 different methodologies and software design approaches within the larger ITT labs.

ITT was also a multi-national corporation with labs in many countries in Europe, North and South America, the Far East, and the Middle East. It was obvious to those who worked in software within the corporation that single-purpose tools would never be satisfactory for such a diverse enterprise.

After Software Productivity Research (SPR) was formed, the strategy was to build estimating tools that supported quality and productivity estimation for any kind of software, in any country.

In 1985 our SPQR/20™ software estimating tool was released. The acronym "SPQR" stood for "Software Productivity, Quality, and Reliability." So far as can be determined, this was the first commercial software estimating tool to feature integrated defect predictions and to estimate defect removal efficiency levels. This tool also estimated the reliability of software at various intervals, starting with the day of the initial release.

A pragmatic reason for including quality estimates as standard features of software cost estimating tools is that for large systems, the time and effort devoted to finding and fixing bugs constitute what is often the most expensive work of the entire project. It is not possible to create accurate overall software cost estimates if the major cost driver is left out of the equation.

SPR's second tool, CHECKPOINT, came out in 1989 and added very detailed quality estimates that provide the basis for discussion here. There are three major subtopics to explore when discussing software quality estimation:

1) Predicting the probable number of defects that might be encountered.

2) Estimating the probable kinds of defect removal operations to be used.

3) Estimating the defect removal efficiency of the operations utilized.

Note that all three aspects of software quality estimation must be based on empirical data taken from several thousand software projects. As with every other kind of estimating, accurate measurement is the starting point. Without solid empirical data as a starting point, accurate estimation is essentially impossible.

Predicting Defect Potentials

As mentioned elsewhere in this book, the defect potential for a software application consists of the probable numbers of bugs or errors that will be encountered in five key software deliverables:

1) Requirements bugs

2) Design bugs

3) Coding bugs

4) User documentation bugs

5) Bad fixes, or secondary bugs created while repairing previous bugs

Two other kinds of defect predictions are not yet supported in software estimating tools but will probably be added within the next year:

6) Test case errors

7) Data quality errors

The ranges of defects encountered in each category are very broad. Factors which influence the ranges include the experience levels of the technical staff, the experience levels of the clients, schedule pressure, creeping requirements, the technical novelty of the application, the size of the application, the complexity of the application, certified reusable components, and the methodologies and programming languages that will be utilized while building the application.

The best-case situation would consist of a very experienced and capable technical staff working with experienced clients building a well-understood kind of application where certified reusable components are available and where tools and programming languages are both very familiar and well suited to the nature of the application. Here the overall defect potential can drop to or even below 1 bug per function point.

The worst-case situation would consist of inexperienced technical personnel working with inexperienced clients, under significant schedule pressure, on a highly complex new kind of application with excessive creeping requirements while using tools and programming languages that are unfamiliar or unsuitable coupled with close to zero availability of certified reusable material. In the worst-case, the overall defect potential can be equal to or greater than 15 bugs per function point.

Between the best-case and worst-case situations are countless intermediate possibilities. Since all of the variables are essentially independent, a great deal of historical data must be analyzed in order to derive any pattern or order to the probabilities of various kinds of defects occurring. Nonetheless, U.S. averages for the projects analyzed by myself and my colleagues typically run between 4 and 6 bugs per function point.

To determine the probable number of defects of each type requires knowledge of a number of supplemental facts such as the experience levels of the team for this particular kind of application, the availability of certified reusable components, and a number of others.

Predicting software defect potentials brings to mind a quote from Samuel Johnson when he observed a dog that had been trained to walk on its hind legs: "It isn't done well, but it is surprising that it can be done at all."

Table 1 shows the minimum, average, and maximum numbers of defects noted during SPR assessment and benchmark studies between 1986 and 1996.

Table 1   Observed Ranges in Software Defect Potentials Between 1986 and 1996

(Data expressed in terms of defects per function point)

	Minimum	Average	Maximum
Requirements	0.15	1.00	2.50
Design	0.30	1.25	4.25
Code	0.25	1.75	5.75
User Documents	0.25	0.60	1.50
Bad Fixes	0.05	0.40	2.75
TOTAL	1.00	5.00	16.75

Note that Table 1 shows defects found over the life of a software project from the start of requirements through the first year or two of deployment. The table does not show the number of delivered defects. Before delivery, the defect potential will be reduced to a greater or lesser degree by the set of defect removal operations that are utilized.

Estimating the Sequence of Defect Removal Activities to Be Used

The total number of defect removal operations observed on software projects can range from 0 to a total of more than 20. There are characteristic patterns based on the size and class of the software being developed.

Consider three examples of the defect removal activities that might be performed on software projects of 1,000 function points in size. One of the examples is a civilian management information systems (MIS) project such as might be built by a bank, one of the examples is a civilian systems software project such as might be built by a telecommunications company, and the third example is a military software project such as might be built by a defense contractor.

Table 2   Differences in Defect Removal Patterns for Three Software Classes

(Assumes all three examples are 1,000 function points in size)

Civilian MIS Projects	Systems Software Projects	Military Software Projects
	Design inspection	Design review
	Code inspection	Code inspection
		Ind. verif. & valid.
Subroutine test	Subroutine test	Subroutine test
Unit test	Unit test	Unit test
System test	Integration test	Integration test
Acceptance test	Performance test	Performance test
	Regression test	Regression test
	System test	System test
	Field test	Independent test
		Acceptance test

The MIS project performed only four defect removal operations; the systems software project performed nine defect removal operations; and the military software project performed 11 defect removal operations.

Although these examples are simplified and hypothetical, they reflect real-life differences in defect removal patterns. There is no constant set of defect removal operations which are always performed on every project. However, there are patterns of typical defect removal operations that are associated with various industries, with various classes of software applications, and with various sizes of software projects. (See the sections on Defect Removal Efficiency and Testing for additional information.)

A knowledge of software defect removal patterns can best be acquired by examining several thousand software projects from different industries and companies. Since this is of necessity a lengthy process, the software estimating companies that have done this might regard their findings as proprietary trade secrets.

Note that in this simplified set of examples, the number of defect removal operations for software of exactly the same size, 1,000 function points, ranged from a low of only three test steps to a high of seven test steps preceded by three non-test defect removal operations.

The function point metric provides an interesting general rule for predicting the number of defect removal operations that must be included in the series if you wish to go above 95% in cumulative defect removal efficiency. Raise the size of the application in function points to the 0.3 power and express the result as an integer.

Using this rule (which is only a rough approximation by the way) an application of 100 function points would require four defect removal stages. An application of 1,000 function points would require eight defect removal stages. An application of 10,000 function points would require 16 defect removal stages.

Estimating the Defect Removal Efficiency of the Series of Operations Used

Each kind of software defect removal operation used will have a characteristic defect removal efficiency. Here too there are wide ranges of performance. What is surprising and perhaps even depressing is that the average defect removal efficiency for almost every kind of test step hovers around 30%. That is, most forms of testing will only find approximately one bug out of every three that are actually present.

Only a handful of defect removal operations top 60% in removal efficiency under controlled conditions. Every now and then a gifted programmer might go above 60% in unit testing, and sometimes systems test can reach that mark as well. There are only four defect removal operations that stand out from the pack as having a very good probability of going over 60% almost every time they are utilized:

1) Formal requirements inspections

2) Formal design inspections

3) Formal code inspections

4) High-volume Best testing with more than 10,000 clients

Although the calculations for defect removal efficiency are discussed elsewhere in the book (in the section on Defect Removal Efficiency), it is useful to repeat the basic method here. During development keep a record of all bugs or defects that are found. For example, suppose a total of 90 bugs are found during development. After the project is released to customers, keep records of all the bugs which customers find for a fixed interval, such as one year. Suppose the customers find a total of 10 valid, unique defects. (Duplicates are not for defect removal efficiency calculations.)

After one year, add the 10 user-reported bugs to the 90 bugs found during development. It is obvious that the cumulative defect removal efficiency during development was 90%, since 9 out of 10 bugs were discovered prior to release.

In real life, defect removal efficiency is a great deal more complicated. For example, each kind of defect removal operation can have a differential efficiency against various kinds of defects. Code inspections might be 85% efficient against coding defects, and also find 30% of remaining design defects and even 15% of requirements defects.

An illustration can reveal some of the complexity associated with calibrating defect removal efficiency levels. Assume a software project is 100 function points in size and has a defect potential of 460 defects or 4.6 per function point.

Also assume that four different defect removal activities will take place: a design inspection, a code inspection, unit test, and system test.

In addition, assume four different classes of software defects: requirements defects, design defects, coding defects, and user documentation defects.

(Note that bad fix defects are omitted from Table 3. The reason is simply to keep the table within the bounds of the printed page without resorting to very small type. Also, the results are shown with integer values, which is normal for defect removal calculations.)

Table 3   Software Defect Removal Efficiency Patterns for Four Origin Points

	Requirements Defects	Design Defects	Code Defects	Document Defects	TOTAL DEFECTS
Defect Potential	100	125	175	60	460
Design Review	25.00%	60.00%	0.00%	0.00%	
Remaining	75	50	175	60	360
Code Inspection	40.00%	40.00%	60.00%	25.00%	
Remaining	45	30	70	45	190
Unit Test	20.00%	20.00%	50.00%	20.00%	
Remaining	36	24	35	36	131
System Test	25.00%	25.00%	50.00%	40.00%	
Remaining	27	18	18	22	85
Total Removed	73	107	158	38	376
Removal Efficiency	73.00%	85.60%	90.00%	64.00%	81.72%

What this table illustrates is out of the original number of 460 defects, the combination of two inspections and two testing steps found and eliminated 376. The number of latent defects still present at the time the project is released to customers is 85.

Expressed in terms of function points, 4.6 bugs per function point was the starting value. A total of 3.76 bugs per function point were removed during development. There were 0.85 bugs per function point still present at the end of the removal cycle.

The overall defect removal efficiency against all four categories of defects was 81.72%. However the range of efficiencies ran from only 64% against user documentation defects to 90% against coding defects.

This kind of information can be used to improve weak areas where defect removal efficiency is undesirably low. It can also be used to plan out the set of defect removal operations that will be needed to achieve any desired target level of removal efficiency.

Suppose a mission-critical system such as air-traffic control is being built where total reliability was a major criteria. In this case a cumulative defect removal efficiency level of more than 99.9% would be needed to achieve this which is not an easy task.

The choices are to add defect removal stages to the sequence that will be deployed, and to train and encourage the staff so that their performance moves to the high side of the defect removal probability curve.

However, if in real life defect removal efficiency levels in excess of 99% are required, be prepared to deploy several formal defect prevention activities and more than a dozen consecutive defect removal operations including both non-test defect removal and multiple stages of testing.

Table 4   Sequence of Operations Yielding > 99% Defect Removal Efficiency

Defect Prevention
Formal requirements gathering
Prototyping
Quality function deployment (QFD)
Non-Test Defect Removal
Requirements inspections
Design inspections
Code inspections
Test case inspections
User manual inspections
Screen inspections
Testing Defect Removal
Subroutine test
Unit test
Complexity analysis (and reduction) test
New function test
Regression test
Capacity test
Performance test
Integration test
System test
Field test

Evaluating the cumulative defect removal efficiency of multi-stage removal operations is a difficult job with a great many calculations involved. I regard the job as being too complex for easy or accurate manual calculations. The company will either need to construct its own automated defect removal efficiency model or utilize one of the commercial estimating tools with removal efficiency calculation functions such as CHECKPOINT®.

The more sophisticated software quality estimation tools have other features in addition to the ones described here. For example, these features may also be present:

- Estimating defect severity levels

- Estimating duplicate defects from multiple clients

- Estimating "abeyant" defects that will require special handling

- Estimating the impact of defect prevention methods

- Estimating inspection costs

- Estimating test-case preparation costs

- Estimating defect repair costs

- Estimating customer support costs

- Estimating mean time to failure (MTTF)

- Estimating mean time between failures (MTBF)

As this book is being written in 1996, there are approximately 72 commercial software estimating tools on the world markets. In the near future, this number will probably increase. Indeed, new estimating tools have been coming out at about monthly intervals for several years. For the longer range, there will probably be a series of mergers, acquisitions, and perhaps business failures because there are so many players in a finite market.

Many of top commercial estimating tools such as CHECKPOINT®, ESTI-MACS™, GECOMO, PRICE-S, SEER™, SLIM™, or SPQR/20™ now include quality estimates and/or reliability estimates either as an integral part of the tool or as an add-on that can be acquired separately.

Since defect removal is such a major cost driver for software projects, it is obvious that software cost estimating tools which lack quality estimation capabilities can never be very accurate since they omit a major cost element.

Because so many vendors are involved in quality estimation, there is no overall figure as to how accurate the commercial tools themselves are. SPR has data on its own company's tools, and the quality prediction results were described by one client as "frighteningly accurate" since they matched their measured results within 1% for an entire series of reviews, inspections, and tests. However this is a best-case example.

The only companies capable of estimating software defects without using one of the commercial estimating tools are those with extensive historical data derived from accurate quality measurements. Companies that do not measure quality cannot estimate it either.

By interesting coincidence, almost all of the companies with accurate quality data are also customers of the commercial estimating tools which can predict software quality. Although such companies can and sometimes do estimate quality using their own data and manual methods, they are also alert to the fact that running an independent estimate of quality can be valuable, too.

COST OF QUALITY

The phrase "cost of quality" is unfortunate, since it is the lack of quality that really drives up costs. While the basic cost of quality approach generates useful information for manufactured products, it is not totally adequate for software.

However, a number of software companies utilize the "cost of quality" concept which originated with Joseph Juran and was made popular by Phil Crosby's well-known book, *Quality is Free*. Among our clients, about 75 companies out of roughly 600 have at least partial cost of quality data.

The cost of quality concept utilizes three general cost buckets for exploring software quality economics:

1) Prevention costs

2) Appraisal costs

3) Failure costs

The cost of quality concept originated in the manufacturing sector, and is not necessarily an optimal concept for software quality. From both an economic and a psychological point of view, some of the concepts need to be expanded and tailored to the needs of software quality. Further, the value factors and return on investment figures associated with software quality also needs expansion.

A cost structure more suited to the nature of software work would expand upon the three cost buckets of the original cost of quality concept, and resemble the following:

Costs of Ensuring Software Quality

1) Defect prevention costs

2) User satisfaction optimization costs

3) Data quality defect prevention costs

4) Data quality defect removal costs

5) Quality awareness/training costs

6) Non-test defect removal costs (reviews, inspections, walkthroughs, etc.)

7) Testing defect removal costs (all forms)

8) Post-release customer support costs

9) Warranty support and product recall costs

10) Litigation and damage award costs

11) Quality savings from reduced scrap/rework

12) Quality savings from reduced user downtime

13) Quality value from reduced time-to-market intervals

14) Quality value from enhanced competitiveness

15) Quality value from enhanced employee morale

16) Quality return on investment (ROI)

The purpose of this expanded set of quality cost buckets is to allow accurate economic measurement of the impact of various levels and severities of software defect rates. Economic measurement also includes the value of quality, and the return on investment for quality-related activities.

A short hypothetical example can illustrate some of the basic premises involved. Assume a commercial software house is building two products at the same time. Both are 1,000 function points in size. One achieves high quality levels, and the other is of low quality. The burdened compensation rates are the same for both, and are $6,000 per staff month.

Assume that the "high quality" product uses a synergistic combination of defect prevention, inspections, and formal testing. It had a defect potential of 3 bugs per function point and an overall removal efficiency of 96% so the number of delivered defects was 0.12 per function point.

Assume the "low quality" product invested nothing into defect prevention or inspections, but did have formal testing. It had a defect potential of 5 bugs per function point and an overall removal efficiency of 90%, so that 0.5 bugs per function point were delivered. (This is more than 4 times the quantity of the high quality product.)

The following table shows development costs and the expenses for the first 12 months of customer use. The revenue and profit figures also reflect one year of sales. All of the data is expressed in terms of costs per function point.

Table 1   Comparison of Low and High Quality Software Defect Removal Expenses

(Data expressed in terms of cost per function point)

Activity	Low Quality	High Quality	Difference
Pre-Release			
Prevention	$0	$50	$50
Inspection	$0	$125	$125
Testing	$375	$175	-$200
Subtotal	$375	$350	-$25
Post-Release			
Support	$250	$200	-$50
Maintenance	$250	$125	-$125
Subtotal	$500	$325	-$175
TOTAL	$875	$675	-$200
Revenue	$850	$1,100	$250
Profit	($25)	$425	$450

As can be seen, the investment in defect prevention and pre-test inspections generates a small saving of $25 per function point during development. However, both customer support costs and post-release maintenance costs are substantially reduced, so the tangible cost savings are significant.

Even more significant, the sales volumes of the high-quality product ramped up very quickly while the sales volumes of the low-quality product lagged due to the fact that the first customers were dissatisfied and "flamed" the product via the Internet and CompuServe online forums. Thus the high-quality product made a profit in its first year on the market, while the low-quality product lost money.

This hypothetical example merely indicates the kind of information that can demonstrate the comparative value of high versus low quality levels in terms of both direct cost reduction and higher levels of sales volumes and profitability.

Although the data is hypothetical, it is not unrealistic. High quality for commercial software usually pays off with both direct cost reductions and higher sales volumes. Vendors should be sensitive to the fact that not only do customer associations exist that share information about software quality, but the Internet has opened up a whole new way of transmitting information anywhere in the world instantly.

COST PER DEFECT

The widely used "cost per defect" metric is highly unreliable, and appears to be economically invalid under a number of conditions. The popular software anecdote that "it costs 100 times to fix a bug in the field as in development" and its many variations has become a commonplace but may not be accurate in many cases. (See the example in the section under Barriers to Software Quality Measurement.)

One of the problems with the cost per defect metric is that it tends to ignore fixed costs, and hence can fluctuate in counter-intuitive ways. Here are two simplified examples to illustrate the problem:

Case 1: Suppose a poorly developed Ada program of 25,000 LOC is being tested, and a total of 500 bugs are found during test. Assume that test-case preparation cost $5,000; executing the tests cost $20,000; and fixing the bugs cost $25,000. The entire testing cycle cost $50,000 so the cost per defect of the 500 bugs is exactly $100.

Case 2: Assume that the application used modern defect prevention approaches, so that the number of bugs found during testing was only 50 instead of 500, which is an order of magnitude improvement. In this scenario, test-case preparation cost $5,000; executing the test cases cost $17,500; and fixing the bugs cost only $2,500. Now the total testing cost has declined to $25,000. However, the cost per defect for the 50 bugs has risen to $500.

Obviously, test-case preparation is a fixed cost, and test-case execution is comparatively inelastic and only partly dependent upon the number of defects encountered.

As can be seen, the cost per defect metric tends to escalate as quality improves and does not capture the real economic advantages of higher quality. Fortunately the function point metric is now being used for economic studies of quality control. Since Ada applications average about 70 statements per function point, let us assume that both examples are 350 function points in size. The testing cost per function point in Case 1 was $142.87 for the low quality example. The testing cost per function point in Case 2 was $71.42 for the high quality example. As can be seen, the function point metric correlates exactly with the real economic gains while the cost per defect metric would be invalid in this example.

The following graph illustrates the general tendency of cost per defect to rise as potential defects decline. The graph illustrates the costs associated with testing software and assumes a burdened salary level of $10,000 per staff month and a separate test group.

Before examining the table itself, consider the extreme conditions which the table illustrates:

1) Test cases must be created whether there are many bugs, only a few, or none at all.

2) Test cases must be run whether there are any bugs or not, although tests will be run more often for buggy software.

3) While the testing is going on, some programming time will be spent waiting for bugs to be found. If a lot of bugs are found, slack time will be close to zero. If few bugs are found, slack time can be extensive. Programmers will still get paid whether they are fixing bugs or waiting for bugs to be found.

These three factors coalesce in such a way as to make "cost per defect" a very hazardous metric for serious quality economic studies, as can be seen:

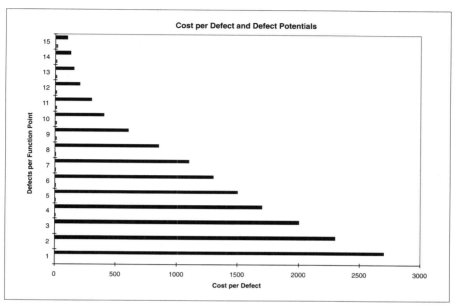

Figure 1: Cost per Defect Ascending as Defect Volumes Decline

As can easily be seen, cost per defect is inversely related to the overall defect potentials of software projects, assuming your cost collection system captures test-case preparation and test-case execution time plus slack time on the part of the programming staff should few defects be discovered.

By contrast, a graph of defect removal costs per function point using the same assumptions correlates perfectly with declining defect potentials. There will still be some slack time and there will still be fixed costs for test-case preparation, but at least the cost per function point data moves in the right direction as quality improves.

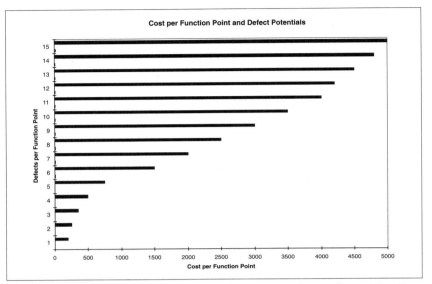

Figure 2: Cost per Function Point Declining as Defect Volumes Decline

Both charts make a number of simplifying assumptions are intended only to show the directions of the two metrics under various conditions. Neither chart should be used for serious business purposes such as estimating real defect repairs on real projects. To do that, one of the commercial software estimating tools which includes testing cost estimates such as CHECKPOINT, PRICE-S, SEER, or SLIM should be utilized.

The basic reason why "cost per defect" ascends is due to fixed costs. Test cases must be created and run, even if few or no defects are found.

Case Study of Cost Per Defect and Cost per Function Point

A simple example can illustrate the impact of fixed costs and how both cost per defect and defect repairs per function point respond to the same numbers of defects and the same repairs.

Assume that software project is 100 function points in size, and it contains exactly 100 defects. Assume that this project will go through a series of six consecutive test steps, each of which is approximately 50% efficient and this will find half of the defects that are present.

Assume that for each of the six testing steps, preparation of test cases costs $500 and execution or running of the test cases also costs $500. These are fixed costs and do not vary in this example.

Now assume that each defect encountered will cost exactly $100 to repair, exclusive of the preparation and execution costs. Examine the six-stage test series when preparation and execution costs are part of the picture. The origin of the software legend that "it costs 10 times as much to fix a defect at the end of the development cycle than at the beginning is easy to see."

What happens is that the fixed costs for preparation and execution gradually overshadow the variable repair costs. This means that as the number of defects found declines, the cost per defect will go up. On the other hand, both total costs and cost per function point match the real economic observation that costs go down as defect volumes go down.

Table 1 Comparison of Cost per Defect and Cost per Function Point for Six Consecutive Testing Stages

Defect Potential		100	
Test 1	*Defects found*	50	
	Preparation	$500	
	Execution	$500	
	Repairs	$5,000	
	TOTAL	$6,000	
	Cost per defect	$120	
	Cost per function point	$60	
Test 2	*Defects found*	25	
	Preparation	$500	
	Execution	$500	
	Repairs	$2,500	
	TOTAL	$3,500	
	Cost per defect	$140	
	Cost per function point	$35	

(continued)

Table 1   *(continued)*

Defect Potential		100
Test 3	*Defects found*	*12*
	Preparation	$500
	Execution	$500
	Repairs	$1,200
	TOTAL	$2,200
	Cost per defect	$183
	Cost per function point	$22
Test 4	*Defects found*	*6*
	Preparation	$500
	Execution	$500
	Repairs	$600
	TOTAL	$1,600
	Cost per defect	$267
	Cost per function point	$16
Test 5	*Defects found*	*3*
	Preparation	$500
	Execution	$500
	Repairs	$300
	TOTAL	$1,300
	Cost per defect	$433
	Cost per function point	$13
Test 6	*Defects found*	*1*
	Preparation	$500
	Execution	$500
	Repairs	$100
	TOTAL	$1,100
	Cost per defect	$1,100
	Cost per function point	$5

When the project is released to customers and maintenance begins, the cost per defect metric will grow even larger because it is necessary to train at least one person to maintain the software. Further, that person must spend at least part-time answering client questions and assisting clients during the installation and start-up period.

The following data assumes that only a single bug or defect was reported in the first year of use, but that the customers were provided with a trained support person who assisted in installation and answered start-up questions during the first year:

Year 1	*Defects found*	*1*
	Preparation	$2,000
	Execution	$1,500
	Repairs	$100
	TOTAL	$3,600
	Cost per defect	$3,600
	Cost per function point	$36

As can be seen from the flow of data through the series, the cost per defect metric rises steadily as defect volumes decline. However, this phenomenon is decoupled from the real economic situation where overall repair costs decline but are affected by fixed costs.

The data just presented used a constant $100 for each defect repaired. However, by including fixed and inelastic costs, the apparent "cost per defect" ranged from $120 early in the removal cycle to $3,600 after delivery, which is a 30 to 1 difference. Had the project in question been commercial software with field service as part of the picture, a range of 100 to 1 could easily occur. However, these ranges are artificial and not economically valid.

By contrast, analyzing the economics of a testing and maintenance series using "defect repair costs per function point" gives a much better picture of the real value of quality and how fixed and variable costs interact.

See also the section on Barriers to Software Quality Measurement earlier in this book for additional information on the flaws of cost per defect, and on the hazards of "lines of code" metrics as well.

CREEPING USER REQUIREMENTS AND SOFTWARE QUALITY

Requirement changes or creeping requirements are an important topic for both quality control and for change management and configuration control. Requirements changes become progressively more troublesome after the nominal completion of the requirements phase.

During the subsequent design phase, the average rate of requirements change may exceed 3% per month for many software projects. This burst of rapid requirements changes may last as long as a year for large systems but would occur only for about three months on smaller projects.

The burst of new requirements slows down to about 1% per month during coding, and eventually stops by the time testing commences. (Requirements changes don't really stop, of course, but the requirements tend to get pushed down stream into follow-on releases.)

For systems software and for commercial software, changes may be due to market needs or competitive products. The average rate is about 2% per month from the end of initial requirements until start of testing. But if a competitor suddenly announced a new product monthly change rates can top 15%.

For internal software, requirements changes are driven by user needs and average about 1% per month from the start of design until well into coding. For military software, the average is about 2% per month.

Military software requirements call for very strict "requirements traceability." This means that all down-stream deliverables need to identify which requirements they include to a very granular level. This implies, ideally, that software requirements would be the base for hypertext linkages to other down-stream software artifacts.

The fact that military software has strict requirements traceability plus fairly good defect tracking has allowed an important discovery: the defect rates associated with new features added during mid-development are about 50% greater than those of the artifacts associated with the original requirements. Defect removal efficiency levels are depressed as well, sometimes by more than 15%. This combination means that a very significant percentage of delivered defects can be traced back to creeping user requirements.

To minimize the harm from late requirements, formal change management procedures and state-of-the-art configuration control software tools are both strongly recommended. Formal design and code inspections are also useful.

Other technologies associated with minimizing the harm from late requirements include joint application design (JAD), prototyping, and rapid application development (RAD) for smaller projects of less than 1,000 function points.

An emerging method for dealing with creeping user requirements in the context of outsource and contract agreements is to base the agreement on "cost per function point" metrics.

Under this method, there will be a mutually agreed to quantity of function points in the contract for a fixed cost. Assume that the initial agreement calls for 1000 function points to be delivered at a cost of $500 per function point, or $500,000 in all.

The agreement would then have a clause with a sliding scale of costs for changes that modify the basic agreement. For example, features that are added during after requirements and during design might have costs of $600 per function point. Features added after design and during coding might have costs of $750 per function point. Features added after coding and during testing might either jump to $1,500 per function point, or be deferred until a future release.

The contract might also include clauses for deletions or removals of features. For example, client-initiated removal of features during design that reduce the overall scope of the agreement might have a cost of $100 per function point assigned to them.

The costs shown here are hypothetical and simply illustrate what appears to be an interesting and effective application of function point metrics to a problem area that has long been troublesome for the software community, and troublesome for contract and outsource agreements in particular.

Creeping user requirements and all other kinds of changes to software projects become more difficult as the project proceeds. The usual response to this situation is to cut off changes at a certain point, and defect all subsequent changes to the next release of the product. There is no fixed point where cut-offs always occur, however.

If you correlate the overall probability of a requirements change introducing fairly serious errors, it is obvious that the safest policy is to stop changes to the current release before the design phase, and defect any other requirements changes to a follow-on release.

Table 1   Impact of Creeping Requirements on Error Injections

Development Phase	Error Injection Probability
Requirements	Moderate
Design	High
Coding	Very High
Testing	Catastrophically High
Follow-on Release	Moderate

Although it makes technical sense to defer late requirements changes to future releases, the real world is not always obliging. For example, abrupt changes in state law, tax law, or any other government mandate may have to be implemented at once, whether doing so is convenient, safe, or very hazardous. The same caveat occurs with changes in mission-critical software where the changes are necessary to complete the mission.

Most requirements originate during an early feasibility study or during the requirements phase itself. The following graph illustrates the story by showing the steep cost increase in requirements that are delayed until after the conclusion of the formal requirements phase.

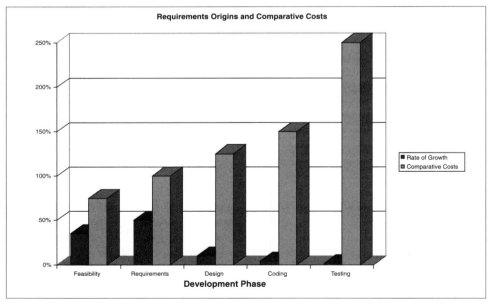

Figure 1: Requirements Creep by Phase of Software Development

Because the costs of creeping requirements climb steeply as the development cycle proceeds, there are strong economic reasons for being very thorough early. For requirements that are unavoidably late, the most economical solution is to defer them to a future release.

It is also advantageous to plan for changes and utilize architectures, design strategies, planning tools, cost estimating tools, and coding strategies that are flexible enough to permit late-arriving requirements to be added without catastrophic consequences.

CURRENT U.S. AVERAGES FOR SOFTWARE QUALITY

Based on a study published in one of my books *Applied Software Measurement* (McGraw Hill, 1991; 2nd edition 1996), the average number of software errors is about five per function point. This data has been comparatively stable for the United States as a whole between the mid-1980s and 1995.

The value of about five bugs per function point was first determined circa 1990 using about 4,000 projects as the base. Today's section is drawn from a larger sample of about 7,000 projects, but the value of roughly five defects per function point is still more or less a good approximation of the U.S. average for potential defects prior to the removal caused by various reviews and testing stages.

The overall range of defects is very broad, and from less than one defect per function point to more than 16 defects per function point have been noted.

Specific companies, however, have been able to make notable reductions in their potential defects and to do so rapidly. In fact, the best results have been quality improvements that approximate 40% per year, compounded for several years in a row. Both between and within industries the range of quality results is alarmingly large. Note that software defects are not found only in code, but originate in all of the major software deliverables, in the following approximate quantities.

Table 1   U.S. Averages in Terms of Defects per Function Point

Defect Origins	Defects per Function Point
Requirements	1.00
Design	1.25
Coding	1.75
Document	0.60
Bad Fixes	0.40
Total	*5.00*

These numbers represent the total numbers of defects that are found and measured from early software requirements throughout the remainder of the life cycle of the software. The defects are discovered via requirement reviews, design reviews, code inspections, all forms of testing, and user-reported problem reports.

For those who still utilize the ambiguous "defects per KLOC" metric, following is the equivalent data for the C programming language.

Table 2   U.S. Averages in Terms of Defects per KLOC for the C Programming Language

Defect Origins	Defects per KLOC in C
Requirements	7.8
Design	9.7
Coding	13.7
Document	4.7
Bad Fixes	3.1
Total	*39.0*

One of the problems with the LOC metric for quality analysis is that the coding defects are directly related to the specific programming language used, but the requirements, design, and document defect categories are not.

Also, the LOC metric needs to be calibrated for each specific programming language. You cannot perform comparisons between languages using LOC metrics for the same mathematical reason that you cannot do a direct comparison between costs when multiple currencies such as dollars, yen, and Deutschmarks are involved. All values have to be converted to the same base for the comparisons to be valid.

U.S. averages lend themselves to a graphical representation. The following graph shows defect potentials and defect removal efficiency levels as the two axes. The graph also identifies three zones of some significance:

1) The central zone of average performance where most companies can be found.

2) The zone of "best in class" performance where top companies can be found.

3) The zone of professional malpractice.

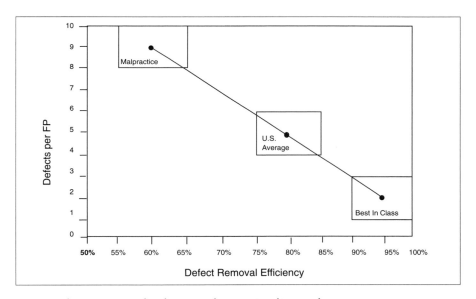

Figure 1: Graph of U.S. Software Quality Performance Ranges

It is very revealing to overlay a sample of an enterprise's software projects on this graph. Indeed, readers are encouraged to do this. Note that the "Defects per FP" axis refers to the total defect potential, which includes errors in requirements, specifications, source code, user manuals, and "bad fix" categories.

Software defect potentials vary over quite a broad range associated with the size of software applications. In general, smaller projects in the 1 through 1,000 function point band have lower defect potentials and higher removal efficiency rates than larger systems above 10,000 or 100,000 function points in size.

The following table shows approximate U.S. software defect potentials in terms of six discrete size plateaus an order of magnitude apart, from 1 function point to 100,000 function points.

Table 3   Relationship Between Software Size and Defect Potentials

(Data expressed in terms of defects per function point)

Size	Require.	Design	Code	Docum.	Bad Fixes	Total
1	0.10	0.10	0.50	0.20	0.10	1.00
10	0.20	0.40	1.30	0.40	0.25	2.55
100	0.65	1.00	1.65	0.50	0.45	4.25
1000	1.10	1.35	1.85	0.60	0.55	5.45
10000	1.30	1.65	2.10	0.70	0.65	6.40
100000	1.60	2.00	2.20	0.90	0.85	7.55
Average	0.83	1.08	1.60	0.55	0.48	4.53

The reason that this table varies somewhat from the nominal average of five defects per function point that is often cited as the average value is because this table uses simple arithmetic averaging rather than a weighted average that matches the distribution of software sizes. That is, there are very few one function point applications and even fewer 100,000 function points systems.

Note that below 1,000 function points, coding errors are the dominant problem category. However for large systems in the 10,000 to 100,000 function point range front-end errors attributed to requirements and design become the dominant sources of error. The implication of this data is that testing, by itself, is not adequate for large systems. Pre-test reviews and inspections are necessary in order to achieve acceptable quality levels.

Defect removal efficiency also varies with size, as does first-year defect discovery rates by software clients and users. The following table uses the last column of the prior defect potential table as its starting value.

Table 4   Relationship Between Size and Defect Removal Efficiency Levels

(Data expressed in terms of defects per function point)

Size	Defect Potential	Defect Removal Efficiency	Delivered Defects per F.P.	1st Year Discovery Percent	1st Year Reported Defects per F.P.
1	1.00	99.00%	0.01	90.00%	0.01
10	2.55	97.00%	0.08	80.00%	0.06
100	4.25	90.00%	0.43	70.00%	0.30
1000	5.45	89.00%	0.60	50.00%	0.30
10000	6.40	87.00%	0.83	40.00%	0.33
100000	7.55	83.00%	1.28	30.00%	0.39
Average	4.53	90.83%	0.54	60.00%	0.23

In general, the larger the project the higher the levels of potential defects and the greater the difficulty of removing them prior to release. Small projects can be built carelessly and the results are sometimes OK. Large systems demand serious quality control by trained specialists or the results can be catastrophically bad.

Although average results are not very good for large systems, note that several industries and many individual companies can top 95% in cumulative defect removal efficiency for projects of almost any size, even those approaching 100,000 function points.

In general, the industries that have the best defect removal are those whose main products are large and complex physical devices that depend upon high-quality software to operate: computer manufacturers, telecommunication manufacturers, aerospace manufacturers, defense manufacturers, medical instrument manufacturers, and the developers of major operating systems such as Microsoft and IBM.

Average results are interesting, but predicting the quality for a specific software project requires a great deal of information about the project itself, the experience of the team, the methods and tools available, and even the experience and cooperation of the clients.

To make a parallel with medical data, statistics on the average life expectancy in a country give an overall view of the health status of the country. However, average life expectancy has no immediate impact on any specific citizen. To evaluate any real person's chances requires knowledge of family history, smoking and drug use, occupational hazards, and many other factors.

DATA QUALITY AND DATA METRICS

The topic of data quality was not included in the original 1992 SPR quality survey from which this book derives. However, data quality is a topic of growing significance as more and more of the world's important records are stored in computerized form. Data quality is also very difficult to measure and is outside the scope of normal software quality assurance since much of the data comes from clients using the application long after development rather than from the software development process itself.

Among SPR's clients almost all of them (about 600) have data quality problems, but only about 75 have begun any kind of formal data quality improvement programs. The normal trigger for data quality improvement is the desire to move toward data warehousing, data mining, online analytical processing (OLAP), and other approaches where data from various sources needs to be consolidated. As a result, about another 50 of SPR's clients are discussing data quality and will probably move toward formal data quality approaches in 1997.

Data and databases can have any of the same four kinds of kinds of defects discussed earlier in the section of this book dealing with error categories:

- Errors of omission (something missing, such as the zip code in an address)

- Errors of commission (something incorrect, such as a misspelled name)

- Errors of clarity and ambiguity (primarily with complex search or join criteria)

- Errors of speed or performance (primarily sluggish transactions with large databases)

Unlike software, data has another kind of error condition too. Data errors can occur due to changes in the real-world situation which the data describes or models. Thus records that are correct at a specific time and date can become erroneous as time passes without any change in the record itself but because of changes in the reality which the data describes.

For example, suppose on January 1 of 1997 a corporate personnel database has records for an employee named Jane Doe, who is employed as a database administrator, with a salary of $50,000 per year.

Now suppose that on February 1 of the same year the employee marries and changes her name. On March 1 of the same year the employee is promoted and becomes a "senior database administrator" with a salary of $60,000 per year.

Unless these real-world changes are reflected in the data describing the employee, the records will be no longer be correct although they were correct when the data was first put into the database.

For data errors brought about by gradual changes in the real, external world which the data models, there is no easy solution. Active and frequent comparisons between the data and reality must be performed.

These comparisons may require voluntary participation on the part of humans and companies whose information is contained in the databases. As a trivial but very common example, when a person moves or changes addresses, it is up to that person to notify at least the post office in order to continue to receive mail.

However, most people end up notifying a large number of vendors, journals, credit card companies, and professional service groups such as doctors, dentists, attorneys, and accountants. What these people are really doing is participating in a number of database update transactions, even if they are not consciously aware of it.

Another and very serious example of a situation where reality will change and cause data errors is the approaching "Year 2000" problem. Not only do millions of software applications contain two-digit date fields which will fail when 1999 becomes 2000 AD, but so do databases, repositories, and data warehouses.

Since many companies often own larger volumes of data than they own software, the Year 2000 problem will generate tremendous data quality problems as well as tremendous software repair problems, although the data quality aspects of the Year 2000 issue are not as well understood.

Data has been a difficult topic to perform research on. A major source of difficulty has been the lack of useful data-related metrics. Unfortunately, as this draft is written in 1997 there are no satisfactory normalizing metrics for expressing the volume of data a company uses, the quality levels of the data, and the costs of creating data, migrating data from platform to platform, correcting errors, or destroying obsolete data.

Also, unlike software errors which are found only in computerized applications, data errors are not restricted to data stored magnetically or optically in computerized databases, repositories, and warehouses. Data errors can also occur in data stored on paper, on microfiche, on video or audio tape, on CD-ROM, or on any other known medium. Indeed, data errors are far older than the computer era and have been occurring since the invention of writing and symbolic representations for mathematics.

There are many data errors to be found in ordinary office file cabinets containing paper documents. Data quality is also of concern during transmission of data via optical or copper cable, microwave, or by radio or television signals since errors and noise can be introduced during the transmission process.

Even the word "data" itself is ambiguous and hard to pin down exactly. What the word "data" means in the context of data quality are symbolic representations of facts (i.e., pi = 3.14159265358, etc.), encoded representations of objects (i.e., valves, bolts, chairs, etc.) or encoded representation almost any kind of idea the human mind can envision.

Data is not necessarily static, and indeed some kinds of data can change very rapidly. For the data on the actual and predicted trajectory of an incoming Exocet missile picked up by a ship's radar can change very rapidly indeed.

Associated with the definition of data is the concept that data can be structured in the form of models that deal with various aspects of the world: physical objects, business rules, mathematics, images, and so forth.

Although the function point metric was created to measure the size of software applications, it is interesting to evaluate whether function points might be extended to deal with the size and quality of databases, or whether an equivalent "data point" metric might be developed for similar purposes.

Recall that the function point metric is comprised of the weighted totals of five external aspects of software applications:

- Inputs   Forms, screens, sensor-based values etc., entering the application
- Outputs   Reports, screens, electronic signals etc., leaving the application
- Inquires   Question/answer pairs to which the application responds
- Logical files Record sets maintained within or by the application
- Interfaces   Record sets passed to or received by external applications

These five elements are then adjusted for complexity to provide the final total of function points for the application. There are 14 adjustment factors for the U.S. function point defined by the International Function Point Users Group (IFPUG) and 19 adjustment factors for the British Mark II function point.

While all five of the function point elements overlap data to a certain degree, they do not seem to capture some of the topics of concern when exploring data quality. Perhaps a set of factors similar to these may move toward the development of a data point metric:

- Logical files The number of record sets maintained within or by the application

- Entities   The number of kinds of objects within the database

- Attributes   The number of qualifications for the entities within the database

- Inquires   Question/answer pairs which the database responds to

- Interfaces   Record sets passed to or received by the database

While the above is only a preliminary suggestion, there is an urgent need to develop a data point metric without which research into data quality and database economics are severely handicapped.

Right now, there is so little empirical, quantified information on data quality that this topic is included primarily to serve as a warning flag that an important domain is emerging, and substantial research is urgently needed.

Several commercial companies and Dr. Richard Wang's data quality research group at MIT have begun to address the topic of data quality. Dr. Wang and his colleagues are definitely broadening the horizon of the data quality domain. Indeed the MIT data quality research group is the sponsor of perhaps of the first international conference on data quality in October of 1996.

In spite of good preliminary research, there is still a long way to go before data quality becomes a well-understood topic. To date, there are no known published statistical studies that include the volumes of data errors in either paper or computerized data bases, the severity levels of data defects, or the costs of removing data errors. Even reliable information on the sizes of data bases is difficult to come by, as is corollary information on the costs of collecting the data, validating it, or removing outdated information.

Yet another of the unknowns and ambiguities of the database domain is that of extraneous information and redundancy. There is a tendency to store information that may never be used again, on the grounds that "it is there if someone needs it." It would be very interesting to do a statistical analysis of a full corporate database or repository in order to ascertain how much data is used daily, weekly, monthly, annually, rarely, or not at all. Very preliminary observations indicate that perhaps as much as half of the entire volume of data might fall under the "rarely used" or "never used" categories.

Redundancy in data is also a troubling topic, although better covered in the literature that extraneous data. Most corporations maintain multiple copies of a significant portion of their data. Sometimes the copies are maintained for reasons of security or disaster recovery. Sometimes the copies are maintained for reasons of transaction processing efficiency.

However, some redundancy has no rational explanation and is difficult to explain except under the hypothesis that few companies actually know what kind of data they store, so redundancy is a natural byproduct of partial data dictionaries or catalogs of stored information. Another reason for redundancy between paper data and computerized data is the lack of simple, portable reading devices that would make access to online data easy and facile.

In terms of data quality, anecdotal reports on both manual and computerized databases indicate that errors are both plentiful and severe. Samples of things like employee personnel records, credit records, and mailing lists tend to indicate that errors can occur more than 1% of the records stored. However, much more research is needed to examine the interaction of data errors with the nature and volume of the data itself.

As this book is written, there is not even any accepted standard method for exploring the "cost of quality" for data errors in the absence of any normalizing metrics. This is an important research project and all technical contributions would be welcome.

A cost structure that might be suited to the nature of the database domain would resemble the following, which is similar to the expanded cost structure discussed in the Cost of Quality section earlier in this book.

Costs of Ensuring Data Quality

1) Data defect prevention costs

2) User satisfaction data optimization costs

3) Data quality defect prevention costs

4) Data quality defect removal costs

5) Data quality awareness/training costs

6) Non-test data defect removal costs (reviews, inspections, walkthroughs, etc.)

7) Testing data defect removal costs (all forms)

8) Data-related customer support costs

9) Data-related warranty support and product recall costs

10) Data-related litigation and damage award costs

11) Savings from reduced data scrap/rework

12) Savings from reduced data-related computer downtime

13) Data quality value from reduced time-to-market intervals

14) Data quality value from enhanced competitiveness

15) Data quality value from enhanced employee morale

16) Data quality return on investment (ROI)

Here, too, this is a preliminary list of cost elements that are being presented to elicit further research on a topic of significant economic consequence.

Database and Information Usage Within Large Corporations

I worked for IBM for a 12 year period. During the latter part of this period, I performed a study on the volumes of information required to create IBM's major software products. Although the study did not cover other kinds and uses of information, such as hardware manufacturing, marketing, or sales, it was obvious that information was a major component of IBM's annual expenses and the company utilized enormous volumes of information. The same observation has held true when consulting with other corporations and government agencies: both data and information are major but largely invisible components of operating expense.

The following is an attempt to put together a rough estimate of the volume of data or information typically owned by major corporations. Assume a high-technology manufacturing corporation with a total employment of 250,000 personnel. Roughly 150,000 of those personnel might be engaged in manufacturing activities, while 100,000 would be engaged in various business and operational activities such as engineering, marketing, sales, finance, human resources, administration, purchasing, and the like.

The total number of discrete products and services which corporations of this size typically have on the market would amount to perhaps 5,000 different hardware products and perhaps 500 different software products. Information about these products would be a major component of the company's databases, repositories, and data warehouses.

In addition, a company of this size would have created more than 1,500 internal software tools for use within the company, and would have bought or leased an equivalent number from outside vendors. Both hardware and software would be supported and surrounded by various kinds of sales, marketing, training, repair, and maintenance services. (Although these tools are important and were expensive to acquire or build, it is interesting that even IBM did not have a complete inventory or database of all tools owned or leased by the corporation. This is also true of my other corporate and government clients.)

A corporation of this size would typically have a client base of perhaps 500,000 corporations and government agencies on a global basis. Here too, this is a major kind of information that would be stored in corporate data bases and repositories.

Since many of the client organizations would be large enterprises in their own right, the total number of customer sites served would be in the range of 2,000,000. The total number of real people that are clients or prospects of a company this size would probably approach or exceed 10,000,000 on a global basis.

These three statistics are significant in calculating the volume of information a company maintains as permanent records to conduct basic business operations. Information on personnel, products, and clients constitute the basic operating information that drives modern businesses. The table shows approximate volumes of information stored by a large corporation for these three major kinds of business data might total to the following:

Table 1   Volumes of Primary Business Information Used by A Large Corporation

Information Item	Number of Pages	Number of Words
Personnel Information	12,500,000	3,500,000,000
Product Information	26,500,000	7,950,000,000
Customer Information	65,000,000	19,500,000,000
TOTAL	*104,000,000*	*30,955,000,000*

The latter two kinds of information, on products and customers, have close logical ties and often need to be coupled together for business operations. Indeed, relating clients and products is a major form of transaction for database software in all corporations.

Personnel and staff information, on the other hand, is usually kept rigorously separate from other kinds of information for reasons of confidentiality. Usually it is not possible to even determine the identities of the employees who worked on a product, except in the case of some kind of litigation where the records are produced due to a court order.

Although the three basic kinds of business information constitute, by volume, the bulk of the information which corporations store and utilize in order to conduct business, there are many other kinds of information utilized in the course of business activities.

From studies carried out by the author on technical specifications and user documentation for software products, roughly 30% of the pages contained some kind of graphical illustration or image. Marketing materials and training materials approach 50% graphics and illustrations by volume: that is, every other page contains an illustration. Assuming these ratios hold for hardware products as well as software (hardware was not studied by the author) then the approximate volume of images and graphical information within the case study company would amount to about 10,000,000 discrete images or graphical illustrations.

Although not "pages" in the traditional sense, the volume of data required to encode a typical image or graphic device is much larger than a page of text. However, for convenience in expressing the data in this article, each image or graphic will be deemed equivalent to "one page." It is reasonable to assume about a 50% split between paper and online storage for graphics and images.

One of the data warehouse topics needing additional research is a better survey of the ratios of graphics, images, text, and tabular information utilized by enterprises. Since graphics and images are more troublesome to store and transmit electronically, and since many commercial databases are cumbersome for images and graphics, this is a topic needing substantial future research.

Among military and scientific communities, data can also consist of various kinds of electronic signals from sensors or bit streams coming in from ships, aircraft, satellites, etc. These data items tend to be voluminous and also have the characteristic that they may represent dynamic phenomena in rapid motion.

However, the following case study deals only with "ordinary" business data in the form of alphanumeric information plus standard graphics and some photographic illustrations. Let us now consider three views of information storage and usage in large corporations:

1) The total volume of information stored

2) The volume of information kept in paper form

3) The volume of information kept in magnetic or optically encoded form

Note that there is a high margin of error in this kind of analysis, and the approximations for the ratios of paper to online storage are only hypothetical. An important point for data quality purposes is that errors in paper-based data can be just as severe as errors in computerized data.

The following table summarizes the approximate overall volumes of information in rank order:

Table 2   Relative Volumes of Stored Information for Case Study Example

Kind of Information	Pages Stored	Percent Stored Online
Customer information	90,000,000	50%
Product information	50,000,000	50%
Software applications	40,000,000	75%
E-mail messages	30,000,000	95%
Reference information	15,000,000	20%
Personnel information	12,500,000	50%
Graphics/images	10,000,000	50%
Correspondence	5,000,000	10%
Defect information	2,500,000	50%
Supplier information	1,500,000	25%
Tutorial/training material	1,000,000	50%
Litigation/legal information	1,000,000	25%
Total Volume	*272,000,000*	

Since the case study corporation was stated to have 250,000 employees, it is interesting to note that the total volume of corporate information stored by the case study corporation amounts to more than 1,000 pages per employee. Let us now turn to the volumes of paper information, once again shown in declining order by volume.

Table 3   Relative Volumes of Stored Paper Information for Case Study Example

Kind of Information	Pages Stored
Customer information	45,000,000
Product information	25,000,000
Reference information	12,000,000
Software applications	10,000,000
Personnel information	6,250,000
Graphics/images	5,000,000
Correspondence	4,500,000
E-mail messages (printed)	1,500,000
Defect information	1,250,000
Supplier information	1,125,000
Litigation/legal information	750,000
Tutorial/training information	500,000
Total Volume	*112,875,000*

To give a human context to the volumes of paper information, consider that 250 pages of ordinary 20-pound office paper make a stack one-inch high. The volume of paper information stored by the case study corporation is roughly equal to a stack of paper 37,625 feet high, or more than seven miles of paper information. Expressed another way, if the paper information were divided equally among each employee, then about 451 pages would be assigned to every worker. If the 2,250,000,000 pages of personal reference information stored privately by employees is considered, then it would constitute a stack 750,000 feet high, or more than 142 miles.

This is equivalent to about 9,000 pages for every employee. For example, my office at Software Productivity Research contains one wall of shelves that are six feet high and seven feet wide. The shelves contain almost 40 linear feet of books, reports, and data from our own and secondary sources.

In addition, I have about six cubic feet of lockable storage in a file cabinet, and another dozen or so cubic feet reserved for my data in our main file room. However, the file cabinets contain corporate data and client studies. It is interesting that I more more private data in my shelves than corporate or business-related data. Most of the SPR consultants, managers, and technical staff have similar arrangements with books and articles that they find interesting and relevant.

Currently no known data warehouse could absorb this volume of personal and private reference, so it is fortunate that much of this kind of information is treated as personal property and not as a corporate asset. Eventually, however, for data warehousing to become a truly effective business technology this private information must be absorbed.

Let us now consider the volumes of information stored online in magnetic or optical formats.

Table 4   Relative Volumes of Online Information for Case Study Example

Kind of Information	Pages Stored
Customer information	45,000,000
Software applications	30,000,000
E-mail messages (online)	28,500,000
Product information	25,000,000
Personnel information	6,250,000
Graphics/images	5,000,000
Reference information	3,000,000
Defect information	1,250,000
Tutorial/training material	500,000
Correspondence	500,000
Supplier information	375,000
Litigation/legal information	275,000
Total Volume	*145,625,000*

Since this case study reflects a large and sophisticated corporation, it is interesting to note that even though more than 53% of the total volume of business information is available online in magnetic or optical form, there is still almost 47% of the total information is stored in paper form.

Moreover, if the 2,250,000,000 pages of private reference information kept in individual offices in the form of paper is considered, the total volume of online information for the case study company is less than 6%.

Also significant is the redundancy between paper and online storage. For several kinds of information necessary to business operations, such as basic product and customer information, training, and tutorial information, there is almost 100% redundancy between paper and online storage of information.

There is also an approximate 100% redundancy between paper and online storage for many kinds of financial and accounting data, and for many aspects of the data associated with litigation. In these two situations, various government audit trail requirements or court rulings on the admissibility of evidence are among the reasons for the redundant storage.

However, the dominant reasons for redundancy between paper and online information storage are convenience and accessibility. It can by hypothesized that much of the redundancy between online and paper forms of information can be traced to the lack of convenient portable access devices for extracting and utilizing online information.

If hand-held, portable devices were available which had screens equivalent in clarity to printed pages, and were about as easy to carry and use as normal books, then the need for printed information should decline significantly. This kind of device is technically achievable and indeed products such as the SONY Data Diskman are steps in the right direction.

If the amount of information in the case study example is multiplied by all the major corporations and government agencies of the world, it can be seen that huge volumes of information are a major contributor to a number of escalating social problems such as rising taxes and increasing health-care costs.

It can be hypothesized that a major portion of global tax dollars and medical costs are tied up in the production and storage of enormous volumes of words and diagrams, rather than the provision of actual services.

Error Densities of Stored Information

Data quality, or the prevention and elimination of errors in databases and data warehouses, is notoriously difficult to quantify. As already stated, data quality is perceived to be an important topic but there is a severe shortage of empirical data on the volumes and severity levels of data errors. There is also a lack of fundamental metrics for normalizing data quality.

The current U.S. averages for software defect potentials is a total of about 5 bugs or errors per function point, coupled with an approximate 85% defect removal efficiency so that at deployment the volume of latent errors is about 0.75 defects per function point.

Assuming that a hypothetical "data point" metric existed that approximated software function points for sizing purposes, the error densities of data errors appears to be much higher, and the defect removal efficiency levels much lower, than for software.

From analysis of errors in the SPR client databases and repositories, I hypothesize that the data defect potential for the United States is around 8 errors per "data point" and the removal efficiency is only about 75%, so that the number of data errors deployed would be about 2 per "data point" or more than twice the volume of software errors at delivery.

This assertion poor of data quality measured with hypothetical "data point" metrics is of course purely speculative. However, from thoughtful comparisons of data quality and software quality, it does appear that the error densities associated with data may be high, and everyone knows that it is extremely difficult to remove data errors. What is needed, of course, are exact metrics that can capture both the data quality defect potentials and the data quality defect removal efficiency levels. Without quantification of these two factors, data quality research is little more than subjective opinion.

In the context of this case study, my observations of printed reference manuals and tutorial information indicates a rough "defect potential" of about three errors per page of information when it is initially created.

Normal proof reading and fact checking of textual information is fairly efficient. Studies of magazines and book publishers indicate that careful proof reading by a single proof reader can eliminate about 90% of minor typographical errors, and the use of two pairs of proof readers can top 99%.

However, there are no equivalent studies for ordinary business databases. However, based on the number of errors reported the efficiency appears lower. From my preliminary analysis, assume that out of three errors per page fact checking might eliminate 2.75 of them, so there would be roughly 0.25 errors per page still latent in information when it is stored in a database or one error for every four pages of stored data.

Assuming that these preliminary results are true for the entire mass of information considered as part of this case study, then the total number of potential errors in the data would have amounted to 816,000,000. Assuming that roughly 92% of them would have been eliminated, the total volume of latent errors still remaining would total to about 65,280,000. This is a significant volume of latent errors.

Even if only 2% of the latent data errors are important enough to cause serious damages (i.e., errors in tax information, errors in payroll information, errors in customer orders, errors in shipping address, etc.) that is still more than 1,000,000 data errors, which is quite a significant volume. The twin topics of data errors and data quality are obviously very important, and deserve serious research.

The literature on database design, data warehousing, and the "information superhighway" tend to deal with only portions of the kinds of information recorded and utilized by corporations and government agencies. There is a growing need for careful exploration and thoughtful analysis of all of the kinds of information stored in paper from, magnetic or optical form, or stored redundantly in multiple forms.

This hypothetical case study attempts to construct a profile of all of the kinds of information recorded and used by major corporations in carrying out their business and personnel operations.

Although hypothetical, the case study strongly suggests that several topics are in need of significant future research in order to develop truly effective data warehouse and data quality concepts and tools:

- The need for an effective "data point" metric similar to function points for software is a critical gap. Without effective normalizing metrics for size and quality, database research, data quality research, and all derivative fields of research are severely handicapped.

- Future research is also needed in the related topics of information creation costs, information defect repair costs, information storage and transmission costs, and the almost totally unexplored topic of the costs of eliminating or destroying unwanted and obsolete information.

- The topic of the current near 100% redundancy between paper and online storage for some information deserves continued study. (The main reasons for the redundancy appear to be security, performance, the lack of light-weight hand-held reading devices, and lack of effective catalogs that describe information already available.)

- The topic of the ratios of graphics and images to alphanumeric information needs additional study. Currently graphics are more or less ignored in standard database products.

- The topic of sensor-based data also needs to be included in data quality research. Otherwise data coming in from satellites, radar, or electronic sensing devices such as those controlling aircraft flight systems cannot be evaluated under data quality criteria.

- The topic of the enormous volumes of personal and private reference information stored in individual offices, which collectively are far larger than any other kind of data storage, and far larger than any known data warehouse, is essentially unexplored and is not part of any current studies on data warehousing or repositories.

- The topic of the "Year 2000 problem" in databases, repositories, and data warehouses needs urgent research. It is suspected that the problem is as severe for databases as for software, but much less has been published on the data issues of the Year 2000 problem.

- One of the emerging and very serious problems with data storage is long-range retention. I remember reading an article recently where I said that if archeologists dug up the ruins of our civilization in 1,000 years and found CD-ROMS, magnetic disks, magnetic tape, and books, only the books would probably be decipherable. The problem is not so much that the physical media decays, but rather that there is no really long-range format for encoding data that is universal and has longevity.

As computers expand in usage throughout the worlds of business, government, and military operations data and data quality will be growing in importance in the 21st century. Data quality research is only in start-up mode as this book is written, and needs to mature into a fully developed subdiscipline of quality control.

DEFECT DISCOVERY RATES BY CUSTOMERS AND USERS

When software is delivered to customers or users, bugs and defect start being reported back to the development organization. However, the discovery of bugs by users is not instantaneous. The following table shows typical results for several years in a row, with the data showing the percentage of the original delivered defects reported.

Table 1   Three Year Discovery Rate of Initial Software Defects After Release

	End-User	MIS	Outsource	Systems	Commerc.	Military	Average
Year 1	80.00%	30.00%	40.00%	60.00%	65.00%	70.00%	57.50%
Year 2	15.00%	35.00%	35.00%	30.00%	25.00%	25.00%	27.50%
Year 3	5.00%	25.00%	20.00%	9.00%	9.00%	4.00%	12.00%
Latent	0.00%	10.00%	5.00%	1.00%	1.00%	1.00%	3.00%
Total	100.00%	100.00%	100.00%	100.00%	100.00%	100.00%	100.00%

Of course long before three years have passed new defects will be injected due to updates, enhancements, bad fixes, and the like. However this table shows only the decline in the original defects from release 1. The data is derived from studies performed by the QA teams in IBM, ITT, and also several other SPR clients.

As a general rule software that controls physical devices such as systems software and military software will discover bugs more rapidly than software that deals only with information. The early discovery of software bugs that affect hardware devices is due to the nature of such products. They don't work without reliable software, and if they fail the consequences may be grave.

Indeed, hardware manufacturers such as telecommunication companies tend to have special testing laboratories where the hardware and software are both installed and used by clients under conditions that replicate actual usage patterns after deployment. These special testing labs are designed to ensure that critical problems will be found early.

There are two general rules that determine the rate at which users of software find and report bugs:

- Rule 1: Defect discovery is directly related to the number of users.

- Rule 2: Defect discovery is inversely related to the number of defects.

The first rule is simple and intuitive. The second rule is counter intuitive and needs some explanation.

For the first rule, defect discovery correlates strongly with usage patterns and also with hours of execution. The more customers running the software, the greater the variety of usage patterns and the greater the amount of execution, so defect discovery rates accelerate.

However, end-user software is something of an exception since there is usually only a single user. The reason for the anomaly is because end-user applications are so small (averaging only about 10 function points). Hence the user tends to find all of the bugs in the application fairly quickly. It is much easier to find bugs in a 10 function point application than in a 10,000 function point application.

However, if you ship software with too many bugs in it, say more than one latent defect per function point or seven latent defects per KLOC, the quality and reliability of the application will be so bad that customer usage will probably stop. Zero users report zero defects, and the product will probably be recalled or withdrawn from service.

DEFECT PREVENTION METHODS

A host of technologies have some effect in defect prevention, or reducing the probable number of errors which might occur in software projects. There are too many to discuss all of them, but a few of the most successful defect prevention methods include: Joint Application Design (JAD), prototyping, and various flavors of reusability such as reusable designs and reusable source code.

Among SPR's clients only about 40 companies out of 600 have some kind of formal research programs on-going to explore methods of data prevention. The other companies recognize the importance of defect prevention and utilize quite a few preventive approaches, but they do not actually attempt to explore the impact of prevention on defect totals.

It is an interesting fact that formal design and code inspections, which are currently the most effective defect removal technique, also have a major role in defect prevention. Programmers and designers who participate in reviews and inspections tend to avoid making the mistakes which were noted during the inspection sessions.

It is obvious on theoretical grounds that object-oriented (OO) analysis and design should be an effective defect prevention mechanism. Unfortunately, as of 1996 there is no empirical evidence to support the theory, and indeed there is some evidence that the steep learning curve associated with OO analysis and design may result in higher than normal front-end defect levels for at least the initial projects that use OO approaches.

Following are observations on various flavors of defect prevention and what kind of software they might be appropriate for, or not, as the case may be.

Table 1   Software Defect Prevention Approaches by Application Type

Defect Prevention Approach	Software Classes With Good Results	Software Classes With Questionable Results
Class libraries (certified)	All classes	None
Clean-room development	Systems software	MIS software
Complexity analysis	All classes	None
Configuration control tools	All classes	None
Defect estimation tools	All classes	None
DoD standards	Military software	All others
Error-prone module analysis	All classes	None
Formal code inspections	All classes	None
Formal design inspections	All classes	None
Formal test plan inspections	All classes	None
Function point defect metrics	All classes	None
ISO 9000-9004 standards	Commercial software	Most other classes
Joint application design (JAD)	MIS software	System software
LOC metrics	None	All classes
OO analysis and design	Ambiguous results	Ambiguous results
Prototyping	All classes	None
Reverse engineering	COBOL primarily	Many languages
Quality circles	Ambiguous results	Ambiguous results
Quality function deployment (QFD)	Most classes to date	Still experimental
Quality measurement tools	All classes	None
Reusable code (certified)	All classes	None
Reusable designs (certified)	All classes	None
Reusable test cases (certified)	All classes	None
Reusable test plans (certified)	All classes	None

(continued)

Table 1   *(continued)*

Defect Prevention Approach	Software Classes With Good Results	Software Classes With Questionable Results
Risk analysis protocols	All classes	None
Test coverage tools	All classes	None
Test library tools	All classes	None
Total quality management (TQM)	Systems software	MIS software
Zero-defect programs	Systems software	MIS software

Defect prevention is a more difficult concept to grasp, and a more difficult concept to measure, than defect removal. This should not be a surprise, since preventive medicine is also more difficult to justify than curative medicine. In both domains, there is a strong synergy between prevention and cures and both are necessary.

It is useful to construct a simple matrix that shows defect origins on one axis and defect prevention effectiveness on the other axis. It is obvious from such a graph that there is no "silver bullet" that will magically eliminate all sources of error.

	Requirements Defects	Design Defects	Code Defects	Document Defects	Performance Defects
JAD's	Excellent	Good	Not Applicable	Fair	Poor
Prototypes	Excellent	Excellent	Fair	Not Applicable	Excellent
Structured Methods	Fair	Good	Excellent	Fair	Fair
CASE Tools	Fair	Good	Fair	Fair	Fair
Blueprints & Reusable Code	Excellent	Excellent	Excellent	Excellent	Good
QFD	Good	Excellent	Fair	Poor	Good

Figure 1: Software Defect Origins and Defect Prevention Effectiveness

Graphs such as this are useful for clarifying the kinds of defect prevention and defect removal methodologies that need to be utilized to achieve satisfactory quality levels. It is obvious that each source of error should utilize prevention methods that are "good" or "excellent" in order to minimize down-stream problems.

DEFECT PREVENTION AND REMOVAL VARIATIONS BY INDUSTRY

There are very significant differences in defect potentials, defect prevention methods, and in the patterns of defect removal approaches among a variety of industries. The following are overall results for six different software domains, taken from the second edition of my book *Applied Software Measurement* (McGraw Hill 1996).

Table 1 Software Defect Origins for Six Domains

	End-User	MIS	Outsource	Commer.	System	Military	Average
Requirements bugs	0.00%	15.00%	20.00%	10.00%	10.00%	20.00%	12.50%
Design bugs	15.00%	30.00%	25.00%	30.00%	25.00%	20.00%	24.17%
Source Code bugs	55.00%	35.00%	35.00%	30.00%	40.00%	35.00%	38.33%
User Document bugs	10.00%	10.00%	10.00%	20.00%	15.00%	15.00%	13.33%
Bad Fix bugs	20.00%	10.00%	10.00%	10.00%	10.00%	10.00%	11.67%
Total bugs	100.00%	100.00%	100.00%	100.00%	100.00%	100.00%	100.00%

The concept of "defect prevention" is the most difficult to study and quantify. Here is an example of how assumptions on defect prevention are derived.

Assume two projects of the same size and nominal complexity, say 1,000 function points. Assume that one of the projects developed a prototype, while the other project did not.

When the defects for the two projects are accumulated, assume that design reviews found 200 bugs or errors in the project that did not build a prototype, and only 100 bugs or errors in the project that did build a prototype. It can be hypothesized that the prototype had the effect of preventing 100 potential bugs or errors that might otherwise have occurred.

Of course, one example is not enough to really form such a hypothesis. But if 50 projects that built prototypes were compared to 50 similar projects that did not, and the number of design defects had a 2-to-1 average difference in favor of prototypes, then the hypothesis would be reasonable.

It would also be helpful to construct controlled experiments of various defect prevention factors such as prototypes, but controlled experiments for software are difficult and fairly uncommon. However, field data collected from hundreds or thousands of projects can gradually build up a body of knowledge about software quality and what works and what does not.

The concept of defect removal efficiency is a very important one for quality control and quality assurance purposes. Defect removal efficiency is normally calculated on the anniversary of the release of a software product. Suppose that during development, a total of 900 bugs or errors were found. During the first year of use, customers found and reported another 100 bugs.

On the first anniversary of the product's release, the 900 bugs found during development are added to the 100 bugs customers reported to achieve a total of 1,000 bugs for this example. Since the developers found 900 out of 1,000, their defect removal efficiency can easily be seen to be 90%.

The measurement of defect removal efficiency levels is one of the signs of a "best in class" software producer. Not only do best in class organizations measure defect removal efficiency levels, but they average more than 95% removal efficiency levels for their entire software portfolio.

It is comparatively easy to go above 95% in defect removal efficiency levels for small applications of less than 100 function points in size. As the size of the application grows, defect removal efficiency levels typically decline unless very energetic steps are taken.

For applications larger than 10,000 function points and especially so for those approaching 100,000 function points defect removal efficiency levels in excess of 95% are only possible by using a multi-stage set of pre-test removal activities such as formal inspections, coupled with an extensive suite of formal testing stages.

The following table illustrates the approximate variations in typical defect prevention and defect removal methods among the six domains.

Table 2   Patterns of Software Defect Prevention and Removal Activities

	End-User	MIS	Outsource	Commer.	System	Military
Prevention Activities						
Prototypes	20.00%	20.00%	20.00%	20.00%	20.00%	20.00%
Clean Rooms					20.00%	20.00%
JAD sessions		30.00%	30.00%			
QFD sessions					25.00%	
Subtotal	*20.00%*	*44.00%*	*44.00%*	*20.00%*	*52.00%*	*36.00%*
Pretest Removal						
Desk checking	15.00%	15.00%	15.00%	15.00%	15.00%	15.00%
Requirements review			30.00%	25.00%	20.00%	20.00%
Design review			40.00%	45.00%	45.00%	30.00%
Document review				20.00%	20.00%	20.00%
Code inspections				50.00%	60.00%	40.00%
Ind. Verif. and Valid.						20.00%
Correctness proofs						10.00%
Usability labs				25.00%		
Subtotal	*15.00%*	*15.00%*	*64.30%*	*89.48%*	*88.03%*	*83.55%*
Testing Activities						
Unit test	30.00%	25.00%	25.00%	25.00%	25.00%	25.00%
New function test		30.00%	30.00%	30.00%	30.00%	30.00%
Regression test			20.00%	20.00%	20.00%	20.00%
Integration test		30.00%	30.00%	30.00%	30.00%	30.00%
Performance test				15.00%	15.00%	20.00%
System test		35.00%	35.00%	35.00%	40.00%	35.00%
Independent test						15.00%
Field test				50.00%	35.00%	30.00%
Acceptance test			25.00%		25.00%	30.00%
Subtotal	*30.00%*	*76.11%*	*80.89%*	*91.88%*	*92.69%*	*93.63%*
Overall Efficiency	52.40%	88.63%	96.18%	99.32%	99.58%	99.33%
Number of Activities	3	7	11	14	16	18

It is obvious that the more effective subindustries and companies use a multi-stage sequence of defect prevention and defect removal operations in order to achieve their results. The minimum sequence of defect removal operations necessary to ensure good to excellent quality consists of the following:

Defect Prevention Approaches

Formal requirements analysis such as Joint Application Design (JAD)
Formal risk-analysis early in development
Prototyping
Structured or formal specification methods
Structured programming methods
Certified reusable design and code components

Non-Test Defect Removal Methods

Requirement inspections
Design inspections
Code inspections
Test plan reviews
Test-case inspections
User documentation editing or reviews

Testing Defect Removal Methods

Unit test by individual programmers
New function testing
Regression testing
Performance testing
Integration testing
System testing
Field test (External Beta test)

The reason for so many discrete stages of defect removal operations is because the average efficiency of each stage will hover around 30%. To build up to a cumulative defect removal efficiency level exceeding 95% requires quite a few stages.

DEFECT REMOVAL EFFICIENCY

Complementing the function point metric are measurements of defect removal efficiency, or the percentages of software defects removed prior to delivery of the software to clients. Defect removal efficiency measurement is comparatively easy, and extremely effective.

The measurement of defect removal efficiency merely requires accumulating defect statistics for errors found prior to delivery, and then for a predetermined period after deployment (usually the first year of usage).

Among SPR's clients, about 50 companies out of 600 have developed their own measurement methods for dealing with defect removal efficiency from requirements through deployment. Another 100 can deal with defect removal efficiency from testing on. The remaining 450 have only partial or anecdotal data, or compare their results against secondary data from external sources.

Surprisingly, at least 100 of these organizations actually had the raw data available for calculating defect removal efficiency levels (i.e., running totals of defects before and after delivery) but had not attempted to calculate removal efficiencies because they did not realize that such a calculation was possible and useful.

The calculation of defect removal efficiency is simple in concept, although tricky in real life. If the development team for a software product found 950 defects during development, and the users reported 50 defects in the first year, it can be seen that the cumulative defect removal efficiency for the application is approximately 95%.

Of course, there will still be latent bugs after the first year, but there will also be new features and updates to the package. Therefore calculating defect removal efficiency with data reflecting more than 12 months of usage is very complicated, due to the introduction of fresh defects in the follow-on releases of the software. Using the first 12 months of usage as a standard period at least provides a common basis for discussion and comparison.

The U.S. average for defect removal efficiency, unfortunately, is currently only about 85% although top-ranked projects in leading companies such as AT&T, IBM, Motorola, Raytheon, and Hewlett Packard achieve defect removal efficiency levels well in excess of 99% on their best projects.

All software defects are not equally easy to remove. Requirements errors, design problems, and "bad fixes" tend to be the most difficult. Thus, on the day when software is actually put into production, the average quantity of latent errors or defects still present tends to be about 0.75 per function point, with the following distribution.

Table 1   Defect Removal Efficiency By Origin of Defects

(Data Expressed in Terms of Defects per Function Point)

Defect Origins	Defect Potentials	Removal Efficiency	Delivered Defects
Requirements	1.00	77%	0.23
Design	1.25	85%	0.19
Coding	1.75	95%	0.09
Document	0.60	80%	0.12
Bad Fixes	0.40	70%	0.12
Total	5.00	85%	0.75

Note that at the time of delivery, defects originating in requirements and design tend to far outnumber coding defects. Data such as this can be used to improve the upstream defect prevention and defect removal processes of software development.

The best companies are using state-of-the art methods to lower their defect potentials, and coupling that with state-of-the-art methods for removing defects with high efficiency. The results can be quite impressive: Defect potentials of less than 2.0 defects per function point coupled with removal efficiencies in excess of 99%.

Table 2 shows the equivalent results for "defects per KLOC" using the C programming language.

Table 2   Defect Removal Efficiency by Origin of Defects

(Data Expressed in Terms of Defects per KLOC in C)

Defect Origins	Defect Potentials	Removal Efficiency	Delivered Defects
Requirements	7.8	77%	1.8
Design	9.7	85%	1.5
Coding	13.7	95%	0.7

(continued)

Table 2   *(continued)*

(Data Expressed in Terms of Defects per KLOC in C)

Defect Origins	Defect Potentials	Removal Efficiency	Delivered Defects
Document	4.7	80%	0.9
Bad Fixes	3.1	70%	0.9
Total	*39.0*	*85%*	*5.5*

Note that companies that use the "lines of code" metric for data normalization usually don't count defects in user documents, requirements, or design. Therefore the only value from Table 2 that would apply to a pure "lines of code" measurement approach is the 0.7 data point shown here for coding defects.

The best results in terms of defect removal are always achieved on projects that utilize formal pre-test inspections of design, code, and other major deliverables such as user manuals and even test cases.

Following are the approximate ranges of defect removal efficiency levels for selected kinds of defect removal activities. The data is derived from SPR clients who record such information as well as from secondary studies. In other words, the data comes from companies such as AT&T, Hewlett Packard, IBM, Microsoft, Motorola, Raytheon, and similar companies with formal defect tracking and measurement capabilities.

Table 3   Ranges in Software Defect Removal Efficiency Levels by Activity

Defect Removal Activity	Ranges of Defect Removal Efficiency		
Non-Test Defect Removal	Min	Avg	Max
Requirements inspections (limited samples)	25%	35%	50%
Informal design reviews	25%	30%	40%
Formal design inspections	45%	65%	85%
Informal code reviews	20%	30%	45%
Formal code inspections	45%	65%	85%
Formal test case inspections (limited samples)	35%	50%	65%

(continued)

Table 3   *(continued)*

Defect Removal Activity	Ranges of Defect Removal Efficiency		
Testing Defect Removal	Min	Avg	Max
Unit test by developers	15%	30%	55%
New function test	20%	30%	40%
Integration test	25%	35%	45%
Regression test	10%	15%	30%
Performance test	20%	15%	30%
System test	25%	35%	55%
Low-volume Beta test (<10 clients)	20%	30%	40%
High-volume Beta test (>1000 clients)	60%	75%	90%

If this entire sequence of six non-test and eight testing stages were performed, the ranges of cumulative defect removal efficiency would range from about 96% to a high of 99.999%. The mode would be about 98% cumulative defect removal efficiency.

All of these are far higher than the current U.S. average of about 85% cumulative defect removal efficiency. However, few U.S. software producers utilize a 14-stage suite of defect removal operations. Only companies that build very complex physical devices such as airplanes, telephone switching systems, or mainframe computers utilize so many defect removal steps.

Indeed, some client/server projects have been noted that used only two forms of defect removal: unit testing by individual programmers and an overall system test after integration. It is no wonder that client/server quality is often suspect.

It is obvious that no single defect removal operation is adequate by itself. This explains why "best in class" quality results can only be achieved from synergistic combinations of defect prevention, reviews or inspections, and various kinds of test activities.

Companies that can consistently average more than 95% in defect removal efficiency levels, and keep defect potentials below about 3.0 per function point are moving toward "best in class" status.

As with defect prevention, not every form of defect removal is equally effective against all sources of software errors. Here, too, it is useful to construct a simple matrix that relates defect origins and defect removal methods.

	Requirements Defects	Design Defects	Code Defects	Document Defects	Performance Defects
Reviews/ Inspections	Fair	Excellent	Excellent	Good	Fair
Prototypes	Good	Fair	Fair	Not Applicable	Good
Testing (all forms)	Poor	Poor	Good	Fair	Excellent
Correctness Proofs	Poor	Poor	Good	Fair	Poor

Figure 1: Software Defect Origins and Defect Removal Effectiveness

Note a significant weakness of current defect removal activities: there are no techniques for removing requirements defects that rank higher than "good." It is obvious that to minimize the effect of requirements errors, defect prevention methods must be part of the strategy.

A useful way of showing the combined impacts of various defect removal operations is to show the permutations that results from using various methods singly or in combination. Since four factors generate 16 permutations, the results show that high quality levels need a multi-faceted approach. Table 2 shows the cumulative defect removal efficiency levels of all 16 permutations of four factors.

The phrases "design inspections" and "code inspections" refer to formal inspections following the protocols defined by Michael Fagan: i.e., training of participants, careful selection of participants, materials delivered well prior to the inspection day, both a moderator and recorder present, adequate time and facilities provided, and defect statistics kept for subsequent analysis.

The phrase "quality assurance" refers to an active software quality assurance group, as defined earlier in this book. That is, the QA staff will be in the range of about 3% to 5% of the software development population, so that each QA analyst will support no more than 20 to 30 developers.

The phrase "formal testing" refers to tests carried out by testing specialists under these conditions: 1) a test plan was created for the application; 2) the specifications were complete enough so that test cases can be created without notable gaps; 3) test library control tools are utilized; and 4) test coverage analysis tools are utilized.

The data shown in the following table is hypothetical, but derived from empirical studies carried out in corporations whose quality data is precise enough for this kind of analysis. Examples of such companies include AT&T, Bellcore, Hewlett Packard, IBM, Microsoft, Motorola, and Raytheon.

Table 4   Defect Removal Efficiency Levels and Permutations of Four Factors

	Worst	Median	Best
No design inspections No code inspections No quality assurance No formal testing	30%	40%	50%
No design inspections No code inspections **Formal quality assurance** No formal testing	32%	45%	55%
No design inspections No code inspections No quality assurance **Formal testing**	37%	53%	60%
No design inspections **Formal code inspections** No quality assurance No formal testing	43%	57%	66%
Formal design inspections No code inspections No quality assurance No formal testing	45%	60%	68%
No design inspections No code inspections **Formal quality assurance** **Formal testing**	50%	65%	75%

(continued)

Table 4   *(continued)*

	Worst	Median	Best
No design inspections **Formal code inspections** **Formal quality assurance** No formal testing	53%	68%	78%
No design inspections **Formal code inspections** No quality assurance **Formal testing**	55%	70%	80%
Formal design inspections No code inspections **Formal quality assurance** No formal testing	60%	75%	85%
Formal design inspections No code inspections No quality assurance **Formal testing**	65%	80%	87%
Formal design inspections **Formal code inspection** No quality assurance No formal testing	70%	85%	90%
No design inspections **Formal code inspections** **Formal quality assurance** **Formal testing**	75%	87%	93%
Formal design inspections No code inspections **Formal quality assurance** **Formal testing**	77%	90%	95%

(continued)

Table 4   *(continued)*

	Worst	Median	Best
Formal design inspections	83%	95%	97%
Formal code inspections			
Formal quality assurance			
No formal testing			
Formal design inspections	85%	97%	99%
Formal code inspections			
No quality assurance			
Formal testing			
Formal design inspections	95%	99%	99.99%
Formal code inspections			
Formal quality assurance			
Formal testing			

As may be seen from the progression through the 16 permutations, achieving high levels of software quality requires a multi-faceted approach. No single method is adequate. In particular, testing alone is not sufficient; quality assurance alone is not sufficient; inspections alone are not sufficient.

Since the ranges of defect removal efficiency levels are rather broad, it is of interest to discuss how many projects have achieved various levels of removal efficiency. Using only more recent data collected since SPR was formed in 1984, the next table gives approximate distribution of defect removal efficiency for about 1,500 projects where such data is known. (Note that this data has a bias toward systems software and military projects since more companies in these domains keep defect removal efficiency data than for MIS, commercial, or outsource groups.)

Table 5   Distribution of 1,500 Software Projects by Defect Removal Efficiency Level

Defect Removal Efficiency Level (Percent)	Number of Projects	Percent of Projects
=> 99%	6	0.40%
95-99%	104	6.93%
90-95%	263	17.53%
85-90%	559	37.26%
80-85%	408	27.20%
< 80%	161	10.73%
TOTAL	1500	100.00%

The picture this data presents is interesting. Obviously achieving high defect removal efficiency levels is a technical possibility since it has been done. Also obviously, quite a few companies do not know how to go about achieving high levels of defect removal efficiency.

Although the results have nothing to do with software, a plot of the time 1500 army recruits could run a mile would have a similar distribution. One or two of the recruits might be able to approach a four-minute mile, and maybe 25 or so in less than five minutes, but hundreds would have trouble running a mile in less than 10 minutes. In both track and software, if you want to be really good you have to work at it.

(See also the sections on Testing and on the "Good Enough" Quality Fallacy for information on how defect removal efficiency correlates with software development schedules.)

DEFECT REPAIR RATES

Although finding and fixing software defects constitutes the largest identifiable expense for the software industry, there is surprisingly little solid data on this topic in the software quality literature. Even worse, some of the published data does not satisfactorily deal with either the impact of fixed costs or with slack time while waiting for defects to be reported.

There are a number of factors that affect software defect repair rates, and they pull the rates in different directions:

- Defect repair rates usually decline as cyclomatic and essential complexity go up although there are sometimes exceptions to this rule.

- Defect repair rates increase as staff experience levels go up: 1) experience in the application being repaired; 2) experience with the programming language or languages used; 3) experience with design and code inspections; and 4) experience with structured design and structured coding methods.

- During maintenance, defect repair rates are higher for maintenance specialists than for generalists who do both development and maintenance work. Indeed assigning both maintenance and development responsibilities to the same person tends to degrade performance at both ends. Defect repairs are driven by high-severity random interrupts which make it difficult to predict development schedules. If development tasks are running late, there is a tendency to skimp on maintenance testing and validation so bad fix rates go up.

- During maintenance, defect repair rates are lowest for defects involving special configurations so that the maintenance team cannot replicate the defect or make the problem occur at their repair facility.

- For defect repairs of source code, repair rates generally correlate with the density of comments. Somewhat surprisingly, an IBM study found an optimum node point of about 18% comment density (i.e., 18% of the statements in the application were commentary statements). Too many comments slowed down repairs, as did too few comments or none at all.

- The IBM study on maintenance defect repairs also found that detailed flow charts of application structure had no visible affect on the time needed to either find or repair defects. The most useful information for maintenance purposes were very accurate error messages and cross-references that associated error messages with the modules that issued them and were involved in the trouble that triggered them.

- Maintenance effort is difficult to measure with function point metrics because many maintenance changes are so small (< 10 lines of code or 0.1 function points) that they are below the size at which function points can even be counted, since the counting rules deal with integer values and not fractional function points. In any case, function points are inaccurate below 10 function points in size due to the fact that the 14 adjustment factors have too large an effect for precision with very small projects. A kind of "micro function point" is needed for the range below 10 function points, which include very small adjustment factors and would also support at least two decimal places (i.e., 1.25 function points).

Because local conditions and experience levels vary, every company and software group should determine their own defect repair intervals from their own measurement system. However, the following ranges may be useful when getting started. The following table deals only with repairs after a defect has been found, had its symptoms described, and been routed to the personnel responsible for repairs.

In other words, this table excludes activities such as inspection preparation or creating and running test cases. Note that the time shown assumes work-hours during business, so that a time of "24 hours" would imply three separate business days. (Since weekends and holidays can occur, the number of calendar days may be as long as six.) Of course, some companies have three-shift, 24-hour maintenance teams and under this condition "24 hours" would be a single calendar day.

Table 1   Software Defect Repair Rates for Selected Defect Removal Activities

(Repair rates expressed in terms of staff hours after defect is reported)

Defect Report Origin	Lowest	Mode	Highest
Non-test Defect Removal			
Requirement inspections	0.25	2.0	16.0
Design inspections	0.50	6.0	24.0
Code inspections	0.10	2.0	16.0
Test plan inspections	0.20	1.5	4.0
User manual inspections	0.10	0.6	3.0
Pre-test average		2.5	
Testing Defect Removal			
Unit test	0.10	0.5	4.0
New function	0.50	2.0	8.0
Regression test	2.00	6.0	16.0
Stress/performance test	2.00	12.0	24.0
Integration test	3.00	6.5	18.0
System test	3.50	6.5	18.0
Field test	4.00	7.5	40.00
Testing average		5.85	

(continued)

Table 1   *(continued)*

(Repair rates expressed in terms of staff hours after defect is reported)

Defect Report Origin	Lowest	Mode	Highest
Post-Release Defect Removal			
Severity 1 (critical) code defects	8.00	18.0	40.0
Severity 2 (serious) code defects	5.50	10.5	40.0
Severity 3 (minor) code defects	1.75	4.5	16.0
Severity 4 (cosmetic) code defects	1.50	3.0	8.0
Invalid (user error, hardware, etc.)	1.00	6.5	24.0
Duplicate (defect already reported)	0.10	0.5	4.0
Abeyant (can't reproduce problem)	8.00	24.0	60.0
Post-release average		9.57	
Average of Averages		5.97	

Note three special cases are included in the post-release defect repair section of the table: abeyant defects, duplicate defects, and invalid defects.

The phrase "abeyant defects" originated in IBM and refers to customer-reported defects where the change team could not recreate the problem or make it happen at the repair site. Usually abeyant defects were due to some special hardware or software configuration at the client's site. Whatever the cause, abeyant defects are the most time consuming and expensive forms of defects since it is necessary to gather additional data and sometimes even to visit the client site.

The phrase "duplicate defects" simply refers to problems that have already been reported, and have been found by another customer (or many other customers). If a software vendor has a good defect tracking and reporting system that includes symptoms of incoming defects, then duplicates can be dealt with very quickly. However, if the repair team does not recognize a defect as a duplicate and has to explore its implications, then duplicates can accumulate quite a lot of wasted energy.

The phrase "invalid defects" refers to errors that are reported against a software product, but upon investigation turn out not to be errors in the product at all. Sometimes the reported defects are due to user errors, sometimes the reported defects are hardware problems, and sometimes the reported defects are true bugs, but the bugs reside somewhere else in another software package. For example a bug might be reported against a software application that turns out to be a bug in the operating system rather than in the application itself. Sometimes too the reported defect is converted into a possible future enhancement.

Surprisingly, invalid defects are among the most troubling and expensive to deal with. Even though the problem may not exist at all, the problem to be dealt with might be the task of explaining to indignant customers that they might have made a mistake. Invalid defects are not a trivial problem.

Pure defect repairs are not a good indicator of the actual turn-around or elapsed time between when a customer reports a defect and when the repair becomes available. The total interval from reporting to repair availability can sometimes take weeks or even months. (See the Case Study of Software Quality Improvement section earlier in this book for a discussion of factors that influence total repair intervals.) In general, the quickest elapsed times through the whole process are for companies and clients that have direct computer connections for defect reporting and downloading of repairs.

DEFECT SEEDING

The concept of "defect seeding" is to insert a set of known errors into a software deliverable prior to a review, inspection, or testing. For example, if 100 known bugs are inserted into a system just prior to integration test, and the test cases only detect 30 of them, you have an immediate basis for asserting that integration testing is about 30% efficient.

Among SPR's U.S. clients only half a dozen out of 600 have experimented with defect seeding. Among our overseas clients, Japan seems to be the country where defect seeding is most widely utilized. Although defect seeding is not universal in Japan either, the approach is not uncommon for calibration of the testing efficiency for large-scale systems software.

The only other way to ascertain defect removal efficiency is to wait for the remainder of the development cycle plus at least a year of field usage, and then retroactively calculate defect removal efficiency from the total numbers of bug reports.

The defect seeding approach is not often used for software, except in the context as a teaching aid when preparing courses on testing, design inspections, or other forms of defect removal. Whenever defect seeding is used, the results that can be gathered are valuable and may give new insights.

Once when I was developing a new course on design inspections, I carefully seeded 10 known errors into the case study I had prepared. When I first presented the course, my students found all 10 of the known errors, and also detected four others that I had not realized were there. While the results were personally embarrassing, they demonstrated the value of both defect seeding and also of formal inspections.

The idea of deliberately putting defects into software is unpleasant to most of us. Also, there is no guarantee that the "tame" bugs that we insert will be true replicas of the "wild" bugs that are already in the software. However, the entire concept of vaccination is logically similar to defect seeding. Vaccine serums are based on weakened or dead cultures of "wild" bacteria or viruses and their presence triggers the production of antibodies that can lead to immunity. While it is unwise to carry the analogy too far, the practice of defect seeding is currently the quickest known way of determining defect removal efficiency levels.

However, the ratio of seeded bugs to real bugs is still an unknown quantity. Very preliminary data indicates about a 20% differential between efficiency in finding seeded bugs versus real bugs; i.e., if a particular test stage finds 65% of the seeded bugs, it may not find more than 45% of the real bugs.

One interesting variant of the defect seeding approach has become a fairly large new subindustry within the past five years, and is a rather good replica of medical vaccination. The new and fast growing subindustry of protecting computers and software against known viruses (and hopefully potentially unknown ones too) depends upon seeding of known viruses in order to judge the effectiveness of the viral protection software.

Currently there is no definitive data of the kinds of problems which are amenable to defect seeding, and the kinds for which the method may be inappropriate. Obviously deep logical problems are not a good candidate for defect seeding, while superficial problems such as branching errors or loop cycle errors are an obvious choice.

DEFECT SEVERITY LEVELS

Most software defect tracking systems include a multi-tier "severity level" scale. Three, four, and five-level scales have been observed. For example, AT&T uses a three-level severity scale and IBM uses a four-level severity scale.

Most of these scales use a similar structure regardless of the number of steps included. As a general illustration of the principle, Software Productivity Research uses a four-level scale derived from the IBM model with these definitions:

Severity 1   Total failure of application
Severity 2   Failure of major function(s)
Severity 3   Minor problem
Severity 4   Cosmetic problem that does not affect operation

The distribution of defects among the various severity levels will vary in response to a number of factors. For example, most companies fix severity 1 bugs as rapidly as possible: sometimes within a few hours. Severity 2 bugs are also fixed rather rapidly but severity 3 and 4 bugs are usually aggregated and repaired during the next formal release of an application, sometimes many months down-stream.

The results of this bias in defect repair intervals (which customers usually know about) tends to create an artificially high percentage of severity 2 problems, since customers who find errors usually want them fixed fairly soon. Following are the approximate distributions of defects by severity level for bugs found after release in the United States, associated with the overall sizes of software applications, derived from the 2nd edition of my book *Applied Software Measurement* (McGraw Hill 1996).

Table 1   U.S. Averages for Delivered Defects by Severity Level

	Severity 1 (Critical)	Severity 2 (Significant)	Severity 3 (Minor)	Severity 4 (Cosmetic)	Total
1FP	0	0	0	0	0
10FP	0	0	1	0	1
100FP	1	4	14	20	39
1000FP	6	78	222	250	556
10000FP	127	1,225	4,224	2,872	8,448
100000FP	2,658	15,946	66,440	47,837	132,880
Average	465	2,875	11,817	8,497	23,654
Percent	1.97%	12.16%	49.96%	35.92%	100.00%

As can be seen, severity 1 and severity 2 defects constitute a small percentage of the overall volumes of delivered defects, but this is where the bulk of the costs tend to be concentrated.

Some commercial software products there tend to encounter unusually large numbers of severity 2 defects. This is because most vendors repair high-severity defects quicker than low-severity defects, so any bug that is annoying tends to have its severity level raised a notch. It is hard to fake severity 1 defect levels (i.e., the application is dead in the water and does not operate at all) but severity 2 is ambiguous enough so that many defects are assigned that level by clients just to speed up the repair intervals.

While it is mildly surprising that severity 3 defects outnumber severity 4, it should be recalled that severity 4 defects are so minor and inconsequential that large volumes of them are never even reported. Also, many severity 4 bugs are not fixed even if they are reported.

DEFECT TRACKING

Until 1993, accurate and automated defect tracking was a capability that few companies had, because it was necessary to build custom defect tracking systems. Therefore, only companies such as AT&T, Hewlett Packard, IBM, Microsoft, Motorola, Raytheon, Siemens-Nixdorf, and the like had fully automated defect tracking systems.

Starting in early 1993, and continuing forward through today, many new commercial defect tracking tools are entering the U.S. commercial market on various platforms such as DOS, Windows, OS/2, and UNIX. Accurate and automated software defect tracking is now within the grasp of any company that chooses to do it.

Among SPR's clients, the number of enterprises adopting formal defect tracking is increasing rapidly as commercial tools become available. In 1992 only about 60 companies out of 500 were using defect tracking automation, but in 1996, about 125 out of 600 are using defect tracking automation.

The overall functions of these commercial defect tracking tools include: tracking defects by severity level and by origin, and routing the defect to the appropriate repair facility. Some have even more advanced functions such as keeping records of duplicate defects, invalid defects submitted by mistake, and the like.

It is an interesting observation that some of these new commercial defect tracking tools were created by former employees of the companies that had built internal defect tracking systems. Having used such systems and seen their capabilities, it is obvious that a growing commercial market exists.

For those interested in purchasing or leasing software defect tracking tools, the following capabilities should be included:

- Defects from all major sources should be capable of being recorded; i.e., defects in requirements, design, source code, user documents, and bad fixes or secondary defects. It would also be useful to be able to add other sources of defects, such as errors in test cases or data errors.

- Defect causes should be included, i.e., errors of omission, errors of commission, errors of ambiguity, and errors of capacity or performance.

- Duplicate reports of the same defect should be recorded and noted, although for quality analysis purposes most statistics are based on valid unique defects. However, a large number of duplicate defect reports for a high-severity defect is an important topic that should be noted.

- In addition to real bugs or defects, it will often happen that invalid defect reports are received. (I once received a bug report against a direct competitor's software product which was mailed to us by mistake.) Examples of invalid defect reports include: hardware problems misdiagnosed as software problems; user errors, and problems with things like the operating system misdiagnosed as being an error in an application running under the operating system. Since invalid defect reports are both numerous and expensive, they should be recorded as a standard feature of defect tracking systems.

- Although not critical to the repairs of defects, it is helpful to record the method through which the defect report was received. The major channels for reporting defects to vendors include: telephone calls, faxes, e-mail, direct communication via computer to computer linkages, or face to face discussions in situations where there is on-site service. This kind of data is useful in planning staffing resources for things like hot lines and customer support desks.

- Defect severity levels should be recorded, ranging from critical down to minor. However, assigning defect severity is a very subjective field, so provisions are needed to allow the severity levels to change if needed.

- A small but significant number of defects are eventually turned in to suggestions for future enhancements. Therefore, a capability is needed to convert defect reports into possible new features.

- The date that defects are first reported should be recorded, as should the date when other key events occur, such as turning the defect over to the repair team, and the date of the final defect resolution, plus the date when the repaired software was released back to clients.

- The defect tracking tool should have a built-in warning system so that defects that have aged beyond user-specified boundary points are highlighted. For example, a critical severity 1 defect that is more than one week old without being repaired is in need of some kind of alarm signal.

- Some defect tracking systems also record the effort needed to repair the defect. If this feature is included, it should be granular enough to capture all relevant activities such as defect analysis, design changes, code changes, creation of new test cases, testing, etc.

- A significant number of defects cannot be replicated by the vendor's repair team. This situation is usually because of some special or unique combination of hardware and software used by the customer. The term for these difficult problems used by IBM was "abeyant" defects. The word meant that repairs had to be postponed until additional information could be elicited about the special conditions that caused the problem to occur. Abeyant defects are usually the longest to repair and often the most expensive, so defect tracking systems need to be able to highlight them when they occur.

The overall cumulative costs of finding and fixing bugs is usually the most expensive cost element for building large software systems. Therefore, an effective defect tracking tool is very useful for both quality and productivity improvements.

DEMING PRIZE

W. Edwards Deming is the well-known quality expert who lived in Japan for many years in the post-World War II era. Deming started lecturing in Japan circa 1950 and was very influential in introducing statistical quality control to Japanese industry. Deming and Joseph Juran were very important figures in both Japanese and world quality research in the early post-war era.

In honor of Deming's work, the Japanese government introduced the Deming Prize for quality in 1951. It is remarkable that the prize was created only about a year after Deming's message on statistical quality control was broadcast. The

Deming Prize has a level of prestige even higher than the Baldrige Award in international circles.

The Deming Prize has six subcategories:

1) Companies

2) Small enterprises

3) Divisions

4) Work Sites

5) Overseas companies

6) Individuals

The variable scale of the Deming Prize is notably different from the American Baldrige Award. Also different is the fact that a Deming Prize category is reserved for overseas companies and for individuals.

Like the Baldrige Award, the Deming Prize is based on a full history of quality practices and requires substantial preparatory work. Also like the Baldrige, the Deming Prize is not aimed specifically at software, which is not surprising since it originated in 1951 when software was barely started on the path to becoming a separate industry.

Although my colleagues and I at SPR have done on-site consulting studies in Japan, we have not worked directly with any Deming Prize recipients. It is probable that winning a Deming Prize has the same kind of energizing effect as winning a Baldrige, but that is a supposition.

DEMOGRAPHIC DATA ON SOFTWARE QUALITY PERSONNEL

So far as can be determined, there is no accurate census of software quality assurance personnel, test personnel, or other related occupations in the overall quality domain. SPR demographic data on the overall software population of the United States suggests that out of the total of about 2,000,000 professional software personnel in 1996 that the full-time software quality assurance community totals to about 30,000. The set of testing specialists, or software professionals who devote most of their time to testing, is in the range of perhaps 225,000. The U.S. total of customer support personnel is growing rapidly, and may now top 100,000. Indeed, the customer support community is now large enough to have national conferences devoted to this topic alone. However, SQA, customer support, and testing demographic numbers have a high margin of error.

Maintenance and enhancement specialists are heavily involved in quality-related matters and are a very significant percentage of the overall U.S. software population, since they total to perhaps 600,000. However, most of SPR's clients lump maintenance (i.e., defect repairs) and enhancements (i.e., adding new features) together so it is difficult to separate the quality-related demographics from other kinds of work.

Table 1 shows the approximate ratios of various kinds of software occupations observed in SPR consulting studies, with quality-related positions highlighted in bold.

Table 1   Approximate Ratios of Technical Specialists to General Software Populations

Specialist Occupations	Specialists	Generalists		Generalist %
Maintenance and enhancement specialists	1	to	4	25.0%
Testing specialists	1	to	8	12.5%
Technical writing specialists	1	to	15	6.6%
Quality assurance specialists	1	to	25	4.0%
Customer support specialists	1	to	25	4.0%
Database administration specialists	1	to	25	4.0%
Configuration control specialists	1	to	30	3.3%
Systems software support specialists	1	to	30	3.3%
Function point counting specialists	1	to	50	2.0%
Integration specialists	1	to	50	2.0%
Measurement specialists	1	to	50	2.0%
Network specialists (local, wide area)	1	to	50	2.0%
Performance specialists	1	to	75	1.3%
Architecture specialists	1	to	75	1.3%
Cost estimating specialists	1	to	100	1.0%
Reusability specialists	1	to	100	1.0%
Package acquisition specialists	1	to	150	0.6%
Process improvement specialists	1	to	200	0.5%
Education and training specialists	1	to	250	0.4%
Standards specialists	1	to	300	0.3%

Note that this list of specialists is incomplete, since more than 100 specialized occupations exist in the overall software domain. However, ratios are not available for many kinds of specialists. This lack of good demographic data is a significant barrier to research in many important topics.

In the 1995 study of software demographics, which was commissioned by AT&T and carried out by SPR with the assistance of Dr. Bill Curtis of TeraQuest, one of the interesting problems noted was the deliberate refusal to record demographic data by a number of software human resources and personnel departments.

Keeping accurate records of the numbers of on-board personnel and open requisitions for 100 job categories would be quite a lot of work for the human resources group. It would also require very flexible software and position descriptions that could deal with new and emerging areas of specialization such as "Web master" or "JAVA programmer" or "SAP analyst."

What typically occurs is that the human resource policy is to lump multiple occupations together under a few generic titles such as "member of the technical staff." This, of course, eases the work load of the human resource group, but makes serious demographic research very difficult.

An interesting and potentially significant observation from our interviews with software managers and technical workers is that a clear majority regarded their corporate human resources group as unhelpful and unresponsive to the needs of the software community.

DEPARTMENT OF DEFENSE QUALITY STANDARDS

Since U.S. military software ranks among the best in the world in terms of quality levels, it must be concluded that the software quality methods included in various military and Department of Defense (DoD) standards have had a positive and beneficial impact on quality.

However, there is another aspect of military standards which should also be addressed. Of the six industries which typically create software with the highest quality levels (aerospace manufacturers, computer manufacturers, defense manufacturers, telecommunication manufacturers, commercial system software developers, and medical instrument manufacturers) the military software producers typically create twice as much paperwork as the second-place industry (telecommunications) and more than three times the volume of paperwork than civilian averages.

Further, the costs of military software averaged more than 100% higher than most civilian projects of the same size, and more than 50% higher than the other industries which consistently create high-quality software.

Also, military software project schedules average between 20% and 50% longer than equivalent schedules for civilian projects of equal size and technical complexity levels. Part of the lengthy military schedule duration is due to the time required to create the paper materials, part to the DoD need to review and understand the paper materials (although this does not always occur), and part to the rather baroque oversight requirements built into military contracts.

One additional aspect of lengthy military schedules is the fact that a substantial number of projects (both hardware and software) are slow getting started because of the litigious nature of military contract bidding.

I recall hearing a speech by a deputy undersecretary of defense at an Air Force seminar that cited about 30% of the initial awards of defense contracts were challenged in court by disgruntled vendors who did not get the work. Indeed, contract litigation is so common in the defense community that a whole body of military contract law, appeals, arbitration methods, specialized attorneys and expert witnesses, and even special courts have come into existence.

Several of my military colleagues have stated that the contract litigation is sometimes so protracted that it tends to slow down replacement of obsolete defense systems (both hardware and software) and often adds 18 months or so to the beginning of any major defense system upgrade.

However, once the projects get started when pure technical work is considered, such as programming; the military community and the civilian community are more or less equal. Indeed, for some projects developed in Ada9X the military software community would be in the upper quartile of software coding productivity for the United States.

In spite of very respectable coding productivity and the comparative success of the Ada programming language, pure programming comprises a very small percentage of military software costs. Coding is usually less than 20% of the cost of military software projects, while paperwork can top 50% of military software costs.

Much of the paperwork and oversight associated with military software projects do not appear to be technically necessary. Lloyd Mosemann, former deputy undersecretary of software acquisition for the Air Force, has remarked in conversation and speeches that much of the paperwork is because the Department of Defense and the military services essentially don't trust the defense contractors.

As this book is written, U.S. military standards are undergoing a profound transformation in response to a 1994 directive by William Perry, Secretary of Defense, to move toward civilian practices and adopt commercial standards. To minimize disruption and discontinuity, existing contracts and proposals based on military standards would continue, but the overall push is to move closer to civilian practices.

Since the military standards world is somewhat chaotic and undergoing transformation, there is little purpose in writing an extended treatise on how military standards affect quality if those same standards are on the verge of being eliminated. Therefore, only short discussions of some of the more notable military standards will be included here.

As computers and software began to expand through the military community during the 1950s and 1960s, a host of more or less independent standards were developed to deal with the emergence of this new technology.

By the late 1970s, the standards had multiplied to such an extent that it was difficult to follow any of them without violating others. In 1979, a military workshop held in Monterey, California recommended a standards consolidation. Two general principles were elucidated as the overall purpose of military standards:

1) To ensure that software was built properly with high quality.

2) To ensure that quality could be independently evaluated and measured.

These two principles have continued to be used, and have resulted in two general streams of standards dealing with construction on one hand, and evaluation and validation on the other hand.

While the military community does build many pure software applications, it is important to realize that most key weapons systems are hybrid projects that entail simultaneous construction of physical devices and the software which controls it. Consider something like the F-115 fighter airplane, the B2 bomber, or an Aegis class ship. The major operational components require both hardware and software concurrently. Therefore, a great deal of military software is termed "embedded" with the sense that the software is resident inside a physical device, which the software controls to a greater or lesser degree.

Therefore, military software standards must be considered in context with hardware standards, and the two sets of standards are used for the same systems in cases where hardware and software are both needed for the project in question.

DoD 2167, DoD 2167A, and DoD 2168

The standard termed DoD 2167 was issued in 1985 and was utilized until about 1988. This standard dealt with both software development and software quality control.

In 1988 the standard was segmented into two components. DoD 2167A dealt with software development, while DoD 2168 dealt with software quality control. However, there was some unavoidable overlap between the two.

There are also a number of related standards which augment the 2167A and 2168 primary standards. For example, MIL-STD-1521B describes formal reviews and audits. MIL-STD-480B and 481B describe configuration control and submission of change requests.

In addition, there is also DoD-STD-7935A which is similar but not identical to 2167A and covers automated information systems but not hybrid hardware/software weapons systems. It is used for the equivalent of ordinary information systems for things like payroll and compensation software packages.

The well-known DoD 2167A tended to assume a classic "waterfall" model of system and software development with five general phases:

- Concept exploration and definition

- Demonstration and validation

- Engineering and manufacturing

- Production and deployment

- Operations and support

Also, seven discrete activities are defined for system and software development:

- System requirements (hardware and software)

- Software requirements

- Preliminary design

- Detailed design

- Coding and unit testing

- Integration and testing

- System integration and testing (hardware and software)

The DoD-STD-2168 was the primary standard for software quality for a number of years. It was reasonably effective from the standpoint of quality, although not perfect by any means.

One interesting aspect of 2168 was the requirement that some portions of the quality assurance work be performed by personnel other than the developers, in order to ensure a truly independent evaluation.

This requirement led to several more or less unique solutions that are almost never used for civilian software: Independent Verification and Validation (IV&V) by a separate company other than the prime contractor, and sometimes independent testing by either the same subcontractor as the one performing IV&V, or by yet another subcontractor.

The IV&V concept is well intentioned, but in practice it has not exerted anything but a marginal impact on quality. Often the IV&V contracts have such severe cost limits (i.e., the work is performed by consultants for a billing rate of around $25.00 an hour) that the personnel doing the work are seldom "top guns" in the software quality and verification domain.

Mostly the IV&V process discovers or looks for surface-level mechanical problems such as whether or not all of the required documents have been produced and have included the correct sections. Deeper problems having to do with architecture or design issues are seldom uncovered.

The 2167-2168 family of standards were in effect for many years, and have been reasonably effective for software quality control. However, they unintentionally triggered the production of more paper documents than any other known standards in human history, although the ISO 9000-9004 standards are becoming strong contenders for generating excessive paperwork.

DoD 2167, 2167A and other military standards introduced a series of acronyms and abbreviations which are standard nomenclature within the military software community and essentially unintelligible outside the military world. However, if you expect to do any military software contract work or even read the literature on military software practices then an understanding these terms is a necessity. A sample of the military acronyms includes:

CID   Critical Item Description
CRISD   Computer Resources Integrated Support Document
CSCI   Computer Software Configuration Item
CSC   Computer Software Component

CSOM	Computer Software Operators Manual
DID	Data Item Description
ECP	Engineering Change Proposal
FSM	Firmware Support Manual
HWCI	Hardware Configuration Item
IDD	Interface Design Document
IRS	Interface Requirement Specification
IV&V	Independent Verification and Validation
PID	Prime Item Description
SCP	Specification Change Notice
SDD	Software Design Document
SDP	Software Development Plan
SPM	Software Programmers Manual
SPS	Software Product Specification
SQPP	Software Quality Program Plan
SRS	Software Requirement Specification
STD	Software Test Description
STP	Software Test Plan
STR	Software Test Report
SUM	Software Users Manual
VDD	Version Description Document
SSS	System/Segment Specification

Note that the abbreviations are shown before the definitions. This is because much of the military software literature uses the acronyms and may not even bother to define what they mean on the assumption that everyone already knows. Someone reading a military software standard or a journal article about military software development practices for the first time is in for a confusing experience unless a table of acronym expansions is readily available.

Overall, in spite of the baroque and arcane structure of some of the military standards, they performed a creditable job in making sure that the quality levels of military software were generally higher than many other industries. As mentioned elsewhere in this book, the top six industries in terms of software quality are:

- Aerospace manufacturers

- Commercial systems software manufacturers

- Computer manufacturers

- Defense system manufacturers

- Medical instrument manufacturers

- Telecommunication manufacturers

All six of these have one major factor in common. The main software products of all six industries support complex physical devices which require high-quality software in order to operate successfully.

From the work that my colleagues and I have done with various military software groups, two interesting phenomena have been noted: 1) military or at least weapons systems defect potentials are higher than civilian norms; and 2) military or at least weapons systems defect removal efficiency levels are also higher than civilian norms.

Table 1 shows the approximate "average" overall results noted for Ada83 projects during the years 1998-1994 to give a rough indication of how military software compares to civilian norms, shown earlier in the section on Defect Removal Efficiency.

The following table is derived from a combination of Air Force and Navy projects that were built following the basic 2167A and 2168 standards. (Neither the author nor his colleagues at SPR have done any substantial measurement work with the Army, Marine Corps, or the Coast Guard.)

Table 1   Military Software Defect Removal Efficiency by Origin of Defects for Ada83 Software Projects Under DoD 2167A and 2168

(Data Expressed in Terms of Defects per Function Point)

Defect Origins	Defect Potentials	Removal Efficiency	Delivered Defects
Requirements	1.60	87%	0.20
Design	1.70	90%	0.17
Coding	1.25	96%	0.05
Documents	0.65	80%	0.13
Bad Fixes	0.30	75%	0.08
Total	*5.50*	*89%*	*0.63*

In both military and civilian domains, the best projects have lower defect potentials (< 3 per function point) and higher defect removal efficiency levels (> 95%) than averages. Compared to similar civilian projects, front-end requirements and design defect potentials are slightly elevated, but coding defect potentials are reduced.

For military and defense weapons systems, complexity is often very high. Also, the front-end of the software development cycle which deals with requirements and design has elevated volumes of defects compared to simpler civilian applications.

In addition, although not shown here, military software requirements tend to have a very high rate of "creep" which can sometimes exceed 2% per month during the design and coding phases. This means that military software projects often add more than 30% of their final features after the initial requirements are first specified.

Since military creeping requirements have always been high, a whole set of methods and protocols for dealing with ECRs (engineering change requests) has built up over the years in the defense community.

Indeed, several colleagues have commented that the whole military procurement process tends to encourage high rates of change. This is perhaps due to the fact that the initial bid of a defense system is competitive in nature, but once the contract is let the engineering change costs are non-competitive. Therefore a common strategy for defense projects would be to submit a low bid for the initial contract and assume that engineering change requests will be of sufficient volume to end up making a profit.

Note that at the time of delivery of military software projects, defects originating in requirements and design tend to far outnumber coding defects for Ada projects. This is because requirements and design defects are both very plentiful and also much harder to find and isolate than coding defects.

Data such as this can be used to improve the upstream military defect prevention and defect removal processes of software development.

The best defense projects tend to use state-of-the art methods to lower their defect potentials, and couple that with state-of-the-art methods for removing defects with high efficiency such as civilian-style formal design and code inspections. The best military results can be quite impressive: Defect potentials of less than 2.5 defects per function point coupled with removal efficiencies in excess of 99%.

Following are the equivalent results for "defects per KLOC" using the Ada83 programming language as the base. Note that this table assumes logical statements rather than physical lines (users of the SEI core metrics concepts should take note of this difference).

On average, it requires about 71 logical Ada83 statements to encode one function point. One of the many problems with using physical lines is the lack of empirical rules of thumb for conversion between LOC and function point metrics.

Table 2 Military Software Defect Removal Efficiency by Origin of Defects for Ada83
Software Projects Under DoD 2167A and 2168

(Data Expressed in Terms of Defects per KLOC in Ada83)

Defect Origins	Defect Potentials	Removal Efficiency	Delivered Defects
Requirements	22.5	87%	2.93
Design	23.9	90%	1.39
Coding	17.6	96%	0.70
Document	9.1	80%	1.82
Bad Fixes	4.2	75%	1.05
Total	77.3	89%	8.89

While the Ada83 language has been rather robust and capable of reducing coding errors compared to many other languages, those advantages have not been noted in military requirements nor military design approaches. In these two domains, the defect potentials are somewhat higher than civilian norms, although in the same range as large and complex civilian systems software projects such as operating systems.

If the previous tables on military defect densities were to substitute other programming languages, the results would be somewhat different. For example, Jovial and CMS2 would generate coding defect rates that are somewhat greater than Ada83, while Ada9X would presumably generate coding defect rates that are slightly lower. Changing programming languages, however, does not affect the non-coding error rates in requirements, specifications, or user manuals.

A library of certified reusable components in any language would reduce defect potentials. Reuse is also capable of minimizing other sources of error too, such as design problems if reusable design elements are available.

However, for reusable material to make significant improvement in quality, the materials slated for reuse must approximate zero-defect quality levels. It cannot be overemphasized that attempts to reuse materials not certified to extremely high quality levels is a disastrous mistake.

Unfortunately, the KLOC metric is very unreliable using either the physical lines or logical statement forms. As pointed out earlier in the section on Barriers to Quality Measurement KLOC penalizes high-level languages such as Ada83. To understand the essential difference between military and civilian defect potentials and removal efficiency, use only the function point data.

Even more unfortunate, the military community is the last remaining industry to attempt to use "lines of code" or KLOC as a normalizing metric, although many of the more enlightened defense measurement specialists also utilize function points.

MIL-STD-490A

This standard is not about quality, rather it is about specification practices. This particular standard is the origin of some of the peculiar terminology associated with military projects of various kinds. For software projects, three general forms of specifications are required called a "Type A" specification a "Type B5" specification and a "Type C5" specification, with all being named after the sections of the standard discussing them.

The Type A specification is a description of the system requirements and couples both hardware and software requirements into one. The Type B5 specification for software is called a Computer Software Configuration Item or CSCI for short. The Type C5 specification is a detailed description that drops down to the major elements of the B5 contents.

Collectively, much of the enormous bulk of military paperwork can be traced back to the rather arcane structure of the 490 standard. The 490 standard is not about software per se, but has overlaps some of the military software standards.

MIL-STD 498

As this book is written, Secretary of Defense, William Perry has recognized certain inefficiencies and cumbersome aspects of traditional military standards, there is a drive among the military community to move closer to civilian practices.

The new MIL-STD-498 was approved in November of 1994, and is one of the first attempts to achieve both simplification and a measure of "civilian style." Indeed, 498 is perceived as a stepping stone on the path leading to adoption of the civilian ISO/TEC Software Lifecycle Standard.

The new 498 standard was produced by all of the military services working jointly. Selected civilian agencies also participated, as did the departments of defense of Germany, Canada, and the United Kingdom whose own military standards have often been based on U.S. standards.

In 1994, the new DoD 498 standard was issued. It is a substantial replacement of the older DoD 2167 and 2167A and, for that matter, for 7935A (information systems) as well. The new 498 standard is still finding its way, and has not been in effect long enough to have garnered a substantial amount of empirical data.

It is interesting that it took almost three years to develop the 498 standard, but its anticipated life expectancy is only two years. When either ISO or IEEE civilian standards are approved, it is planned that 498 will be phased out and the civilian standards substituted.

However, preliminary reports indicate that the DoD 498 standard may be somewhat more flexible (or ambiguous depending upon your point of view) and hence not quite so burdensome as the former military software and quality standards.

Since the new 498 standard is based on the older 2167A, 2168, and 7935A standards, it is not a complete break with everything that went before. Many of the terms and concepts still remain, as do the baroque sets of acronyms and abbreviations.

However, the 498 standard does recognize many of the areas of inefficiency of the older standards and attempts to minimize or eliminate them. For example, the enormous and expensive formal project reviews with large volumes of overheads are, in 498, replaced by smaller less formal reviews of the actual work products being developed, as opposed to overheads and secondary data.

The 498 standard attempts to reduce the volume of paperwork required for software by substituting generic requirements to define and record certain kinds of information, rather than mandating the production of specific documents in a fixed format.

However, among my military and defense clients, this freedom has led to some uncertainty about what really needs to be done. Under 2167A, 2168, 7935A, etc., there was no real doubt concerning what was needed and what it should look like. (In fact, contractors could always produce variations and modifications, although not everyone took advantage of this.)

As a result of the freedom allowed under 498 coupled with long familiarity of 2167A and 2168, many defense contractors continue to roll out similar paper documents simply because they have done it before and know the older rules. Since 498 does not prohibit the de facto adherence to the older 2167A standard, a significant portion of newer projects are almost indistinguishable from older projects in terms of what gets produced.

The new 498 standard also envisions usage of metrics and measurements to indicate progress. However, my view on much of the military work on metrics is that it lags civilian best practices by many years. (In fact, the SEI core metrics proposal to utilize not only lines of code, but physical lines of code rather than logical statements, is professionally embarrassing. It is almost as if SEI deliberately ignored all of the relevant civilian literature on software measurement for the past 20 years. When I asked the SEI metrics personnel why they did not discuss or deal with the problems of "lines of code" for cross language-comparisons, they did not even know that the problems occurred.)

Only recently has the defense community discovered function points, and most military measurement specialists have so little empirical data available that they do not really understand the problems and hazards associated with metrics such as "cost per defect" and "lines of code."

The new 498 standard attempts to remove the implicit assumption that software will be built using a "waterfall" model. The new standard does not suggest a specific alternative, but does support some of the concepts of both incremental development, the object-oriented paradigm, and various flavors of reusability.

From a distance, the 498 standard appears to be a step in the right direction. Whenever there are major changes in standards, and especially when standards such as 2167A that are widely understood, are modified or made more flexible there is a chance of new problems arising.

As this book is written, there is not yet enough empirical data available to quantify the impact of 498 on quality, schedules, costs, or other quantitative dimensions. If indeed the 498 standard is soon replaced by civilian standards, there is a chance that 498 can pass into history without enough empirical data to ever judge its overall effect.

DOWNSIZING AND SOFTWARE QUALITY

As the data for this handbook is collected, many of the clients of the author and his company have gone through periods of severe downsizing: Data General, DEC, IBM, and Wang for example. Other companies are announcing downsizing, but they have not yet occurred as this handbook is prepared: AT&T, for example.

The short-term visible impact that downsizing has on software quality is often severe and harmful. One unmistakable observation is that quality assurance personnel are regarded as "expendable" and tend to be laid off with much higher frequency than the general technical populations that the QA groups support. The inevitable result is a degradation of quality assurance capabilities. For example, one IBM software quality assurance group was reduced by 80%. A similar QA group in DEC was reduced by more than 50%.

After such massive reductions in force, the role of the QA organization changes inevitably from "active" to "passive" at best. Often there are not even enough QA people left to support the "passive" model, so the remaining QA group can only be termed "token." That is, the company wants to have the visible appearance of supporting quality, but does not want to pay for a full QA function.

(QA personnel are not the only occupation that has a higher than average attrition during periods of downsizing. As a general rule, most occupations regarded as indirect or in support of direct or line activities are hit more severely than line occupations.)

Against the approximate background of U.S. averages, companies undergoing severe and traumatic downsizing do not look very good. It is hard to get good data on quality after downsizing, because both measurement programs and consulting studies are eliminated. However, following are some informal observations based on discussions with the residue of software QA groups. The data is expressed in terms of "defects per function point."

Table 1   Impact of Software Downsizing on Software Quality Effectiveness

	Performance Before Downsizing	Performance After Downsizing
Defect Potentials	5.00	5.75
Defect Removal Efficiency	85%	80%
Delivered Defects	0.75	1.15

What would be interesting would be a long-range study of both pre-downsizing and post-downsizing quality results. However, such a study would be hard to achieve because the companies engaging in severe downsizing operations often cut off funding for measurements and for external consulting groups.

ECONOMIC AND COMPETITIVE VALUE OF SOFTWARE QUALITY

An interesting point about software quality is the fact that achieving high levels of software quality tends to have a very positive economic and business value. The author and his colleagues at SPR perform assessment, benchmark, and user-satisfaction studies on a global basis. When we compare the software projects with high quality and low defect rates against similar projects with mediocre to low quality, we find these facts to be generally true:

- High quality software applications have shorter development schedules than low quality applications because they do not get hung up in integration and testing due to excessive defect levels. Effective quality control is on the critical path to schedule reduction. For typical Windows 95 applications of a nominal 1000 function points in size, those topping 96% in defect removal efficiency require about 14 months from initiation to delivery. Those dropping below 90% in defect removal efficiency require about 16 months from initiation to delivery and those below 85% require about 18 months.

- High quality software applications have lower development and maintenance costs than low quality applications. This is because the cumulative costs of finding and fixing bugs is often the major cost driver for software projects. Typical commercial Windows 95 applications of 1,000 function points that top 96% in defect removal efficiency cost about $1,300 per function point to build, versus more than $1,500 per function point for those below 90% and more than $1,600 for those below 85%. There are even more extreme variances in post-deployment maintenance costs. Annual maintenance per function point for applications topping 96% in removal efficiency is usually less than $150 per function point, as opposed to more than $400 per year for projects below 85% removal efficiency.

- High quality software applications have better reliability levels and longer mean times to failure than low quality applications. Although the reliability literature is ambiguous on the correlation between software defects and reliability, this appears to be due to the fact that many reliability authors do not have enough solid data on defect levels to have noted the correlation.

- High quality commercial software packages have larger market shares that low quality commercial software packages. This should not be a surprise, because quality is a key to market shares for all kinds of high-technology products.

- High quality software achieves better user-satisfaction ratings than low quality software. Here, too, this should not be a surprise because defect levels correlate with user-satisfaction levels for scores of products including automobiles, electronic equipment, and many kinds of consumer goods.

- High quality software projects score better on employee morale surveys than do low quality software projects. Further, companies that can build high quality software projects repeatedly have lower levels of voluntary attrition. Although there is not a direct correlation, companies averaging more than 95% in defect removal efficiency have much higher morale levels than those averaging less than 85%. (Companies averaging > 95% also pay more.) These findings should not be too surprising, since achieving high software quality levels implies the presence of capable managers and technical staffs. Good teams always have better morale and lower attrition than groups that are poorly managed.

- High quality software produced under contract or an outsource agreement has a much lower probability of ending up in court for breach of contract or malpractice litigation than low quality software. My colleagues and I at SPR are often commissioned to serve as expert witnesses in law suits involving allegations of poor quality so we know from personal experience that low quality leads to expensive litigation. Almost every software project that ends up in court for breach of contract is found to have had inadequate quality control.

- High quality software benefits or augments the performance levels of users, while poor quality tends to degrade worker performance. This fact is particularly true for workers who deal with large volumes of information (such as insurance claims handling) or with many customers (such as sales personnel).

- Poor quality software can trigger truly massive unplanned expense levels. The fact that the opening of the new Denver Airport was delayed for a year at a cost of $1,000,000 a day due to software bugs is a recent example of this topic. In the near future, the costs of repairing the "Year 2000" software problem is likely to trigger the largest one-time business expense in human history. Indeed, some companies may go bankrupt and others lose their assets due to the effects of the anticipated litigation surrounding this problem.

To sum up, achieving high software quality levels is one of the most effective business strategies that a company can follow. High quality will benefit user-satisfaction, employee morale, costs, schedules, and competitiveness. Nothing else is so pervasive.

Conversely, poor quality is a drain on expenses, damages worker performance, annoys or alienates clients, and in extreme conditions can lead to litigation, bankruptcy, or both.

ERROR-PRONE MODULES

In the middle 1960s, an IBM researcher named Gary Okimoto at IBM's Endicott lab, did a study of the distribution of customer-reported bugs in IBM's major operating system, OS/360 (which later evolved into the MVS operating system). Since conventional wisdom called for a relatively equal distribution of defects across all modules, Gary was surprised to find a decided skew in the data. About 4% of the modules had received 38% of all customer defects. Gary's report identified these as "error-prone modules" and the name has continued to be used.

Upon finding out about Gary's results, my colleagues at IBM's San Jose lab and I did a similar study of the IMS database product, which in the early 1970s ranked as one of the products with the largest number of customer-reported defects ever shipped by IBM.

Here the results were even more skewed. At the time of the study the IMS product had about 425 modules in total. The study found that 58% of all customer-reported bugs were being reported against only 31 modules. Equally surprising in a product with a bad reputation for quality, the product contained more than 300 modules that were at the zero-defect level and had never received any bug reports at all.

The discovery of error-prone modules was a significant turning point for dealing with the quality of aging legacy applications. By isolating and repairing the error-prone modules, it was possible to make significant quality improvements for comparatively low costs. In the case of the IMS database product, defect reports were reduced by almost an order of magnitude simply by eliminating the error-prone modules.

These results have been replicated by many other organizations. Indeed, a hallmark of "best in class" software quality is a continuous analysis of the factors that might lead to error-prone modules.

Many reasons exist for error-prone modules, but all of them can be eliminated by the use for formal design and inspections. Inspections approach or achieve 100% efficiency in eliminating error-prone modules.

Some of the factors associated with error-prone modules include:

- Excessive schedule pressure on the programmers.

- Poor training or lack of experience in structured methods.

- Rapidly creeping requirements which trigger late changes.

- High complexity levels with cyclomatic complexity ranges greater than 15.

Once a company is alerted to the presence of error-prone modules, a complete eradication is possible within a year or two. Eradication is highly recommended in terms of both quality and cost improvement. Maintenance of error-prone modules is the most expensive activity in the entire software world, and the costs of defect repairs in error-prone modules are actually the major expense of the entire maintenance period.

Error-prone modules are very buggy indeed. Compared to typical U.S. coding errors which average about 1.75 per function point, some error-prone modules have been observed that top 10 defects per function point. However, an "average" error-prone module will contain about 6 bugs per function point.

Since coding errors are the easiest to remove, many software projects can top 95% against coding errors. Here, too, there are significant differences, and error-prone modules seldom top even 85% and average only about 70% in cumulative defect removal efficiency.

The combination of high volumes of potential defects coupled with depressed levels of removal efficiency leads to horrendous volumes of delivered defects: 6 bugs per function point minus 70% defect removal efficiency leaves a total of 1.8 bugs per function point still present after the software is delivered. Thus the volume of delivered defects is higher than the coding defect potential of normal modules. Error-prone modules can have almost 20 times the average amount of latent defects, which explains why error-prone modules are so expensive to repair.

Also, since error-prone modules are usually unstable and highly complex, the existence of so many bugs accelerates the onset of fatal entropy. Within a short period (less than a year of use in some cases) the bad fix injection rate for error-prone modules begins to approach 100%. That is, almost every change triggers a fresh bug. Eventually there is no solution but a complete redevelopment of the offending module.

Even with redevelopment the situation is not always eliminated. If the same person or group that developed the original error-prone module is assigned responsibility for replacement, they may build a brand new error-prone module. To successfully eliminate error-prone modules you normally need some kind of coach or technical guru who truly understands the essence of structured programming and complexity analysis.

The net result is that a company can end up paying the equivalent of 500% for an error-prone module before finally eliminating it. They pay once to develop the original module. The costs of maintenance very quickly total to the same level as development, so that is another 100%. The module is so unstable it can no longer be maintained, so they pay a third time for redevelopment. If the new replacement module is also error-prone, they pay a fourth time for fixing bugs in the new version. Finally they bring in someone who knows how to build software properly, so they pay a fifth time get it right.

Paying five times for a defective product is not exactly a land-mark of modern business practice, and explains why quality control often has a positive economic value. Any company whose software process leads to error-prone modules needs urgent remedial training in software quality control and software economics. They might also benefit from the replacement of a few executives and managers along the way.

Fortunately, error-prone modules are a treatable condition. A combination of formal inspections, formal risk-analysis, professional testing, and an active quality assurance group can immunize a project against error-prone modules.

EUROPEAN SOFTWARE QUALITY INITIATIVES

Some of the most active and interesting software quality approaches have been taking place in Europe and the United Kingdom. About 10% of the data collected by my colleagues and I at Software Productivity Research are from various European projects (around 700 European projects as of mid-1996). In 1994, 1995, and 1996 we have had assessment and benchmark studies going on almost continuously in Europe (except for August which is a slow month in much of Europe).

Over the years my colleagues and I at SPR have performed assessment and benchmark studies in Austria, Belgium, England, Denmark, France, Germany, Italy, the Netherlands, Norway, Portugal, Spain, Sweden, and Switzerland. (SPR's basic assessment questionnaire has been translated into French, German, Portuguese, and Japanese and our assessment and benchmark analysis tool, CHECKPOINT, has been translated into French and Japanese.)

In addition to SPR's data, our personnel also reviews the findings of other international researchers such as Michael Cusumano, Tom DeMarco, Tom Gilb, Watts Humphrey, Andrew McGettrick, Howard Rubin, Richard Thayer, and Ed Yourdon. (See the section on International Quality data later in this book and in the annotated bibliography at the end.)

The combined software population of Western Europe and the U.K. is somewhat larger than the software population of the United States and very energetic in terms of quality initiatives, standards, conferences, and Internet communication channels. Indeed, some quality initiatives with a largely European origin, such as the ISO 9000-9004 standards, now have global impact.

Europe is advancing rapidly in software research under the impact of consolidation and the software research funding made available from the Community of the European Communities (CEC) which has no exact counterpart in the United States.

The closest equivalent source of government funds for software in the U.S. would be the Defense Advanced Research Project Agency (DARPA) which funds the Software Engineering Institute (SEI) and some of the specific projects funded by the Small Business Innovation Research (SBIR) pool of funds.

The newly-created National Software Council (NSC) in the U.S. is intended to assist the U.S. in international competition, but funding for the NSC itself is only barely adequate so the NSC is hardly in a position to fund extensive research programs.

When comparing European software quality results with those from other parts of the world such as Canada, Japan, and the United States there are similarities and differences. Both are interesting.

In terms of similarities, the same industries tend to achieve the best quality results in every industrialized country in Europe, North America, South America, the Middle East, and the Pacific Rim:

- Aerospace manufacturers

- Commercial systems software manufacturers

- Computer manufacturers

- Defense system manufacturers

- Medical instrument manufacturers

- Telecommunication manufacturers

These six industries share a common characteristic that their software supports large and complex physical devices which need close to zero-defect software in order to operate successfully.

This finding is true on a global basis. Looking at the software quality approaches of AT&T in the United States, Siemens Nixdorf in Germany, Bell Northern Research in Canada, Alcatel in France, LM Ericsson in Sweden, Standard Telephone and Cables in the U.K., and Nippon Telephone and Telegraph in Japan, they approach software quality in similar fashions, as indeed they must to compete in the same global telecommunications market.

In terms of differences, several industries where software quality lags in the United States appears to be rather good in much of Europe: insurance and banking software, for example.

In the United States the insurance and banking software development practices tend to be somewhat less formal and more casual than the six industries with the best quality results. The financial and insurance industries have also been rushing to get into the client/server world, where quality is often marginal and even worse than equivalent mainframe applications.

By contrast, financial and insurance software in Austria, Belgium, France, Germany, the Italy, Netherlands, the U.K., etc., has a higher probability of rigor during development, more care in quality control, and a greater use of non-test defect removal methods such as inspections.

Interestingly, banks and insurance companies on both sides of the Atlantic tend to use joint application design (JAD) or local variants as a way of gathering requirements initially.

There are of course wide ranges within every industry, and it may be that the smaller samples that we have for Europe have biased the results. Although 700 projects is not trivial, it only amounts to about 50 projects per country when you consider all of Western Europe.

Another interesting difference, and here the samples are very small, is that the quality of government software seems somewhat better in several European countries than here in the United States. Unfortunately, software produced by some of the civilian agencies of the Federal Government in the United States tends to lag the private sector in terms of defect prevention and defect removal operations, and hence gets deployed with substantially more errors than commercial norms.

(The civilian agencies of the U.S. government run around 83% in defect removal efficiency or 2% less than average. State governments and municipal governments are not usually outstanding either. A notable exception is the National Aeronautics and Space Agency or NASA which is equivalent to the better military and defense software developers and usually tops 95% in defect removal efficiency.)

By contrast, government-produced software in Belgium, Italy, France, Sweden, and the U.K. is sometimes equivalent to information systems software produced by public company or their outsourcing partners.

The most visible differences between the United States and Europe from the vantage point of international consultants such as myself and my colleagues are these:

- Requirements and design approaches are often more formal in Europe, and some of the European front-end approaches are technically very sophisticated such as Merise and Warnier-Orr in France; the Jackson method and SSADM (structured systems analysis and design) in the United Kingdom, and the Vienna Definition Method (VDL) in Austria. On the whole, formal methodologies are used more often than in the United States, and much more often in the information systems and client/server domains where U.S. practices tend to be rather careless. The overall result is that European MIS software projects often run about 10% to 20% below equivalent U.S. projects in requirements and design errors.

- The patterns of programming language usage tend to differ between the U.S. and Europe. Logic-based languages such as ALGOL, Prolog, and Miranda have a higher frequency of use as do strongly-typed languages such as PASCAL and Modula-2. The usage of Ada83 for civilian projects is far more common in Europe than in the United States. Programming language research is very strong in much of Europe.

- Usage of commercial software cost estimating tools and other software project management aids are less common in Europe than in the United States, although both sides of the Atlantic are now experiencing rapid growth in project management technologies.

- Usage of function point metrics for data normalization is roughly equal between the United States and Europe in terms of frequency of use. Membership in various function point users' groups is growing at about 50% per year in every industrialized country, while usage of "lines of code" is declining by about 10% per year. In Europe, large function point associations have been formed in France, Italy, the Netherlands, the United Kingdom, and also a multi-country Scandinavian function point group. Function point usage is growing but not yet formally organized in Austria, Belgium, Germany, Greece, Portugal, or Spain.

- Although the factor is more important for productivity studies than for quality studies, the rather lengthy European vacation periods (running to more than 30 days per year in some cases) tend to favor countries with more working days per year, such as the United States, Japan, and India.

- Although a difficult topic to explore since many tracking systems don't record it, the amount of unpaid overtime applied to software projects (i.e., unpaid work in the evenings, on weekends, and on public holidays) appears low in Europe and the United Kingdom compared to the United States and Japan. Unpaid overtime is so often part of software projects that it can exert an overall productivity influence that approaches 20%.

One of the problems of doing direct international comparisons between the United States and Europe is that the metrics are sometimes different. For example, all of the function point data in this book is based on Version 4 of the counting standards published by the International Function Point Users Group (IFPUG).

By contrast, function point data published in the United Kingdom is partly derived from IFPUG standards, and partly derived from the indigenous "Mark II" function point method developed by Charles Symons of the consulting company of Nolan and Norton (now part of Peat Marwick).

By interesting coincidence, the Mark II function point counts tend to differ from IFPUG function point counts by about as much as a British Imperial gallon differs from a U.S. gallon: roughly 20%.

Also, the Netherlands function point users group has developed local counting rules that differ from U.S. norms, too. This means that some kind of conversion is necessary before doing comparisons between U.S. and European data unless you are sure that the European data used standard IFPUG function points, which are currently at the Version 4.0 level as this book is written.

There are also wide and wild variations in European data that is based on the older "lines of code" metric. However, variations in LOC counting have been endemic to that metric for more than 50 years and wide ranges are noted in every country.

Indeed, a survey of refereed software engineering journals which I carried out a few years ago noted that about one-third of the articles using "lines of code" were based on physical lines; one-third were based on logical statements; and the remaining third did not even state the basis of the lines of code count. Almost 20% of the articles, surprisingly, did not even identify the languages from which the study was based.

Since the difference between a count of physical lines and a count of logical statements for some languages can exceed 400% failure to state which method was utilized leads to rather significant potential ranges when trying to understand or replicate a published study.

Of course, there are function point variants in the United States too: Boeing has developed a variant called "3D function points" and some years ago I developed a variant called "Feature Points" as well as a simplified method of counting standard function points that used only three complexity variables.

Between the United States and Europe, at least a dozen function point variations can now be enumerated. The logical necessity of all these variants is questionable, but until IFPUG and the International Organization for Standards (ISO) publish the new joint standard, the variants are a fact of life. On a global basis, however, standard IFPUG function points have about 90% penetration in terms of published books, articles, and data.

There are far too many individual quality initiatives going on in Europe to discuss all of them in a book of this size. Indeed, it would take a book of about 1,000 pages to do justice to all of the European research and approaches.

Some of the methods and concepts that tend to cause differences between software quality levels in the United States and quality levels in Europe include the following, listed alphabetically.

The AMI Methodology

AMI is an acronym with two meanings. It started in the early 1990s as "application of metrics in industry" under the sponsorship of the Commission of the European Communities. The AMI acronym is also more or less a good choice for "assess, analyze, metricate, improve" which is what the original study ended up with.

The AMI concept is a framework for exploring methods that might improve software engineering effectiveness. The AMI approach is a hybrid that freely utilizes concepts from other sources, such as the Software Engineering Institute (SEI), the Shewart cycle (plan, do, check, act), and also from Deming and Juran.

Even though "metricate" is one of terms comprising the AMI acronym I have not found much quantitative data available on how effective AMI is in either reducing defect potentials, raising defect removal efficiency, or both. My view is that the metricate portion of AMI should move in the direction of function points as the basis for normalizing data.

Speakers about AMI at various conferences often cite the AMI interest in better estimation, but few of the speakers seemed to be aware of the more than a few of the 75 or so commercial software estimation tools now available.

The Bootstrap Process Assessment

Bootstrap is a form of software process assessment starting to be deployed throughout much of Europe. The Bootstrap approach is a combination of concepts found in the ISO 9000-9004 quality standards, the Software Engineering Institute (SEI) capability maturity model (CMM), and the U.S. Department of Defense 2167A standard.

No significant quantitative results have yet been published, nor has my company yet been commissioned to explore the impact of Bootstrap (the U.S. Air Force commissioned us to study the quality impact of the SEI CMM however). Given the antecedents of Bootstrap, it is a promising approach. Here too, quantification of empirical results in terms of defect potentials and defect removal efficiency levels would be useful.

The Bootstrap methodology is coordinated from Belgium: Bootstrap Institute, Avenue de Beaulie 25, 1160 Brussels-Belgium; Telephone +32 2 675 7208; fax +32 2 675 85 13.

The Council of the European Communities (CEC)

The Council of the European Communities or CEC is a very influential organization which funds a number of research programs in various high technology areas, and a substantial number of software research programs such as those under the ESPRIT and EUREKA umbrellas. Indeed, the funding and influence of the CEC has a strong chance of making Europe the leading software research center of the world.

There is no equivalent organization in the United States for funding civilian software research, although the U.S. Department of Defense spends a great deal of money on software research through the Defense Advanced Research Project Agency (DARPA) which funds the Software Engineering Institute (SEI) among other things.

The European Software Institute (ESI)

The European Software Institute or ESI was founded in 1993 by a number of software-intensive companies in the form of an international consortium. In a sense, the ESI concept is similar to the Software Productivity Consortium (SPC) in the United States: a central research facility funded by and supporting a set of client organizations. One notable difference is that SPC was started by defense contractors, while ESI was started by civilian organizations.

ESI has launched a number of ambitious research programs, and is also very active in training, seminars, and dissemination of software data and articles. ESI has also established a software quality program that performs research and offers seminars and publications.

The most surprising gap in the ESI studies is the apparent failure to come to grips with software measurement. One would think ESI would be a European leader in function point analysis, but in fact that topic is not even mentioned in any of the current ESI brochures and publications. Given the failure of "lines of code" to actually measure either software quality or productivity, the lack of ESI utilization of functional metrics will probably reduce their effectiveness in generating solid data.

ESI is located in Bilbao, Spain, and the address is: Parque Tecnologico, Edificio 204, E-48016 Zamudio (Bilbao). The telephone is +34 4 420 95 19 and the fax is +34 4 420 94 20. The ESI World Wide Web site is http://www.esi.es.

The European Strategic Program of Research and Development in Information Technology (ESPRIT)

The European ESPRIT research program in various software domains is one of the most ambitious technology programs in human history and certainly the most ambitious to deal with software issues. This book is written in 1996, and the ESPRIT program has been in existence for roughly 10 years and has established a very solid base of interesting research programs in many high-technology areas including software.

ESPRIT was created more or less in reaction to the U.S. dominance in the computer and software business segments (i.e., in reaction to companies such as IBM and Microsoft).

Although the origin of ESPRIT was somewhat reactive, the current research programs appear to be proactive and indeed to rank among the very best in the world in terms of breadth of topics included. ESPRIT operates by providing partial funding to research proposals by companies within the European community. With more than 70 projects underway in a host of different areas, the full scope if ESPRIT-based research is too extensive for the purpose of this book.

Some of the topics funded under the ESPRIT umbrella include software reusability, programming environments, complex system testing, formal methods, interfaces, and graphical representations for visualization.

There is nothing in the United States that correlates exactly to the ESPRIT program. The military research programs under the Defense Advanced Research Project Agency (DARPA) spends quite a bit of money on software and has been funding the Software Engineering Institute (SEI). However, the DARPA emphasis is on defense issues while ESPRIT is looking at software as an important civilian technology as well as a military technology.

In reaction to ESPRIT, among other things, the United States has created a National Software Council (NSC) that includes military and government agencies, commercial enterprises, and academia. However, the NSC does not issue research grants nor does it have any funding other than the bare minimum needed to handle its own operations using largely volunteer officers.

Although the ESPRIT program does not have the same "clout" with businesses, it has some of the same attributes of the Japanese Ministry of International Trade and

Industry (MITI) in the sense that it suggests and approves the direction of important strategic and tactical research programs.

The European Research and Coordination Agency (EUREKA)

Both EUREKA and ESPRIT operate under the umbrella of the Council of the European Communities (CEC). Here too as with ESPRIT, funding is provided for research programs in high-technology areas including software. The purpose of EUREKA is to give the European community a competitive advantage in global high-technology markets.

However, EUREKA differs from ESPRIT in that there is no central approval committee and individual projects are not necessarily strategically linked to others.

The European Quality Network (E-Q-Net)

The European Quality Network is a confederation of some 14 non-profit quality organizations representing most of the countries of Europe. The purpose of the E-Q-Net is to ensure consistency and cooperation on topics of common interest.

The E-Q-Net organizations recognize one another's ISO audits and certification programs, which minimizes transnational disputes within the European community. The E-Q-Net is not a software group, but rather an organization concerned with quality of all kinds of products including manufactured goods, medicines, and food products.

However, the concept of cooperation and mutual recognition could usefully be applied to various U.S. quality approaches. For example, in the United States there are several organizations that issue certification in quality issues, such as the American Society of Quality Control (ASQC) and the Quality Assurance Institute (QAI). These organizations do not currently recognize one another's certification prerogatives.

At a global level, the E-Q-Net concept could usefully be extended to include Eastern Europe, the Pacific Rim, North and South America, and the Middle East. In particular, there is a strong need for global coordination and cooperation in the area of software quality.

The ISO 9000-9004 Quality Standards in Europe

The International Organization for Standards (ISO) is headquartered in Geneva, Switzerland. (Note that the "ISO" acronym is based on the Greek word "isos" meaning equal, rather than on the initials of the organization itself.)

Although the American National Standards Institute (ANSI) and other U.S. organizations collaborated with ISO on the ISO 9000-9004 quality standards, much of the technical content is of European and United Kingdom origin.

The ISO standards are used intermittently in the United States, Japan and the Pacific Rim, South America, the Middle East, and Eastern Europe. The ISO standards have had far and away their greatest deployment in Europe and the United Kingdom. Indeed, they are now often required for marketing products (including some software products) within the European Community (EC).

Not every company utilized the ISO standards in Europe, but the penetration is probably now in excess of 20% in Western Europe and the U.K. as opposed to perhaps 3% elsewhere based on interviews with software managers and QA personnel. (A few U.S. companies that produce only domestic software respond to questions about ISO standards with a question of their own: "What are they?")

ISO 9001 is the primary standard on how products are built, and a guideline numbered ISO 9000-3 explains the ISO approach in a software context. In common usage, all of the various ISO documents are simply identified by the umbrella term "ISO 9000" even though the total set includes ISO 9000-1, 9001, 9002, 9003, 9004, 9004-2, and 9000-3. (See the section on the ISO 9000-9004 standards later in this book for additional information on how software is affected.)

The SPICE Software Capability Assessment Method

SPICE is the acronym for "Software Process Improvement and Capability Evaluation." The SPICE approach is a composite software assessment method based in part on the Software Engineering Institute (SEI) capability maturity model (CMM); in part on the Bell Northern Research TRILLIUM assessment approach; and in part on the International Standards Organization (ISO) 9000-9004 standard series.

The SPICE approach is moving toward an international standard for software process assessments that is intended to improve the relationship between software contractors and clients. Many of the SPICE concepts are derived from the needs of large corporations and large government agencies whose software contracts might run to many millions of dollars for key contracts, and billions of dollars in aggregate.

SPICE is a bold and ambitious program, and like many bold programs, also has some risks associated with it. As this book is written it is premature to judge the overall impact of SPICE since it is still evolving. The direction is promising, but when so many organizations are involved in standards the results are often cumbersome and unsuitable for small projects and small companies.

One problem that is immediately apparent with SPICE is the lack of utilization of functional metrics as part of the contract discussion. The use of things like "cost per function point" and "defects delivered per function point" are starting to be used in U.S. software contracts and outsource agreements, and are eliminating many previous sources of trouble. For example functional metrics allow direct measures of creeping user requirements and can quantify anticipated defect levels in both code and non-code deliverable items.

The TickIT Software Quality Method

TickIT is a method of evaluating software quality that originated in the late 1980s by the British Computer Society. (The phrase "TickIT" is based on the British usage of the word "tick" as a synonym for "check" in American English. Thus, "TickIT" would be roughly expanded to "checking information technology.")

The TickIT approach is based on the ISO 9000-9004 standards, and is intended to serve as a consistency check on auditing ISO standards as applied to software. The TickIT concept includes both training and certification of auditors, who are then qualified to perform ISO audits.

The TickIT approach includes on-site interviews and assessments and envisions the production of a number of quality-related plans and reports. TickIT is widely used throughout the United Kingdom, and especially so for projects involving the government. However, the TickIT concept is not limited only to the United Kingdom and is moving globally, including to the United States.

Since the ISO standards did not originate for software, there is a strong need to customize or tailor the ISO standards and audits to the software world. The TickIT concept is to serve as a translator of ISO philosophy into the software domain.

Unfortunately, as this book is being prepared empirical data on the effectiveness of the TickIT approach is sparse. Also, the both the TickIT concept and the ISO standards ignore both functional metrics and defect removal efficiency measurement.

Functional metrics plus both estimation and measurement of defect removal efficiency levels would seem to be useful advances for the TickIT and ISO approaches. Indeed, without accurate quantification of defect potentials, defect removal efficiency, and delivered defect levels and their correlation to software costs and schedules, software quality will remain ambiguous and unconvincing.

Overall, Europe is advancing rapidly in the software domain. Although the United States dominates the global software market at the end of the 20th century, the combined effect of the European software initiatives should increase European market shares in the 21st century.

Of course, both the United States and Western Europe will be facing increasing software competition from Brazil, China, India, Russia, the Ukraine, and a host of other countries who are anxious to enter global software markets.

However, the overall coordination of focus of software issues by the Council of the European Communities may give Europe a new competitive edge vis-à-vis the United States where software research is either dominated by military considerations or fragmented among individual companies.

The U.S. lacks a true national coordination group for software, although the emerging National Software Council (NSC) is trying to hatch into something useful. The NSC would do well to imitate the already visibly successful approach to software research found in Europe under the ESPRIT concept.

However, substantial government (or private) funding would be needed to perform the same functions as ESPRIT, and in the United States the Federal Government can barely handle the annual budget without embarrassment and has shown no sign of putting large amounts of money into civilian software research.

FORMAL DESIGN AND CODE INSPECTIONS

Although formal design and code inspections originated more than 25 years ago, they still are the top-ranked methodologies in terms of defect removal efficiency. (Michael Fagan, formerly of IBM Kingston, first published the inspection method.) Further, inspections have a synergistic relationship with other forms of defect removal such as testing, and also are quite successful as defect prevention methods.

Recent work on software inspections by Tom Gilb and his colleagues continues to support the early finding that the human mind remains the tools of choice for finding and eliminating complex problems that originate in requirements, design, and other non-code deliverables. Indeed, for finding the deeper problems in source code formal code inspections still outrank testing in defect removal efficiency levels.

Among SPR's clients about 75 enterprises out of 600 are using formal inspections more or less the way the method was designed and intended. However, another 200 are using semi-formal inspections, design reviews, structured walkthroughs, or one of a number of local variations on the inspection process.

The most effective usage of formal inspections among our clients occurs among large corporations that produce systems software such as computer manufacturers, telecommunication manufacturers, aerospace manufacturers and the like. These companies have learned that if software is going to control complex physical devices it has to have state-of-the-art quality levels, and only inspections can achieve the necessary quality.

Most forms of testing are less than 30% efficient in finding errors or bugs. The measured defect removal efficiency of both formal design inspections and formal code inspections is sometimes more than 60% efficient, or twice as efficient as most forms of testing. Tom Gilb, one of the more prominent authors dealing with inspections, reports that some inspection efficiencies have been recorded that are as high as 88%. So far as can be determined, this level of efficiency would be a "world record" that is never even approached by testing with the possible exception of high-volume Beta testing involving more than 10,000 simultaneous Beta test sights.

A combination of formal inspections, formal testing by test specialists, and a formal (and active) quality assurance group are the methods which are most often associated with projects achieving a cumulative defect removal efficiency higher than 99%.

Formal inspections are manual activities in which from four to six colleagues go over design specifications page by page, using a formal protocol. Code inspections are the same idea, but go over listings or screens line by line. In order to term this activity an "inspection" certain criteria must be met, including but not limited to:

1) There must be a moderator to keep the session moving.

3) There must be a recorder to keep notes.

4) There must be adequate preparation time before each session.

5) Records must be kept of defects discovered.

6) Defect data should not be used for appraisals or punitive purposes.

The original concept of inspections was based on actual meetings with live participants. The advent of effective online communications and tools such as the Honeywell Bull system for supporting remote inspections now means that inspections can be performed electronically, which saves on travel costs for teams that are geographically dispersed.

Any software deliverable can be subject to a formal inspection, and the following deliverables have now developed enough empirical data to indicate that the inspection process is generally beneficial:

- Architecture inspections
- Requirements inspections
- Design inspections
- Database design inspections
- Code inspections
- Test plan inspections
- Test-case inspections
- User documentation inspections

For every software artifact where formal inspections are used, they range from just under 50% to more than 80% in defect removal efficiency and have an average efficiency level of roughly 60%. This is overall the best defect removal efficiency level of any known form of error elimination.

Further, thanks to the flexibility of the human mind and its ability to handle inductive logic as well as deductive logic, inspections are also the most versatile form of defect removal and can be applied to essentially any software artifact. Indeed, inspections have even been applied recursively to themselves, in order to fine-tune the inspection process and eliminate bottle necks and obstacles.

"If inspections are so good why doesn't everyone use them?" The answer to this question reveals a basic weakness of the software industry. Inspections have been in the public domain for more than 25 years. Therefore, no company except a few training companies tries to "sell" inspections while there are many vendors selling testing tools. If a company wants to use inspections, it must seek out the tools and adapt them.

Most software development organizations don't actually do research or collect data on effective tools and technologies. They make their technology decisions to a large degree by listening to tool and methodology vendors and adopting those where the sales personnel are most persuasive. It is even easier if the sales personnel make the tool or method sound like a "silver bullet" that will give miraculous results immediately upon deployment with little or no training, preparation, or additional effort. Since inspections are not sold by tool vendors and do require training and effort they are not a "glamorous" technology. Hence many software organizations don't even know about inspections and have no idea of their versatility and effectiveness.

The companies that are most likely to use inspections are those that for historical or business reasons have some kind of research capability that looks for "best practices" and tries to adopt them.

It is a telling point that all of the "top gun" software quality houses and even industries in the United States tend to utilize pre-test inspections. For example, formal inspections are very common among computer manufacturers, telecommunication manufacturers, aerospace manufacturers, defense manufacturers, medical instrument manufacturers, and systems software and operating systems developers. All of these need high-quality software to market their main products, and inspections top the list of effective defect removal methods.

One of the most effective ways of illustrating the effectiveness of formal inspections is to produce graphs that connect the point where software defects are *discovered* with the point in software development where the defects *originate.*

Whenever there is an acute angle in the line connecting defect discovery and origin points, there is a serious problem with software quality control since the gap between making an error and finding it can amount to many months.

The goal of defect removal is to have the angle connecting defect origins and discoveries approach 90 degrees. Although a 90 degree angle is unlikely, formal inspections can at least bring the angle up from perhaps 30 degrees to more than 60 degrees.

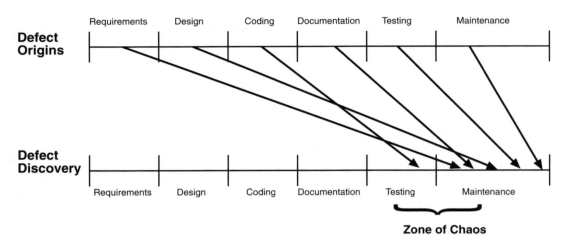

Figure 1 Defect Origins and Discovery Points without Usage of Formal Inspections

As can easily be seen, software projects that do not utilize formal inspections enter a "zone of chaos" during the test cycle. This is because deep problems with requirements and specifications suddenly emerge that require extensive and expensive repair and rework.

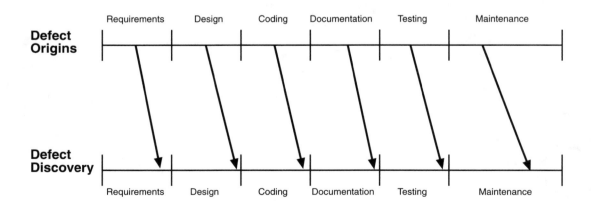

Figure 2 Defect Origins and Discovery Points with Usage of Formal Inspections

Note how the lines connecting the discovery points of defects with their origins have obtuse angles. Even more important, note how defects that originate within a phase tend to be eliminated during that phase, and do not pass on to downstream activities.

There are enough users of software inspections and reviews so that they have formed a non-profit organization called SIRO (Software Inspection and Review Organization). The SIRO mailing address is:

Software Inspection and Review Organization (SIRO)
P.O. Box 61015
Sunnyvale, CA 94088-1015

When this book was first being planned, SIRO published an interesting newsletter. The organization has subsequently decided to switch from a paper newsletter to an Internet World Wide Web page. However, the URL has not been settled as this draft is written.

FUNCTION POINT METRICS AND SOFTWARE QUALITY

Since this book utilizes function point metrics, it is appropriate to include a short discussion of what function points are, and why they have become so common for normalizing both quality and productivity data for software projects.

As this book is written, the function point community seems to know quite a bit about software quality. However, the software quality community does not always know much about function points.

Among SPR's clients, about 500 out of 600 companies now use function points. Of these, about 450 use standard IFPUG function points and the remaining 50 use one or more of the variants such as Mark II function points, feature points, or Boeing 3D function points.

The large number of function point users among our clients is due to a bias in our data. SPR has been well-known for its work in function point metrics since 1985 when our first estimating tool based on function points was released. Also in 1986 Allan Albrecht, the inventor of function points, retired from IBM and created SPR's first course in function points counting. Therefore, companies using function points tend to seek us out more than companies that don't use function points.

Interestingly, about 400 of SPR's clients use lines of code and function point metrics concurrently. For these corporations "backfiring" or direct conversion of older lines of code data into function point form is the most common motivation for using both metrics. A strong secondary motivation is because some of our clients own clients (i.e., the U.S. military services) may require lines of code under some situations.

The function point metric was invented in the middle 1970s by Allan J. Albrecht of IBM White Plains in association with several colleagues. The function point metric was put into the public domain by IBM at a conference in Monterey, California in October of 1979 where Allan Albrecht gave the first public speech on the metric. From that beginning, the usage of the function point metric has spread rapidly throughout the world.

In 1986, a non-profit organization was created in Toronto, Canada of companies that were using function points. This organization was originally staffed only by part-time volunteers, but quickly grew to such a size that formal incorporation and a permanent staff appeared desirable.

In 1988, the non-profit International Function Point Users Group (IFPUG) was incorporated in Westerville, Ohio and hired a small permanent office staff to handle administration. In 1996, this group is now the largest software measurement association in the United States. Affiliated function point users groups are the largest software measurement associations in perhaps 20 countries.

The function point metric is a way of determining the size of a software application by enumerating and adjusting five visible aspects that are of significance to both users and developers. Standard IFPUG function points consist of five key external factors:

- **Inputs** that enter the application (i.e., input screens, forms, commands, etc.)

- **Outputs** that leave the application (i.e., output screens, reports, etc.)

- **Inquiries** that can be made to the application (i.e., queries for information)

- **Logical** files maintained by the application (i.e., tables, text files, etc.)

- **Interfaces** between the application and others (i.e., shared data, messages, etc.)

Note that the British Mark II variant of standard IFPUG function point metrics also include counts of **Entities** and **Relationships**. Note also that the feature point variant of function point metrics includes the five standard IFPUG factors plus a count of Algorithms.

Once the raw total of these five factors has been enumerated, then an additional set of 14 influential factors are evaluated in order to adjust for complexity. These adjustment factors are evaluated for impact using a scale that runs from 0 (no impact) to 5 (major impact).

The 14 adjustment factors are outside the scope of this book, but include topics such as whether the application requires distributed functions, uses data communications, will have high transaction volumes, and a number of similar topics.

The adjustment factors are converted into a weighing scale that can modify the initial raw total by a range that runs from about 65% of the initial value for rather simple applications to 135% of the initial value for highly complex applications. After complexity adjustment the final value is termed the "adjusted function point total" of the application and this is the value that is used when discussing quality or productivity in terms of function points.

From the standpoint of quality, function points can be used for a number of useful purposes including but not limited to:

- Normalizing defect data across requirements, design, coding, documentation, and bad fix defect categories.

- Estimating the numbers of test cases and test runs that may be required.

By interesting coincidence the five standard IFPUG factors for counting function points, plus the inclusion of algorithms (from feature points) and the inclusion of entities and relationships (from Mark II function points) provides a useful set of the key software features for which test cases are normally constructed. These features include:

- Algorithms

- Inputs

- Outputs

- Entities and relationships

- Logical files

- Inquiries

This means that companies that utilize function point metrics are in a very good position to predict the number of test cases and test runs that will be needed as early as the requirements phase. Further, rather accurate defect estimates can also be made, as can opportunities for applying defect prevention methods.

Although the data is preliminary and has a high margin of error, the use of function point metrics also offers new insights into the origins and frequency of software defects.

Table 1   Software Defect Origins Related to Function Point/Feature Point Key Factors

Category	Software Defects	Document Defects	Data Defects	Test Case Defects
Algorithms	<u>35%</u>	15%	5%	<u>30%</u>
Inputs	10%	<u>35%</u>	15%	5%
Outputs	20%	10%	15%	20%
Entities and relationships	10%	0%	<u>35%</u>	5%
Logical files	5%	0%	10%	10%
Inquiries	20%	40%	20%	<u>30%</u>

(Note: Underscored percentage denotes the highest rate for each category.)

From preliminary analysis of software defect patterns for projects where function points and/or feature points have been enumerated, it appears possible to assign a preliminary distribution of errors to the essential factors of functional metrics. Thus, for errors in software, algorithms are the dominant error source. For user documentation, errors in describing how users input information or commands is the dominant error source. For data defects, entities and relationships are the dominant error source. For errors in test cases themselves, errors in inquiries and algorithms appear approximately equal as dominant error sources.

Although function point metrics were not invented for quality assurance purposes, they have been found to be very synergistic with the goals and approaches of software quality. Indeed, they open up some new forms of quality research such as exploration of front-end requirements defects and the rate at which requirements changes "creep" that could not easily be studied before function points were developed.

For additional information and instructions on counting function points, if your company joins the non-profit International Function Point Users Group (IFPUG) a copy of the latest counting rules (Version 4.0 as this book is written) will be supplied.

There are also several primers and introductory text books such as Dr. Brian Dreger's *Function Point Analysis* (Prentice Hall, 1989), Charles Symons' *Software Sizing and Estimating—MK II Function Point Analysis* (John Wiley & Sons, 1989), or a new book that covers version 4.0 counting rules, David Garmus and David Herron's *Measuring the Software Process: A Practical Guide to Functional Measurement* (Prentice Hall, 1995).

Counting and adjusting function points for an application is not trivial, nor is it overwhelmingly difficult. The normal training course for those who set out to learn function point counting runs for two days, and includes several hands-on counting exercises. To ensure precision and consistent application of the counting rules, the International Function Point Users Group (IFPUG) offers periodic certification examinations.

The accuracy of certified function point counters was measured by Dr. Chris Kemerer (who was at MIT's Sloan School at the time) under a research contract issued by IFPUG. Certified counters generally came within about 9% in reaching the same total of adjusted function points, which is in the same range of accuracy as usually found in financial accounting, and actually much better than the error range made by the Internal Revenue Service in tax calculations.

By contrast, I did a study on the errors associated with counting lines of code. I found errors of about 500% for counting COBOL lines of code in U.S. businesses and almost an order of magnitude across other languages. In one instance, four different counting methods were noted in a single company with a range of almost 500% for projects that were in the same building and located not more than 100 feet from one another. Even lines of code data in refereed software journals varies widely. About one third of the articles count physical lines, one-third count logical statements, and the other third fail to state which method is used.

IFPUG also codifies and maintains the formal counting rules, which are revised as needed. For example, this book assumes Version 4.0 of the IFPUG counting rules. However, IFPUG is working with the International Organization of Standards (ISO) to develop a formal standard for function point counting.

The modifications to the function point counting rules are usually made in response to changes in fundamental software technologies. For example, there was a need for better definitions of the factors found in graphical user interfaces (GUI) applications, in client/server software, and in embedded and real-time software. Future rule changes may be required to deal with Internet applications in JAVA, HTML, and other modern approaches.

The normal raw materials used to determine function point totals are the requirements and functional specifications for the software application. Since function points are independent of the code, the counts need not be delayed until coding is underway or complete. Several companies such as Bachman and Texas Instruments have developed commercial function point "engines" that can estimate function point totals by direct analysis of software specifications without any particular human intervention.

For existing or legacy applications it is also possible to derive approximate function point totals using a technique called "backfiring" or direct conversion from "lines of code" counts based on logical statements. (Backfiring from counts of physical lines is too ambiguous and uncertain to be recommended.)

Here, too, there are commercial tools available that support the backfiring concept, such as those from Viasoft which can parse COBOL and return approximate function point values. Many commercial cost estimating tools such as CHECK-POINT, COCOMO II, GECOMO, SLIM, SPQR/20, etc., also support bi-directional sizing. When normal forward function point counts are the input, the tools will predict source code volumes. In reverse, if source code volumes are the input the tools will backfire and produce function point totals.

The algorithms for converting source code statements into equivalent function point counts were published in 1991 in the first edition of my book *Applied Software Measurement* (McGraw Hill). This same book also defined the counting rules for logical statements on which the backfiring algorithms are dependent.

Several software tool companies have utilized the published algorithms, and it is now possible to generate at least approximate function point totals by parsing source code in common programming languages such as COBOL and C. For more obscure languages which lack plentiful tools (i.e., CHILL, CORAL, SNOBOL, etc.) the algorithms can be applied manually.

Since several days of effort is required to learn how to count function points, and the work of manually counting the function point sizes of applications is significant (certified function point counters can only count up to a few thousand function points per day) the question arises as to why bother? Why not continue to use lines of code?

In order to understand why anyone would bother to use function points, it is necessary to consider the limitations of the "lines of code" metric which function points replace or augment. The function point metric is normally used in place of or in addition to the older software metric based on the number of *source lines of code (SLOC)* in a software application.

My own company, SPR, routinely captures software project data using both function points and lines of code data. I strongly recommend multiple metrics if for no other reason than understanding how they all work under different conditions. Although a count of physical lines is the least useful for software estimation and quality measurements, even this metric can be useful because it is helpful to know the ratio of physical lines to logical statements.

For some reason there seems to be a dogma in the software world that only one metric should be used. There is another dogma in the software world that only "easy" metrics should be used regardless of whether such metrics are accurate or inaccurate. These are ridiculous and arbitrary limitations. Imagine the state of progress if electrical engineers only used volts and not ohms or watts "because they are too complicated."

For that matter, consider all of the complex but useful metrics that require some effort to calculate: caloric content of food; cholesterol levels in food and blood serum; blood types, octane ratings of gasoline; British Thermal Units of heating and cooling equipment; horsepower ratings of motors; emission ratings of gasoline engines; the Dow Jones stock market indicators; and the pollution levels of rivers and lakes.

Let us now consider why the "lines of code" metric originated and what it was used for when it first appeared.

Rationale for the Source Lines of Code (SLOC) Metric

When the software industry began in 1943, computer programs were all written in a very complex code called "machine language." This code or language was so difficult to understand that very few people could write computer programs at all, and no one could write computer programs rapidly.

From about 1945 to about 1950, software applications averaged less than 250 lines of code in total size. The effort for coding in machine language was so difficult that coding itself took about 90% of the total effort needed for constructing an application. Requirements, design (if any), and user materials required only the other 10%.

The era of machine language programming only lasted about five years. After that time, other computer languages were developed that were easier for human beings to understand and work with.

The first programming language that attempted to be clear to human programmers was called "assembly language." Assembly language was essentially computer machine language, made somewhat easier to use by means of commands based on English words or standard mathematical symbols.

Programmers were able to write programs using these words and symbols, and then their work was converted into true machine language by a special process called "assembly" from which the name of the language is derived.

The code statements in programs written by the programmers were called the "source code" and the final version of the program that ran on the computer was called the "object code" or the "executable code."

When software began to be used for business purposes, there was significant interest in measuring the productivity of creating new programs. It was natural to measure software productivity using source lines of code or SLOC, because most programs were small and coding absorbed more than 90% of the total effort needed to make a computer perform work.

Rationale for the Function Point Metric

By the early 1960s, computers and software were beginning to be used so widely in business and industry that the labor associated with writing computer programs in assembly language was becoming burdensome and expensive for corporations and government agencies and also the military services.

Software researchers began to develop more and more powerful programming languages that did not have a 1-to-1 correspondence with computer machine language. These languages were called "higher-level" languages because one statement in such a language could cause the execution of several machine languages.

Since the process of converting higher-level programming languages into machine code took several passes, the term "compilation" was used in place of "assembly" for creating the executable programs that actually operated in the computer. This triggered the generic term "compiled languages" for the overall set of higher-level languages. (Another set of higher-level languages such as BASIC used a different conversion method and are called "interpreted" languages. The process of interpreting source code lends itself to immediate execution of software, while compilation requires additional steps before the software can be executed.)

These higher-level compiled or interpreted languages were often created for special purposes. For example the language FORTRAN was created for mathematics and scientific work (FORTRAN stands for "Formula Translator"). The COBOL language was created for business applications (COBOL stands for Common Business Oriented Language).

As more and more programming languages and special purpose languages were created, the concept of a "line of code" became less useful for measuring the productivity of software development. Indeed for many modern languages such as Visual Basic, some parts of application development are derived from using controls, buttons, or manipulating graphic symbols, so the entire concept of a "line of code" is losing relevance.

For example, the APL programming language was about 10 times as powerful as assembly language, in that one APL statement on the average could cause the execution of 10 machine instructions.

With a 10-to-1 increase in the power of programming languages, pure coding was no longer the dominant cost driver of software development. It was soon discovered that other tasks cost more than coding.

As fourth-generation languages, application and program generators, "visual" languages, object-oriented languages, database languages, and specialized languages began to multiply pure coding steadily declined in both absolute effort and as a percentage of the total effort needed to build software applications. The following table oversimplifies the situation, but shows the general trend over time.

Table 2   Evolution of Programming Languages and Software Effort at 10 Year Intervals

Year	Coding Percent	Non-Coding Percent	Most Common Programming Languages
1950	90%	10%	Machine language
1960	80%	20%	Assembly
1970	70%	30%	COBOL, FORTRAN, Assembly, + 200 others
1980	60%	40%	COBOL, BASIC, + 300 others
1990	50%	50%	Visual Basic, COBOL, 4GLs, +400 others
2000	30%	70%	Visual, Object-Oriented, COBOL + 600 others
2010	15%	85%	Reuse, Visual, OO, COBOL, + 800 others

While better programming languages were reducing coding costs, military standards and other methods for dealing with the increasingly large systems that were occurring were ballooning specifications, plans, and paper documents which are necessary for controlling large systems in excess of 100,000 lines of code or 1,000 function points.

By the 1970s, software applications in excess of 100,000 lines of code were starting to appear in systems, military, and information systems contexts rather often. A few systems such as IBM's MVS operating system were larger than 1,000,000 lines of code. IBM's planned but not implemented Future System (FS) operating system would have topped 10,000,000 lines of code. The Department of Defense worldwide military command and control system (WIMMIX) was larger than 20,000,000 lines of code. The famous "Star Wars" missile defense system might have approached 100,000,000 lines of code had the system gone to completion. For these larger systems, requirements, specifications, user manuals and other paper documents were increasingly large and expensive to produce and cost far more than the code itself.

Also, since bugs or defect levels increase with size, larger systems had much more expensive inspection and testing activities associated with them than did the smaller applications of an earlier day.

For large applications written in higher-level languages such as COBOL, PL/I, Ada, or one of the Visual languages coding became only a minority cost element. In descending order, the four major cost drivers of the initial release of large software applications include but are not limited to:

1) Testing and defect removal

2) Production of paper planning and specification documents

3) Meetings and communication among team and with clients

4) Coding

Unfortunately, the "lines of code" metric is not a good choice for normalizing the three top cost elements of software—defect removal costs, paperwork costs, and meeting and communication costs. This means that economic studies of full software lifecycles were difficult to perform using "lines of code" metrics and major research topics tend to be under reported, or worse, reported incorrectly.

By the middle 1970s when Albrecht developed the function point metric, there were more than 200 different programming languages and dialects of programming languages in use throughout the world: ALGOL, APL, Assembly, C, COBOL, CORAL, CHILL, FORTRAN, LISP, PL/I, RPG, SMALLTALK, and a host of others.

By the 1970s in IBM where Albrecht worked, coding was averaging less than 65% of the total costs of building software, while other kinds of work such as producing paper documents or testing, was averaging more than 35%. For military software with their enormous paperwork requirements, coding had dropped below 45% of the effort while non-coding tasks routinely topped 55% and were basically invisible when the metrics used for productivity or quality were lines of code.

The available programming languages ranged in power over a span of about 20-to-1. Albrecht recognized that with so much variation, measurements based on "lines of code" could not be used to perform economic or quality comparisons of programs written in different programming languages.

For example, a program that took 1,000 lines of code in Assembly language might need only 50 statements in the SMALLTALK language. It might take 20 days to develop the program in Assembly language and only one day to develop the same program in SMALLTALK. But, if both versions of the same program were measured using the lines of code or LOC metric, their productivity would be identical: 50 lines of code per day. Thus, a real improvement in economic productivity of 20 to 1 would be invisible when measured using lines of code metrics.

What Albrecht was attempting to create was a software metric that would stay constant based on the functions performed for users, regardless of the programming language in which it was written.

Since non-coding costs had become larger than coding itself, Albrecht was also building a metric that could be aimed at planning, requirements gathering, design, specifications, user manual creation, training, installation, and the host of other activities associated with software that could not be directly evaluated in terms of lines of code metrics.

In the two examples just cited, both the 1,000 lines of Assembly language code and the 50 lines of SMALLTALK code would create the same visible functions for users, so the function point total of both versions would be identical. Assume that these two programs were both 5 function points in size. Now, when productivity is measured using the function point metric, it can easily be seen that the more powerful SMALLTALK language is more productive. The SMALLTALK version was created at a rate of 5 function points per day. The Assembly language version was created at a rate of only 0.25 function points per day.

Expressed in another fashion, and assuming that each work day contains five hours devoted to programming, the SMALLTALK version required one hour to build a function point, and the Assembly language version required 20 hours to build a function point.

Thus, the function point metric highlights the 20-to-1 difference in the real effort devoted to the two examples, while the lines of code metric makes both versions seem the same, which is an economic fallacy.

As can easily be seen by these simple examples, the function point metric matches the standard economic definition of productivity:

"Productivity is the amount of goods or services produced per unit of labor or expense."

In this case, a function point is a very practical, workable surrogate for the "goods" which a software program provides to users.

By contrast, a line of code is not an effective surrogate for software "goods" because there is no advantage to the users in having a lot of code in a language such as Assembly, when they could have identical features with much less code in other programming languages.

The ability of the function point metric to perform very accurate software economic studies explains why this metric has become the most widely used in the software industry.

The failure of the lines of code metric to deal with economic topics (or quality either) explains why so many companies are abandoning measurements based on lines of code, and switching over to measurements based on function points.

As of 1997, the function point metric has become the most widely utilized software metric in the United States, Canada, and approximately 20 other countries. Usage of function points is expanding to all countries, and the function metric is being used in countries such as China, Brazil, India, Cuba, and Russia as well as in Europe and the major Pacific Rim countries. The primary forms of function point usage include these common metrics:

- Function points produced per staff month

- Work hours required to produce one function point

- Work hours required to support one function point

- Work hours required to maintain (fix bugs) per function point

- Cost per function point for development

- Cost per function point for maintenance

- Defects per function point during development

- Defects per function point for released software

The usage of function points is now so common that the U.S. Internal Revenue Service, and the revenue services of many other countries, are now exploring function points for determining the tax value of software.

Function Points and Software Quality Data

Function point metrics were presented at a public conference in October 1979, and began to be used for software quality studies later that same month. I had been analyzing software quality at IBM's Santa Teresa lab and had been troubled by the failure of either "lines of code" or "cost per defect" to match the reality of software projects written in high-level languages that were approaching zero-defect levels.

As soon as I heard Allan Albrecht's talk about function points, I began to retrofit the data using function point metrics and was delighted to find that the decline in defect repair costs with high-level languages and near zero-defect quality levels could be correctly evaluated using function points.

Ironically, although IBM invented the function point metric, they were not the first to report the effectiveness of function points for software quality research. The same month that I heard Albrecht's speech on function points I left IBM and joined ITT. Therefore, the initial research on the correlation of function points and quality was not published by IBM, although I had published the first report on the hazards of lines of code and cost per defect measures in the *IBM Systems Journal* in 1978. Indeed, the IBM Santa Teresa QA lab where I had worked did not come to realize how effective functional metrics were for quality control and still struggled on with "lines of code" for quite a few years.

When Allan Albrecht, the inventor of function points, retired from IBM in 1985 and joined Software Productivity Research the correlation between function points and software quality was well established. Our first commercial software estimating tool in 1985 was SPQR/20 (SPQR stands for "software productivity, quality, and reliability"). This was the first software estimating tool to utilize function point metrics for predicting both defect levels and test-case volumes, as well as for sizing programming languages, specifications, and other deliverables.

Function points are now the norm for sizing various software deliverables in the commercial estimating world. As this book is written at least 30 out of the 50 or so commercial estimating tools sold in the United States now use function points for sizing paper documents, source code, defect levels, test cases, and other deliverables.

For example, the first step in any software estimate is to predict the sizes of the deliverables that must be constructed. The older software cost estimating tools such as COCOMO did not include sizing logic, and size information had to be provided by the user. However, the invention of function point metrics has made full sizing logic for all deliverables a standard feature of estimating tools from 1985 forward. Indeed the new COCOMO II estimating tool will also support function point metrics.

Here are selected size examples, drawn from systems, MIS, military, and commercial software domains. In this context, "systems" software is that which controls physical devices such as computers or telecommunication systems. MIS software stands for "management information systems" and refers to the normal business software used by companies for internal operations. Military software constitutes all projects which are constrained to follow various military standards. Commercial software refers to ordinary packaged software such as word processors, spreadsheets, and the like.

Table 3   Number of Pages Created Per Function Point for Software Projects

	Systems Software	MIS Software	Military Software	Commercial Software
User Requirements	0.45	0.50	0.85	0.30
Functional specifications	0.80	0.55	1.75	0.60
Logic specifications	0.85	0.50	1.65	0.55
Test plans	0.25	0.10	0.55	0.25
User tutorial documents	0.30	0.15	0.50	0.85
User reference documents	0.45	0.20	0.85	0.90
Total document set	3.10	2.00	6.15	3.45

This kind of sizing for software documentation is now a standard feature of several commercial software cost estimating tools. At least one commercial software estimating tool can even predict the number of English words in the document set, and also the numbers of diagrams that are likely to be present, and can change the page count estimates based on type size.

Indeed, work is under way in using function points for estimating translation costs from one language to another, such as the cost of translating user manuals, comments, HELP text, screens, etc. into French, German, Japanese, etc., for international sales.

The second major sizing capability associated with function point metrics is the ability to predict source code size for any programming language, or even for applications that use two or more languages at the same time such as COBOL and SQL or Ada and Jovial.

There are far too many languages to do more than illustrate the concept, but source code sizing consists of predicting the number of logical statements that will be needed to encode one function point. (Note that conversion rules between programming languages and function points are based on logical statements rather than physical lines. This is an important distinction since the two can vary by several hundred percent.)

Table 4   Ratios of Logical Source Code Statements to Function Points

Language	Nominal Level	Source Statements Per Function Point		
		Low	Mean	High
Basic assembly	1.00	200	320	450
Macro assembly	1.50	130	213	300
C	2.50	60	128	170
FORTRAN	3.00	75	107	160
COBOL	3.00	65	107	150
PASCAL	3.50	50	91	125
ADA 83	4.50	60	71	80
C++	6.00	30	53	125
Ada 9X	6.50	28	49	110
SMALLTALK	15.00	15	21	40

The relationship between logical statements and function points has created an alternative method for deriving function point total for legacy systems where the code already exists. As mentioned, this method is called "backfiring" and consists of direct mathematical conversion between code volumes and function points. The accuracy of backfiring is not very good (usually within plus or minus 25%) but for some aging legacy software it is the only practical method since the specifications are missing and the original personnel may no longer be available.

Most commercial software estimating tools now include code sizing derived from function points and many include backfiring support as well. For greater accuracy, it is necessary to include adjustments for both complexity and for reusable code. It is also necessary to deal with applications that include multiple programming languages. However, all of these capabilities are now available in commercial software estimating tools.

Another useful sizing capability associated with function point metrics is the ability to predict the number of test cases that are likely to be created for the application. Because the five basic topics included in function points are the same topics that need test cases constructed (inputs, outputs, inquiries, logical files, and interfaces) function points are surprisingly effective in test-case estimation.

Here, too, there are major differences in test-case numbers by industry, with military software and systems software producing much larger totals of test cases than information systems. There is now at least preliminary data available for all standard kinds of testing. Table 5 are some representative examples.

Table 5   Number of Test Cases Created per Function Point

	Systems Software	MIS Software	Military Software	Commercial Software
Unit test	0.30	0.20	0.50	0.30
New function test	0.35	0.25	0.35	0.25
Regression test	0.30	0.10	0.30	0.35
Integration test	0.45	0.25	0.75	0.35
System test	0.40	0.20	0.55	0.40
Total test cases	1.80	1.00	2.45	1.65

The total number of kinds of testing covered is now up to about a dozen discrete forms. The sizing logic for test cases in the best commercial software estimating tools also includes adjustments for enhancements rather than for new projects, for complexity factors, and for the impact of ancillary tools such as test-case generators and test coverage analysis tools.

In addition to sizing test cases, some commercial estimating tools such as CHECKPOINT and SPQR/20 also include estimating capabilities for defect levels and defect removal efficiency.

Function point metrics can be used to predict not only coding defects, but also defects in non-code items such as requirements and specifications.

Table 6   U.S. Averages for Software Defect Levels

Defect Origin	Defects per Function Point
Requirements	1.00
Design	1.25
Code	1.75
User documents	0.60
Bad fixes	0.40
TOTAL	5.00

Thus, function points open up quality research for both front-end defect levels and also peripheral defect levels such as user manuals and screens, as well as continuing to support research in coding defect levels.

Also, for economic research on the cost of quality and the economics of various quality technologies, function points provide the only viable metric for normalizing data. As discussed in the Barriers to Software Quality Measurement and Cost per Defect sections of this book, the lines of code metric and cost per defect metric behave paradoxically under certain conditions and actually move backwards.

International Function Point Users Group (IFPUG)

The non-profit International Function Point Users Group (IFPUG) was formed in Toronto, Canada in the mid-1980s. In 1986, IFPUG became large enough to need a permanent administrative home, so it moved to the United States and became a formal non-profit corporation.

IFPUG is included in this handbook because the function point metric is rapidly becoming one of the most widely used metrics for normalizing software quality data.

In 1986, function point users formed a non-profit association, the International Function Point Users Group, commonly known as IFPUG. (For additional information, IFPUG headquarters is located in Blendonview Office Park, 5008-28 Pine Creek Drive, Westerville, Ohio 43081-4899; telephone 614 895-7130.)

Note that in 1994 the IFPUG organization voted to change its name, as a result of broadening its scope from only function points to a full range of metrics and measurement topics. The new name is the North American Software Metrics Association (NASMA). However, so many people know the organization by its old name that IFPUG is still a valid identifier.

The IFPUG organization has established relationships with software measurement groups and other national function point associations in a number of countries.

Australian Software Metrics Association (ASMA)
P.O. Box 1
Kensington, NSW Australia
Phone 61 2 697 4450
FAX 61 2 662 4061

Centre D'Interet sur les Metriques (CIM)
1193 Carre Philips Sal C5435
CP 8888 Succ A
Montreal, Quebec, Canada H3C 3P8
Phone 514 987-8900
FAX 514 987-8477

Computer Society of South Africa
P.O. Box 3710
Birnam Park 2015
Johannesburg, South Africa 1763
Phone 27 11 885 2408
FAX 27 11 786 1868

Deutschsprachige Anwendergruppe fur Software Metrik und Aufwandschatzung
(DASMA)
HS Bremerhaven
Fachbereich 2, Mozart strasse 37
D-27570 Bremerhaven, Germany
Phone 49 471 26142
FAX 49 471 207 386

French Function Point Users Group (FFPUG)
6 Rue du Palais de Justice
69 005 Lyon, France
Phone 33 78 92 86 63
FAX 33 78 42 33 94

Italian Users Group of Function Points (GUFPI)
c/o SOGEI
Via Mario Carucci 99
Rome, Italy
Phone 39 6 502 52396
FAX 33 78 42 33 94

Netherlands Function Point Users Group (NEFPUG)
Oosterzijweg 43
1851 PC Heiloo, Netherlands
Phone 31 7233 1417
FAX 31 7234 0617

United Kingdom Function Point Users Group (UFPUG)
TOK Brameur LTD
Mead House, Heathfield Lane
Chislehurst, Kent, England BR7 6AH
Phone 44 81 295 0234
FAX 44 81 467 7843

It is an interesting phenomenon that because of the usefulness of function points as a quality metric, the international function point user community may have more quality data available than any of the major quality associations. In any case, there is a need for coordination and communication between the function point organizations and the software quality organizations, since both share common goals of better measurement and better quality.

Function Points and the Internet

Like everything else in the modern world, function point data and information about using function points are now available over the Internet and other online services such as CompuServe. (Incidentally, function points can be used to estimate the quality levels of JAVA and HTML applications both of which can contain interesting volumes of bugs.)

There is a very large Internet LISTSERV dealing with function points with well over 500 members and growing rapidly. It is managed by Denis St. Pierre and his colleagues from the Computer Research Institute of Montreal (CRIM). Denis can be reached by e-mail at Denis.St.Pierre@CRIM.CA.

To join the LISTSERV group use the following address and protocol:

To:..CIM@CRIM.CA
Subj: (leave blank – do not include a subject)
Content: SUB FUNCTION.POINT.LIST "Your name"

Note that the e-mail subject field must be left blank.

There is also a function point "frequently asked questions" or FAQ on the Internet. This was established by Ray Boehm, function point consultant. The address of this list of questions and answers is:

http://ourworld.compuserve.com/homepages/softcomp/fpfaq.htm.

My company, Software Productivity Research Inc., also has a Web site which connects to most of the other function point sites. Our Web address is http://www.spr.com.

In addition, the International Function Point Users Group (IFPUG) also has a World Wide Web address: http://ifpug.org/ifpug.

The CompuServe network has several forums that often discuss function points. The CASE forum deals with function points almost daily. There are forums for information management and for cost estimating where function points are also discussed.

FUNCTION POINT RULES OF THUMB FOR SOFTWARE QUALITY ESTIMATION

Commercial estimating tools require some significant input data on experience, skills, tools, etc., in order to estimate accurately. For rough sizing and casual estimating, function points also provide rough rules of thumb that are not very precise, but can easily be used with a pocket calculator or even in your head. Here are a few simple but interesting quality estimation rules:

Rule 1: Function points raised to the 1.20 power predicts the approximate number of test cases created.

A simple corollary rule can predict the number of times each test-case will be run or executed during development: assume that each test-case would be executed approximately four times during software development.

Recall that the "defect potential" of an application is the sum of bugs or errors that will occur in five major deliverables: 1) requirements errors; 2) design errors; 3) coding errors; 4) user documentation errors; and 5) bad fixes, or secondary errors introduced in the act of fixing a prior error.

Rule 2: Function points raised to the 1.25 power predicts the approximate defect potential for new software projects.

A similar corollary rule can predict the defect potentials for enhancements. In this case, the rule applies to the size of the enhancement rather than the base that is being updated: Function points raised to the 1.25 power predict the approximate defect potential for enhancement software projects. The higher power used in the enhancement rule is because of the latent defects lurking in the base product that will be encountered during the enhancement process.

The defect potential will be reduced by somewhere between 85% (approximate industry norms) and 99% (best in class results) prior to actual delivery of the software to clients. Thus, the number of delivered defects is only a small fraction of the overall defect potential.

Two interesting rules approximate the defect removal efficiency of various reviews, inspections, tests, and also the number of consecutive defect removal operations needed to top 95% in cumulative defect removal efficiency levels:

Rule 3: Raising function point totals to the 0.3 power predicts the number of consecutive defect removal operations needed to exceed 95% in cumulative defect removal efficiency.

Rule 4: Each software review, inspection, or test step will find and remove 30% of the bugs that are present.

The implication of these rules mean is a series of between six and 12 consecutive defect removal operations must be utilized to achieve very high quality levels for large software projects. This is why major software producers normally use a multi-stage series of design reviews, code inspections, and various levels of testing from unit test through system test.

One final and important aspect of function point sizing is dealing with the rate at which requirements "creep" and hence make projects grow larger during development. Fortunately, function point metrics allow direct measurement of the rate at which this phenomenon occurs. For example, assume that the initial requirements for an application total exactly 100. One month later, new features are added to the application that raise the function point total to 110.

The following table shows the approximate monthly rate of creeping requirements for four kinds of software.

Table 1   Rate of Requirements Creep after Initial Size is Determined

Software Type	Monthly Rate of Changes to Requirements
Information systems software	1.5%
Systems software	2.0%
Military software	2.0%
Commercial software	3.5%

The ability to deal with creeping requirements illustrates one of the new estimating capabilities that are now becoming part of software estimating tools.

For estimates made early in the lifecycle, a general rule of thumb for dealing with creeping requirements in the absence of full knowledge follows.

Rule 5: New requirements will occur at a rate of 2% each month during the design and coding phases of a software project.

Software cost estimating tools can now predict the probable growth in unplanned functions over the remainder of the development cycle. This knowledge can then be used to refine the estimate, and to adjust the final costs in response.

Function points are useful but not perfect. There are still a number of important issues where function point metrics are difficult to apply or inappropriate. For example, data quality is outside the scope of function point metrics.

Another area where function points are difficult to utilize is for small enhancements and defect repairs. Many defect repairs are small and involve changing only a few lines of code. Since function points are normally expressed as integers, changing 10 lines of COBOL is equivalent to only about one-tenth of a function point. The current rules for counting function points do not support fractional values, and in fact are not very accurate below about 10 function points.

There is a dogma among many developers of real-time, systems, and embedded software that asserts "function points are only for management information systems." This is nonsense. Allan Albrecht who invented function points is an electrical engineer, and he had always designed function points to work on engineering projects. It is only a historical accident that IBM first used function points for management information systems.

Function points can and are being used for real-time and embedded software such as fuel injection systems, operating systems, telephone switching systems, ship-board gun control systems, the embedded software in the Tomahawk cruise missile, aircraft flight control software, and many other applications.

GAPS IN SOFTWARE QUALITY DATA

There are several common gaps in the collection of software quality data. Normally we do not ask individuals to testify against themselves, so any defects found privately by desk checking or unit testing do not show up in defect totals or defect removal statistics.

While this practice is very reasonable and common, it raises a major question: "How many bugs can people find in their own work?"

There is no definitive answer to this question, but several companies such as IBM and ITT have performed experiments with volunteers who have agreed to record their own mistakes or defects and note how many were found via activities such as unit testing or desk checking. Indeed, I was formerly a professional programmer and served as a volunteer to record this kind of information.

The problem with data collected from a few volunteers is that there is no guarantee that the results will actually match those of the entire community of programmers and software engineers. However, suspect data is probably better than no data at all.

When working as a programmer, I tended to make mistakes or bugs that were in the range of 20 to 25 per KLOC or perhaps 2.0 to 3.5 per function point in languages such as Assembly, PL/I, or various dialects of Basic. In candor, I only regarded myself as an "average" programmer for the day (circa 1965-1975).

My own unit testing and desk checking usually found between 25% and 35% of the errors that were made, with the others being found via inspections, external testing, and users of the my software after the software had passed down-stream.

The results of volunteer colleagues who would rank as "excellent" programmers were a bit better than mine: coding defects in the 10 to 15 per KLOC range (1.0 to 2.0 per function point) and defect removal via desk checks and unit testing that could rise above 50%.

The lack of empirical data dealing with private desk checking and unit testing creates an unfortunate "black hole" in our ability to predict overall defect removal efficiency levels.

The volunteer studies that I participated in were all more than a decade ago and the recent literature has not stressed self-discovered defect removal efficiency levels. This gap is therefore of unknown dimensions for a number of modern methodologies, software languages, and even classes of software, such as:

- Personal defect removal for client/server applications.

- Personal defect removal for modern languages such as:

  Eiffel
  Realizer
  Visual Age C++
  Visual Basic

- Personal defect removal for object-oriented design (Booch, Rumbaugh, etc.)

- Personal defect removal under ISO 9000-9004 standards.

- Personal defect removal under the SEI capability maturing model.

- Personal defect removal under European initiatives such as ESPRIT and TickIT.

- Personal defect removal under rapid application development (RAD).

For almost 50 years controlled experiments on software defect removal efficiency by individual programmers has indicated a very broad range for efficiency. Studies dating from the 1960s and 1970s within IBM found ranges that ran from about 10% to about 70% for detecting "seeded" defects that were deliberately injected.

It is interesting that participation in software design and code inspections has proven to be very effective in raising personal defect removal. The observation of the kinds of defects which are found in other people's work tend to make us more aware of similar problems in our own work. Indeed, over and above the errors which inspections find, the process of inspections ranks among the best in terms of both defect prevention and elevating personal defect removal efficiency levels.

The overall average for seeded errors seems to be about 55%, but some people are much better than that, while a few are much worse. Unfortunately, seeded errors may differ from real errors in unknown but significant ways. The preliminary data indicates a 15% to 25% differential between efficiency in finding seeded errors and efficiency in finding real errors, with real errors on the lagging side. Thus, if a programmer finds 50% of a set of seeded errors, perhaps only 30% of the real errors might be found.

It is strongly recommend that this topic be revisited with a new generation of volunteers who are willing to report on their own defect removal efficiency levels in the interest of software engineering research while using modern languages such as Eiffel, Forte, JAVA, HTML and the like.

Given the wide availability of commercial defect tracking tools in the 1990s, this kind of research should actually be common even though the literature is sparse.

GLOBAL SOFTWARE QUALITY LEVELS

One of the advantages of functional metrics is the ability to perform very large-scale comparisons of industries and even of countries. Of course at the national level it is hard to achieve a truly valid statistical sample, but the fact that this kind of research can be performed at all is a tribute to the power of functional metrics.

The author and his colleagues at SPR have collected quality data from about 23 countries. In addition, we also study the secondary sources of data such as international quality conferences.

Two other researchers, Ed Yourdon and Dr. Howard Rubin, were commissioned by the Canadian government in 1994 so there is some substantial global information starting to become available. In addition, may other researchers such as Dr. Michael Cusumano, Watts Humphrey, Dr. Richard Thayer, Tom DeMarco, and Dr. Victor Basili have worked enough in Europe and the Pacific Rim to make valuable observations about differences in approaches and quality results.

The following data is originally derived from my book *Software Productivity and Quality Today—The Worldwide Perspective* (Information Systems Management Group, Carlsbad, CA, 1993).

This data has been updated in 1994, 1995, and 1996 so the results differ from the original publication. Also, the original book used the Feature Point variant of function points, while IFPUG function points are assumed here. There is still a high margin of error and the overseas results still have small sample sizes of less than 50 projects per country on average.

Table 1   International Software Defect Potentials and Defect Removal Efficiency Levels

Country	Defect Potential per Function Point	Defect Removal Efficiency	Delivered Defects per Function Point
Japan	4.50	93%	0.32
Canada	4.55	86%	0.64
Sweden	5.00	86%	0.70
England	4.85	85%	0.73
United States	5.00	85%	0.75
Belgium	5.00	85%	0.75
Italy	4.85	84%	0.78
Norway	4.95	84%	0.79
France	4.95	84%	0.79
India	5.10	85%	0.84
Germany	4.95	83%	0.84
South Korea	5.20	83%	0.88
Ukraine*	5.30	82%	0.95
Russia*	5.50	80%	1.10

* Note: Data on the Ukraine and Russia are from secondary sources only.

It is interesting that international averages are actually clumped rather closely together. The range of defect potentials and defect removal efficiency on a global basis are more or less equivalent to the ranges observed within any single country, such as the United States.

It is also interesting that the way requirements are analyzed in Japan, and the more widespread usage of formal design methods in Europe, tend to reduce front-end defects compared to U.S. norms. U.S. MIS software projects usually top 1 defect per function point in requirements and 1.25 defects per function point in design-related problems. By contrast, Japanese software projects may have less than 0.6 defects per function point in requirements and less than 1 defect per function point in design. Many European MIS projects may drop below 1 defect per function point in design-related problems, although requirements problems are similar to U.S. volumes.

While high-technology industries (telecommunications, computer manufacturing, aerospace, etc.) are virtually equal everywhere in the world, the management information systems community in the United States tends to lag behind both Europe and Japan in front-end quality control.

The U.S. defense industry is a world-leader in software quality but this basic fact is tempered by the observation that the U.S. also builds the largest and most complex defense software systems in human history. It is fortunate that U.S. defense software quality control is as good as it is, otherwise many weapons systems might not work at all, much less work reliably.

Overall, global defect potentials run from a low of just over about 1 defect per function point to a high that approaches 20 defects per function point. Defect removal efficiency levels run from a low of about 50% to a high of 99.999% although both extreme ends are rare and modal results hover close to 85%.

Table 2 summarizes the ranges observed from my international data. The table is only approximate and is derived from data accumulated during requirements reviews, design and code inspections, testing, and customer-reported defects during the first year of usage.

Table 2   International Ranges of Defect Potentials by Origin Point

	Lowest	Mode	Highest
Requirements	0.20	1.00	2.50
Design	0.25	1.25	7.75
Code	0.50	1.75	5.00
User documents	0.25	0.60	2.00
Bad fixes	0.00	0.40	1.50
TOTAL	1.20	5.00	18.75

Note that this data is pieced together from many clients and many projects in more than 20 countries. Once again, the margin of error with this data is high. However, it is encouraging to know that the topic of international variances in software quality can at last be studied and placed on a quantitative basis.

From the international studies and data collected by myself and my colleagues, India is a country with a very interesting combination of fairly low labor rates, fairly good training for software personnel, and a growing appreciation of the importance of quality for international software markets. Other countries where similar combinations exist include the Ukraine, China, and Thailand.

"GOOD ENOUGH" QUALITY FALLACY

Starting in about 1993, the topic of "time to market" began to garner an increasing amount of business and software press coverage. At the same time, the topic of "good enough" software quality also began to garner press coverage. The essence of "good enough" thinking is that rather than striving for zero-defect levels or striving to exceed 99% in defect removal efficiency, it is better to ship software with some defects still present in order to speed up or shorten time to market intervals.

The justification for "good enough" software quality is the fact that all major commercial vendors (i.e., Microsoft, Computer Associates, Lotus, Novell, IBM, etc.) are known to have latent defects at the time the initial release of new applications comes out. From the observed fact that most commercial software contains bugs at delivery, the "good enough" enthusiasts have formed the hypothesis that leaving bugs is a deliberate and even clever strategy on the part of the commercial software houses, which might advantageously be imitated by other software developers.

What most people don't realize, of course, is that the major commercial software vendors are running more than 95% in cumulative defect removal efficiency and some projects approach or exceed 99%. That it, the major commercial software vendors are 10% to almost 20% more efficient than in-house information systems developers in finding errors prior to delivery.

Companies such as Microsoft do not deliberately ship software that contains bugs. It simply happens that for large systems in the 10,000 to 100,000 function point range, zero-defect software at the moment of release is currently outside the envelope of defect removal technologies.

The "good enough" concept is a very dangerous one for ordinary companies whose defect removal efficiency levels are only in the 80% to 85% level such as small software houses and internal management information system groups. It is also dangerous thinking for contractors, consultants, and outsource companies.

The normal impact of "good enough" thinking is a certain carelessness about software quality. For an average company, its software quality is already pretty marginal. If it gets any worse, there is a strong chance that the software will not work at all when it is released, or that the software will contain errors with catastrophic consequences.

The "good enough" concept is seldom found in companies that understand the importance of quality; i.e., telecommunication manufacturers, medical instrument manufacturers, aerospace manufacturers, and the like. The "good enough" concept is particularly hazardous for information systems producers such as banks and insurance companies. These companies are usually behind the state-of-the-art in software quality matters, and any slacking off from their already mediocre quality control can lead to hazardous situations.

What is the worst feature of the whole "good enough" concept is that it is based on fundamental flaw derived from having little or no solid empirical data. One of the major rationales for the "good enough" concept is the notion that software can be delivered earlier and schedules will be shorter if inspections are missing or perfunctory and if testing is minimized or truncated early.

In fact, all of the empirical data on the relationship of schedules and software quality is counter to the "good enough" hypotheses. The most severe schedule delays usually occur when testing begins, when it is discovered that quality is so poor that the software application either fails completely or cannot possibly achieve even minimal stability levels.

Some years ago, I was part of IBM's quality assurance team on the IMS (Information Management System) database product in Palo Alto, California. When IMS was first transferred into the division its quality was so bad that integration and system testing ran around the clock for more than four calendar months.

Indeed, IMS testing was so difficult that it interfered with other projects because the test team was utilizing almost all of the IBM Palo Alto lab computing capacity on a three-shift basis. Some of the my colleagues who were actually members of the IMS test team sometimes did not get to go home for two or three days in a row since testing was running around the clock.

When IBM began a serious quality push on the IMS product that included formal design and code inspections and error-prone module removal, these methods made a reduction in overall schedules and a highly visible reduction in integration and system testing schedules.

Integration and system testing was transformed from a three-shift, four-month cycle, down to a one-shift, one-month cycle. In the course of about 24 calendar months of quality improvement, incoming IMS customer-reported defects dropped by roughly a ratio of 10-to-1 while the IMS development schedule shrank by one month overall and the testing portion by three months. The formal inspection process added two months upstream so the net saving was a one-month shortening of a typical release cycle.

This kind of data on the relationship of quality and schedules has been replicated by many other companies and many other software projects: AT&T, Hewlett Packard, ITT, Microsoft, Motorola, Raytheon, and many more have all noted that a synergistic combination of defect prevention and defect removal shortens schedules at the same time that quality goes up.

The following table shows the general relationship of quality and schedules for 10,000 function point systems software projects:

Table 1   Relationship of Software Development Schedules and Defect Removal Efficiency Levels for 10,000 Function Point Systems Software

Defect Removal Efficiency	Schedule (Calendar Months)
50.00%	55
55.00%	58
60.00%	57
65.00%	56
70.00%	55
75.00%	52 Malpractice
80.00%	50
85.00%	49
90.00%	48 Average
95.00%	46
96.00%	44
97.00%	40
98.00%	38 Minimum
99.00%	39
99.99%	42

Table 1, above, shows that the approximate U.S. average of 90% for large systems software projects in cumulative defect removal efficiency is far from optimum in terms of software development schedules.

Even worse, projects that are below 75% in defect removal efficiency (i.e., the malpractice zone) have very elongated schedules due to the fact that the software does not work well enough to be delivered to clients.

There is no schedule advantage whatsoever from dropping below 95% in cumulative defect removal efficiency, which is the current threshold value for "best in class" software organizations.

Minimum schedules for 10,000 function point applications today occur when the defect removal efficiency level is in the zone of about 97% to 99%, which is where the "top gun" organizations can typically be found.

Achieving > 95% in cumulative defect removal efficiency requires a synergistic combination of defect prevention approaches, pre-test defect removal approaches such as inspections and testing by testing specialists. This is exactly the combination of technologies used by "top gun" software quality organizations such as AT&T, Hewlett Packard, IBM, and Microsoft.

Similar relationships between quality and schedules exist for other size categories, too, and the current optimal schedules and defect removal efficiency levels are roughly the following for six size plateaus an order of magnitude apart:

Table 2   Software Defect Removal Efficiency and Minimum Development Schedules

Size in function points	Removal Efficiency For Minimum Schedule	Schedule (Calendar months)
1	99.99%	< 0.25
10	99.99%	< 1
100	99.00%	< 4
1000	98.00%	< 16
10000	97.00%	< 38
100000	96.00%	< 48

The overall conclusions that can be reached about the "good enough" fallacy are the following.

- If the company's defect removal efficiency is unknown, it is probably no better than U.S. averages (roughly 85% when all classes and sizes of projects are aggregated). In this case the "good enough" concept should not even be dreamed of. If defect removal gets worse, schedules will get longer, not shorter and the company will probably be sued, forced out of business, or both. The current schedules are already too long, and the company is probably getting hung up in integration and test because its major applications don't work.

- If the company's defect removal efficiency is known, and it is in the zone of 85% to 90% then pre-test reviews and inspections should be added to shorten the company's schedules. Going the other way and reducing emphasis on quality will lengthen the company's schedules; not make them any shorter.

- If the company's defect removal efficiency is known, and it is higher than 95%, the "good enough" concept is irrelevant because its own data will show the relationship of quality and schedules. Indeed, if the company is topping 95% in cumulative defect removal efficiency, it is already at or approaching the minimum schedule node and any reduction in quality control would stretch things out.

- If the company is entering into a contract to have software built for it, or it is considering acquiring a commercial software package, it should stay away from "good enough" quality concepts. For contracts, the "good enough" fallacy is a frequent cause of litigation. For commercial software, vendors attempting "good enough" products tend to go out of business fairly soon.

- If a company's building in-house software for itself, and it attempts to utilize "good enough" concepts, its internal clients will probably suggest to its CEO that outsourcing may be a viable option since the development team clearly does not know how to build software properly.

- If a company depends purely upon testing and does not use any kind of pre-test inspections, its quality will never be very good and its schedules will always be longer than necessary. In this case, any move toward the "good enough" concept will make its schedules longer and raise its litigation potential if it is a contractor or building commercial software. If the company is building in-house software, its CEO will probably eventually get tired of disaster and replace the in-house systems personnel with an outsource group.

Unfortunately, the "good enough" concept is one of those appealing fallacies that attracts people who don't have any empirical data on either quality or schedules. It is appealing because it gives a blanket endorsement to sloppy development and casual quality, so that software personnel who are sloppy and casual can have some kind of a justification for not doing anything to improve.

The "good enough" concept is also popular with the software press as this book is written. Here there is no clear reason why so many articles are published on the "good enough" topic, other than the fact that journalists are constantly looking for new things to write about and this one is fairly new. Also, journalists don't have much empirical data either.

HIGH VOLUME BETA TESTING

Commercial software producers with large numbers of clients (more than 10,000 for example) sometimes approach software quality in a fashion that is not possible for custom software with low usage.

The number of bugs found during testing is roughly proportional to the number of test personnel that are executing the software. The high-volume commercial software producers sometimes have more than 1,000 customers simultaneously participating in external Beta tests.

Any software product with more than 1000 concurrent users testing it at once is likely to have a rather good defect removal efficiency: 75% or higher. However, this method of testing is only available to companies such as Computer Associates, IBM, or Microsoft who have many thousands of customers.

Even within this restricted set, not every product has enough customers to allow the kind of high-volume testing that is extremely efficient.

Since both in-house software packages and commercial software products are often tested by clients, the following table shows the rough defect removal efficiency levels associated with six plateaus of external Best test sites.

Table 1   Number of Client Sites and Beta Test Defect Removal Efficiency

Number of Clients in External Best Test	Approximate Defect Removal Efficiency
1	25.0%
10	50.0%
100	75.0%
1000	95.0%
10000	99.0%
100000	99.9%

Note that external Beta testing occurs pretty late in the software development cycle, so many of the "easy" bugs are already removed.

Another limiting factor on external Beta testing efficiency levels is the fact that not everyone who says they will participate actually runs the software at all! If 10 companies volunteer to participate in an external Beta test, two or three will really exercise the product, two or three will run it a few times somewhat gingerly, and almost half who may not even install it or run it at all.

Unless the product has features that are urgently needed by clients, the pressure of their own work and their suspicion that what they are being sent may be unreliable provides ample justification for not bothering.

IEEE QUALITY STANDARDS

The Institute of Electrical and Electronic Engineers (IEEE) is one of the largest non-profit associations of technologists in the world. As the name implies the IEEE was created in response to the explosive growth of electrical apparatus in the early part of the 20th century.

The portion of the IEEE which concentrates on software and computing-related issues is the IEEE Computer Society, which is a separate organization under the general IEEE umbrella. Both the IEEE and the IEEE Computer Society have very active publication programs that includes many books, monographs, and well-regarded journals such as *IEEE Computer, IEEE Software,* and *IEEE Spectrum* all of which contain interesting software articles in every issue.

The IEEE has been active in standards development since its formation. The IEEE standards have been jointly published with the American National Standards Institute (ANSI) so they are commonly referenced using the nomenclature "ANSI/IEEE Std nnnn" where nnnn is the number assigned to the standard. However, both ANSI and the IEEE have issued standards without the other, so ANSI standards and IEEE standards also occur.

IEEE standards and IEEE Computer Society standards can be ordered directly from the IEEE Standards Department whose address is 445 Hoes Lane, Piscataway, NJ 0885-1331 USA. Their P.O. Box 1331 should be used for letters. The telephone number is (908) 562-3805 and the fax is (908) 582-1571.

The IEEE Computer Society's publications group can also be reached by E-mail and on the World Wide Web. The e-mail address is cs.book@computer.org and the Web address is http://www.computer.org.

LIVERPOOL JOHN MOORES UNIVERSITY
LEARNING SERVICES

Although the IEEE quality standards have many interesting and some useful concepts included within them, they differ from Department of Defense (DoD) standards and International Organization for Standards (ISO) standards in that there is no enforcement criteria. In other words, IEEE standards can be used or not used at the discretion of any company or project.

As a result of the lack of any strong need for utilization, there is only sparse empirical information on whether the IEEE quality standards have had any tangible impact on software quality. Among my clients, it happens that the defect removal efficiency levels of the companies that utilize the IEEE quality standards is often above 90% which is about 5% higher than U.S. norms. However, these same companies also utilize other standards (their own, ISO 9000-9004, and sometimes DoD) so the impact of the IEEE standards is hard to isolate.

It is an interesting observation that I, and my colleagues at SPR, have never been commissioned by any client to evaluate the effectiveness of the IEEE standards, even though we have received such commissions for various DoD and ISO standards and also for evaluating the effectiveness of the SEI CMM. So far as can be determined, there is very little follow-up associated with most software standards to determine their effectiveness using empirical data under field conditions.

Some of the IEEE standards that are aimed at software quality or have a potential impact on software quality include but are not limited to the following (in chronological order):

- ANSI/IEEE Std 0983-1986 (Standard for Software Quality Assurance). This standard has been replaced by IEEE Std 0730.1 in 1989.

- ANSI/IEEE Std 1012-1987 (Standard for Software Verification and Validation)

- ANSI/IEEE Std 1016-1987 (Recommended Practices for Software Design)

- ANSI/IEEE Std 1063-1987 (Standard for Software Documentation)

- ANSI/IEEE Std 1058-1987 (Standard for Software Project Management)

- ANSI/IEEE Std 1028-1988 (Standard for Software Reviews and Audits)

- ANSI/IEEE Std 0828-1990 (Standard for Software Configuration Management)

- ANSI/IEEE Std 1074-1991 (Standard for Software Life Cycle Process)

The various standards committees within the IEEE umbrella are quite active, and there are even annual conferences which deal with IEEE standards. One key feature of IEEE standards, which is often missing from other standards, is the fact that the standards are updated rather often in response to new information and changing software technologies.

However, there are still some embarrassing gaps. For example, the IEEE standard glossary of software engineering (ANSI/IEEE Std 610-1990) managed to omit all terms relating to "function points" even though function points are now the most widely utilized software metric in the world.

ISO 9001-9004 CERTIFICATION

It should be noted that ISO 9000-9004 certification only became mandatory in 1992, so there is still very little data yet available even in 1996. ISO 9001 is the standard that appears most relevant to software projects while ISO 9000-3 is a guideline document that interprets the ISO 9001 standard for software projects.

In the course of the SPR assessment, benchmark, and quality surveys, a number of companies were contacted that were in the process of completing their ISO certifications or which had recently been certified. Similar companies were also contacted which were not applying for certification. So far as can be determined, there is not yet any tangible or perceptible difference in the software quality levels of companies which have been certified when compared to similar companies in the same industries which have not been certified.

The ISO concepts have some merit and are certainly important standards in terms of their international impact. Preparing for ISO certification and for visits by ISO or TickIT auditors will certainly focus attention on a number of quality issues.

However, as of 1997, there is still a remarkable lack of quantified results associated with the ISO 9000-9004 standard set. To date it does not seem to have happened that with several years of history, the ISO-certified groups have pulled ahead of the non-certified groups in some tangible way. Currently the most tangible aspects remain the higher costs of the ISO certification process, larger volumes of planning and control documents, and the time required to achieve certification.

After several years, it is obvious that the ISO standards have had a polarizing effect on software producers, as well as on hardware manufacturers. Some companies such as

Motorola have challenged the validity of the ISO standards, while others such as ViewLogic have embraced the ISO standards fully.

The reaction to ISO certification among U.S. software groups to date has been so negative that several other industries were contacted (fiber optics, electronics manufacturing). Here the reactions are also polarized, and the ISO certification process has been asserted to be ineffective for quality control as currently performed on one hand, while it has been embraced and endorsed for both quality control and marketing purposes on the other hand.

Objections to the ISO standards from companies that have no quality measurements in place and whose own hardware and software quality is marginal can be discounted. However, objections to the ISO standards from a company such as Motorola that does have quality measurements and a serious presence in the quality world is more thought provoking. The Motorola objections were based on two key points:

1) ISO certification was used for marketing purposes with an implied assertion that achieving ISO certification meant high quality levels regardless of the lack of empirical data demonstrating that point. Richard Butow, Motorola Vice President of Quality, bluntly stated that was false advertising.

2) The ISO standards themselves lacked some of the key quality elements found in Motorola's own quality standards and could be viewed as a step back rather than a step forward in terms of quality methodology.

Motorola had achieved ISO certification itself at the time Butow published the statement, so it was not just a case of sour grapes.

Some ISO users have observed that it is not the place of the ISO 9000-9004 standards to actually improve quality. Their purpose is simply to ensure that effective practices are followed, and are not in and of themselves a compilation of best current practices. Indeed, many companies have pointed out that compliance is fairly easy if a good quality control approach is already in place, and ISO certification tends to raise the confidence of clients even if quantification of results is elusive.

On the whole, the data available from the ISO 9001 domain as of early 1997 remains insufficient to judge the impact of the ISO standards on these topics:

• Does ISO 9001 reduce software defect potentials below 5 per function point?

• Does ISO 9001 raise defect removal efficiency levels above 95%?

• Does ISO 9001 reduce the number of bad test cases below 15%?

- Does ISO 9001 reduce the rate of "bad fix" injections below 7%?

- Does ISO 9001 increase reliability under field conditions?

- Does ISO 9001 increase customer satisfaction levels?

- Does ISO 9001 have any affect on data quality?

- Does ISO 9001 reduce the number of canceled or delayed projects?

- Does ISO 9001 reduce the incidence of litigation for breach of contract?

- Does ISO 9001 reduce the incidence of litigation for poor quality control?

Quite a bit of information about ISO 9000-9004 is available via the Internet and various information utilities such as CompuServe. Attempts to find empirical data that ISO 9001 improves quality using these channels elicited no useful factual information. However, many ISO enthusiasts responded with the surprising message that the ISO standards were not actually intended to improve quality and hence should not be faulted if they failed to do so.

Among SPR's clients the set of ISO certified companies do average more than 90% in defect removal efficiency, which is more than 5% above U.S. norms of about 85%. However, this appears to be because most of the companies that are ISO certified are in industries that also average above 90% (i.e., commercial software houses, aerospace, computer manufacturers, telecommunication manufacturers, medical instrument manufacturers, and the like).

Another observation of the set of ISO certified companies is that the volumes of planning and control documents produced under the ISO 9001 standard approximates the volumes produced under the DoD 2167 and DoD 2168 military standards, or about three times larger than civilian norms (i.e., paperwork approaches 6 pages per function point versus 2 pages per function point).

However, when the comparison is restricted to companies in the same industries as the ISO-certified companies, the difference in document volumes is only about 50% since a number of high-technology industries already produce specifications and planning documents of significant volume.

Even though the sample is small and comprises less than 50 projects from five companies, it is interesting to attempt to construct patterns of how ISO 9001 affects software. The following table assumes commercial systems software of about 10,000 function points in nominal size, created using the C programming language.

Table 1   Approximate Defect Potentials and Removal for 10,000 Function Point
Software Systems With and Without the ISO 9001 Standard

(Data Expressed in Terms of Defects per Function Point)

	Average Project Defect Potential	ISO 9001 Defect Potential	Best Practices Defect Potential
Requirements	1.25	1.15	0.85
Design	1.50	1.25	1.00
Code	1.75	1.50	1.15
User Documents	1.10	1.00	0.75
Bad Fixes	0.40	0.30	0.10
TOTAL	6.00	5.20	3.85
Defect Removal Efficiency	90%	93%	96%
Delivered Defects	0.60	0.36	0.15

Among SPR's clients, the ISO 9001 certified projects are somewhat better than average, for systems software projects in the 10,000 function point range although as with everything else there are substantial ranges around nominal averages.

However, when compared to similar projects that use "best practices" but are not ISO 9001-certified, it can be seen that ISO certification, by itself, is not sufficient to achieve "top gun" quality levels.

There is obviously a lot of overlap between the ISO standards and the best current practices in terms of software quality, because the ISO standards were produced by people who know a lot about quality even if software quality was not the original intent.

However, some of the approaches that are found in the "best practice" group are not required and sometimes even discussed in the ISO 9001 standard or the ISO 9000-3 software guidelines. Of course standards are not fixed and unchanging, and no doubt future releases of the ISO 9001 and 9000-3 standards will expand the topics and eliminate some of the gaps in the current versions.

The following list highlights the set of best practices for software quality and includes both factors that are part of the ISO standards and those that are currently outside it. I have moved the non-ISO factors to the top of the list for convenience in highlighting them.

Software Quality Best Current Practices Versus ISO 9001 Practices

- Early defect estimates   (Not discussed in ISO standards)
- Defect removal efficiency measurements   (Not discussed in ISO standards)
- Function point normalization of quality data   (Not discussed in ISO standards)
- Quantified executive quality targets   (Not discussed in ISO standards)
- Availability of certified reusable components   (Not discussed in ISO standards)
- Formal requirements gathering and analysis
- Defect tracking by severity levels
- Defect tracking by age or duration from report to resolution
- Automated defect tracking tools utilized
- Automated configuration control of all major deliverables
- Active quality assurance groups
- Formal inspections of design and code
- Formal testing by trained specialists
- Formal test library control and automation
- User satisfaction analysis
- Training of management in software quality concepts
- Training of technical staff in software quality concepts
- Quality control of subcontract work
- Software quality warranties (for commercial vendors)

The ISO quality approaches and the best current practices seem to be converging but are not yet in perfect synchronization. The most notable flaw of the ISO approach is the failure to realize that accurate quantification of software quality based on functional metrics and defect removal efficiency measures are major contributors to software quality.

Because of the importance of the ISO 9001 standard to the world software community, the quantification of ISO results using function point metrics is an important research topic.

The author and his colleagues at SPR will collect new data as it becomes available in both the United States, Europe, and elsewhere. However, both the ISO and TickIT organizations should also collect data and should encourage ISO and TickIT auditors and assessors to move toward quantification and empirical results rather than subjective opinions. Also, the usage of function points for normalizing quality data and the direct measurement of defect removal efficiency levels would add a great deal of pragmatism and reality to the underlying ISO approaches.

In fact, software standards groups such as ISO, the IEEE, DoD, ANSI, etc., should consider the methods through which medical and pharmaceutical standards are set. Although medical standards are not perfect, their concept that a therapy should be proven to be effective and its side effects understood before it becomes a standard is missing from many software standards including ANSI, DoD, IEEE, ISO, and many others as well.

Software standards are normally totally published in a way that is totally devoid of empirical data regarding their effectiveness when the standards are first promulgated. The fact that there may possibly be negative or harmful side effects from following the standards is usually not even discussed, although negative side effects are a major section of medical and pharmaceutical standards.

It would be a strong statement that software is approaching the status of a real profession if software standards included information similar to medical and pharmaceutical standards on efficacy, counter-indications, known hazards, and potential side effects.

JAPANESE SOFTWARE QUALITY APPROACHES

Considering that Japan is an island country with minimal natural resources used by modern industry, the fact that it has developed one of the strongest economies in world history is largely intertwined with the fact that Japanese products have also achieved the highest quality levels in world history.

The success of modern Japanese products in electronics, automobiles, motorcycles, shipbuilding, optics, and other complex devices may lead to the conclusion that the quality of Japanese manufacturing is a recent phenomenon. However, Japan has a history of quality and craftsmanship that is several thousand years old.

In a number of technologies, such as lacquer ware, silk production, ceramics, steel making and sword making, fine carpentry, and jewelry making, Japanese quality levels have been high for as long as such artifacts have been created. For example, the steel itself and the quality of Japanese swords produced more than a thousand years ago rank as among the best in human history.

In the United States it is common to take some credit for the quality of Japanese manufactured goods since the work of the Americans W. Edwards Deming and Joseph Juran were so influential among Japanese manufacturers in the late 1940s and early 1950s.

However, neither Deming nor Juran would have been given much attention if there had not already been a strong interest in quality on the part of their Japanese students. What Deming and Juran accomplished was essentially showing how a strong personal drive to achieve quality could be channeled toward large-scale production where products were created by huge teams of workers rather than by individual craftsmen working alone.

Deming and Juran facilitated the industrialization of Japanese quality in large-scale manufacturing enterprises, but they did not have to awaken a basic interest in achieving high quality levels. That was already present in Japan.

In a software context, the on-site work which SPR has done in Japan indicates a tendency toward careful gathering of requirements and somewhat more careful design of software applications than U.S. norms, with a corresponding reduction in front-end defect levels.

For programming itself, Japanese programmers, U.S. programmers, and European programmers are roughly equivalent in making errors, although obviously there are huge personal differences in every country. However, Japanese programmers tend to be somewhat more industrious at desk checking and unit testing than is typical in the United States, with a corresponding elevation in defect removal efficiency. Very noticeable is the fact that "bad fix" injection rates tend to be lower in Japan than in the United States. Only in the case of documentation errors does the balance of software defects favor the United States.

Most Japanese programmers would be quite embarrassed if they turned over source code to a test or quality assurance group that would not even compile properly and had obvious bugs still present in it on the day of turnover. However, the phenomenon of programmers throwing buggy code "over the wall" to a test or QA group is distressingly common in the United States.

The following table gives rough differences between the United States and Japan, although the margin of error is high. It should be noted that much of SPR's work with Japanese companies has been in the area of high-technology products and software, and not so much with information systems, so there is a visible bias.

Of the six industries that stand out globally as having the best quality levels, SPR's data from Japan includes four: 1) computer manufacturing; 2) telecommunication manufacturing; 3) aerospace manufacturing; and 4) medical instrument manufacturing.

SPR has not been commissioned to explore Japanese defense and military software, although there is no reason to suspect that it would not also be part of the top six since military software has rather good quality levels in every country where studies are performed.

Also SPR has sparse data from Japanese commercial software houses. Another domain where SPR has no data is Japanese computer and software game industry, although observations at a distance indicates that the game industry has better tool capacities than almost any other.

Like every country Japan is heterogeneous in terms of software practices and results. In general the large high-technology corporations do a creditable job on software quality (i.e., Nippon Telegraph, Mitsubishi, Hitachi, Kozo Keikaku, NEC, etc.). Even within this set, not every lab nor every project is identical.

When smaller companies are examined, the results vary widely just as they do in the United States and Europe. However, the tendency to deal with requirements and design somewhat more formally than is common in the United States does tend to occur rather often, as can be seen by the following rough comparison in Table 1.

Table 1   Approximate Comparison of U.S. and Japanese Software Defect Potentials and Defect Removal Efficiency Levels

(Defects expressed in terms of defects per function point)

	U.S. Software Averages	Japanese Software Averages	Difference
Requirements	1.00	0.60	(0.40)
Design	1.25	1.15	(0.25)
Code	1.75	1.75	0.00
User documentation	0.60	0.75	0.15

(continued)

Table 1   *(continued)*

(Defects expressed in terms of defects per function point)

	U.S. Software Averages	Japanese Software Averages	Difference
Bad Fixes	0.40	0.25	(0.15)
TOTAL DEFECTS	5.00	4.50	(0.50)
Defect Removal Efficiency	85%	93%	7.0%
Delivered Defects	0.75	0.32	(0.43)

The average software quality results in Japan are somewhat superior to average software quality results in the U.S. or anywhere else for that matter. However, the "best in class" U.S. companies such as AT&T or Microsoft and the "best in class" Japanese companies such as Hitachi or Nippon Telegraph are virtually indistinguishable in final software quality results, even if they approach quality in slightly different ways.

It is a significant observation that for high-technology products at least, the Japanese attention to software quality tends to minimize time-to-market intervals and allows Japanese products to enter new markets slightly faster than any country from which SPR has collected data.

There is a tendency in the United States to be pejorative toward successful competitors. Many U.S. analysts have asserted that Japanese industry tends to be "fast followers" rather than leaders of innovation. This is a dangerous fallacy. The per capita rate of inventions and major patents (including U.S. patents) in Japan is approximately equal to that of the United States. In a number of high-technology arenas Japanese innovation has been "world-class" and outpaced other countries such as the United States.

The one major area where Japan lags behind both the United States and Europe is the adoption and utilization of function point metrics. While individual companies such as Kozo Keikaku Engineering, Nippon Telegraph, Nippon Steel, and others have experimented with function points and translated some of the function point literature, the overall deployment of function point metrics in Japan is far less advanced than in Australia, Canada, England, the United States, or almost any other industrialized country.

Following are brief discussions of some of the quality approaches that originated in Japan and are now starting to gain international recognition.

The Kaizen Approach to Continuous Improvement

The Kaizen approach is based on the view that improvements in final results can only be derived from continuous examination of both product quality and the process of development, followed by the steady chipping away of things that cause problems or obstacles to progress. In other words, careful analysis of problems and their causes followed by the elimination of those causes can gradually lead to excellence.

The Kaizen approach is the exact opposite of the "silver bullet" approach which is so common in the United States. (The phrase "silver bullet" is based on a famous horror movie called "The Werewolf" where bullets made out of silver were the only thing that could kill werewolves.)

In the United States, there is a tendency to focus on one thing and assume that something like buying a new CASE tool, adopting the object-oriented paradigm, or achieving ISO 9000 certification will trigger a miraculous improvement in software productivity, quality, schedules, or all three at once.

As this book is written, "process improvement" is the current "hot button" throughout the U.S. software domain, having replaced CASE (computer-aided software engineering) as the latest fad for software improvement in the mid-1990s. While both CASE and process improvement have some merit, neither is a total solution to software problems. Other U.S. hot buttons are "client/server projects" and the "object-oriented paradigm." Here, too, both concepts have merits but neither is a "silver bullet" that will create miraculous improvements.

The Kaizen approach leads to a different method of progress in Japan compared to the United States. Kaizen is based upon solid empirical data, statistical analysis, root cause analysis and other methods that are neither trivial nor inexpensive. A substantial amount of time on the part of both management and technical workers in Japan is devoted to analysis of the way things are done and to evaluating possible improvements.

In the United States, by contrast, changes often occur almost like religious conversions based on faith. A topic will become popular and then sweep through companies and even industries, whether there is tangible evidence or not.

Quality Circles

The concept of quality circles originated in the manufacturing and high-technology sectors where it has proven to be valuable not only in Japan but also in the United

States and Europe. The early quality circle approach surfaced in the 1950s as Japan began to rebuild major industries that were damaged during World War II.

The fundamental concept of quality circle is that of a group of employees who work in the same general area sharing data and ideas on improving the quality of their areas products and processes.

Quality circles are not just casual social groups, but are actually registered by a national organization in Japan. The quality circle concept is supported by the Japanese government and the executives of all major corporations.

The number of Japanese companies with quality circles tops 80%, and perhaps one Japanese worker out of every five is a member of a quality circle. Although there is some ambiguity in the data, it appears that quality circles in Japan are perhaps an order of magnitude more common than in the United States.

Quality circle members receive formal training in statistics, graphing methods, and root cause analysis, and they also receive useful tools such as statistical packages, chalkboards, graphic templates, and the like.

In Japan quality circles have also been applied to software and have been generally successful. In the United States quality circles have been attempted for software, but so far, most U.S. software quality circles have faded out in less than six months.

I'm not aware of equivalent research in Japan although no doubt it exists, but psychological studies of U.S. programmers such as those by Dr. Bill Curtis and Dr. Gerald Weinberg have found a very low need for social interaction. Since quality circles are built upon social interaction, this may explain why quality circles have not been visibly successful for U.S. software.

From my own visits to Japan and to Japanese software factories and labs, I have observed a somewhat more extensive set of social interactions among the Japanese programming community than is common among U.S. consulting clients.

Quality Function Deployment (QFD)

The topic of quality function deployment was first applied to manufactured products by Mitsubishi in 1972, and then later moved to software where it has so far been rather effective. The method is also termed "house of quality" because some of the diagrams produced resemble the peaked roof of a house.

The concept of quality function deployment is to create an exhaustive list of the quality factors in a product that are important to users and customers. In fact users and customers are interviewed or participate, so it is obvious that QFD works best for products where potential customers are readily available.

Once the customer quality criteria are collected, the factors which the development group must pay attention to in order to satisfy the requirements are then worked out. The QFD approach utilizes rather large and complex matrices, graphs, and other visual aids for showing the relationship between customer requirements and development responses to those requirements.

Here in the United States, QFD is also being applied to software by high-technology companies such as AT&T, Motorola, IBM, and the like. Here, too, the method is proving to be valuable.

The QFD method in the United States has thus far been applied primarily to large and complex systems software projects such as telephone switching systems, process control systems, and engineering software projects. However, the QFD approach would also be valuable for management information systems and also for outsource projects such as the software Electronic Data Systems (EDS) builds for General Motors.

By fortunate coincidence QFD fits nicely into the requirements gathering method known as Joint Application Design or JAD which is one of the most effective software front-end approaches for collecting and clarifying user requirements.

Adding QFD sessions during the early requirements gathering stage appears to be one of the most effective defect prevention methods yet discovered. Although the data from the United States is still sparse, the combination of Joint Application Design, Quality Function Deployment, and prototyping as used on some Japanese MIS projects appear to reduce the rate of creeping requirements from roughly 2% per month down to less than 0.5% per month.

Software Factories

The phrase "software factory" normally refers to a significant critical mass of software technical personnel and ancillary personnel who work in a shared facility with very good tool sets, communication facilities, education facilities, and the like. The typical sizes of software factories run from about 150 total personnel up to more than 5,000 software personnel.

The name "software factory" was first applied to Japanese software facilities such as those run by Hitachi, Toshiba, and Fujitsu. Because "software factory" has a certain appeal, the name quickly became popular in the press in the 1970s and was usually associated with Japan.

However, similar software development and research facilities can be found all over the world, although they are not always called "factories." For example, since the 1960s IBM's systems software has been built in large software laboratories averaging more than 1,000 personnel. Similar organizations can also be found in other large corporations such as AT&T, Siemens-Nixdorf, Microsoft, Motorola, and the like.

There is comparatively little difference between an IBM software laboratory, an AT&T software development lab, Microsoft's campus in Redmond, and a Japanese software factory. The Motorola software lab in India is also the logical equivalent of a software factory, and that particular facility has achieved a level of 5 on the SEI capability maturity model (CMM).

Regardless of the country in which they occur, software factories have shown themselves to be very efficient in terms of both software quality and software productivity. For example, among SPR's client base, the software that originates in software factories and/or large software laboratories approaches 95% in cumulative defect removal efficiency levels, or 10% higher than U.S. norms.

As a class, software factories tend to be effective in a number of important quality control approaches: 1) defect prevention; 2) non-test defect removal; 3) quality measurements; 4) testing by trained specialists; 5) quality education and training; 6) quality analysis and root cause analysis; and 7) post-release software quality control.

Net productivity rates for software factories are somewhat higher than U.S. averages, but still only about 6 function per staff month. However, given the fact that the projects created in software factories are both large and complex, that level of productivity is remarkably good and roughly twice what results from isolated software groups attempting to build large systems.

There are some social and career advantages associated with software factories too. For one thing, having a concentrated critical mass of software personnel means that on-site education and training are readily available. So are opportunities for informal discussions and information sharing with colleagues.

The software factories also interact with universities and in several cases have formed collaborative arrangements with universities whose curricula support the needs of the factory.

In addition, the factories provide a very useful resource for the universities in several ways. For one, the factories often fund academic research programs and provide consulting opportunities for faculty members. For another, the factories tend to have large-scale summer intern programs which employ many software engineering and computer science undergraduates. (Microsoft's summer hire program is so extensive that it tends to fill up the parking lots, available offices, and even convert some conference rooms into temporary offices to hold all the students who have temporary jobs.)

The large numbers of software personnel also open up technical and managerial career paths. When software organizations are scattered through a company in little pockets, they usually don't offer many long-range opportunities for advancement. This means that a well-managed software factory with 1,000 technical staff will have many possible career paths. This results in higher morale levels and lower levels of voluntary attrition than are typical with scattered and fragmented software groups.

In addition, software factories are usually well equipped with tools (> 75,000 function points of tools per software engineer) and also are well supported by specialists such as quality assurance, testing, maintenance, technical writing, database administration, and the like. Indeed, both Japanese and U.S. software factories often have measurement specialists in both quality and productivity areas, although the U.S. is far ahead in employing certified function point specialists.

Roughly 35% of the technical employment in large software factories consist of ancillary personnel who are not programmers or software engineers but whose jobs make software engineering more efficient and effective. Overall, the software factory concept works well in every country and the large Japanese software factories are proving to be highly effective, as are equivalent factories in other countries.

Total Quality Management (TQM)

There is some interesting debate in the literature on whether the concepts of total quality management (TQM) originated in Japan, the United States, or elsewhere. The lineage of total quality management is studded with well-known quality researchers from multiple countries such as Phil Crosby, W. Edwards Deming, Armand Feigenbaum, Kaoru Ishikawa, Joseph Juran, and W.A. Shewart.

The earliest citations on TQM appear in the 1940s just after World War II, which is long before software was a major industry. Regardless of who first invented the concepts of TQM, there is no doubt that the TQM approach has been more widely deployed in Japan than anywhere else, and that it was deployed earlier.

Based on defect statistics of product failures and in stereo equipment, television sets, appliances, automobiles, and high-technology electronics published in journals such as *Consumer Reports,* it also looks as though TQM is somewhat more successful in Japan than elsewhere. At any case the first-year failure rates of Japanese products are usually among the best in the world.

The exact origin of TQM is less important than two key questions:

1)   Does TQM work for software?

2)   Does software TQM work better in Japan than in the U.S. or Europe?

Unfortunately, all three of the terms in total quality management are somewhat ambiguous when applied to software:

1)   What exactly does "total" mean in a software context?

2)   What exactly does "quality" mean in a software context?

3)   What exactly does "management" mean in a software context?

The fundamental concepts of total quality management are that quality in a delivered product is the result of quality in the process used to build the product. Thus, the word "total" must include everything delivered to customers and all of the methods used in production.

Further, the kind of quality that is important is based on opinion of the users of a product. What they think is more important than what the software developers or QA personnel think. Thus, the word "quality" must center around the user perception of quality.

Finally, quality in either products or process cannot occur unless the entire organization wants it to occur. That is executives, managers, and technical staff must all have a common vision of quality and their actions must be congruent with that vision. Since technical workers cannot independently achieve high quality levels if management obstructs the process, the word "management" implies that all supervisory and management personnel are supportive of quality.

From observations on both sides of the Pacific and both sides of the Atlantic as well, the TQM approach seems a better fit in Japan than elsewhere, but even in Japan it has not yet demonstrated an overwhelming impact on software projects.

Among SPR's clients using the TQM approach, their software quality levels are sometimes better than the norms for their industries, sometimes average, and sometimes worse. There is no clear-cut empirical evidence that TQM reduces software defect potentials or raises software defect removal efficiency levels of software, although there is such evidence in the hardware and manufacturing domains.

JOINT APPLICATION DESIGN (JAD)

The requirements analysis method of joint application design (JAD) originated in the IBM Toronto programming laboratory circa 1984. The JAD approach rapidly proved to be valuable for gathering the requirements of management information systems (MIS) and is now possibly the most widely utilized method for MIS requirements in Canada, the United States, and much of the rest of the world. Among our MIS clients, about 80% now utilize the JAD approach or a variant.

The distribution of usage patterns among our clients is interesting. At the corporate or enterprise level, about 500 out of 600 client organizations utilize JAD on at least some of their projects. However, at the project level those which utilized JAD constitute only about 1,500 out of 7,000.

The reason for this anomaly is because JAD is aimed at projects where the users are active participants in the requirements sessions. This fact means that many kinds of software may not find JAD to be appropriate, such as high-volume software with millions of users or specialized software embedded in hardware.

With the JAD concept, both the client side and the MIS software side work together in a structured manner to develop the requirements, using the services of a trained facilitator to keep the process on track. The facilitator can either be an outside consultant from one of the many JAD consulting groups, or an in-house employee who has received training in the JAD methodology.

Both the client and MIS sides agree to an uninterrupted time commitment and the JAD sessions are often held off-site to minimize disruptions. A typical JAD requirements gathering and analysis session can take as little time as a few days, or as much time as six weeks based upon the size and complexity of the resulting application. A rough planning guideline for JAD sessions would be expressed in Table 1.

Table 1   JAD Staffing and Schedule Durations for Requirements Gathering and Analysis

Size of Application in Function Points	Schedule in Work Days	Software Representatives	Client Representatives
1	0.5	1	1
10	1.0	1	1
100	2.0	1	2
1000	5.0	2	4
10000	15.0	5	6
100000	30.0	10	15

The results of a JAD requirements process are single requirements specification which both the client side and the software development side agree to. This specification will average about 0.25 pages per function point, so for larger systems it can be seen that the requirements are rather substantial. The advantage of JAD-based requirements versus "traditional" requirements is that they are more complete, and also have fewer "rough edges" that can slow down development later.

It is an interesting observation that IFPUG function points, British Mark II function points, and feature points can all be derived very easily from JAD-based requirements because such requirements include the topics that are used for function and feature point sizing, i.e.,

- Algorithms

- Entities and relationships

- Logical files

- Inputs

- Outputs

- Inquiries

In addition to these basic elements, the supplemental complexity adjustment factors are also defined during the JAD sessions themselves. This means that a rather accurate quantification of application size using functional metrics is a useful output from JAD-based requirements gathering.

Indeed, sometimes software cost estimating tools are used toward the end of the JAD sessions to determine the approximate costs, schedules, and quality of the application in a near real-time fashion.

The observed empirical effects of JAD-based requirements offer three benefits compared to gathering requirements in a "traditional" unstructured manner:

- JAD-based requirements usually contain less than 0.15 defects per function point as opposed to about 0.75 defects per function point for traditional requirements.

- The rate of requirements "creep" with JAD-based requirements is less than 0.25% per month later, as opposed to more than 1% per month with traditional requirements.

- The sociology of JAD requirements minimizes antagonism and friction between the client community and the MIS community.

While JAD-based requirements gathering are often effective, the method is not a panacea. In fact, for some kinds of software JAD-based requirements do not work at all. It is obvious that JAD works best for applications where the client community is finite and has some definite set of requirements to work toward. Thus, JAD is effective for in-house MIS applications for specific departments or work groups where all users will have requirements that are relatively homogeneous.

For other kinds of applications, the JAD method cannot be applied or is not very effective. For example, a commercial software product such as a word processor or spreadsheet might have millions of users, all of whom have slightly different needs and requirements. One cannot find a representative set of users to participate in JAD sessions for this kind of high-volume software.

There are other kinds of software, such as the embedded software controlling automobile fuel injection systems, where the "users" may not even know that software is present. Of course, automotive engineers designing the engine are surrogate users, but for this kind of high-technology application JAD will not affect the users themselves.

The JAD approach can be coupled with other requirements analysis methods in a synergistic manner. See the sections on Prototyping and Quality Function Deployment or QFD for two other requirements approaches that are frequently coupled with the JAD method.

Prior to the development of the JAD approach, requirements gathering and requirements analysis were both informal and often adversarial. The user group would put together a rough statement of the need for a new application and present it to the MIS software director, who in turn would assign one or more analysts to work with the users on expanding and refining the original statement.

The process of gathering and refining the requirements did not satisfy either side. The client side often felt that the software group was unresponsive, critical, and sometimes arrogant. The software side felt that the user community might be asking for impossible results or could not make up their minds about what they wanted. Before very long, both sides disliked each other and the requirements suffered as a result.

KIVIAT GRAPHS

The phrase "Kiviat Graphs" refers to a form of graph that uses multiple axes extending from a central point. In the United States the name "Kiviat Graph" refers to a software researcher, Phil Kiviat, who used this graphic representation.

This is a misnomer, and the actual graphing approach is far older than the software industry. However, this form of graph is very widely used for displaying multiple aspects of software quality information simultaneously.

Figure 1 is an example of such a graph.

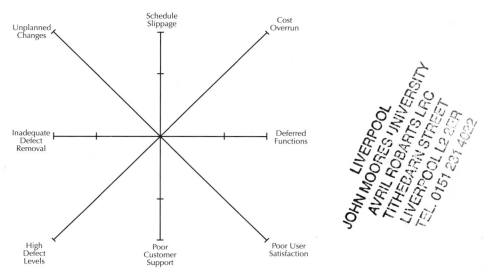

Figure 1 Sample Kiviat Graph of Selected Software Quality Topics

Although such graphs are widely used, there is no consistency in either the contents or the format of Kiviat graphs. For example, the central point can be used either as the origin point or the target point. The number of axes can vary from as few as three to as many as a dozen, and each axis can stand for any desired topic.

The most common use of Kiviat graphs is for executive presentations and for comparisons between projects or business units. The approach has the advantage that it makes quite a few factors visible at the same time.

MICROSOFT'S QUALITY METHODS

Because Microsoft has made so much money in the software marketplace, many companies are attempting to imitate "the Microsoft methods" with varying degrees of success, although most usually do not experience very great success.

A strong caution is indicated to those who are trying to pattern themselves after Microsoft. The capabilities of the Microsoft management teams and the capabilities of the technical personnel are among the best in the world. Microsoft's recruiting and appraisal programs tend to optimize the selection of highly qualified individuals and to rapidly weed out marginal performers.

Unless your company has an extensive summer intern program, uses multi-stage employment interviews, uses pre-employment skill testing to ascertain technical qualifications, and has an appraisal system that rapidly weeds out the marginal performers you may not be able to imitate Microsoft.

Also, since Microsoft has plenty of money to spare, they are not cheap when it comes to tools and support. To do what Microsoft does for quality, a company can plan spending about $15,000 per software staff member and more than $20,000 per project manager for improved tools and better training. It may also have to hire quite a few more testing personnel, as well.

Microsoft is evolving like every other company, and the quality methods used from 1995 are by no means the same as those used 10 years ago in 1985. The evolution of quality control in Microsoft is largely due to the fact that the sizes of Microsoft's applications are now as large or larger than mainframe software. For example, Windows 95 is about 87,000 function points in size, which is roughly the same size as IBM's MVS operating system, and larger than UNIX. Windows NT is in the same size category. Modern PC applications and operating systems are virtually the same size as mainframe software, and need the same kind of rigor.

The essential aspects of Microsoft's quality approaches include the following:

- State-of-the-art evaluation and recruiting methods

- Excellent training of technical and management personnel

- Expanding usage of formal pre-test inspections

- State-of-the-art testing using trained testing personnel

- A ratio of less than 1500 function points per tester

- State-of-the-art configuration control and daily product builds

- State-of-the-art defect tracking methods during development

- High-volume external Beta testing with > 10,000 clients

- State-of-the-art customer defect tracking methods after release

The results of these combined quality approaches places Microsoft among the small set of companies that averages more than 95% in cumulative defect removal efficiency levels, which is about 10% higher than U.S. averages overall, and about 15% higher than the averages found on projects > 5,000 function points which is where almost every Windows-based application is now found.

This is not to say that Microsoft is perfect in terms of quality control and defect removal efficiency. However, among 100 other commercial software companies, it is unlikely to find more than two whose quality results are equal to Microsoft, and none will be found whose quality is significantly better.

Microsoft has integrated the testing and quality assurance functions rather than having separate groups, which is mildly surprising but seems to work for the Microsoft culture. However, Microsoft is not understaffed in terms of testing and quality assurance personnel as are many companies. The Microsoft ratio of test personnel to function points seems to require that each tester deal with less than 1,500 function points, as opposed to each tester dealing with more than 5,000 function points which is common in many companies.

Microsoft itself still has some room to improve. Surprisingly, for a company with such a large research budget, Microsoft lags in software metrics technology and is only just beginning to explore function point metrics.

As might be expected Microsoft is a world leader in pure testing approaches and also in configuration control approaches. In fact, in terms of overall tool capacity Microsoft tends to have more of everything than almost any other company in the world, and why not? A corporation with Microsoft's revenue and profit levels can afford any tools they want, and can build others too.

The "leading" column of the following table of tool capacities illustrates the Microsoft tool set rather nicely. The double asterisks (**) indicate the tool components that Microsoft markets commercially.

Table 1   Software Tool Capacity Expressed in Terms of Function Points

Corporate Business	Lagging	Average	Leading	
Budgeting	500	750	1,250	
Variance reporting		500	750	
Strategic planning		1,000	2,500	
Competitive analysis		1,000	2,500	
Bus. Proc. Re. (BPR)		750	1,000	
Data administration		500	750	
Market planning		250	750	
Software asset mgt.			1,500	
Subtotal	*500*	*4,750*	*11,000*	

General Support Tools	Lagging	Average	Leading	
Spreadsheets	750	1,250	2,500	**
Graphics/presentations		1,250	2,000	**
Word processors	500	1,000	2,500	**
Database	500	1,000	1,500	**
Electronic mail		500	1,500	**
Internet access/browsing		1,500	2,500	**
Intranet support		1,500	2,500	**
Calendar management	100	300	750	**
Phone numbers	100	150	500	**
Subtotal	*1,950*	*8,450*	*16,250*	

(continued)

Table 1   *(continued)*

Project Management	Lagging	Average	Leading	
Project planning	1,000	1,250	2,500	**
Project estimating			2,500	
Risk analysis			1,500	
Resource tracking	300	750	1,500	**
Milestone tracking			500	**
Project measurement			1,250	
Statistical analysis			3,000	
Function point analysis		250	750	
Backfiring: LOC to FP			750	
Lines of code counting		250	250	
Methodology management		750	1,500	
Value analysis support			500	
Assessment support		500	2,000	
Benchmark support			500	
Subtotal	*1,300*	*3,750*	*19,000*	

Requirements Tools	Lagging	Average	Leading	
JAD Support		250	500	
QFD Support			1,000	
Prototyping		1,000	2,500	**
Build/buy analysis			1,500	
Cost/benefit analysis			1,500	
Subtotal	*0*	*1,250*	*7,000*	

Design Tools	Lagging	Average	Leading
General design tools	500	1,500	3,000
GUI design tools	750	1,500	2,500
Data modeling		500	1,000
Database design	500	750	1,000
Reverse engineering		1,000	3,000
Design reuse analysis			1,500
Subtotal	*1,750*	*5,250*	*12,000*

(continued)

Table 1   *(continued)*

Development Tools	Lagging	Average	Leading	
Assemblers	750	1,250	2,000	**
Compilers	750	1,500	2,500	**
Program generators		1,500	2,500	**
Database query languages	1,000	1,500	2,500	**
Code editors	750	1,250	2,500	**
Debugging tools	250	500	750	**
Capture/playback		500	750	**
Virus protection		500	750	**
Configuration control	500	750	2,000	
Code reuse analysis			1,500	**
Subtotal	*4,000*	*9,250*	*17,750*	

Maintenance Support	Lagging	Average	Leading
Customer contact support			1,500
Complexity analysis		500	1,000
Defect tracking	500	750	1,000
Reverse engineering		1,000	3,000
Reengineering		1,250	3,000
Code restructuring		1,000	1,500
Code reuse analysis			1,500
Year 2000 analysis			1,500
Subtotal	*500*	*4,500*	*14,000*

Quality Assurance	Lagging	Average	Leading
QFD Support			1,000
TQM Support			1,000
Quality estimation			2,000
Reliability estimation			1,000
Inspection support			1,000
Defect tracking	500	750	1,000
Complexity analysis		500	1,000
Subtotal	*500*	*1,250*	*8,000*

(continued)

Table 1 *(continued)*

Testing			
Test-case generation			1,250
Test path coverage	100	200	350
Test-case execution		200	350
Capture/playback		500	750
Defect tracking	500	750	1,000
Test library control	250	750	1,000
Complexity analysis		500	1,000
Data quality analysis			1,250
Subtotal	*850*	*2,900*	*6,950*

Documentation Support	Lagging	Average	Leading	
Word processing	500	1,000	2,500	**
Grammar checking			500	**
Spell checking		200	200	**
Dictionary/thesaurus			500	**
Desktop publishing	500		2,500	**
Graphics support	500	500	2,500	**
Hypertext support		250	500	**
Multimedia support		750	2,000	**
Text virus elimination			250	
Scanning support			300	**
Subtotal	*1,500*	*2,700*	*11,750*	
TOTALS	**12,850**	**44,050**	**123,700**	

It is interesting that Microsoft markets tools commercially that cover more than a fourth of the total tool capacity associated with software development. It can be hypothesized that eventually Microsoft would like to market tools that cover 100% of the software engineering space, and probably the project management and quality assurance space as well.

In round numbers, a well-equipped software engineering and management staff will need from roughly 45,000 to more than 125,000 function points per staff member. For companies whose software staffs support multiple platforms (i.e., DOS, Windows, OS/2, UNIX, MVS, VMS, etc.) the needs will be even greater, because of the current need to duplicate at least some tools for each environment.

From performing software assessment and baseline studies for several hundred companies, the tooling differences between the leaders and the laggards are striking and significant. In general, the laggards are under equipped in terms of overall tool capacities and severely under equipped in critical areas such as quality control and project management. The laggards also have a greater tendency to use low-end tools with minimal functionality.

While both the laggards and the leaders may have similar tools available for software engineering, the laggards tend to have less than 500 function points of project management tools, and less than 1,000 function points of quality assurance tools available.

Leaders such as Microsoft, IBM, AT&T, etc., usually deploy more than 15,000 function points of project management tools and more than 5,000 function points of both testing and quality assurance tools. This imbalance leads to significant differences in terms of schedule and cost estimation accuracy, quality levels achieved, and user-satisfaction levels.

There are also interesting differences among industries. For example, software game vendors and the large commercial software vendors such as Microsoft usually have the most extensive suites of software engineering tools, and may exceed 100,000 function points in total capacity.

Yet the companies that build very large systems such as telecommunications companies and computer manufacturers usually have the most complete suites of software project management tools. These same companies, plus defense contractors, are often the best equipped with quality assurance tool suites.

The approach of using function points to evaluate software tools is still new and still experimental. The results to date are interesting, but not yet fully definitive. Even so, a method that can add realism to vendor claims is worth exploring.

The overall impression that Microsoft gives is having some of the best managers and software technical staff members in the world, supported by probably the largest collection of tools in the world.

In terms of methodologies, Microsoft tends to follow its own path and can take or leave what the rest of the industry does. In other words, Microsoft does not bother to blindly follow the current fad although they are certainly interested in keeping current on the state-of-the-art.

For example, as Microsoft's key products grew to mainframe proportions and approached 100,000 function points it became obvious that approaches such as design and code inspections needed to be added to the arsenal of Microsoft approaches.

It will be interesting to see if Microsoft's continued rapid growth allows it to keep the same approaches that have been successful to date.

MULTIPLE RELEASE QUALITY MEASUREMENTS

One of the most troublesome aspects of software quality measurement is that of measuring quality over long time spans and multiple releases of a software product. There are several ways of recording the data, and one of the more common ways tends to exaggerate quality and give an incorrect impression. Following is a simplified example to show the right and wrong ways of dealing with multiple release quality measures. This example uses artificial data and assumes more bugs than would be normal, in order to illustrate the underlying mathematics of the situation.

Assume that release 1 of a software product is 1,000 function points in size, and contains software 1000 defects on the day it is put into production with customers. In the course of the first year of usage, customers find and report 500 defects back to the vendors. For this first release, there is no real ambiguity. The number of reported defects per function point is 0.5.

Assume that release 2 of the product comes out one year later. This is a small release that is 100 function points in size and contains 100 software defects. In the course of the second year of usage, customers find and report 50 of the bugs that are local to the new release, and they find another 250 bugs that were still latent in the original release.

The question that is somewhat ambiguous in the literature is that of normalizing the data for the second release.

Method 1: Aggregation of all data into one set

The first and most common method for reporting the quality data for the second year is to ignore the fact of two releases, and simply aggregate the total results. Under this method, the product is sized at 1,100 function points and the old and new defects are added together, i.e., 300 defects were found. This method gives a result of 0.27 bugs per function point. With this method, quality seems to have improved notably which is not the true situation for the second release.

Method 2: Aggregation of all data against the second release

Another method for normalizing and reporting the data is to report all bugs against the second releases. Using method 2, the 250 old bugs and the 50 new bugs would both be counted against the 100 function point size of the second release. The result is a total of 3 bugs per function point. Using method 2, the follow-on release looks much worse than it really is because all of the older, latent bugs are counted against it.

Method 3: Keep release to release statistics

The most accurate and realistic way of recording data for multiple releases is the most difficult. This method requires keeping statistics from release to release and doing multiple reporting.

With method 3, the 250 bugs found in the original release would be reported against the original 1,000 function points. The 50 bugs found in the second release would be reported against the 100 function points that is comprised. Thus, the first release defect level is 0.25 bugs per function point, but the defect level of the second release is 0.5 bugs per function point.

After the second release, the complexity of the problem is compounded by the fact that now you have latent defects in two prior releases. Most companies cannot continue to track errors against specific releases forever, so the most effective practice is to record defect counts against the current release until the next release comes out. All prior releases are then aggregated together as part of the base product.

The following table shows a 10 year continuation of the situation. Note that although the cumulative results give the impression that quality has been improving steadily and rapidly, in fact each new release has just as many bugs as the one before it.

Table 1   10 Year Sequence of Software Enhancements and Defect Reports

	Release Size in Func. Pts.	Product Size in Func. Pts.	Defects Reported	Current Release Defects per Func. Pt.	Cumulative Release Defects per Func. Pt.
Year 1	1000	1000	500	0.5	0.50
Year 2	100	1100	300	0.5	0.27
Year 3	100	1200	175	0.5	0.15
Year 4	100	1300	110	0.5	0.08
Year 5	100	1400	80	0.5	0.06
Year 6	100	1500	80	0.5	0.05
Year 7	100	1600	80	0.5	0.05
Year 8	100	1700	80	0.5	0.05
Year 9	100	1800	80	0.5	0.04
Year 10	100	1900	80	0.5	0.04

Note that the example as illustrated in the table is artificial, but it illustrates that statistics can be very deceiving. After 10 full years of having the same number of bugs in every release, the overall data is moving toward almost zero-defects and gives the false impression of steadily improving quality levels.

Although the product's development cycle has not shown any real improvement at all in how each release is developed, the overall results appear to grow steadily better over time. This is due of course to the delusional affect of having a steadily growing base product that over time has eliminated the bulk of the original defects.

The only way to judge real progress is to go to the effort of keeping release to release statistics. Whenever specific release defects are divided by total product size, the results will be artificial and look much better than they really are.

OBJECT-ORIENTED QUALITY LEVELS

The object-oriented (OO) world has been on an explosive growth path. The usage of OO methods has now reached a sufficient critical mass to have created dozens of books, several OO magazines, and frequent conferences such as OOPSLA and Object World.

Among SPR's clients, about 150 companies out of 600 are exploring or using object-oriented technologies, although most are still climbing the learning curve. The total number of OO projects in our knowledge base is about 600 out of almost 7000, but about 100 are new projects started since 1994. (Since new data is arriving at a rate of perhaps 50 projects per month, there is no fixed number of projects reflecting any specific technology.)

Unfortunately, this explosion of interest in OO methodologies has not carried over into the domain of software quality. There are a number of citations on software testing, but little or no empirical data on actual software quality levels associated with the OO paradigm.

From SPR's assessment and benchmark results of OO projects, it appears that object-oriented languages such as C++, Objective C, Eiffel, and SMALLTALK may have reduced defect levels compared to normal procedural languages such as C or COBOL or FORTRAN. Defect potentials for OO languages are perhaps in the range of 1.0 to 1.5 defects per function point, as opposed to the range of 1.5 to 3.25 per function point for normal procedural languages.

However, the defect potentials for object-oriented analysis and design have not yet showed any reduction, and indeed often exceed the 1.25 defects per function point associated with the older standard analysis and design approaches such as Yourdon, Warnier-Orr, and Gane & Sarson. Some projects using OO analysis and design for the first time have topped 3.0 defects per function point, which is a very large number indeed and indicative of very complex situations and a steep learning curve.

Unfortunately, not only do OO analysis and design show an increase in defect potentials but OO analysis and design tend to have a high rate of abandonment. In both the United States and the United Kingdom, the first-time users of OO analysis and design give up or bring in other methods about 50% of the time. This is a very significant failure rate.

Some projects that don't abandon OO analysis and design find it necessary to augment the OO approach with standard design methods in order to complete the project. There is obviously a steep learning curve associated with most of the current flavors of OO analysis and design, and steep learning curves are usually associated with high levels of errors and defects.

There is not yet enough data available in 1996 to reach a definite conclusion about what happens after the learning curve is climbed since most of our clients are still on the upward slope. But there is not yet any convincing published evidence that OO quality levels are dramatically better than non-OO quality levels for OO analysis and design. In fact, for analysis and design the weight of current evidence is unfavorable for OO design for the first year, marginally unfavorable for years two and three of OO use, and eventually becomes more optimistic circa the third and fourth years of utilization of the OO paradigm.

The data on OO programming languages is available in larger quantities and is both better and somewhat more convincing, but still needs more exploration. On theoretical grounds it can be claimed that OO quality levels should be better, due to inheritance and class libraries. However, that which is inherited and the class libraries themselves need to be validated carefully before theory and practice coincide.

Against the background of U.S. averages, the empirical quality results observed on OO projects are a mixed bag. Coding defects are reduced, but front-end defects associated with analysis, and design tend to be elevated for the first year after adoption of the OO paradigm due to the steepness of the learning curve.

Following are some preliminary results with a high margin of error that compares "average" procedural projects using conventional structured design and languages such as COBOL and FORTRAN with OO projects using either the Booch or Rumbaugh OO analysis and design methods and OO languages such as Objective C and C++. The data is expressed in terms of "defects per function point."

Table 1   Comparison of Procedural and Object-Oriented Defect Potentials

Defect Origins	Procedural Projects	Object-Oriented Projects	Difference
Requirements	1.00	1.10	0.10
Design	1.25	1.65	0.40
Coding	1.75	1.15	(0.60)
Documents	0.60	0.60	0.00
Bad Fixes	0.40	0.35	0.05
Total	*5.00*	*4.85*	*(0.15)*
Defect removal efficiency	85%	85%	0.00
Delivered defects	0.75	0.72	(0.03)

As this handbook is being prepared, Grady Booch and James Rumbaugh are working on a consolidated OO analysis and design approach that will minimize the differences between their methods, and perhaps shorten the learning curve leading to a full understanding of OO analysis and design. Peter Coad's work on OO design is also gaining favor. However, no data is yet available on the newer versions and the prior versions have had a steep learning curve.

The OO paradigm is on a fast growth path and the theoretical potential looks exciting. Many technologies are troublesome when they are first being developed, and the OO technology is complex enough so that many people do experience start-up problems. My observation is that you should expect a reduction in both productivity and quality for the first 12 months of OO usage, and you can also expect to have very notable problems in your first experience with OO analysis and design.

On the other hand, some people had trouble learning to ski, to drive a car, and to get up on water skis. Learning to play golf well can also take quite a few years. If you persevere, you eventually get past the hard start-up problems and gain the benefits. The same observation may be true for the object-oriented paradigm.

Gaps in the OO Literature and Research Programs

The OO community has been rather lax about collecting empirical data, but rather bold in making assertions of greatly improved productivity, costs, schedules, and quality without enough solid data to make the claims totally convincing.

Much of the OO literature asserts that substantial gains should be accrued in terms of both software productivity and quality as a result using OO analysis, design, coding, and reusable material. However, with few exceptions there are no publications that contain any quantitative data at all.

One of the very few OO books to even attempt such a quantification is Dr. Tom Love's *Object Lessons* (SIGS Books, New York, 1993), but the data is tantalizing rather than definitive. Dr. Love's use of function point metrics to demonstrate the power of the OO approach is commendable, but the lack of any details about how the data was collected and what activities were included makes it difficult to replicate or even analyze the results.

Dr. Chris Kemerer of MIT has been working on the problem of OO metrics, and his initial findings are interesting. However, the set of metrics he proposes have the disadvantage of not being backwards compatible with non-OO projects. Hence, the set of Kemerer OO metrics cannot be used for comparisons between OO projects and non-OO projects.

While some of Kemerer's metric topics such as depth of inheritance and weighted methods per class are relevant to OO projects, there is no easy way of comparing Kemerer's OO results to normal procedural projects.

On the whole, the quantitative results to date of using OO methods is essentially too sparse to either validate or challenge the claims of improved productivity and quality levels. The absence of definitive data makes one wonder what the OO claims are actually based on, however.

Software quality improvements derive from two fundamental principles: 1) reducing defect potentials, and 2) improving defect removal efficiency. It is being claimed on theoretical grounds associated with inheritance and reuse that the OO approach should reduce defect potentials. However, there is a fundamental question:

- What are OO ranges and averages for potential defect levels in requirements, design, source code, user documents, and "bad fix" injections?

This question has basically no citations in the OO literature other than this book and some earlier studies using the similar data such as my article on "The Economics of Object-Oriented Software" in the October 1994 issue of Ed Yourdon's *American Programmer* magazine.

The other part of the quality equation, or defect removal efficiency, has essentially no citations at all in the OO literature. Since formal inspections are the most effective known way of eliminating software defects, software quality assurance personnel are anxiously awaiting some kind of guidance and quantitative data on the use of inspections with OO projects:

- Do OO design inspections have the same defect removal efficiency levels as for older design methods?

- Do OO code inspections have the same defect removal efficiency levels as when inspecting procedural languages?

- What are the ranges of software defects residing within class libraries?

The topic of testing in the OO domain is also sparsely represented in the literature. However, at least for testing there are now several books and a growing sample of conference papers so the topic is not without any citations at all.

However, there are a number of fundamental quality questions for the OO community that are in need of more definitive answers:

- How many test-case per function point are needed for OO projects of various sizes and classes?

- What is the incidence of bad test cases for OO projects?

- What is the optimal series of test stages for OO projects?

- Are there any OO projects that have topped 99% in cumulative defect removal efficiency levels?

- Is the average defect removal efficiency level for OO projects better or worse than U.S. norms of about 85%?

There are many important questions concerning OO quality levels, but a shortage of solid empirical answers.

Since the Internet has made global research easy, it is perhaps significant that I have received no fewer than 50 e-mail requests for OO productivity and quality data that all begin with phrases similar to the following:

"I'm doing research on the quantified effects of object-oriented methods on software productivity and quality, and can find no empirical studies but only vague claims...."

Many of these requests are from university students working on master's theses in software engineering and computer science. It is a step in the right direction that universities are tackling the key issues of the software engineering domain, and I hope these research programs will turn up convincing data and solid studies.

One of the basic problems with collecting empirical data on OO projects is how can they be measured? It can be stated flatly that "lines of code" will not show OO productivity or quality in a satisfactory way.

The newer OO metrics such as Kemerer's MOOSE suite (Metrics of Object Oriented Systems Environment) are probably useful in an OO context, but have no value in doing cross-comparisons between OO projects and older procedural projects. The function point metric seems to be the best current choice for dealing with the OO paradigm and for comparing quality and productivity results between OO projects and conventional procedural projects.

Object-Oriented Reusability

One of the most striking claims of the OO literature is for substantial volumes of reusable material. In theory at least high levels of reuse for some deliverables, such as design and code, would seem to be an integral result from the class library and inheritance concept that is a fundamental part of the OO paradigm.

Here too, unfortunately, there are some notable gaps and omissions in the OO literature on a very important topic. In my book *Patterns of Software Systems Failure and Success* (International Thomson Computer Press, 1996) there are 12 potentially reusable artifacts associated with software projects.

The OO literature to date has addressed four of the 12 in depth, four sparsely, and of the remaining four the OO literature has not yet touched upon the topics at all.

For a technology whose literature stresses reuse as a major virtue, having sparse coverage or no coverage for two-thirds of the potentially reusable artifacts is a sign that the OO community needs much more rigorous study into what "reuse" really means in a software context.

The following table summarizes the status of the dozen reusable software artifacts and divides them into categories of adequate, sparse, and no OO coverage.

Table 2   Gaps in the Coverage of Object-Oriented Reusability Literature

Reusable Artifact	Coverage in the OO Literature
Reusable estimates	No current OO literature
Reusable plans	No current OO literature
Reusable user documentation	No current OO literature
Reusable requirements	No current OO literature
Reusable human interfaces	Sparse citations in OO literature
Reusable screens	Sparse citations in OO literature
Reusable test plans	Sparse citations in OO literature
Reusable test cases	Sparse citations in OO literature
Reusable architecture	Adequate citations in OO literature
Reusable data	Adequate citations in OO literature
Reusable design	Adequate citations in OO literature
Reusable code	Adequate citations in OO literature

The lack of any substantial OO literature dealing with two-thirds of all possible reusable artifacts is a sign that the OO approach has not yet fully come to grips with reusability as a serious technology.

Somewhat surprisingly, even for reusable code which is a key assertion of the object-oriented literature, the current leader in terms of the volume of reusable material available is not an object-oriented programming language at all. Microsoft's Visual Basic has created an entire subindustry of third party companies selling reusable custom controls that work with the basic language and the Visual Basic programming environment. Whether by accident or by design, Visual Basic has more reusable components than any current object-oriented programming language.

A final point about software reuse is that successful reuse programs require essentially zero-defect levels in the reused artifacts. Reusing buggy material will generate massive recalls and catastrophic expense levels which degrade the economic value of reuse to negative levels.

Therefore, reuse and quality control are tightly coupled technologies. As of 1996, quality control in the OO domain does not appear to be sufficiently rigorous to fully support successful reusability of commercial-grade software products.

Object-Oriented Risk and Failure Analysis

One of the major omissions from the OO literature is on a critical topic: the number and kinds of software projects where the OO paradigm is abandoned part way through, or where OO methods produce unacceptable results such as canceled projects or missed schedules.

No technology is perfect, and especially so during its formative years. As mentioned before, reports from both the United Kingdom and the United States lead to the conclusion that the various flavors of OO analysis and design are not yet mature enough to be used on critical systems without augmentation from some of the older approaches such as conventional structured design. At least the OO methods are very difficult to use for the first time, since the start-up rate of abandonment of the OO concept approaches 50%.

Using just the results reported among our clients rather than secondary reports, the following distribution reflects first-time usage of OO analysis and design and OO programming languages.

Table 3   Results of Initial Experience Using Object-Oriented Methodologies

First-Time Results:	Object-Oriented Analysis/Design	Object-Oriented Programming
Termination of project	10%	10%
Abandonment of OO approach	25%	15%
Augmentation of OO approach	45%	25%
Completion using OO approach	20%	50%

The word "termination" means that the project in question was not completed for either business or technical reasons. Sometimes termination was due to OO difficulties, but sometimes to unrelated issues.

The word "abandonment" means that the OO approach was dropped in favor of a more traditional approach; i.e., an OO programming language such as Objective C was the first choice for a project but for various reasons was dropped in favor of something else such as C. For programming, size, and performance issues are common factors for abandonment. More commonly, an OO design method such as Booch, Rumbaugh, Shlaer-Mellor, etc. was started but proved too difficult, so in order to finish the project a more traditional approach such as Yourdon, Warnier-Orr, Jackson, or Merise was brought in and the OO method was shelved.

The word "augmentation" means that the OO approach was used, but traditional approaches such as Warnier-Orr design, SADT (structured analysis and design technique), or one of the other older methods were also utilized due to difficulties in mastering aspects of the OO approach.

The word "completion" means that the OO approach was used as intended and the project was finished.

Also, when the results of using OO analysis and design are thoughtfully compared to similar projects that used conventional structured approaches such as those of Yourdon, Warnier-Orr, Merise, Jackson, Structured Analysis and Design Technique (SADT), Information Engineering (IE), or several other methods, there are not yet any clear-cut advantages that can be perceived from the OO paradigm, or at least from the initial analysis and design portion of the OO paradigm. There are some OO projects where productivity is high, but there are similar projects where productivity is below averages for the industry and class of project.

In terms of quality, the data is more ambiguous because the OO community, to a large extent, does not yet measure nor deal with quality. There are a few books on OO testing, but nothing at all in the literature nor at the many OO conferences on OO defect potentials, removal efficiency levels, inspection protocols, and a host of other key quality topics.

This is a sign that the OO quality methods need more emphasis if the OO paradigm is going to tackle large mission-critical applications.

Summary and Conclusions on Object-Oriented Quality

There is no doubt that the object-oriented paradigm is emerging as an important and exciting contribution to software engineering. But the OO paradigm is visibly deficient in empirical data.

There are also some very significant gaps in the OO literature, with important topics either having no citations or only sparse references. By the end of the century, the current gaps may have been filled. If so then the OO approach might reach its full potential.

As this book is written, the available quality data from global OO projects indicate the following trends:

- The OO learning curve is very steep and causes many first-use errors.

- OO measurement practices are embarrassingly poor for quality and marginal for productivity. The experimental OO metrics themselves are too limited for economic and quality exploration.

- OO analysis and design seem to have higher defect potentials than older design methods.

- Defect removal efficiency against OO design problems seems lower than against older design methods, which is a significant observation if confirmed.

- OO programming languages seem to have lower defect potentials than procedural programming languages.

- Defect removal efficiency against programming errors is roughly equal or somewhat better than removal efficiency against older procedural language errors.

- For OO reusability to succeed in mission-critical or commercial products, OO quality control needs substantial improvement over current practices.

- The OO metrics experiments seem to have ignored two important topics: 1) the ability to measure quality in a meaningful way; and 2) the ability to perform economic studies between OO projects and conventional procedural projects.

The OO community needs much better measurement practices than can currently be found in the software literature. Functional metrics would be a welcome adjunct for both productivity and quality studies in an OO context.

ORTHOGONAL DEFECT REPORTING

In 1992, Dr. Ram Chillarege of IBM's T.J. Watson Research Center published a seminal paper on a new way of identifying and monitoring software defects in the IEEE Transactions on Software Engineering. This method is called "orthogonal defect classification" or ODC since the semantic categories are all related and derived from one another.

Among SPR's clients, only about a dozen have experimented with the new orthogonal approach so there is a shortage of solid empirical data. However, when major software labs at IBM or Hewlett Packard experiment with an approach the results are often worth noting.

The traditional way of dealing with software defects is to simply aggregate the total volumes of bug reports, sometimes augmented by severity levels and assertions as to whether the defects originated in requirements, design, code, user documents, or as "bad fixes." In the ODC method, defects are identified using these criteria:

- Detection Method

- Symptom

- Type

- Trigger

- Source

Examples of *"detection method"* might be design inspection, code inspection, or any of a variety of testing steps.

Examples of *"symptoms"* might be system down completely, performance degraded, or questionable data integrity.

Examples of *"types"* might be interface problems, algorithm errors, missing function, or documentation error.

Examples of *"triggers"* might be start-up of application, heavy utilization of application, termination of application, or installation.

Examples of *"source"* would be the version of the projects using normal configuration control identifications, such as "version 2.3 build 6."

The ODC method seems to provide a very good set of defect statistics that greatly facilitates large-scale statistical analysis of software errors. The ODC method is also starting to have a place in quality economic studies.

Although the ODC method is only four years old as this book is written, early users have all reported favorably on the technique. The ODC concept appears to be a significant advantage over the subjective and troublesome "severity" concept and also offers a much richer set of factors for subsequent analysis.

It is premature to state that the ODC method will replace conventional defect recording, but it is certainly a method with promise and the first real extension to standard severity levels that I've observed. As an augmentation to the standard severity level concept, the ODC method provides useful additional information.

OUTSOURCE AND CONTRACT SOFTWARE QUALITY LEVELS

The topic of outsource and contract software quality is only just beginning to develop useful statistical data on the quality levels, schedules, productivity and other topics concerning external vendors in the United States. There is much less data for the sub-domain of international outsourcing to countries such as India, the Ukraine, or Russia.

Among SPR's clients, about 50 out of approximately 600 have already entered into outsource agreements for either development, maintenance, or both. Another 75 or so companies have issued development contracts for individual projects, rather than large-scale outsource agreements.

However, at least another 75 of SPR's clients are evaluating the prospects of outsourcing and are thinking seriously about at least partial outsourcing of selected activities such as maintenance, Year 2000 repairs, or projects that are not of strategic business importance.

Although the data is still sparse, enough information is coming in so that for my last two books, *Patterns of Software Systems Failure and Success* (International Thomson Press 1995) and *Applied Software Measurement – 2nd Edition* (McGraw Hill 1996) I was able to show outsource contracts as a separate category for the first time when displaying quality, defect removal, schedule, and cost data.

The general results were that outsource vendors usually have higher productivity and shorter schedules than their clients, as well as somewhat better quality control. The volume of reusable material available to the larger outsource companies is also greater, and especially so among vendors that serve vertical markets such as banks, insurance, and health-care where all of the clients need similar software applications.

However, on the down side of outsourcing, my colleagues and I are sometimes commissioned to serve as expert witnesses in U.S. law suits between clients and outsourcers or contractors where poor quality is one of the charges levied by the client. (We have not yet been asked to serve as expert witnesses in international outsource litigation, although we have worked with several companies where such litigation may occur due to dissatisfaction with the delivered projects.)

Although litigation potentials vary from client to client and contractor to contractor, the overall results of outsourcing within the United States approximates the following distribution of results after about 24 months of operations, as derived from observations among our clients.

Table 1   Approximate Distribution of U.S. Outsource Results After 24 Months

Results	Percent of Outsource Arrangements
Both parties generally satisfied	70%
Some dissatisfaction by client or vendor	15%
Dissolution of agreement planned	10%
Litigation between client and contractor (probable)	4%
Litigation between client and contractor (in progress)	1%

From process assessments performed within several large outsource companies, and analysis of projects produced by outsource vendors, our data indicates slightly better than average quality control approaches when compared to the companies and industries who engaged the outsource vendors.

However, this data is still preliminary and needs refinement as of 1996. SPR's main commissioned research in the outsource community has been with clients of the largest outsource vendors in the United States such as Andersen, EDS, IBM's ISSC subsidiary, Keane, and others in this class. There are a host of smaller outsource vendors and contractors where we have encountered only a few projects, or sometimes none at all since our clients have not utilized their services.

Classes and Types of Software Amenable to Outsourcing

Outsourcing and contract development is associated with every kind of software, ranging from small management information systems through large military and defense contracts.

Outsourcing is possible for development projects, maintenance projects (defect repairs), enhancement projects (adding new features to existing software), conversion projects (moving software to a new platform), or all of the above. A special kind of project, fixing Year 2000 problems, is now exploding through the contract and outsource domains.

Although the results vary from situation to situation, the overall results from the outsource data SPR has collected indicates the following in terms of how the outsource world compares to similar projects carried out by client companies that produce management information systems (MIS).

Table 2   Comparison of Outsource Results With Projects Produced by Clients

Project Type	Outsource Results Versus Clients		
	Schedule Reductions	Productivity Levels	Defect Levels
New software projects	- 10%	+ 15%	- 12%
Maintenance projects	- 50%	+ 50%	- 45%
Enhancement projects	- 10%	+ 20%	- 35%
Conversion projects	- 20%	+ 30%	- 30%
Year 2000 projects	- 50%	+ 75%	- 65%
AVERAGE	- 28%	+ 38%	- 37%

The most visible advantage noted for outsource projects are in the domains of maintenance projects and Year 2000 projects, where the specialized staff and tools available within the outsource community tend to be particularly effective.

Note that the performance edge which outsource contractors have over their clients in terms of work effort does not translate into a direct dollars and cents advantage, because the outsource fees and charges include burden rates and enough extra to make a normal profit.

The MIS domain has the most visible difference in performance between outsource and client projects. For other domains, such as military and systems software, the gap between clients and contractors is smaller. Consider the classes of software where outsourcing is now common:

Systems Software Outsourcing

The best overall quality results seem to occur with systems software outsourcing or contracts, such as building software for electronic switching systems, operating systems, and other software packages that control physical devices.

Since high quality is required to operate complex physical systems, quality is often part of the outsource agreement. Also, but both participants in systems software outsource agreements usually know how to go about achieving high quality levels.

Systems software outsourcing is also among the most successful forms of international outsourcing. For example, both India and the Ukraine have established outsource companies with U.S. marketing groups that handle telecommunication software packages for U.S., Canadian, and European telecommunication manufacturers.

Both international outsourcing and also a form of "insourcing" are starting to become popular. For outsourcing, of course, the software development work is done in the country where the outsource vendor resides. For "insourcing" teams of software personnel from that country work in the United States on temporary visas.

International "insourcing" is more expensive than international outsourcing, but has the advantage of almost zero communication lag since the contract personnel are sometimes located in the same building as their clients.

Military Software Outsourcing

Military project contracts and outsourcing seems to be in second place in terms of quality, although many military projects are troubled by cost and schedule overruns. Military contracts are a special class in the United States, and they have developed their own unique terms, conditions, and even attorneys, courts, and arbitration services.

Historically various military standards such as DoD 2167A and DoD 2168 have emphasized quality control (although no military standards ever emphasize cost control), so quality levels have usually ranged from acceptable to excellent.

However, there have been occasional quality failures and quality litigation in the military contract domain. In the conflict and litigation involving poor quality for military projects, there are often strong counter-claims by the vendors that the requirements ballooned excessively and that the client also applied excessive schedule pressure.

One somewhat troubling observation is that a few of the complaints about poor quality on defense applications involve outsource vendors who are at SEI CMM Level 3. In one case, the Navy reported very poor quality levels from a Level 3 contractor, and other similar comments have also come in from the Air Force. These are perhaps isolated instances, but the situation deserves careful monitoring over time.

Commercial Software Outsourcing

Commercial software outsourcing is not as common as other forms of outsourcing, but is beginning to occur more often in the 1990s than in the 1980s. While commercial outsource contracts often end favorably, the litigation potential is rather high.

Several forms of litigation can occur with commercial software outsourcing, including quality problems, breach of contract for lengthy cost and schedule overruns, and even theft of intellectual property based on charges that the outsource group later tried to imitate the products that they worked on. The latter situation is particularly troublesome with offshore outsource agreements in countries whose intellectual property laws may be ambiguous or difficult to enforce from the United States.

Some commercial software vendors who use subcontractors and outsourcers have attempted to ensure high quality levels of third party software by offering various financial inducements and/or penalties.

For example, my colleagues at SPR and a number of our competitors have been commissioned to do on-site assessments and benchmarks of subcontractor quality practices. For some major projects, both SPR consultants and competitive consultants have been used simultaneously to see if our independent methods give results that correlate to create a favorable picture.

In addition, the same vendors have offered bonus incentives to their subcontractors if quality levels and user-satisfaction levels exceed expectations so a positive incentive for ensuring high quality levels exists.

Management Information Systems Outsourcing

Management information systems (MIS) outsourcing is rapidly becoming the most common form of outsource arrangement for what appears to be basic business reasons. First, software does not bring in revenue in the MIS domain, so it is viewed by corporate management primarily as an expense, and a very large and troublesome expense at that.

For banks, insurance companies, manufacturing companies, and many other businesses software is necessary for business operations but is not necessarily of strategic importance.

Further, since many in-house MIS development groups have not established overwhelming track records of achieving high quality levels, low costs, or either short or accurate schedule results it is natural enough for senior executives at the vice presidential and presidential or CEO levels to consider outsourcing as a potential option that can perhaps bring software under control or at least stabilize a situation many executives regard as being out of control.

It is interesting to compare MIS projects produced within companies by their own technical staffs to the results of similar projects produced by outsource vendors such as Andersen, EDS, ISSC, Keane, and the like. On the whole, the quality data slightly favors the outsource community for large systems above 1,000 function points in size, although individual projects can vary widely.

Table 3   Comparison of MIS and Outsource Defect Potentials by Application Size

Size in Function Points	MIS Defect Potential	Outsource Defect Potential	Difference
1FP	1.00	1.00	0.00
10FP	2.00	2.00	0.00
100FP	4.00	3.50	(0.50)
1000FP	5.00	4.50	(0.50)
10000FP	6.00	5.50	(0.50)
100000FP	7.25	6.50	(0.75)
AVERAGE	4.21	3.83	(0.38)

The data in this table has a high margin of error and is only approximate. However consider that the main business of the outsource vendors is software development and they often have rather capable personnel, substantial training, adequate resources, ample tool capacity, and other advantages which their clients may not have in the same degree.

In addition, the outsource vendors may also have substantial volumes of high-quality reusable materials available. This is particularly true of outsourcers who specialize in certain industries such as banking, finance, health care, insurance, or something similar. In these industries all of the client companies need software packages that resemble one another closely, except for minor local customization. Therefore, reuse is a natural adjunct to serving these client companies.

Origins of Conflict and Litigation in Outsource Agreements

When outsource contracts end up in court, the cases are generally remarkably similar. The client charges that the outsource contractor breached the agreement by:

- Delivering the software late or in some cases, not at all.

- Delivering the software in inoperable condition or with excessive errors.

In turn, the outsource vendor claims non-performance on the part of the client and may even countersue, using such assertions that:

- The client changed the original requirements unilaterally and excessively.

- Sometimes the outsourcer may assert that the defect levels are not excessive, but rather the client has redefined the requirements and is labeling things defects which should be termed enhancements.

- The client did not review early deliverables or fulfill their end of the contract.

- The client has refused to pay for work already completed.

By the time the situation has made it to court, both sides of the outsource agreement have become so indignant that it is very difficult to salvage the software in question, although this can sometimes happen.

From the objective vantage point of serving as an expert witness, it seems to me that the fundamental root cause of most contractual disagreements lies in the generalities and ambiguities of the outsource contracts themselves.

Many outsource contracts do not contain language or clauses that deal with creeping user requirements, quality, defect removal efficiency, or any of the other critical issues that are likely to end up in court under litigation.

In modern outsource agreements, function point metrics are starting to be used to quantify the basic dimensions of the agreement. Function points have the useful property of being able to make direct measurements of the rate at which requirements creep. For example, if a contract calls for building a system of 5,000 function points and the client adds creeping requirements which add another 500 and brings the total up to 5,500 this fact is now visible, measurable, and difficult to challenge in court.

Some development contracts even include a sliding scale which charge more for features added down-stream than for the original agreed-to features. For example:

- Initial 5,000 function points $500 per function point or $2,500,000

- Features added > 3 months after contract signing $600 per function point

- Features added > 6 months after contract signing $700 per function point

- Features added > 9 months after contract signing $900 per function point

- Features added > 12 months after contract signing $1200 per function point

- Features deleted at client request $150 per function point

Similar clauses can be utilized with maintenance and enhancement outsource agreements, on an annual or specific basis such as:

- Normal maintenance and defect repairs $125 per function point per year

- Mainframe to client/server conversion
$200 per function point per system

- Enhancements or new features added
$500 per function point

- Special Year 2000 search and repair
$ 65 per function point per system

Another interesting clause that can be inserted into software contracts and outsource agreements deals with the quality of the delivered materials and also with defect removal efficiency levels.

For example, a contract might deal with software quality in any or all of the following ways:

- By specifying permissible levels of defects during the first year of usage, such as no more than 0.05 defects per function point of severity 1 and severity 2 categories in the first year of production as measured by an independent QA organization.

- By demanding that the vendor achieve a specified defect removal efficiency level, such as 97.5%, and keep the records to prove it. (Such records would be counts of all development bugs and counts of all user-reported bugs for a predetermined time period.)

- By demanding that the vendor utilize certain quality control methods such as formal inspections, testing by trained specialists, an active quality assurance group, and a quality measurement and defect tracking tools.

- By demanding that the vendor achieve certain levels of assumed quality control, such as insisting on ISO 9001 certification or SEI CMM Level 3 attainment.

- By requiring, as do some military software contracts, that the quality levels be assessed by independent consultants or subcontractors who are not under direct control of the prime contractor. This is termed "independent verification and validation" (IV&V) and has been a standard part of military software contracts for many years although rare in a civilian context.

Whatever the final language in the contract, software quality estimation, measurement, and control are now good enough so that outsource and software development contracts can easily include quality language that will be acceptable to both sides and also have a good chance of delivering high quality in real life.

PROJECT MANAGEMENT AND SOFTWARE QUALITY

One of the most important topics in the entire software quality domain is the relationship between software quality and software project management. This relationship is also true between quality control and project management for manufactured and engineered products.

Indeed, W. Edwards Deming, Joseph Juran, Phil Crosby, and most other quality experts have asserted that the main source of quality problems can be assigned to management rather than to technical workers.

For software quality, the correlation between project management and quality is both strong and somewhat disturbing. Among SPR's client companies and the software projects we have analyzed, the following correlations have been noted for a sample that comprises more than 100 companies and more than 1,000 software projects.

Project Management Approaches Correlating with Poor Software Quality

- Use of manual project estimation methods

- Use of manual project planning methods

- Failure to estimate or consider software defect potentials

- Failure to estimate or even know about software defect removal efficiency

- Failure to perform even rudimentary risk-analysis

- Failure to provide time for pre-test inspections

- No historical quality data from similar projects available

- Milestone tracking absent or perfunctory

- Defect tracking absent or perfunctory

- Management focus was concentrated only on schedules

- Schedules (and costs) tended to be overrun

By contrast, for projects that had a synergistic combination of low defect potentials, high defect removal efficiency, and high user-satisfaction, the following correlations have been observed.

Project Management Approaches Correlating with High Software Quality

- Use of automated project estimation methods
- Use of automated project planning methods
- Use of early and automated estimates of software defect potentials
- Use of early and automated estimates of software defect removal efficiency
- Formal project risk-analysis
- Provision of adequate time for pre-test inspections
- Historical quality data from similar projects available
- Milestone tracking automated and thorough
- Defect tracking automated and thorough
- Management focus was concentrated on achieving excellent results
- Schedules (and costs) tended to be achieved

Although the correlations are indirect, a very useful approach is to examine the set of software project management tools utilized. To a surprising degree, software quality levels can be correlated with the usage of a robust set of project management tools, although the correlation with a set of quality assurance and testing tools is even stronger.

The following table shows the range of software project management tools observed in leading, lagging, and average enterprises. Of this suite of software project management tools, seven stand out as having a significant impact on software quality:

1) Project planning
2) Project estimating
3) Risk analysis
4) Milestone tracking
5) Resource tracking
6) Methodology management
7) Assessment support

These tools are highlighted by double asterisks (**) in the following table to illustrate how they relate to other tools in the project management family.

Table 1   Software Project Management Tools in Leading, Average, and Lagging Enterprises

(Tool Capacities Expressed in Terms of Function Point Size)

Project Management	Lagging	Average	Leading
Project planning **	1,000	1,250	2,500
Project estimating **			2,500
Risk analysis **			1,500
Resource tracking**	300	750	1,500
Milestone tracking **			500
Project measurement			1,250
Statistical analysis			3,000
Function point analysis		250	750
Backfiring: LOC to FP			750
Lines of code counting		250	250
Methodology mgt. **		750	1,500
Value analysis support			500
Assessment support **		500	2,000
Benchmark support			500
Subtotal	*1,300*	*3,750*	*19,000*

Following are brief definitions of the seven project management tool categories that have a tangible impact on software quality. (See also the sections in this book on Quality Assurance Tool Capacities and on Microsoft's Quality Methods for additional information on tools.)

Project planning tools are the standard general-purpose tools for performing critical path analysis, producing Gantt charts, and in general laying out the sequence of activities associated with projects of any type, including software. These tools are often called "project management" tools but for software they perform such limited functions that "project management" is actually a misnomer.

Examples of project planning tools include Artemis, Microsoft Project, Primavera, Time Line, and at least 80 others in the United States alone. They affect quality in the hands of expert software managers because they can show the time needed for effective quality approaches such as formal inspections. For software, project planning tools are not sufficient but usually are coupled to software estimating tools.

Project estimating tools are specialized predictive tools aimed specifically at software projects. These tools include sizing capabilities, schedule and cost estimating capabilities, and for several, quality and reliability estimating capabilities as well. Many support both function point and lines of code estimates and include automatic conversion in either direction.

Examples of software estimating tools include Bridge Modeler, CHECKPOINT, COCOMO, Estimacs, Price-S, Seer, SLIM, SPQR/20, and perhaps 50 others in the United States alone. These tools are particularly important for software quality because they include "what if" modeling capabilities that can demonstrate the impact of various QA approaches such as formal design inspections, formal code inspections, testing specialists, and so forth. Several software estimating tools include a "side-by-side" capability which can show the same project as it might appear using two different development scenarios so the value of effective QA methods can be seen easily. These tools are often closely coupled with project planning tools.

Risk analysis tools are either special custom-built tools usually found within large corporations or they are add-on features associated with software project estimating tools or methodology management tools. Whether they work in standalone mode or as part of another tool, they usually predict technical risks (i.e., inadequate defect removal, requirements volatility). A few can also predict sociological risks (i.e., excessive schedule pressure, staff burnout). Some risk-analysis tools can predict the probability that a software project will run late, exceed its budget, or even have a high probability of litigation.

Milestone tracking tools record both planned and actual events that are deemed critical for software projects. Examples of typical milestones include completion of high-level design, completion of design inspections, completion of low-level or detailed design, completion of coding, completion of code inspections, completion of first drafts of user manuals, and so forth.

Milestone tracking tools are seldom found as standalone tools, although custom milestone tracking tools circa the 1970s sometimes are still used. More often, they are noted as add-ons to either project planning tools, project estimating tools, or methodology management tools. These tools have a role in software quality because they can highlight quality events. Indeed, within leading companies the quality milestones are the major drivers of software development processes and the rest of the development cycle is built around quality milestones such as completion of design and code inspections and various test stages.

Resource tracking tools are one of the oldest forms of project management capability, and have existed in standalone mode since the late 1950s and have been part of other project management tools ever since. Resource tracking tools accumulate data on the human effort and costs expended on software projects. Ideally, these tools will support a very granular chart of accounts so that costs can be apportioned to specific activities. However, sometimes the charts of accounts are too coarse to be really useful.

For quality cost and resource measurements, the charts of accounts should identify the effort devoted to inspections, all forms of testing, and to some kinds of defect prevention approaches such as joint application design (JAD) and quality function deployment (QFD). These tools, properly used, allow retrospective economic analysis to be performed.

One strong criterion for precision in the quality domain, which is often lacking, is that these tools should capture unpaid overtime and show this as a separate category. Unpaid overtime is a major component of quality control, because more than half of the total volume of unpaid overtime usually occurs during late-night and weekend testing marathons.

Methodology management tools are a fairly new category of software project management tool. These tools may include planning and estimating support and also aspects of risk management and even quality estimation. They are usually keyed to one or more of the standard software development methodologies such as information engineering, rapid application development (RAD), Merise, or conventional structured analysis and design. Within this context, they provide guidance for what deliverables are needed, scheduling, planning, and other management topics.

The concept of the methodology management approach is to aggregate a number of managerial functions under one umbrella. Here too, these tools may be coupled to software project planning and software estimating tools, or planning and estimating capabilities may be integrated into the methodology management tool itself.

Assessment support tools are another fairly new class of automated tools that are keyed to one or more of the standard forms of evaluating software methods and approaches, such as the Bootstrap approach, the ISO 9001 approach, the Software Engineering Institute Capability Maturity Model (SEI CMM), or the Software Productivity Research (SPR) assessment method.

When used near the beginning of major projects (i.e., > 5,000 function points) they can highlight both strengths and weaknesses. Obviously, the weaknesses will need repair prior to moving into full development. Assessment tools can either be standalone tools or add-ons connected to software estimating tools or software methodology management tools. The more sophisticated assessment tools can also serve to gather data that can modify cost, schedule, and quality estimates. In fact several software cost estimating tools such as CHECKPOINT, SLIM, and COCOMO II have assessment gathering input capabilities.

See also the sections on quality assurance and testing tool capacities later in this book, because the correlations with software quality are not limited to project management tool capacities. The combination of project management tools, quality assurance tools, and testing tools have the most significant differences between leading, lagging, and average enterprises. There may be a 10-to-1 differential in the tool capacities for these three categories, while differences in software engineering or standard CASE tools are comparatively minor.

PROTOTYPING AND SOFTWARE QUALITY

There are three common varieties of prototyping for software projects. Two of them (disposable prototypes and time-box prototypes) tend to reduce creeping requirements and serve as effective defect prevention approaches for software quality. The third method, (evolutionary prototypes) unfortunately, tends to be hazardous for software quality and may even end up in court if it used for contract software or for projects such as medical systems with significant liability issues.

Among SPR's clients, prototyping is a very common practice. For projects between about 100 and 5,000 function points in size, about 80% of them have had some form of prototype prior to full development. Of the prototypes, about 65% were disposable, 10% were time-box, and 25% were evolutionary in nature.

To have an optimal effect, prototypes should serve as a method for augmenting written requirements and written specifications, not replacing them. When prototypes are used in place of written specifications, the results are hazardous rather than beneficial. The reason for the hazard is because the prototype is not a sufficient source of information to enable formal design and code inspections, effective test-case construction, nor to facilitate later down-stream maintenance.

Prototypes are an interesting technology because they are most successful for mid-sized projects. For very small projects, they are usually not needed. For very large systems, they may not be effective. The following table shows the size ranges where prototypes give the best results.

Table 1   Relationship of Software Project Size and Effects of Prototyping

Size of project in Function Points	Size of Prototype in Function Points	Effect of Software Prototyping
1	0	Not needed
10	1	Seldom needed
100	5 to 10	Minimize requirements defects
1000	50 to 100	Reduce requirements defects and creep rate
10000	100 to 250	Marginal benefits
100000	300 to 750	Difficult, but minor benefits

As can be seen, prototypes are most beneficial for software projects from about 100 function points in size up to perhaps 1000 function points in size. Below these sizes, the application may be too small for prototyping to do much of value. Above these sizes, it is hard to prototype a critical volume of features and functions because the prototype itself would become a major application. For example, prototyping 10% of a 10,000 function point application would yield a project of 1000 function points, which is a substantial size in its own right and might take a year to complete.

Disposable Prototypes

As the name implies, disposable prototypes are created to demonstrate aspects of a software project and when they have served that purpose, they are no longer needed so they are discarded.

Usually disposable prototypes focus on visible aspects of software projects such as input forms or output screens. For many projects, as well as for my own company's software products, disposable prototypes are also used to illustrate the operation of key algorithms. We tend to use Visual Basic for prototypes, but C and C++ for our commercial products. The use of a different language for the prototype more or less ensures that the prototypes will be disposable.

Both SPR and many of our clients do not limit the development of prototypes to the requirements phase of software development. At any point in the development cycle, if an algorithm is difficult or there is some question as to how a screen element should appear, we continue to build disposable prototypes as the need arises.

Compared to the final application, the total volume of disposable prototypes seldom tops 15% of the features and functions, and the average volume is probably between 5% and 10%. It is difficult to make a definitive statement, because disposable prototypes vary from project to project.

For a typical Windows 95 application of 2,500 function points in total size, here are some observations of the trail of disposable prototypes that might be constructed during development.

Table 2   Disposable Prototype Construction for a 2,500 Function Point Application

(Prototype Size Expressed in Terms of Function Points)

Development Phase	Input/Output Screen Prototypes	Key Algorithms Prototypes	TOTAL PROTOTYPES
Requirements	100	20	120
Design	50	75	125
Code	10	50	60
Testing	0	10	10
TOTAL	160	155	315

In this example, the volume of the prototypes total to 12.6% of the entire application and are almost equally divided between prototypes of screens and prototypes of key algorithms. Note that screen prototypes peak during requirements, but algorithm prototypes peak later during the design phase when the inner workings of algorithms require careful analysis.

In this particular example, the prototypes are more or less independent rather than forming a partial replica of the full application. Although not shown in the table, the total number of discrete prototypes built during the development cycle would be about 20.

Disposable prototypes are usually done rapidly without formal specifications or much in the way of up-front planning. High-speed prototyping using tools such as Visual Basic, Realizer, or even special prototyping tools such as the Bricklin Demo tools are rather common.

The observed effect of disposable prototyping is a reduction in requirements defects and a very significant reduction in the rate of creeping requirements. Requirements creep for prototyped projects is usually well below the 1% to 2% per month range noted with conventional requirements gathering.

Interestingly, disposable prototypes also yield a reduction in design defects and coding defects, although they yield no discernible impact on user documentation or bad fix defect categories. Prototypes also seem to have no little or no impact on bad test-case defects or data errors either, although this may be just a gap in our data.

Disposable prototypes interact in a synergistic fashion with two other requirements approaches: Joint Application Design (JAD) and Quality Function Deployment (QFD). Indeed, disposable prototypes are often produced in real time during JAD or QFD sessions.

Time-Box Prototypes

The concept of time-box prototypes originated circa 1986 in DuPont. A specific time period such as one month or six weeks is dedicated to developing a prototype of the final project, in order to demonstrate that it is feasible and implementable.

Compared to disposable prototypes which are often discrete and not unified, time-box prototypes are often partial replicas of a full application and are intended to show how the features and functions interact. If the average size of disposable prototypes sums to 10% to 15% of the eventual features, the average size of time-box prototypes is about 12% to 20% of the eventual features. Compare the following table of time-box prototyping to the prior table of disposable prototyping.

Table 3   Time-Box Prototype Construction for a 2,500 Function Point Application

(Prototype Size Expressed in Terms of Function Points)

Development Phase	Input/Output Screen Prototypes	Key Algorithms Prototypes	TOTAL PROTOTYPES
Requirements	200	150	350
Design	0	0	0
Code	0	0	0
Testing	0	0	0
TOTAL	200	150	350

As can be seen, the time-box prototype volume is 14% or slightly larger. The most notable difference is the concentration of the prototype effort during the requirements phase.

Because the time-box period may be less than a month and is almost never more than three months, it is obvious that time-box prototypes are most effective for projects that range from about 500 function points up to a maximum of about 5,000 function points with an optimal node point of about 1,000 function points.

For really large systems that top 10,000 function points the time-box would either have to stretch out to more than six months, or either too few features could be prototyped to solve technical problems.

Time-box prototyping works best for new kinds of applications where the development team needs to practice in order to be sure that they can build the final product. While time-box prototypes are often constructed using languages such as Visual Basic, Realizer, or Objective C, they are sometimes built using conventional procedural languages such as C.

The observed effects of time-box prototypes are twofold: 1) many requirements defects are prevented; and 2) the rate of requirements creep is significantly reduced and is often less than 0.5% per month after the prototype is finished.

Although harder to validate, time-box prototypes also seem to benefit design and coding defects slightly although perhaps not as much as a staggered set of disposable prototypes.

Time-box prototypes are usually too extensive to be part of joint application design (JAD) or quality function deployment (QFD) sessions. Often the time-box method serves as a replacement for JAD, although QFD can still occur for high-technology projects.

The time-box concept sometimes overlaps the hazardous "evolutionary prototype" form if the time-box prototype is used as the actual base for growing a final product. This situation is dangerous for a number of reasons as will be explained in the section on evolutionary prototypes.

Evolutionary Prototypes

As the name implies, evolutionary prototypes are intended to grow into finished products. Often the evolutionary prototypes are used as part of a methodology discussed elsewhere in this book called "rapid application development" or RAD. Whether the evolutionary prototype is labeled RAD or not, there are some decided hazards associated with the approach that need to be dealt with very carefully.

By definition "prototypes" are built without formal specifications or much in the way of quality control such as design or code inspections. This carelessness means that the structure of the application may be far from optimal, the comment density may be below safe levels, and the number of latent defects in the application can be significant.

For low-end applications (below 1,000 function points in size), the carelessness of the evolutionary prototype can be partially offset by testing, although in fact this seldom occurs.

However, for a really large system in the 10,000 function point range and higher, attempting to grow a prototype into a final product is a very dangerous practice. Indeed, for contract software, such systems show up in court often enough for evolutionary prototypes to be considered professional malpractice for larger applications.

Compare the sequence of evolutionary prototyping with the two prior tables for disposable and time-box prototypes.

Table 4   Evolutionary Prototype Construction for a 2,500 Function Point Application

(Prototype Size Expressed in Terms of Function Points)

Development Phase	Input/Output Screen Prototypes	Key Algorithms Prototypes	TOTAL PROTOTYPES
Requirements	100	50	150
Design	375	175	550
Code	850	450	1300
Testing	225	275	500
TOTAL	1550	950	2500

As can be seen the evolutionary prototype method leaves a lot of important issues more or less unresolved until the coding and testing phases. This means that testing itself is severely handicapped by the lack of any kind of formal specification document as the basis for constructing test cases.

Indeed, unless the development personnel are also the test personnel, it is difficult to do any serious testing at all because the details of the evolutionary prototypes are not stable and may not even have been worked out at the normal time when test-case construction should be ramping up during the design and coding phases.

Also, the evolutionary prototype method usually does not have any finished materials that are capable of going through formal design and code inspections. This explains why inspections are almost never used in conjunction with evolutionary prototypes.

Obviously users and developers have whatever levels of prototypes are available at the moment, but a casual examination of a prototype is far less efficient in finding errors than formal design and code inspections.

The hazards of evolutionary prototyping and of the related RAD approach for software applications larger than roughly 1000 function points are these:

- Design rigor is often absent

- Design inspections are seldom utilized

- Written specifications are missing or perfunctory
- Coding structure may be questionable
- Code inspections are seldom utilized
- Both cyclomatic and essential complexity levels may be high
- Comments in code may be sparse
- Test plan development is difficult and uncertain
- Test cases may have major gaps in coverage
- Quality and reliability levels are usually below average
- Maintenance costs are usually well above average
- Follow-on releases are expensive and troublesome
- Customer support is difficult
- User satisfaction levels are often below average
- Litigation probability is alarmingly high

These problems occur most severely at the larger end of the size spectrum. It is not fair to be totally dismissive of the evolutionary prototyping approach because it has been used more or less successfully on hundreds of applications by our clients.

However, the literature on both RAD and evolutionary prototyping has manifested a common software flaw. There has been a tendency to assume that because the evolutionary prototype method works well on small applications of < 1,000 function points, it can be scaled up for larger applications. This is a dangerous fallacy, although a common failing in the software engineering literature.

Also, the evolutionary prototype method would be very dangerous for software that affects the operation of complex physical devices. This means that extreme caution is indicated when attempting evolutionary prototypes for weapons systems, aircraft flight control applications, medical instrument systems, or any other kind of application where failure can mean death, injury, or the probability of major disasters.

Against the background of average results for MIS projects using disposable prototypes, evolutionary prototypes are a decided step backwards in terms of quality results. For projects of a nominal 1,000 function points in size developed in COBOL, the following results have been noted in Table 4.

Table 5 Defect Levels for 1,000 Function Point Average MIS Projects, Disposable Prototypes, and Evolutionary Prototypes

(Defect data displayed in terms of defects per function point)

	Average Projects	Disposable Prototypes	Evolutionary Prototypes
Requirements	1.00	0.80	0.80
Design	1.25	1.15	1.40
Code	1.50	1.45	1.80
Bad Fixes	0.60	0.60	0.70
User Documents	0.40	0.40	0.40
Total	4.75	4.40	5.10
Defect removal efficiency	85%	85%	80%
Delivered defects per function point	0.72	0.66	1.02

With evolutionary prototypes, the short-term advantages derived from working out the requirements early are quickly offset by sloppy design and poor coding structure, which elevates overall defect volumes and degrades defect removal efficiency levels.

QUALITY ASSURANCE DEPARTMENTS

Among the 600 or so enterprises comprising our client base, less than about 250 have any kind of formal quality assurance departments while more than 350 either have no QA function or assign QA duties to development personnel. Even the companies with QA departments do not utilize their services on every project, or even on every class of project. While most external projects that go to customers have some kind of QA analysis applied, internal MIS projects, internal tools, and some incoming software from contractors or vendors may have no visible QA activity.

The empirical results of having formal quality assurance departments ranges from very good to negligible. The very good results come from well staffed and well funded software quality assurance groups that report directly to the CEO and are able to take a proactive role in quality matters. Two important issues regarding software quality assurance groups are: 1) where should they be placed organizationally? and 2) how big should they be for optimal results?

The most effective quality assurance groups typically average about 5% of the total software staff in size. The top executive is usually a director or VP of Quality, who is a peer to other senior operational executives. Figure 1, following, shows how an effective and active QA fits with other operating groups in high-technology companies such as computer manufacturers.

This figure assumes a large high-technology corporation that will have at least 5,000 total software personnel. The software engineering and product side will have about 1,250 technical personnel building and enhancing software products, 750 personnel maintaining existing software products; 500 personnel in testing roles; 250 in customer support; 200 building in-house tools and internal applications; 150 in quality assurance roles; and 500 in specialist roles such as technical writing, database administration, measurements, network management, system administration, and the like. Thus, the product software personnel total to about 3,600 (of whom management and administrative personnel are assumed to comprise about 15%).

The MIS community would total to about 1,000 personnel who are building and maintaining internal management information systems. Note that unlike the product side, the MIS community often assigns development and maintenance work to the same teams, even though this approach optimizes neither development nor maintenance.

The remaining 400 software personnel would comprise the personal staffs of the top executives and the VP level (roughly 100) and also various liaison and specialist personnel such as those responsible for training and education, standards, process improvements, productivity measurements, and the like.

The usual practice in the high-tech world is for the product software groups to report to their own VP of software, while the MIS software groups report to a chief information officer (CIO).

Figure 1 highlights the overall top levels of executives and management observed in large high-technology companies.

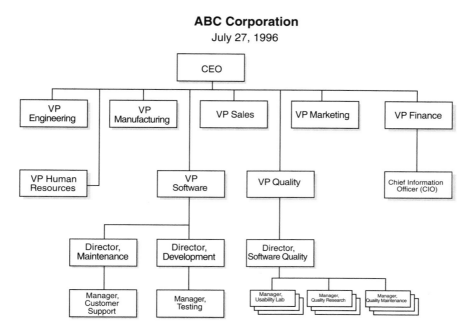

ABC Corporation
July 27, 1996

Figure 1 Software Quality Assurance and Testing Placement within Large Enterprises

Note that the QA organization has its own chain of command up to the VP level, and that the top Quality VP reports directly to the CEO. This is necessary to prevent coercion. It is an unwise practice to have the QA group subordinate to the executives whose products they are ensuring. QA appraisals and salary levels should not be in the hands of the managers whose products are being assessed, for obvious reasons.

The QA vice president is responsible for more than software quality of course. The QA vice presidential position on this diagram is identical to the position Phil Crosby occupied when he worked for Harold Geneen, the Chairman of ITT, prior to founding his own company. It is worthwhile to read Phil's famous book *Quality is Free* (Mentor Books, 1979) to get an idea of how a VP of quality operates in a large multinational corporation.

Underneath the corporate VP of quality, who handles both hardware and software, would also be found a VP or director of software quality depending upon the overall size of the company.

An interesting anomaly in the diagram which is based on real-life experience is that the software QA function is usually focused externally on the software products that reach customers. For reasons of corporate culture and historical accident, the QA groups are seldom utilized on two key classes of software projects:

- Management information systems built for internal use by the company itself.

- Tools and testing software built for internal use by the company itself.

When performing assessments and benchmark studies in large corporations it is an interesting phenomenon that software reaching customers usually has much more rigorous quality control and even better testing than in-house software.

In high-technology organizations, such as those shown in the figure, the QA executives have the authority to stop products from being shipped or even announced if the quality levels are below satisfactory corporate targets. While the development side can appeal, the appeal usually goes directly to the president or CEO (or a divisional president in really large companies).

The marginal to poor results from quality assurance departments are often associated with understaffing and underfunding. For example, QA groups with staffing of less than 2% of the software development staff, can't keep up with the work.

Note that quality assurance is not just testing. Indeed, testing should normally be carried out in combination by the development teams themselves for unit testing, by testing specialists in a formal test organization for stress, regression, and system testing.

Although the QA group does not handle the mainstream of testing, the QA group may have an independent test library and serve as an in-house independent test team. The QA group might also handle usability testing, and in large corporations might even run a special usability lab, as shown in the diagram here.

One important topic which is not often stressed in the literature, but which is interesting and significant, is the fact that the independent QA organizations in really large companies (AT&T, IBM, Hitachi, Siemens-Nixdorf, etc.) actually do research and may even have formal quality research laboratories.

In fact, most of the "best practices" for software quality tend to originate within the QA research labs of large multi-national corporations. To cite a few examples of quality innovations coming out of QA research labs, consider design and code inspections, joint application design (JAD), quality estimation tools, quality reliability models, quality function deployment (QFD), and both the measurement of defect potentials and defect removal efficiency levels originated in various QA labs.

The QA research labs are not usually large in numbers and seldom exceed more than 8 to 15 personnel. However, the researchers are usually free from day to day QA tasks and concentrate most of their time on quality exploration and technology development.

At IBM there was a very fruitful collaboration between the QA research lab and the software development labs. Many joint studies and combined reports were produced. For example, the QA research lab at IBM Palo Alto in conjunction with the development lab built IBM's first quality estimation model in the 1970s.

Another "best practice" in the software QA domain is that of a quality measurement department. Here, too, the sizes are not large, and from about 5 to 12 personnel would handle the formal analysis and reporting. The diagram also shows the normal position of a formal software quality measurement department, which reports in to the director of VP of software quality.

(All QA personnel assigned to specific projects plus the software development, maintenance, and testing managers and team members provide the raw data.) The QA measurement department analyzes the results, performs various statistical studies and correlation analysis, and produces the monthly executive reports and the quality portions of the annual report.

The monthly quality reports show both current month and at least a 12 month rolling average of open and closed defects, severity levels, defects by product, by country, ages of defects, and a number of other basic statistical facts.

User satisfaction data is measured too, but the data is usually collected by the sales and marketing organizations who are in direct daily contact with customers. Eventually the user-satisfaction and defect data come together for correlation analysis and special studies.

The quality measurement data and the user-satisfaction data is consolidated with productivity, cost, and schedule data (not shown in the diagram) to put together an overall annual picture of software operations.

Quality data itself is reported monthly to the top executives of the company (including the CEO) but in addition there is an annual software report that shows all important aspects of software within the company; i.e., portfolio size, software personnel on board; personnel turnover rates, quality, defect removal efficiency; user-satisfaction, project failures versus successes; schedules, costs, etc.

See also the section on Active, Passive, and Token Quality Assurance Organizations earlier in this book. Active quality assurance organizations are often associated with better than average quality results. They are almost always found in the "best in class" organizations with low defect potentials and high defect removal efficiency levels.

QUALITY ASSURANCE TOOL CAPACITIES

A new way of evaluating the capacity of tools using function point metrics was first published in 1991 in Capers Jones' book *Applied Software Measurement* (McGraw Hill). This new methodology is based on quantifying the function point totals of the tools utilized for various business purposes.

It is interesting that since first using this approach in 1991, the volumes of tools available for all software engineering, project management, and quality purposes have been increasing at a compound rate of about 15% per year. This is a strong sign that the software tool business is growing rapidly in all directions.

One of the strongest correlations to date is in the domain of software quality assurance and testing tools. The leading quality assurance organizations such as AT&T, Motorola, Microsoft, Raytheon, the large IBM labs, etc. have roughly 10 times the quality assurance tool capabilities as lagging companies, and about four times the capabilities of average companies. There are also differences of about 2-to-1 in testing tools between leaders and average enterprises.

Variances in software tool capacities can easily be observed during assessment and baseline studies. These variations constitute one of the more striking "best in class" indicators. "Best in class" companies have rather large and sophisticated collections of quality and testing tools, while laggards tend to have very few or even none at all.

The methodology of using function points for correlating tool capacity with performance is still an experimental method, but the initial results are proving to be very interesting. For software quality assurance, testing, and also for software project managers, the correlation between tool capacity and job performance is rather strong.

Following are the major kinds of quality assurance and testing tools and their approximate function point size totals.

Table 1   Function Point Sizes of Software Quality and Testing Tools

Quality Assurance	Lagging	Average	Leading
QFD Support			1,000
TQM Support			1,000
Quality estimation			2,000
Reliability estimation			1,000
Inspection support			1,000
Defect tracking	500	750	1,000
Complexity analysis		500	1,000
Subtotal	*500*	*1,250*	*8,000*
Testing			
Test-case generation			1,250
Test path coverage	100	200	350
Test-case execution		200	350
Capture/playback		500	750
Defect tracking	500	750	1,000
Test library control	250	750	1,000
Complexity analysis		500	1,000
Data quality analysis			1,250
Subtotal	*850*	*2,900*	*6,950*

This method of analysis is leading to some interesting results. For example, the most significant differences in tool capacities between leading and lagging companies are in the domains of quality assurance tools, testing tools, and project management tools.

As just shown there is about a 10-to-1 differential in terms of quality tools. For project management tools the results are even more dramatic, with almost a 30-to-1 differential in tool capacities for project managers between the leaders and the laggards.

However, average companies, leaders, and laggards are seldom very far apart in basic software development tools: The values run from about 30,000 function points to more than 50,000 function points for software engineering tool suites encompassing normal analysis, design, development, configuration control, and testing tools.

Following are short descriptions of the major quality tool categories noted in "best in class" software quality shops.

Quality Assurance Tools

This family of tools is normally run by the software QA personnel when they are operating in "active" mode and are taking a proactive part in software projects during requirements and design phases:

Quality function deployment (QFD) tools support the rather extensive and complicated graphics methods used during QFD sessions. Recall that another name for QFD is "house of quality" because some of the graphs and matrices which link customer quality needs with development responses are drawn in the shape of a house with a peaked roof. Obviously graphics packages such as AutoCAD and PowerPoint can be used for such drawings.

Total quality management (TQM) tools support the "fishbone" and root-cause analysis diagrams that are associated with the TQM concept. Many standard graphics packages such as AutoCAD and PowerPoint can draw these diagrams. In addition, specialized templates and stencils of TQM diagram shapes are also available for "drag and drop" drawing packages such as Visio.

Quality estimation tools can be either custom standalone tools or part of commercial software cost estimating tools. In either mode, they predict the volumes of software defects by origin point (i.e., requirements defects, design defects, coding defects, documentation defects, and "bad fix" defects). The more sophisticated quality estimation tools also predict the defect removal efficiency levels of various reviews, inspections, and test steps and allow "what if" modeling of various combinations of defect removal activities. Some quality prediction tools can also handle defect prevention, and can show reductions in defect potentials associated with team experience, programming languages, formal methods, etc.

Quality estimation tools also predict defect severity levels. For commercial software, the tools can predict special categories such as duplicate defects, abeyant defects, and invalid defects. Quality estimation tools are surprisingly accurate and often outperform human quality predictions. As this book is written, defect levels in test cases themselves and also data defects are outside the scope of most commercial quality estimation tools, but will probably be included as enough empirical data becomes available to develop accurate predictive algorithms. Commercial quality estimation tools have been on the market since about 1985 although in-house quality estimation tools were being build in the early 1970s by IBM and other large software companies.

Reliability estimation tools can also be either custom standalone tools or part of commercial software cost estimation tools. These tools predict mean time to failure (MTTF), mean time between failures (MTBF), and sometimes the "stabilization period" or the amount of usage before a software product can be utilized safely for production work. To work well, reliability models need data on the expected usage patterns of the software package. There are a number of competing reliability models, but all are based on statistical analysis of various collections of software packages. Commercial reliability estimation tools have been on the market since about 1975.

Inspection support tools can facilitate holding inspections of software artifacts remotely, without having the inspection team assemble in a single room. These tools are rather new, having surfaced in the 1990–1995 half-decade. These tools are particularly useful for outsource projects and for distributed development where project teams may be in different cities or even different countries. It is interesting that while inspections themselves have existed since the 1960s, automation for assisting in finding and recording errors using inspections is quite recent.

Defect tracking tools, as the name implies, keep records of software defects when they are found. These tools also record supplemental information such as severity level, platform, symptoms, origin of defects, and repair responsibility. They also include statistical analysis capabilities for aggregating defects from multiple projects and producing summary reports for managers and executives.

The more sophisticated defect tracking tools can also calculate defect removal efficiency levels, since they record pre-release defects as well as customer-reported defects. The better defect tracking tools save a lot of effort, and also prevent defect reports from getting lost, which often occurs with manual systems. Proprietary software defect tracking tools have been around since the early 1960s making this one of the oldest families of quality tools. Commercial defect tracking tools have been marketed since the 1970s but as quality grows in importance, many new and sophisticated defect tracking features have started appearing in the 1990s.

Complexity analysis tools scan source code and calculate cyclomatic and essential complexity levels as their basic function. The complexity analysis tools also produce useful graphs of control flow structure and can highlight regions of "dead" code that is in the system, but no longer operational. Sometimes complexity analysis tools are precursors to full code restructuring capabilities and are embedded in larger hybrid tools. Sometimes these tools can also be used for "backfiring" and can issue approximate counts of function point totals in the applications for which they are used.

Many complexity analysis tools can also generate counts of logical statements, since they work at the statement level rather than the physical line level. The commercial complexity analysis tools have been on the market since the early 1980s. In addition to commercial tools, this category is popular enough so that shareware and even freeware versions can be downloaded from the Internet, various bulletin boards, and information services such as CompuServe.

There are more than 500 programming languages in use, and not every language can be analyzed via complexity analysis tools. However, at least 25 of the more common languages (i.e., COBOL, FORTRAN, C, PASCAL, etc.) are supported by commercial complexity analysis tools.

In addition to code complexity analyzers, a totally separate (and older) category of tools can analyze the complexity of text passages and calculate factors such as the levels of readability or the FOG index. These tools are widely used by professional writers and journalists and could usefully be applied to software requirements, specifications, and other text documents. However, the technical writing world is so different from the software development world that few software development groups utilize the complexity analysis tools that operate on text rather than code, and many software personnel do not even know of their existence. This category of complexity analysis is more than 100 years old and predates the computer era, although such tools were not automated until the 1970s.

Over and above the standard QA tools, there is another useful category of quality tool: code restructuring. Code restructuring may be recommended by the SQA organization, but the tools themselves are usually under the control of the software development and maintenance organizations, since these groups are the "owners" of the code in question.

Code restructuring tools are usually based on graph theory. Their purpose is to simplify the structure of applications and reduce accidental complexity levels to safe values. Supplemental functions include renaming modules, ensuring that various coding standards are followed, and sprucing up the comments. These tools are surprisingly effective in lowering maintenance costs since they generate consistent structures and allow maintenance personnel to move from application to application without undue trouble. The commercial code restructuring tools are aimed at high-volume programming languages such as COBOL and C. There are a number of commercial code restructuring tools on the market, and this class reached commercialization about 1985.

Software Testing Tools

This family of tools is usually owned and operated by testing departments. However since some companies assign test responsibilities to development and maintenance teams, they may also be run by development or maintenance personnel. Other companies use the name "quality assurance" for their testing groups, so in some enterprises the QA department will operate the tools. The family of software testing tools follows:

Test-case generation tools operate by parsing requirements and text specifications and creating a suite of test cases that match the statements and assertions in the specifications. As a byproduct, some can also find errors in the specifications such as missing assertions or contradictory requirements. These tools are usually found only as custom-built tools in very large companies that have quality research laboratories and are only just beginning to reach the commercial markets in 1996. The combination of text complexity analysis logic and code complexity logic could lead to interesting new capabilities for test-case generation.

Test path coverage tools are embedded temporarily in software applications and monitor the relationship of test cases and instruction sequences. Their main purpose is to ensure that a test suite will in fact test all branches and changes of control flow. The outputs from test path coverage tools are charts or indications of testing gaps. These tools have been commercially available since the 1970s and are steadily improving in capabilities.

Test-case execution tools are used to record the running of specific test cases, and to also record (and later playback) the keystrokes and commands utilized. These tools are very useful for testing client/server applications or other programs with high levels of interactive user participation. As tools for supporting online software testing, test-case execution tools are increasing in popularity in the latter 1990s although they originated in the 1980s.

Test library control tools are used for keeping track of hundreds or even thousands of test cases that support multiple releases and multiple projects. Test library tools have been available since the 1960s, and improvements are steadily occurring. Theses tools identify which applications and sections specific test cases support. They are very useful in eliminating accidental redundancy that is likely to occur when different teams create test cases for the same system.

Complexity analysis tools scan source code and calculate cyclomatic and essential complexity levels as their basic function. The complexity analysis tools also produce useful graphs of control flow structure and can highlight regions of "dead" code that is in the system but no longer operational. This explains why complexity analysis tools are used by both quality assurance and testing groups. Indeed, sometimes development and maintenance groups also use complexity analyzers. Both commercial and proprietary in-house complexity analyzers have been observed, but so many complexity analysis tools are available on the commercial market that only special needs such as unique programming languages would trigger in-house development.

Data quality tools are a fairly new category of tool that appeared in commercial form in the early 1990s. These tools analyze databases and look for various anomalies such as duplicate records, missing fields, and the like. As repositories and data warehouses grow in number and volume, data quality tools should also increase in numbers and capabilities.

Year 2000 analysis tools, as the name implies, analyze source code and look for instances of the two-digit date format. This is a new category of tool and the sizes have not yet been fully analyzed. Around 500 function points to 1,000 function points is the apparent range, however. Some of these tools can repair obvious situations, but some date format repairs are so tricky that human intervention is needed. For many instances the tools merely highlight the occurrence so that live programmers can inspect the situation. The more sophisticated Year 2000 tools also deal with cross-references and inference trees.

Not all programming languages have Year 2000 tools available, although obviously COBOL and C have such tools in large supply. Assembly language is the most difficult language for automatic Year 2000 analysis. Some of the Year 2000 tools originated in the 1980s for other purposes, and have simply been renamed or remarketed for Year 2000 repairs. However the most sophisticated Year 2000 tools that are fairly new, circa 1995. These tools can find other problems, of course, and once the Year 2000 crisis is past will be used for finding and repairing many other kinds of field truncations.

For an additional discussion of function points and tool capacities used by various kinds of software personnel, refer to the section on Microsoft's Quality Approaches earlier in this book. See also the section on Project Management and Software Quality.

QUALITY DEFINITIONS

Unfortunately the quality domain is troubled by severe problems with ambiguous terminology. The quality domain is also troubled by excessive pedantry involving a number of minor or secondary terms that are of only marginal utility in dealing with major quality issues. For example, the distinction between "failure" and "fault" and "defect" is essentially irrelevant to the work of repairing quality problems.

Few terms used in modern business are as controversial or ambiguous as the word "quality." In performing the SPR surveys, many different concepts of what quality means were encountered. Unfortunately, some of the more common definitions for quality are unmeasurable, illogical, or both. A few examples can illustrate some of the problems encountered.

The definition of quality that it means "conformance to requirements" was encountered in a majority of MIS software organizations, but seldom less frequently among commercial, military, or systems software producers even though it is included in several IEEE standards.

The most obvious problem with this definition is that requirements themselves contribute about 15% of the total volume of errors associated with software projects, and an even higher percentage of serious or fatal errors. For example, the requirement that dates be recorded with only 2 digits rather than with 4 digits is the origin of the Year 2000 problem that will soon become the most expensive requirements error in human history.

Any definition of quality that means conformance to a key source of errors prevents the direct measurement of requirements defects themselves and leaves a major gap in quality data record keeping.

Also, the observed rate at which new requirements are created during software development projects is about 1% to 3% per month during the design and coding phases. This phenomenon raises serious logical questions about exactly when conformance to requirements starts and stops.

Among the definitions of quality contained in various IEEE and ISO standards are a number of aspects under the general topic of quality: Portability, reliability, efficiency, accuracy, error, robustness, and correctness. Each of these terms, in turn, is defined more fully. (Refer to ANSI/IEEE Std 729, IEE83, IEEE Std 610, ISO 9000-9004, for more extended discussions of quality terms.)

These definitions were originally created in the 1970s, long before software warranties were common and very long before the specter of litigation and consequential damages was on the software horizon.

Several of these nominal quality factors seem to be irrelevant to quality in any normal usage of the word, and should probably be removed in the future. For example, the concept of "portability" is an important business topic, but irrelevant to quality. In a similar fashion, "efficiency" is a significant topic, but has nothing to do with quality.

Many of the companies contacted utilized pragmatic definitions of quality that included these three general aspects: 1) low defect rates after delivery; 2) high user-satisfaction levels after delivery; and 3) rapid response to customer service requests.

From serving as an expert witness in several lawsuits where software quality was an issue in the case, I recommend paying particular attention to the following six quality factors since they are the ones most likely to cause litigation if botched up:

1) Low levels of defects when deployed, ideally approaching zero-defects.

2) High reliability, or the capability of running without crashes or strange results.

3) A majority of users who express satisfaction with the software when surveyed.

4) A structure that minimizes "bad fixes" or insertion of new defects during repairs.

5) Effective customer support when problems do occur.

6) Rapid repairs for defects, and especially for high-severity defects.

No matter what definition is used for quality, it is necessary to be pragmatic rather than pedantic. Think about what kinds of problems are annoying to real people when they use software, or experience some failure on the part of software.

Conformance to requirements is often dealt with in a pragmatic manner. If the requirements are rational, technically achievable, and defined early in the development cycle then they should be met. If the requirements occur too late or are technically impossible, or worse, are dangerously wrong or foolish, then they cannot be dealt with in the context of the current release and the client should be apprised of the situation promptly.

Because of the ambiguity and uncertainty of quality terms, it is sometimes neces-sary to seek a consensus or group opinion. During inspections, for example, the inspection team is queried as to whether a problem should be deemed a defect or a potential enhancement.

Another topic where subjectivity reigns is that of the severity levels assigned to defects. In fact, severity levels are not constant but can change repeatedly. A typical pattern would be that the initial report of a defect by a client or user would assign a rather high severity level (1 or 2 on a standard 4-point scale) based on how annoyed the client is at the time.

The QA manager, change team, or customer support group who evaluates the problem might well assign a lower severity level, or in some cases even convert the defect report into a potential enhancement request.

In litigation involving quality matters, a great deal of time and effort on both sides is devoted to determining whether the problems involved in the law suit are true errors made by the development team, or the result of inaccurate or even incor-rect requirements on the part of the client.

Following are some of the terms used in this book or in other software quality books and articles whose definitions may cause trouble. This is not a full glossary, but rather a short list of terms that are either used in special ways in a software quality context, or which are ambiguous in common software usage.

Abeyant defect: In software quality this phrase refers to bugs or failure situations which the maintenance team cannot replicate or make happen. Abeyant defects are usually caused by unique hardware or software configurations. Abeyant defects are expensive to repair because extra information must be collected.

Assessment: This term is used to define a subjective but thorough study of software development and maintenance practices. Several varieties of assessment are in current use, but all attempt to explore factors which influence the outcomes of software projects.

Audit: This term predates software, but in a software context it is similar to "assess-ment" and refers to a review of the practices, standards, and documents being utilized on software projects.

Bad fix: This term refers to a new bug or error which is an accidental byproduct of attempting to repair a prior or bug or error. Often bug repairs fix the original prob-lem, but inject a new problem in the fix itself. These new bugs are also called "regressions."

Bad test-case: This term refers to an error in a test-case itself. The problem of bad test cases is a common one.

Benchmark: For software, this term refers to a quantitative comparison of an enterprise against similar enterprises in terms of annual software costs, schedules, productivity, quality, or other tangible factors.

Baseline: This term refers to quantitative performance levels at a particular point in time, such as results for a calendar or fiscal year. Baselines are used to judge improvement over time from the initial starting values.

Bug: This term was created in the 1950s by the late Admiral Grace Hopper who found that an insect had shorted out the contacts in a computer relay board. For software, the term is the general one used for defects, errors, faults, or any other with the general meaning of a mistake made during development.

Certification: This term means the issuance of a diploma or certificate to indicate that the recipient has passed an exam or achieved acceptable levels of performance in selected topics. The concept is ambiguous for software due to overlapping issuing bodies. There is no current legal or professional status to the majority of software certification programs.

Complexity: This is a highly ambiguous term for software. The most common software usage assigns a numeric value to the structured or unstructured control flows of software applications based on the number of branches. Other meanings include the difficulty of problems and algorithms, or the number and kinds of relations of data elements in a database.

Configuration control: This term refers to a method for keeping track of the current status and changes to software specifications, source code, and defect reports. The phrase may also include keeping status reports of hardware changes, too.

Consequential damages: This is a legal term that refers to harm that is secondary attribute of a specific error. The term is starting to show up in software quality litigation. For example, in a law suit involving the Lotus Corporation the plaintiff asked for consequential damages to cover the probable fees for a contract that was not awarded to the plaintiff because of alleged errors in the Lotus 123 spreadsheet.

Cost of quality: This term originated in the 1920s with Joseph Juran and was made popular by Phil Crosby in a well-known book *Quality is Free.* The phrase refers to a set of accounting "buckets" for recording cost elements associated with defect repairs. The usage of standard accounting methods allows comparisons between companies and projects. However, the term originated for manufacturing and needs some adjustment to work for software.

Cost per defect: This term attempts to define the average effort or expense for repairing a software bug or failure. The term is highly ambiguous in use because there are no standard accounting practices for which activities should be included or excluded. Due to inclusion of fixed costs, the cost per defect usually rises as quality improves, and will approach or hit infinity for zero-defect software applications.

Cyclomatic complexity: This term defines one of the more common metrics for evaluating source code complexity. It evaluates the complexity of a graph of a program or module's control flow. The general formula for evaluating the graph is "edges minus nodes plus 2." Software with no branch logic at all has a cyclomatic complexity of 1. As cyclomatic complexity rises above 10, the number of test cases goes up and full coverage becomes difficult. For cyclomatic complexity levels above 50, full testing may be impossible because the number of test paths would start to approach infinity. Many commercial and shareware tools are available to parse source code and generate cyclomatic complexity levels. Some also produce interesting graphs of program structure. See also "essential complexity."

Data quality: For software this term deals with errors in databases, data warehouses, repositories and the like. There are no effective metrics for normalizing the numbers or data errors found, or even for evaluating the size or volume of the data being considered.

Defect: For software this term means some kind of error or bug in a software artifact such as a requirements, specifications, source code, or anything else. The term "defect" was used in IBM as early as the 1950s and is common throughout the United States. The similar term "fault" is equivalent and widely used in Europe.

Defect origin: This term refers to the specific document or event which caused a defect to enter the stream of software development. Five common origins are often evaluated for statistical quality control purposes: requirements, design, source code, user documentation, and bad fixes or secondary defects made while repairing a primary defect.

Defect potential: This phrase refers to the total universe of errors or bugs that might be expected in a software project. Errors in requirements, design, source code, documentation, and bad fixes are the usual elements since these five categories are all likely to be discovered by users if not eliminated.

Defect removal efficiency: This phrase refers to the percentage of potential defects eliminated prior to releasing a software project to customers. It is usually measured by comparing the volume of bugs found prior to release with the volume of bugs reported by users in the first year of deployment.

Duplicate defect: This phrase refers to the 2nd, 3rd, or Nth report of the same bug. Usually duplicates are associated with commercial software with large numbers of users.

Error: This term can be used generically for any kind of bug or mistake. It also has a more specific meaning as a deviation from requirements which might cause failure if not eliminated.

Essential complexity: This term is similar to "cyclomatic complexity" with an important difference. Before calculating the essential complexity level the graph of program flow is analyzed and duplicate segments are removed. Thus, if a module or code segment is utilized several times in a program, its complexity would only be counted once rather than at each instance. Thus, essential complexity eliminates duplicate counts of reusable material and provides a firmer basis for secondary calculations such as how many test cases might be needed. This form of complexity is usually derived by tools which parse source code directly. See also "cyclomatic complexity."

Failure: For software this term refers to a software application that stops working completely or produces results that are wrong and in error.

Fault: For software this term means some kind of error or bug in a software artifact such as a requirements, specifications, source code, or anything else. The similar term "defect" is equivalent and widely used in the United States, while "fault" is widely used in Europe. However, both terms are found on every continent.

Feature point: This term refers to a 1986 variant on standard function points. The feature point metric added "algorithms" to the set of five function point elements (inputs, outputs, inquiries, logical files, and interfaces). For quality, it is of interest that the six feature point elements overlap the topics for which testing is usually necessary.

Fiduciary duty: This term is a general business term which means the professional obligations which executives and boards of directors owe to the shareholders of public corporations or to the owners of private corporations. The term is starting to occur in quality-related litigation, often with assertions that executives violated their responsibilities by failing to act in a responsible manner. The term is about to become important for software because failure to correct Year 2000 problems will probably lead to many law suits where violation of fiduciary duty will be part of the case alleged against executives.

Function point: This term refers to a metric developed by IBM in the 1970s and now in the public domain. The function point metric is a synthetic metric based on weighted totals of five factors: inputs, outputs, logical files, inquiries, and interfaces. Function point metrics are used for normalizing quality and productivity data and have the property of staying constant regardless of programming language.

Invalid defect: For software this term refers to a bug report which upon analysis is not actually caused by the software package for which the bug report was sent in. Sometimes invalid defects are due to hardware problems, sometimes to other software packages, and sometimes to user errors.

Inspection: For software this term refers to a formal, manual perusal of software artifacts with the intent of finding errors. Inspections have protocols which must be adhered to, such as the numbers of participants, their roles, the recording of defects, and the scheduling and lead times of the sessions, plus the follow-on activities.

KLOC: In this compound term, "K" is the engineering abbreviation for 1000 (actually 1024) while "LOC" means lines of code. Sometimes KSLOC is substituted with "SLOC" standing for source lines of code. Unfortunately, this term is used interchangeably for more than 20 variations whose total range spans about an order of magnitude, making it among the most ambiguous terms ever used in engineering literature. The most common variance concerns whether physical lines or logical statements comprise the basic element of the metric.

Lines of code: This term is highly ambiguous and is used for many different counting conventions. The most common variance concerns whether physical lines of logical statements comprise the basic elements of the metric. Note that for some modern programming languages that use button controls, neither physical lines nor logical statements are relevant.

Proof of correctness: This term refers to applying mathematical proof techniques to algorithms associated with software.

Prototype: For software, this term refers to building a working version of the interfaces and sometimes key functions of software applications. Although there are wide variations, prototypes often replicate about 10% of the features of the program or system in question.

Quality: This term is among the most ambiguous words in the English language and is ambiguous in all other natural languages, too. For software, quality usually has a hybrid meaning that includes freedom from defects plus adherence to requirements plus other nuances such as fitness for use. There is no single, unambiguous definition.

Quality assurance: This term can be used generically to refer to all activities that affect quality in any way. It also has a number of more specific definitions, such as the label assigned to quality assurance departments and to quality assurance personnel.

Quality control: This term can be used generically for the same concepts as "quality assurance" or more specifically to specific combinations of inspections and test steps applied to software projects.

Reengineering: For software, this term means migrating an aging legacy application to a new version, often using a new programming language, new database package, and even new hardware platforms.

Regression: For software, this term means slipping backward. It usually refers to an error made while attempting to add new features or fix bugs in an existing application.

Regression test: For software, this term means a set of test cases that are run after changes are made to an application. The test cases are intended to ensure that every prior feature of the application still works, and the new materials have not caused errors in existing portions of the application.

Reliability: This term refers to the length of time a software application can run without any bugs or errors being noted. Several kinds of reliability may be measured, such as mean-time to initial failure or mean-time between failures.

Restructuring: For software, this term refers to methods or tools which can reduce the complexity levels of aging legacy software. Commercial code restructuring tools are available for several languages such as COBOL and C. Often they make use of graph theory and operate by creating a graph of the application's control flow, simplifying the graph, and then reconstituting the application using the simplified structure.

Reusability: This term refers to making use of existing artifacts to create new applications. At least a dozen software artifacts are potentially reusable, including specifications, source code, user documentation, test cases, data, screens, and project plans. In the context of software quality, it is important that successful reuse requires very high quality to be effective and economical.

Reverse engineering: For software, this term has several meanings. One meaning is using automated methods to extract latent design information from the source code of aging legacy applications whose specifications are missing or not up to date. A second definition refers to decomposing the operation of a competitive software package so that key features can be imitated.

Severity levels: This term refers to a method of sorting software bugs or defects based on how much trouble they are likely to cause. There is no standard definition for severity, but many companies use severity codes base on IBM's four-part scale. Under this scale, severity 1 means the application does not work at all. Severity 2 means a major function is disabled. Severity 3 means a minor functional deficiency, while severity 4 means a very minor cosmetic problem that does not affect the software package's operation (i.e., a spelling error in an on-screen prompt).

Silver Bullet Syndrome: This unusual phrase entered the software literature via Fred Brooks' famous book *The Mythical Man-Month*. The phrase derives from the myth that only a silver bullet can kill a werewolf. In a software context, this phrase refers to the tendency of software managers to believe that there must be some magical tool or methodology that will eliminate their long-standing problems with schedule slippage, cost overruns, and quality problems.

Six-Sigma: This is a term that originated in Motorola. The meaning of the term is to reduce defect levels down to roughly no more than 3.4 errors in 1,000,000 chances to make an error. The term is derived from the mathematical concept of sigma. For example, an error rate of two-sigma would be 308,700 errors per million; three-sigma would be 66,810 errors per million; five-sigma would be 233 errors per million. Expressed in the more familiar "defects per KLOC metric" the six-sigma value would be approximately 0.0034 defects per KLOC. This value is sometimes achieved for software projects, but not very often.

Although the mathematics are not the same as used by Motorola, another way of envisioning what is needed to achieve six-sigma quality levels is to think of what would have to be done to achieve a cumulative defect removal efficiency level of 99.999999% for a software product of substantial size, say 5,000 function points. Typical defect removal efficiency rates for this size are currently less than 90% although projects by "top gun" software groups approach 99%.

Testing: For software, the word "testing" has come to mean executing all or part of the application against pre-defined data and procedural sequences with known outcomes. This general term has a host of subordinate and secondary definitions.

Test-case: This term defines a specific set of data, ranges, or known outcomes which can be used to validate a software application. For example, to test a software sorting algorithm, a set of data items in random alphabetical or numeric sequence might be presented as input to the application to ensure that the sort will achieve valid sequencing of known outputs.

Warranty: This term refers to a guarantee by a software vendor that a software package will be free from serious defects and/or perform as advertised. However, many software packages have no warranties at all. Many subsidiary and derivative terms are part of the overall concept of a warranty such as "limited warranty" with specific exclusions; "implied warranty" which refers to factors assumed to be obvious; and "explicit warranty" which means a list of specific topics guaranteed by the vendor.

Year 2000 problem: This term refers to the fact that many computer applications store calendar years in two-digit format; i.e., calendar year 1996 is stored as 96. When the 20th century comes to an end, many software applications will fail because the last two digits of 2000 are 00 and hence lower in numeric value than the last two digits of 1999.

QUALITY ESTIMATION TOOLS

It is an interesting phenomenon that most of the Baldrige Award winners and close to 100% of the producers of high-quality software make use of formal quality and defect estimation tools.

The first such tool in the United States that estimated defect potentials and defect removal efficiency was probably IBM's "Interactive Productivity and Quality" model (IPQ) which was developed in 1973 as a proprietary tool and not marketed. Several other large corporations such as AT&T and ITT have also developed proprietary quality and reliability estimation tools, since such tools give them a significant competitive advantage.

Among SPR's 600 or so clients, about 150 currently utilize some form of software quality estimation tool, and about 50 utilize multiple quality estimation tools. It is an interesting observation that from our client set, less than 20 companies that do not use some form of automated quality estimation tool have any kind of manual quality predictions as part of their quality methods.

An even stronger and more interesting correlation, the cumulative defect removal efficiency levels among the enterprises using software quality estimation tools averages about 11% higher than among enterprises that lack such tools; i.e., about 94% versus 83%.

This is not because quality estimation tools themselves raise defect removal efficiency, but rather because the companies with enough interest in quality to use defect prediction tools also have rather sophisticated defect removal activities, including usage of formal inspections.

The first commercial software estimation tool that could deal with defect potentials, defect removal, and reliability was SPQR/20 (SPQR stood for "Software Productivity, Quality, and Reliability") which was marketed in 1985.

There are several powerful quality estimation tools today such as CHECKPOINT, which first entered the commercial market in 1989. In addition the SLIM, cost estimating tool also predicts quality. The general capabilities of quality estimation tools such as CHECKPOINT, SLIM, and others include these quality and reliability estimation features:

- Estimating defect potentials for bugs in five categories (requirements defects, design defects, coding defects, documentation defects, and "bad fixes" or secondary defects).

- Estimating defect severity levels in four categories, ranging from severity 1 (total or catastrophic failure) to severity 4 (minor or cosmetic problem).

- Estimating the defect removal efficiency levels of various kinds of design reviews, inspections, and a dozen kinds of testing against each kind and severity of defect.

- Estimating the number and severity of latent defects present in a software application when it is delivered to users.

- Estimating the number of user-reported defects on an annual basis for up to 20 years.

- Estimating the reliability of software at various intervals using mean-time to failure (MTTF) and/or mean-time between failures (MTBF) metrics.

- Estimating the "stabilization period" or number of calendar months of production before users can execute the application without encountering severe errors.

- Estimating the effort and costs devoted to various kinds of quality and defect removal effort such as inspections, test-case preparation, defect removal, etc.

- Estimating the number of test cases and test runs for all testing stages.

- Estimating maintenance costs for up to 20 years for fixing bugs (some may have a separate estimating capability for enhancements).

- Estimating special kinds of defect reports including duplicates and invalid reports which trigger investigation expenses but no repair expenses.

In addition to commercial software estimating tools a number of large high-technology corporations have constructed or contracted for proprietary quality estimation tools. Already cited is the case of IBM which built a proprietary quality tool in the early 1970s. The AT&T Bell Laboratories also contracted for a proprietary quality estimation tool, and has built a number of specialized reliability models covering both hardware and software. ITT also constructed a proprietary quality estimation tool.

As can be seen from these companies, computer manufacturers and telecommunication manufacturers have a strong business interest in both quality and reliability and are often on the forefront of quality research and development.

Since quality estimation is sometimes a function found within software cost estimation tools, see also the sections on Cost Estimating and Software Quality and Project Management and Software Quality and Quality Assurance Tool Capacities.

QUALITY FACTORS NOTED IN LITIGATION AND WARRANTIES

What constitutes "quality" is an ambiguous term at best. For software, the topic is even more ambiguous due to the well-meaning but incorrect inclusion of factors that actually have nothing to do with quality at all.

For example, many texts on software quality include listings of software quality factors that run from half a dozen to more than a dozen factors. John Marciniak's *Encyclopedia of Software Engineering* (John Wiley and Sons, 1994) summarizes many of these lists. An overall "average" set of quality factors might include these topics:

Table 1 General List of Factors Cited in Software Quality Literature

Quality Factor	Definition
Correctness	Exact adherence to formal specifications
Reliability	Execution without overt failure or error
Efficiency	Amount of computer resources required to execute
Integrity	Protection from viruses and unauthorized use
Security	Protection from penetration by covert means
Usability	Effort to learn software commands and features
Maintainability	Effort to isolate and repair defects
Testability	Effort to test algorithms, boundaries, and ranges
Flexibility	Effort to expand feature set and add new features
Portability	Effort to migrate application to another platform
Reusability	Percentage of software suitable for use by other applications
Interoperability	Effort to port one application to another
Understandability	Effort to read and decipher source code listings

While all of these topics may be important in a business sense, and all are important technical attributes of software products, many of them should be removed from a working definition of quality as being irrelevant or even potentially hazardous to software vendors should they offer explicit warranties. The relevant and irrelevant factors from the above list include:

Table 2 Quality Factors Relevant and Irrelevant to Software Warranties

Relevant Factors	Irrelevant Factors
Correctness	Efficiency
Reliability	Flexibility
Integrity	Portability
Usability	Reusability
Maintainability	Interoperability
Testability	Integrity
Understandability	Security

The factors in the "irrelevant" column are not unimportant or trivial. They may even be vital, but they should be separated from a working definition of "quality" that will be included in an explicit, written warranty of a software package.

Consider "portability" as an example of an irrelevant quality factor. Suppose someone buys a ski rack for a Toyota, and it fits perfectly. Then suppose that person sells the Toyota and buys a Chrysler. Is it a sign of poor quality that the ski rack may not fit the Chrysler?

Now suppose you buy Microsoft Word for Windows 95. Should this same package operate under the UNIX or MVS operating systems?

The same reasoning applies to custom and contract software. If one commissions a software application to be built under Windows 95, whether or not it will also work under MVS or UNIX is irrelevant to the contract unless that was also part of the work requirement.

What should be relevant to a working definition of software quality is the same set factors things that hardware and electronics manufacturers would support under standard warranties; i.e., defects in workmanship and failures under normal operating conditions would be supported by free warranty repairs.

Porting a product to another platform or even having trouble understanding the user's manual is not a warranty situation.

From observing litigation involving claims of poor quality, it is prudent for software contractors and software vendors to narrow down the scope of quality definitions to a set that resembles the kinds of topics that are usually covered under hardware and product warranties. Otherwise, the software vendors may find themselves in court defending why their packages violate their own definitions of quality.

It is a normal business practice to warranty that a product is free from defects or that any residual defects will be repaired promptly. It would not be a normal business practice to warranty that a software package will work on any known operating system or run on any known hardware platform.

QUALITY FUNCTION DEPLOYMENT (QFD)

Quality Function Deployment originated in Japan in the 1970s for dealing with the quality of complex manufactured devices, such as automobiles. (Toyota was one of the pioneers of QFD, for example.)

Like several other Japanese quality approaches, QFD moved to the United States as a manufacturing approach, and was then later deployed for software projects. Only about a dozen of SPR's clients utilize QFD for software and they are all high-technology manufacturing companies (i.e., AT&T, DEC, Ford, General Motors, Hewlett Packard, Motorola, etc.). Further, these same organizations had used QFD for software only once or at most twice, so they were still in start-up mode. Therefore, our total sample of QFD for software projects as this book is written is less than 20.

Because the companies using QFD are already fairly sophisticated in quality control approaches, the apparent success of QFD as a software quality approach may be misleading. QFD is a very formal, structured group activity involving clients and product development personnel. QFD is sometimes called "the house of quality" because one of the main kinds of planning matrices resembles the peaked roof of a house.

In the course of the QFD sessions, the users' quality criteria are exhaustively enumerated and defined. Then the product's quality response to those requirements is then carefully planned so that all of the quality criteria are implemented or accommodated.

For the kinds of software where client quality concerns can be enumerated and where developers can meet and have serious discussions about quality, QFD appears to work very well: switching systems, manufacturing support systems, fuel-injection software controls, weapons systems, and the like. Also, QFD requires development and QA personnel who know a lot about quality and its implications. QFD is not a "quick and dirty" approach that works well using short-cuts and a careless manner.

The QFD software projects that SPR has examined have significantly lower rates of creeping requirements and also much lower than average volumes of both requirements and design defects than U.S. norms. However, the kinds of software projects that use QFD typically do not have highly volatile requirements. Requirements errors identified after QFD is completed have only run to about 0.2 problems per function point versus about 0.75 for the U.S. as a whole. Design problems as found using formal inspections have also been lower than average, and run only to about 0.5 defect per function point rather than 1.0. Coding defects have been lower than U.S. norms but not lower than typical for high-technology software projects using formal structured coding approaches; i.e., about 1.1 coding defects per function point versus U.S. norms of roughly 1.75.

Expressed another way, raising the function point total of an application to the 1.25 power will give a useful approximation of overall defect potentials for "average" software projects in the United States. For projects using QFD raising application size to the 1.15 power gives a better approximation. This indicates a significant impact in terms of defect prevention.

Interestingly, for defect removal efficiency, the QFD projects and similar projects are running about the same: roughly 96% of defects are eliminated prior to deployment. However, it is obvious that any project with a 96% defect removal efficiency level used pre-test inspections and formal testing by testing specialists. These approaches both common among the kinds of high-technology corporations that are also likely to use quality function deployment.

The initial results are favorable enough to recommend at least substantial experiments with the QFD approach. The only caveat is that for certain kinds of software, such as spreadsheets or word processors with thousands of users each of whom might have different quality criteria, it is not possible to gather all of the users together or explore their quality needs completely.

QFD is now finding its way through many of the "high-tech" companies such as AT&T, Motorola, and Hewlett Packard. The more recent experiences with QFD for software are favorable enough so that this methodology can now be added to the lists of approaches with good to excellent empirical results although the sample size is small enough so that caution is indicated.

From observations among SPR's clients who are QFD users, the QFD approach may or may not give the same level of results in companies that lack QA organizations, formal testing, and a tendency to use careful specification and design methods. Since most companies in this class have not yet experimented with QFD and many have not yet even heard of it, there is no empirical data to back up this observation.

QUALITY LAGGARDS

Although the SPR quality surveys concentrates on "best in class" enterprises, the data collected is also capable of highlighting enterprises at the bottom of the quality pyramid. Enterprises with really poor software practices are under represented among our clients, since they do not perform assessment and benchmark studies as often as leading organizations.

However, the following observations have been noted in approximately 25 enterprises out of about 600. (The word "enterprise" is used because almost half of these organizations are government agencies rather than companies.) These lagging enterprises have the following characteristics:

Table 1   Lack of Quality Control Noted in Software Companies with Quality Problems

1) No software quality measurement program of any kind.
2) No usage of formal design and code inspections.
3) No knowledge of the concepts of defect potentials and defect removal efficiency.
4) Either no quality assurance group or a group that is severely understaffed.
5) No trained testing specialists available.
6) Few or no automated quality assurance tools.
7) No quality and reliability estimation capability.
8) Minimal or no software project management tools available.
9) No automated risk assessment or avoidance capability.
10) From a low of one to a high of perhaps four distinct testing stages.
11) No test library or test-case management tools available.
12) No complexity analysis tools utilized.
13) Defect potentials averaging more than 6 defects per function point.
14) Defect removal efficiency averaging less than 80%.
15) Executive and managerial indifference (and ignorance) of quality matters.

In general, organizations that are lagging in quality control tend to be lagging in many other respects as well. Indeed, it would be an interesting large-scale study to explore the relationship between effective quality control and:

1) Staff morale and voluntary attrition.
2) Market shares and competitive positioning.
3) Litigation and product recalls.
4) Replacement of in-house software staff by outsource groups.

It is already clear that the quality laggards are the very companies with the highest probability of canceled projects, several schedule overruns, and severe cost overruns. It is no coincidence that the software groups among the quality laggards also tend to be candidates for immediate replacement by outsource organizations.

In terms of quantification of results, the quality laggards are usually somewhat above U.S. norms in defect potentials. U.S. norms for software defect potentials average about 5 defects per function point, and range from roughly 4 to 6 defects per function point among "average" organizations. The laggards average about or just above 6 and range from 5 to more than 8 defects per function point. The bulk of the imbalance is found in the sub-areas of design defects, coding defects, and "bad fix" injection rates.

In terms of defect removal efficiency, laggards seldom top U.S. norms of about 85% and average about 5% below similar companies, i.e., they average only about 80% in terms of defect removal efficiency.

It is interesting that the quantitative data was quite unknown by the lagging organizations prior to undergoing an assessment and benchmark study. Even then, due to lack of accurate historical data, the results were derived by modeling. That is, upstream data on requirements, design, and user document defects derived by plugging the complexity levels, function point totals, and defect removal steps into a software defect estimation tool. Usually the only kind of quantified quality data available among the set of lagging organizations is a count of customer-reported, post-release defects.

The combination of a visible increase in defect potentials and below par defect removal efficiency levels usually indicates a set of rather unhappy users, coupled with a high exasperation level among corporate executives. The unhappy users and the executive frustration with software results are often what triggered the assessment and benchmark study. Indeed, the managers of lagging software organizations are seldom motivated to perform any kind of process analysis or improvement study unless forced to do so by external pressures.

As a class, the software managers and technical staff employed by the severe quality laggards have a much better than average probability of being replaced by outsource vendors.

Another interesting observation is that the laggards are also candidates for, or even in the midst of, business process reengineering (BPR) studies.

Bringing a really backwards group up to a safe level of software quality performance is an expensive and difficult proposition with a high likelihood of failure. Resistance to change is often severe, coupled with the fact that the software executives and managers of lagging organizations will need really extensive training and retooling to do their jobs properly.

The software technical staff will also need some new tools and probably training in methods such as formal design and code inspections. However, it sometimes happens that the technical staffs in lagging organizations are not actually so bad, but have been handicapped by poor project management and often by questionable executive decisions from higher software management.

From a sociological vantage point, the most difficult aspect of getting lagging software quality enterprises moving is lack of motivation on the part of software management. Yet another problem is the fact that the many of the managers and software executives are ill equipped for their jobs but don't recognize this to be the case.

QUALITY MEASUREMENTS

One of the major factors that differentiates quality leaders from laggards is the existence of a quality measurement program. Among the 600 or so organizations that comprise SPR's clients, about 200 have at least some form of measurement that collect aspects of quality data. The most common measures associated with quality are defect tracking of bugs reported by users after release of software (about 150 clients), which is sometimes augmented by defect tracking during testing (50 clients) or inspections (20 clients).

The rarest form of quality measurements among SPR's clients is the measure of user-satisfaction. Here only about 25 companies have any kind of formal user-satisfaction measurements, and 20 of these are commercial software vendors who have developed or commissioned user-satisfaction surveys.

To really understand quality in all its manifestations, there are two interesting questions that need to be dealt with:

- For quality, what should be measured?

- How often should quality measurements be taken and reported?

The topic of software quality measurements has two broad sub-categories with somewhat different characteristics and frequency intervals:

- Measurement of defects or bugs in software

- Measurement of user-satisfaction levels

Both forms of quality measurement are important. The measurement of defect levels is recommended for essentially 100% of software projects and software organizations.

Measures of user-satisfaction levels are recommended only for software projects where the clients can be queried and actually use the software consciously. For example, software controls many automobile fuel-injection systems but the drivers are often not aware of this fact.

Software Defect Quality Measurements

Defect measurements are often performed by the Quality Assurance (QA) organization although post-release defects may be measured by a customer support or maintenance group. The critical measures and metrics of defect reporting are included in Table 1.

Table 1   Software Quality Measurements Associated with Defect Levels

1) Defect volumes (by product, by time period, by geographic region)
2) Defect severity levels
3) Special categories (invalid defects, duplicates, unduplicatable problems)
4) Defect origins (i.e., requirements, design, code, documents, or bad fixes)
5) Defect discovery points (i.e., inspections, tests, customer reports, etc.)
6) Defect removal efficiency levels
7) Normalized data (i.e., defects per function point or per KLOC)
8) Causative factors (i.e., complexity, creeping requirements, etc.)
9) Defect repair speeds or intervals from the first report to the release of the fix

Defect or bug reports can come in at random intervals, and sometimes many reports can arrive almost simultaneously. However, the natural period for defect data reporting to top management is monthly. Monthly data is shown, usually in the context of a 12 month series of ups and downs. For measurement programs that have been existence for several years, rolling averages are also shown as are comparisons to last year's results.

Over and above standard monthly reports, defect data should also be consolidated into an overall annual report that shows quality in terms of defect rates, user-satisfaction levels, schedules, productivity, assessment results, and other important topics of interest to both software and enterprise executives, management, and technical staff. Some companies even release their software report to clients and shareholders, just as they might release their corporate annual reports to shareholders. Indeed, the production of an annual software report is one of the signs of a true "top gun" software organization.

Software User-Satisfaction Quality Measurements

User-satisfaction measurements are often performed by the marketing or sales organization, although sometimes quality assurance personnel are involved with user-satisfaction measurements, too.

For some commercial software products, user-satisfaction surveys may also be carried out by organizations that are not part of the company at all. For example, for high-volume commercial software user-satisfaction surveys have been noted by these five kinds of external organizations as well as by the vendors themselves:

- User associations (common for many high-volume packages).

- Software magazines (often review related sets of products).

- Direct competitors (often use survey results in advertising).

- User groups or forums on the Internet or other information utilities such as CompuServe or America Online.

- Third-party software survey groups such as Gartner Group, Giga Group, Meta Group, Ovum, Software Productivity Group (SPG), Auerbach, or International Data Corporation (IDC) often sell their survey results to clients or competitors.

The critical measurements of user-satisfaction for software projects and packages include the following topics found in Table 2.

Table 2   Software Quality Measurements Associated with User-Satisfaction Levels

1)	User perception of quality and reliability.
2)	User perception of feature in the software product.
3)	User perception of ease of learning.
4)	User perception of ease of use.
5)	User perception of customer support.
6)	User perception of speed of defect repairs.
7)	User perception of speed of adding new features.
8)	User perception of virtues competitive products.
9)	User perception of the value versus the cost of the package.

The incoming data for user-satisfaction measurements is normally derived from a formal customer survey, and the survey instruments are often created by specialists in this kind of work. Survey design is a complex topic, and therefore consultants, or even cognitive psychologists, may be asked to contribute to the design.

Because survey design is time consuming and tricky the usual frequency for building a survey or modifying one is about once a year. Also, taking the time to fill out a survey is intrusive on customers themselves so companies do not want to risk customers' annoyance by asking them to fill out really massive questionnaires or dealing with frequent requests for new data. As a result of multiple factors, user-satisfaction surveys are often performed either annually or, at most, semi-annually. However, for a brand new product or one that offers new and unique features, a special survey might be performed a few months after release.

For companies such as IBM, Computer Associates, and Microsoft with a host of products in their field, continuous monitoring of user-satisfaction can also occur using the Internet or various online services such as CompuServe or America Online. Most large software companies now have World Wide Web sites and many also have or support user forums on other information utilities as well.

Also, it is too late to correct major flaws in software product usability if developers depend only upon post-release results. Therefore user-satisfaction analysis is a key component of the development of new commercial software packages. The pre-release user-satisfaction data is usually gathered via one or more of these channels:

- Focus groups of customers who are invited to preview prototypes early in development.

- Formal usability laboratories where customers can gain hands-on experience prior to release.

- External Beta tests where selected customers use a near-final but hopefully complete version of the product on their own computers in their own companies.

- Requests from user associations for various improvements in usability.

- Imitation of the usability features of competitive or similar products by other vendors.

The latter form of usability improvement, or imitating features in competitive products, is somewhat hazardous and sometimes leads to one of the software industry's well-known "look and feel" lawsuits.

Indeed, the software industry' tendency to be litigious when it comes to improvements in usability is actually a significant barrier to improving human factors. It is interesting to speculate about automobile driving safety if 75 years ago Ford had sued General Motors over putting their gas, clutch, and brake pedals in the same place and using similar control panel layouts. (Also, for both aircraft flight controls and the positions of motorcycle shift levers and brake levers, identical positioning was mandated by government regulation after the discovery that many accidents had occurred when pilots or motorcycle drivers changed to vehicles with controls in different places and hence reacted incorrectly during emergencies.)

Since quality in terms of defects and quality in terms of user-satisfaction tend to correlate strongly, it is desirable to show both kinds of quality data. Here, too, the production of an annual report that consolidates user-satisfaction findings with numeric defect levels and other topics such as assessment results is a sign of a leading organization.

Quality measurements of both defects and user-satisfaction are not inexpensive, although they are very valuable. Expect a full defect measurement program to require about 1% to 2% of software team effort. The same can be said of user-satisfaction measures, except that they are performed by personnel outside the software development organization. Therefore, a combination of defect and user-satisfaction measures will average about 3%, using the overall budget of the software group as the basis. The range of observed effort for software quality measurements is from less than 1% to just over 5% of budgeted software effort. (Costs may be higher if external consultants are used for specialized tasks such as survey instrument design.)

Quality measurement is not the only aspect of measurement that is important. The following diagram shows how quality measurements fit in context with other significant kinds of software measurement practices.

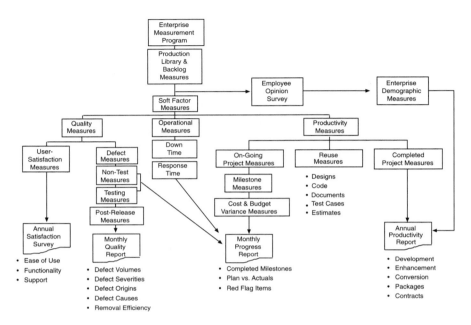

Figure 1 Software Quality Measurement in Context with Other Software Measures

As can be seen, software quality measurements occupy the two columns on the left of the chart. Normally user-satisfaction measures and defect measures are carried out at different intervals and by different groups. The user-satisfaction data is often collected by sales and marketing personnel, while the defect data is often collected by quality assurance personnel. Eventually, all kinds of data are aggregated into monthly reports, and then again for annual reports.

The most important focal point of the whole set of software measurements is the production of the annual report, which integrates quality, user-satisfaction, productivity, schedules, costs, and many other factors into one highly significant document.

The timing and effort to produce an annual software report is roughly the same as the timing and effort to produce a corporate annual report for shareholders. For a major corporation with perhaps 2,000 software personnel (or more) the size of the annual software report is usually in the 50 to 75 page category.

Production of the report normally takes place in the first-quarter after the end of a calendar year or fiscal year, and the effort involved is roughly two staff months assuming that all of the incoming data is available in machine-readable form.

Since the full contents of an annual report include much more than quality, it is not appropriate to show an example here. However, my book *Applied Software Measurement* (McGraw Hill, 1996, 2nd edition) has a complete example of an annual software report in Appendix D.

Among SPR's clients, annual software reports are produced only by about 30 enterprises, and they tend to be among the best in many aspects of software development and maintenance performance.

RAPID APPLICATION DEVELOPMENT (RAD) AND SOFTWARE QUALITY

Techniques that are advertised as improving or shortening software schedules have more or less the same impact on software managers as the discovery of gold in California in 1848. Thousands of people started a mass migration in the hope of becoming rich, and many ended up in poverty or worse off than they were before. For software, methods or tools that are aimed at shortening software development cycles also tend to achieve a stampede of early adopters. Here, too, many end up being worse off than they were before.

Rapid Application Development (RAD) has a very appealing name with "rapid" attracting a great deal of favorable press interest. Some of the concepts associated with RAD, such as prototyping, are often valuable. RAD has also been discussed by a number of highly respected software authors such as James Martin whose book *Rapid Application Development,* (Macmillan, 1991) has been a best-seller. Even before Martin, Fred Brooks also discussed the value of prototyping in his famous book *The Mythical Man-Month,* (Addison Wesley, 1975–2nd edition, 1995).

However, in spite of its name, antecedents, and some examples of success, RAD is often a hazardous approach with a high probability of ending up in court for some kind of breach of contract suit, or even suits alleging professional malpractice because the completed RAD projects have not been reliable enough to be used for their intended purposes.

Among our 600 or so client companies roughly 35 companies have used variations of the RAD approach for a total of perhaps 110 projects out of almost 7,000. The size range of the RAD projects has been from less than 100 function points to about 3,500 function points. This is not a particularly rich sample but my observations from our limited client results indicate the following:

- Below 500 function points RAD is often successful in shortening development schedules, and quality is tolerable although not as good as more formal structured methods.

- Above 1,000 function points RAD is often unsuccessful in shortening development schedules, and quality is poor enough to be alarming.

The typical RAD adoption cycle among SPR's clients has been the following.

Like any new approach, RAD is tried out experimentally on a small project at or below 100 function points in size. The results are usually favorable in terms of schedule reduction and fairly high productivity of > 30 function points per staff month.

Since the results of the pilot experiment are favorable, RAD is then used on one or more projects in the 500 function point size range, and again achieves some level of schedule compression coupled with productivity rates > 25 function points per staff month.

For early uses of RAD, quality may later turn out to be marginal. However, this problem is not immediately visible unless formal defect tracking exists, and for sociological reasons many RAD users tend to lack quality measurements. Therefore it is not known until customer usage builds up that marginal quality levels are occurring. (Note that in-process measurements of quality and post-release measurements of defect removal efficiency are notable gaps in the RAD literature.)

As a result of seemingly successful use on the trial project and other fairly small early projects, RAD is then attempted on a major application in the 1,000 to 5,000 function point range. Here, disaster strikes, and the project may be delayed or canceled because it does not operate well enough to move into production. What is worse, the frequent lack of proper specifications and the poor code structure make it difficult to rescue or salvage the project.

Other consultants and authors who are familiar with the RAD concept assert, with some justification, that the quality problems associated with RAD projects stem from a violation of fundamental RAD concepts. The RAD projects that head into disaster mode are those that abandoned almost every form of written specification and simply jumped into prototyping without adequate planning and preparation. This is not the way RAD is described in James Martin's work, nor is it what Fred Brooks recommends.

The assertion is that evolutionary prototyping in the sense intended by Brooks and Martin is aimed at *augmenting* written requirements and specifications and shortening the time it takes to produce them, rather than total replacement of written requirements and specifications by means of an evolutionary prototype or series of prototypes.

It usually happens that software prototypes are built to either demonstrate key algorithms or to elicit user reaction to interface conventions. Prototypes are usually built without normal quality control procedures such as design or code inspections. This means that the structure of the prototype may be far from optimal, the comment density may be below safe levels, and the number of latent defects hidden in the prototype can be significant.

For disposable prototypes these problems are not too serious since the prototype is intended only to augment understanding of key issues. For evolutionary prototypes, on the other hand, the usual carelessness associated with prototypes can lead to serious problems down-stream.

For large systems of 1,000 function points or larger, attempting to grow a series of evolutionary prototypes into a final product is a very dangerous practice. For contract software evolutionary prototypes may show up in court often enough for evolutionary prototyping to be considered a serious professional hazard for larger applications.

Consider the delay or offset for exploring design decisions when using the RAD approach as a replacement for written specifications. Assume that you were building an application of 1,000 function points in size, using the RAD evolutionary prototyping method.

Table 1   Rapid Application Development (RAD) Construction for an Application of 1,000 Function Points in Size

(Prototype Size Expressed in Terms of Function Points)

Development Phase	Input/Output Screen Prototypes	Key Algorithms Prototypes	TOTAL PROTOTYPES
Requirements	100	25	125
Design	150	125	275
Code	300	200	500
Testing	50	50	100
TOTAL	600	400	1000

As can be seen, the RAD evolutionary prototype method leaves some key issues unresolved until the coding and testing phases. This late exploration means that testing itself may be difficult due to the lack of formal written specifications from which to construct test cases.

For RAD, the development personnel are usually also the test personnel. Since testing is not a common skill, the difficulty in utilizing external testing specialists tends to make it difficult to create full and complete test suites.

Also, because the details of the evolutionary prototypes are not stable and may not even have been worked out at the normal time when test-case construction should be starting, there may be a "crunch" to build test cases late in development. Of course, this is not what the RAD approach recommends, but it is the way the method tends to appear in real life situations.

Another hazard noted with the larger RAD projects is the difficulty of using proper configuration control, since here too prototypes are seldom placed under formal configuration management. The lack of configuration management means that toward the end of development, RAD projects may find conflicting updates occurring.

As often practiced, the RAD method seldom has any finished materials that are capable of formal design and code inspections. This explains why inspections, the most effective known way of quality control, are seldom used in conjunction with RAD projects.

The frequent lack of both configuration control rigor and formal inspections means that RAD would be a poor choice for software that affects the operation of complex physical devices. Thus caution is recommended when attempting to use RAD for weapons systems development, aircraft flight control applications, fuel injection, process control, or medical instrument software systems.

Although the data for RAD has a high margin of error, it is interesting to compare RAD projects against average MIS projects using conventional approaches such as joint application design (JAD). This example shows a project of a nominal 1,000 function points in size developed in COBOL in both normal and RAD flavors.

Table 2 Defect Levels for 1,000 Function Rapid Application Development (RAD) Projects Compared to Average Management Information System (MIS) Projects

(Defect data shown in terms of defects per function point)

	Average MIS Projects	RAD Projects	Difference
Requirements	1.00	0.90	(0.10)
Design	1.25	1.65	0.40
Code	1.50	1.85	0.35
Bad Fixes	0.60	0.75	0.15
User Documents	0.40	0.40	0.00
Total	4.75	5.55	0.80
Defect removal efficiency	85%	78%	0.70%
Delivered defects per function point	0.72	1.21	0.49

With Rapid Application Development (RAD), the advantages derived from early prototyping of user requirements early are frequently offset by sloppy design and poor coding practices, which elevates overall defect volumes and degrades defect removal efficiency levels to hazardous levels.

It is not the intent of this section to be totally dismissive of the RAD concept, since it is often used successfully. However, consider that a number of medicines such as penicillin have hazards and counter-indications associated with them. Penicillin can treat many bacterial infections, but it can also cause a fatal reaction of anaphylactic shock for patients who are allergic to it.

This concept of identifying hazards and counter indications is usually missing from the software literature. For RAD, the hazards and counter-indications lead to the preliminary conclusion that it is not a safe approach for either large systems nor for those where high levels of quality and reliability are indicated.

(See also the sections in this book dealing with Prototyping, Software Quality and Reuse and Software Quality for additional information.)

RELIABILITY AND SOFTWARE QUALITY

Although software quality and software reliability are strongly and fundamentally related, these two topics have developed separate literatures and even separate models for predicting anticipated outcomes.

Among SPR's 600 or so clients, software reliability predictions and measurements are concentrated most heavily in about 100 companies plus military groups that produce large-scale systems software such as operating systems, telecommunications software, medical instruments, embedded software on board weapons systems or aircraft, and other kinds of software that controls the operation of large and complex machinery. Software reliability analysis, prediction, and measurements are comparatively rare among commercial software groups and management information systems although some large commercial shops such as Microsoft do perform reliability studies.

Software reliability is concerned with how software operates under typical field conditions. The most common reliability measurements are those of mean time to failure (MTTF) and mean time between failures (MTBF). These measures are usually based on the number of clock hours of software execution before or between failures or bugs occurring.

Another interesting reliability metric is that of the "stabilization period" or the number of calendar days, weeks, or months before a software project can achieve a specified MTTF or MTBF target. For example, if the target is for a software package to run 40 continuous hours without encountering a bug, it might take six months of usage before that target is approached.

Predicting the reliability of a software package in the hands of users is a complex topic. Some of the factors that need to be known for reliability prediction include:

- Number of users of the software application
- Usage patterns (i.e., intermittent or continuous operation of the software)
- Probable number of latent defects
- Probable severity levels of latent defects
- Complexity of the application in terms of numbers of alternate flow paths

Because the latter three factors are not usually known, some fairly successful reliability models have been built using only the first two factors; i.e., knowledge of probable users and usage patterns. These reliability models use statistical methods derived from observations of similar projects.

From data available primarily within IBM, AT&T, and other large software companies it has been possible to construct a correlation between the number of latent defects in software applications and reliability in terms of mean time between failures (MTBF). The available data on a number of systems software products includes both defect information and reliability information for products at various intervals.

Note that the data in the following table assumes at least 100 users of the software applications. Below about 100 users variations in usage patterns are extreme and hence have a rather strong impact on reliability intervals. Above 100 users, variations in usage patterns tend to level out.

Note also that the table makes a simplifying assumption in terms of the "Defects per KLOC" column. That column is based on a generic expansion ratio of 100 logical statements for each function point. This expansion would be reasonable for a small set of programming languages such as COBOL, FORTRAN, and PASCAL. It is not a suitable expansion for lower-level languages, such as assembly and C, nor for higher-level languages such as Eiffel or SMALLTALK. One of the problems with the KLOC metric is the variability of results from language to language when dealing with topics such as reliability intervals.

This table only shows reliability intervals for a two order of magnitude range of latent defects; i.e., from a high of 1.0 defects per function point down to a level of 0.01 defects per function point. Software with latent defect levels higher than about 1.0 per function point is too unstable to release to users. Software below 0.01 defects per function point have reliability intervals that are better measured in terms of months than in terms of hours.

Table 1   Software Defect Levels and Approximate Reliability Levels in Terms of Mean-Time Between Failures (MTBF)

Defects per Function Point	Defects per KLOC	Reliability in Hours (MTBF)	Interval
1.00	10.00	0.2	
0.90	9.00	0.3	
0.80	8.00	0.4	
0.70	7.00	0.5	
0.60	6.00	0.6	
0.50	5.00	0.8	
0.40	4.00	0.9	
0.30	3.00	1.0	One hour
0.20	2.00	1.5	
0.10	1.00	3.0	
0.09	0.90	8.0	One shift
0.08	0.80	16.0	
0.07	0.70	24.0	One day
0.06	0.60	36.0	
0.05	0.50	60.0	
0.04	0.40	96.0	
0.03	0.30	168.0	One week
0.02	0.20	220.0	
0.01	0.10	280.0	

Although this table has a high margin of error, it does show an interesting correlation between defect densities and reliability intervals. Software that is intended for mission-critical applications such as weapons systems, medical instruments, or national telephone systems must approach zero-defect levels in order to achieve satisfactory reliability intervals.

(See also the sections on Defect Removal Efficiency Levels and Multiple Release Defect Reporting earlier in this book.)

REUSABILITY AND SOFTWARE QUALITY

Software reusability has been a difficult technology to master. However, software reusability is also a very important technology because it holds the promise of making major improvements in quality, schedules, and costs at the same time. Indeed, software reuse has the potential of transforming software construction from a craft into a true engineering discipline.

Among SPR's clients virtually all have at least some kind of reusability in place, with informal code reuse being almost universal in the software industry. Indeed, informal code reuse is much older than the object-oriented paradigm and spans all known programming languages.

However, formal corporate reusability programs that encompass design, code, test materials, and other software artifacts that are both certified and under configuration control are much rarer. Only about 30 of SPR's client companies have such programs, and most are still stocking their libraries.

Of course, the entire commercial software business is a kind of reusability, in that the same applications are sold to thousands or even millions of clients. However, the term "reuse" applies primarily to building custom applications utilizing modules, components, and other artifacts more than one time.

Starting in about 1990, commercial sources of reusable materials began to occur. For example, the Stepstone corporation began to market libraries of reusable components for the Objective C programming language which they called "Software IC's" (the acronym IC is derived from the hardware term of "integrated circuit").

When Microsoft's Visual Basic language and compiler appeared, commercial reuse expanded from a trickle to a river. Indeed, commercial reuse is now on the verge of becoming a new and important subindustry of the overall software industry.

For internal reuse, the most effective way of stocking a library of reusable material is to scan existing applications for modules and functions that occur often, and then develop reusable equivalents that are certified to approximate zero-defect levels.

It is seldom a safe practice to extract modules from aging legacy applications or private libraries and plug them in to a reusable artifact library without careful validation and certification. Recall that from time to time automobile manufacturers are forced to recall large numbers of vehicles and make repairs because of possible hazards that have been noted. This same concept holds true for software reuse. If major or significant errors are found in key reusable artifacts, then product recalls may well be needed.

Just as automotive recalls are sometimes so expensive that they damage the economic value of having reused a defective part, recalling a defective modules or software artifact can turn the positive value of reuse into a negative very quickly. If the recall is accompanied by some form of litigation due to damages, a negative situation can even become a nightmare.

The main effect of software reusability on quality is to reduce defect potentials from today's rather alarming volumes down to safe levels. However, there is a strong caution about the relationship between reuse and quality.

Successful reuse requires that artifacts intended for large-scale reuse achieve zero-defect levels or very close to it. Reusing material that is itself defective and filled with bugs can lead to catastrophic costs and severe project failures.

This means that the task of constructing reusable materials requires state-of-the-art defect removal technologies, and artifacts intended for large-scale corporate reuse must exceed 99% in cumulative defect removal efficiency.

However, once those artifacts are created, certified, and become available, then they in turn become the most effective form of defect prevention discovered for software.

The following table is hypothetical but interesting. It starts with today's observed levels of software defect potentials for six artifacts, and then assumes that various percentages of these artifacts will be replaced by zero-defect reusable equivalents drawn from a corporate library of certified reusable materials.

The table shows 25% reuse, 50% reuse, and 75% reuse in order to illustrate a key point. Reuse is the most effective known technology for achieving substantial reductions in potential defects.

Table 1 Effect of Software Reusability on Software Defect Potentials

(Defect potentials expressed in terms of defects per function point)

Defect Origins	Defects with 0% Reuse	Defects with 25% Reuse	Defects with 50% Reuse	Defects with 75% Reuse
Requirements	1.00	0.75	0.50	0.25
Design	1.25	0.94	0.63	0.31
Source code	1.75	1.31	0.88	0.44
User manuals	0.60	0.45	0.30	0.15
Test cases	1.00	0.75	0.50	0.25
Bad fixes	0.40	0.30	0.20	0.10
TOTAL	6.00	4.50	3.00	1.50

There is no other known way of achieving such low levels of potential defects than to displace custom development by utilization of certified reusable components. Indeed, reuse is the technology that is likely to have the greatest chance of making "six-sigma" quality a viable prospect for the software domain. (See the section on Six-Sigma later in this book.)

Reusability also offers very significant schedule and cost reductions as well as defect potential reductions. As an example of how reuse can benefit costs for a specific project, consider the following hypothetical model.

Assume a financial software project of 1,000 function points (equal to roughly 105,000 COBOL statements) is being constructed with no reuse at all for a net cost of $1,000 per function point or $1,000,000 in total. Then consider three different plateaus of reusability: 25%, 50%, and 75% reuse of key artifacts such as design and source code. The cost breakdown for this project might constitute the following:

Table 2 Cost Per Function Point with 0%, 25%, 50%, and 75% Software Reusability

	0% Reuse	25% Reuse	50% Reuse	75% Reuse
Development				
Requirements	$75.00	$67.50	$52.50	$37.50
Planning & Estimating	$25.00	$20.00	$17.50	$12.50
Design	$150.00	$127.50	$97.50	$67.50
Coding	$225.00	$191.25	$168.75	$112.50

(continued)

Table 2   *(continued)*

	0% Reuse	25% Reuse	50% Reuse	75% Reuse
Development				
Integration	$75.00	$67.50	$60.00	$52.50
Testing	$275.00	$233.75	$192.50	$96.25
User Documents	$75.00	$60.00	$52.50	$45.00
Project Management	$100.00	$80.00	$65.00	$55.00
Subtotal	*$1,000.00*	*$847.50*	*$706.25*	*$478.75*
Maintenance				
Year 1	$250.00	$200.00	$150.00	$75.00
Year 2	$265.00	$215.00	$155.00	$75.00
Year 3	$280.00	$225.00	$165.00	$75.00
Year 4	$300.00	$240.00	$175.00	$70.00
Year 5	$325.00	$260.00	$185.00	$65.00
Subtotal	*$1,420.00*	*$1,140.00*	*$830.00*	*$360.00*
TOTAL	*$2,420.00*	*$1,987.50*	*$1,536.25*	*$838.75*
SAVINGS	*$0.00*	*$432.50*	*$883.75*	*$1,581.25*

It is important to note that there is not a one-to-one linear relationship between the volume of reused material and costs. For example, reusing 50% of the source code in an application does not translate into an exact 50% savings in coding costs. There may be internal charges for acquiring the reusable materials. Even if the reusable component is acquired for free, there is still work involved in linking the reused material to the custom developed material, testing the link, and ensuring that the combination works properly.

There may be subtle impacts on other activities as well. Not all of the impacts are necessarily positive. It may sometimes cost more than normal to handle the requirements, design, configuration control, testing, and user documentation in a way that reflects a high-volume of code reuse. Doing reuse analysis well requires actually requires a much more extensive activity-based reuse model that can deal with all 12 artifacts and their mutual interactions, handle customization of reused materials, deal with acquisition or creation of reused materials, and can amortize the savings or costs across multiple projects and time periods.

There are a dozen software artifacts that are capable of potential reuse in software applications. Since reuse is such a key topic for quality as well as for economics, it is useful to explore the implications of each.

Reusable Architecture

For many kinds of physical structures, the most effective architectural principles have been worked out through trial and error, but these are now well understood by architects, civil engineers, aeronautical engineers, and other scientific and engineering personnel.

For example, the basic architectural principles of suspension bridges, auditoriums, load-bearing walls, athletic stadiums, airframes, catamarans, and countless others are not only well understood but are illustrated and discussed in the relevant literature.

These standard reusable architectural principles are part of the undergraduate and graduate curricula for many kinds of engineers, with the almost unique exception of software engineers. We alone continue to approach every system as though it were a unique artifact with no prior examples anywhere in the world. In fact, most of the kinds of software projects that companies build have been constructed hundreds of times, and a few kinds might have been constructed thousands of times, by other organizations.

For software engineers we have not yet reached the point where the most effective architecture for common kinds of applications is even understood, much less documented and available in published form or taught to software engineering and computer science students.

This is a major gap in software reusability research. For common software applications such as operating systems, compilers, switching systems, payroll applications, insurance claims handling, and a host of others the architectural principles that give effective results should have been worked out by now, but this does not seem to be the case.

As a result, many applications that have been built hundreds or even thousands of times are started from scratch using trial-and-error architectural approaches. The only substantial examples of architectural reuse among SPR's clients is the outsourcing domain among the larger outsource vendors such as Andersen and ISSC who serve multiple clients in the same industries, such as banks, hospitals, or insurance companies.

Reusable Requirements

Although every company is different, what corporations use computers and software for is remarkably similar from enterprise to enterprise. Every company uses software to handle accounting functions, billing, personnel matters, manufacturing support, and other standard business functions.

It should be possible to create a generic requirements statement for common application types that would need only minor customization to be used within various enterprises. Certainly this should be possible for industries where even direct competitors use computers and software for essentially the same things: i.e., insurance, health-care, banking, municipal governments, and so forth.

Unfortunately, understanding of the common elements of the requirements for similar applications is a rare commodity. This means the many software projects must begin with a lengthy and troublesome requirements gathering and analysis phase, rather than starting by scanning a catalog of reusable requirements and using that as the jumping off place.

Even for something so mundane as evaluating possible commercial software packages rather than moving to in-house custom development, there are no standard guidelines for evaluating things that all companies should be interested in, such as ease of learning, ease of use, security, error handling, and the like.

Reusable Designs

For hundreds or perhaps thousands of objects which we use in daily life, reusable designs are available from a host of commercial sources. For example, any reader can purchase reusable designs for summer homes, gazeboes, tool sheds, dinner tables, bookshelves, boats, canoes, small home-built airplanes, and even complete homes of 2,000 square feet or more.

Given the number and variety of reusable designs, one might think that companies who are starting to develop common applications such as point of entry sales support, payroll systems, or order entry systems might be able to acquire a standard reusable design for that kind of application, and customize it to meet local needs.

Unfortunately, reusable designs are not available as commercial commodities for software applications. Nor does the software literature, including the literature on reuse itself and on object-oriented design, contain many tangible examples of reusable designs for common kinds of software applications.

There are a few exceptions, of course, such as the availability of generic reusable designs for sorts and compilers, since these two kinds of applications are often used as tutorial examples in computer science and software engineering curricula.

One of the fundamental barriers to effective reuse of software designs is the continuing difficulty in visualizing software either at the level of complete applications, or at the level of components or specific functions.

Unlike electrical engineering, which has developed standard iconographic representations of electronic circuits and components, there are no standard icons that represent generic software functions such as selection, sorting, error-handling, table updates, or any of the host of common functions that must be joined together to create overall software applications.

Reusable Plans

There are more than 80 project planning tools on the commercial market, such as Artemis, Microsoft Project, Primavera, Project Managers Workbench (PMW), Timeline, and the like.

Given the size of the software market and the number of software project managers in the United States alone (about 250,000) one might expect that these project planning tool vendors would offer templates for planning various kinds of software projects. Unfortunately, the concept of standard planning templates for software projects has not yet reached such a level that software planning templates are commercially available.

Consider these basic questions: for a systems software project of 1,000 function points in size (roughly 125,000 C statements) what is the normal complement of programming personnel? What are the normal schedules in calendar months from the completion of requirements until deployment to customers?

These are not particularly difficult questions to answer, and yet almost every software project deals with these issues as though there had never been any similar projects created anywhere in the world.

A related but more difficult planning question would be how many specialists such as quality assurance, testing, and technical writers, would be required for the project cited above? Here too, the question is not tremendously difficult, but lacks readily available answers available in the form of templates for commercial planning tools.

The root-cause for the lack of reusable plans or readily available software planning templates is primarily due to the fact that software projects have not been measured very well. Poor measurement, in turn, has been due the difficulty of applying "lines of code" metrics to the non-coding portions of software projects such as requirements, design, user documentation, and the like.

Reusable Estimates

Software estimation is a rapidly growing subindustry. As this book is written in 1996, no fewer than 50 commercial software estimating tools are on the market in the United States alone.

Some of the more common commercial software estimating tools include: Before You Leap (BYL), Bridge Modeler, CHECKPOINT, COCOMO, FASTE, GECOMO, Estimacs, PRICE-S, PRO-QMS, SEER, SLIM, and SPQR/20.

These software estimation tools differ from project planning tools in having an attached knowledge base that contains data on hundreds or even thousands of software projects. In fact, most companies that develop and sell software estimation tools also have consulting wings in the software measurement domain. It is the empirical data collected from many software projects that give estimation tools a level of "reusability" that exceeds most other aspects of software reuse.

Because the project planning tools discussed in the previous topic support any kind of project, and software is only one segment of their market, the project planning tool vendors usually do not have a software measurement consulting group nor do they collect enough empirical data on software projects to construct effective planning templates.

The commercial software estimating tools, on the other hand, actually do support reusable software cost estimation. By distilling the results of hundreds or even thousands of software projects and converting them into estimating templates, the software estimation tools are a very good example of the value of reuse applied to a major business problem.

Many of the commercial cost estimating tools also support at least phase-level schedule estimation. A few support activity-level and even task-level schedule estimation. Some commercial estimation tools also support both quality estimation and reliability estimation also.

On the whole, the commercial software estimation world is one of the rare software domains where reuse is both common and reasonably effective and also readily available from commercial vendors.

Reusable Source Code

Every experienced programmer keeps a private library of reusable subroutines derived from prior applications. Among SPR's clients, this kind of informal and personal reuse is both very common and sometimes surprisingly effective. Personal reuse also spans all known programming languages.

However, the volume of personal reusable material is usually small so that the total quantity of reusable code derived from private libraries seldom exceeds 25% of the total volume of the applications being constructed.

Because effective reuse requires high quality levels, most experienced programmers have eliminated the bulk of all errors or bugs from the components and modules that they reuse in multiple applications. Often the bugs have been eliminated by trial and error methods over a period of months or years. As a general rule experienced programmers have learned the hard way the reuse demands high quality levels.

Formal reusability programs at the corporate level are much rarer than informal and personal reuse. Corporate reuse is a much more serious undertaking than casual reuse at the private level too.

Among the hallmarks of formal corporate reusability may be found the following:

- A formal evaluation program for candidates modules for the reuse library

- Certification of reusable components to very high quality levels

- Careful recording of who accesses the reusable library and uses components

- A recall mechanism to deal with errors in reusable components

- An award structure for developers whose work is added to the reuse library

- A browsing capability to ascertain what is available for reuse

- A charge back mechanism for reuse (in some cases)

It is interesting to explore the distribution of reuse among a sample of software applications. As an experiment I evaluated the approximate volume of reusable source code in a sample of 265 new applications (finished between 1993 and 1996) whose size ranged between 100 and 1,000 function points. The programming languages in my sample included C, C++, COBOL, FORTRAN, Ada83, Pascal, and PL/I.

The basic subject of my analysis was simply to enumerate the approximate volume of code in finished applications that had been reused, rather than uniquely developed for the application.

As a trivial example, if a program consists of 100 source code statements in five modules, and four modules were custom developed while one was reused from a prior application, then for this example the reuse volume would be 20% since 20 out of 100 statements were in fact reused.

I did not try to enumerate the exact amount of reuse but only aggregated the results into a series of 10% plateaus. Even so, the results are interesting even if only preliminary and partial in terms of programming languages and application sizes included.

Table 3   Ranges of Reusable Code Volumes in a Sample of 265 Software Applications from 100 Function Points to 1,000 Function Points in Size

Volume of Reused Source Code	Number of Applications	Percent of Applications
0 %	0	0.0 %
< 10 %	50	18.9 %
11 % to 20 %	54	20.4 %
21 % to 30 %	65	24.5 %
31 % to 40 %	38	14.3 %
41 % to 50 %	25	9.4 %
51 % to 60 %	15	5.7 %
61 % to 70 %	13	4.9 %
71 % to 80 %	5	1.9 %
81 % to 90 %	0	0.0 %
> 90 %	0	0.0 %
100%	0	0.0 %
TOTAL	265	100.0 %

As can be seen, at least some code reuse is a very common phenomenon. However, the volume of reuse in terms of the largest number of applications peaked in the range of 21% to 30% which is roughly what might be expected from informal reuse by experienced programmers with private libraries.

This casual study perhaps raises more questions than it answers. For example, what would be the volume of reuse if fully object-oriented languages such SMALLTALK, Objective C, and Eiffel had been included? Unfortunately, SPR's clients have not provided enough projects in these languages within the size ranges I need to research with the topic.

The same is true of many other interesting languages such as Visual Basic. Among a small sample of about 20 applications in Visual Basic, reuse topped 70%, averaged 41% to 50%, and the lowest value was amount was 21% to 30%. However, all 20 of the Visual Basic applications were below 100 function points in size.

If we were to put together a list in descending order of the volumes of reusable code in ordinary software created today for business technical purposes, the probable rank order would be:

- Visual Basic and competitors such as Realizer
- COBOL
- Eiffel
- Objective C
- Ada83
- SMALLTALK
- C++

This ranking is not based on a formal analysis, but from informal observations of the reuse programs among our clients and the volume of reused code in their typical applications.

What is interesting about the list, which admittedly has a high margin of error, is that the top two languages are not object-oriented languages at all. Both Visual Basic and COBOL have accumulated substantial volumes of reusable materials for interesting reasons.

Visual Basic has triggered the creation of a new subindustry of companies that create button controls that can be reused in VB applications. For example, controls are available for Gantt charts, spreadsheets, time accounting, and a host of specialized functions.

COBOL, on the other hand, has not formed a large subindustry of commercial reusable modules but has been around long enough so that most companies have large private libraries of reusable COBOL modules that can be called upon as needed.

Both Objective C and Eiffel were created with reuse in mind, and hence the developers of both languages were careful with how their libraries were controlled. Objective C pioneered the sale of commercial reusable components with their "Software IC" concept in the 1980s. (The phrase "Software IC" stands for "Software integrated circuits" and was an attempt to do for software what hardware integrated circuits did for electronics.)

Eiffel started out as a language for dealing with reuse at the design level, and became a programming language almost as an after thought. Hence, the Eiffel domain is one of the few where reuse can span both design and code.

However, in spite of all the articles and journal articles on software reuse, to say nothing of the claims of the object-oriented domain, empirical studies of software reuse volumes are in very short supply.

There are many articles and some books about the concept of code reuse, but fairly little solid data on how much code is actually reused in day-to-day software development work and even less information on what the code is being used for.

In the 1970s IBM did a fairly detailed analysis of the reusability potential of selected kinds of software applications. I recall that for accounting software packages in COBOL, the IBM study indicated than about 85% of the total volume of code could potentially have been derived from a library of reusable modules had such a library been available.

A more surprising find from the IBM analysis was that less than 30% of the code had any direct relationship to accounting at all, even though the packages were nominally all about accounting. The bulk of the code, and hence the high potential for reuse, was not devoted to the problems of accounting per se, but rather to the problems of moving accounting onto a computer.

Thus, quite a bit of code was devoted to GET and PUT statements, to checking that records being read were valid, loop control, checking that inputs were within permitted ranges, and so forth. All of these things were standard tasks that need to be done for almost any kind of application and had nothing unique to accounting practice associated with them.

Reusable User Documentation

From a distance it is astonishing that reusable user documentation is not far more common that in fact it is. Whenever a software application is documented, there are certain basic things that must be included:

- How to install the application.

- How to start the application.

- How to perform standard application functions.

- How to perform tricky or unusual functions.

- How to deal common errors that novices might make.

- How to deal with errors noted in the application itself.

- How to save and recover any work or files when using the application.

- How to shut the application down.

- How to uninstall the application.

Every author likes to explore topics and demonstrate creativity, of course, but when writing a basic user manual it would be very helpful if the manuals followed a more or less standard sequence of presentation.

What is interesting about the prospect of reusable user manuals is the fact although software vendors themselves don't appear to be very sophisticated with their user manuals, there is a rather large subindustry of third-party publishers who make a good business out of writing better manuals than the vendors themselves.

These third-party publishers such as Howard Sams, QUE, International Thomson Computer Press, McGraw Hill, Sybex, Ziff Davis, and the like often put out series of books using similar general formats and topical outlines, even if the details or specifics vary from application to application.

It is an interesting fact that the object-oriented literature on software reuse is essentially silent on the topic of reusable user manuals, training materials, or any other kind of tutorial information. Since the total costs of instructional and reference material can reach 15% of the overall development budgets of software projects, this is a large omission.

One strong reason that documentation reuse is rather uncommon is the dislike of being accused of plagiarism on the part of most professional authors. Since both plagiarism and copyright violations are serious offenses for literature in general, there is a natural reluctance on the part of authors to reuse materials created by other authors. (However, many authors reuse their own materials with high frequency.)

Reusable Data

Reuse of data and information was long a difficult proposition because early database vendors had a tendency to utilize proprietary formats in a misguided attempt to lock clients in to using their products.

More recently, under the impact of data interchange standards, online analytical processing (OLAP), electronic data interchange (EDI), data warehouses, data markets, and data mining, reuse of various kinds of data has become more common.

However, there was still a problem in that various applications could not consolidate or even access all of the data they needed because of they way they had originally been built. Here the SAP R/3 product has begun to make corporate data sharing a viable proposition.

There is also a significant commercial market for some kinds of reusable data. For example any company can purchase address lists of key executives by industry, demographic data at various levels, and a host of other kinds of interesting data topics.

On the whole, data reuse is now fairly common. What is not common are empirical studies on the volume of reused data versus unique data for common kinds of applications. One of the general weaknesses of research into data reuse is the lack of a suitable metric for normalizing the results. There is no "data point" metric similar to function points for normalizing the volumes of data.

One interesting and important topic is beginning to expand rapidly as data reuse increases: this is the subject of data quality. It is suspected that the error density of databases and repositories may be higher even than the error density of software applications, but as this book is written there is not yet any solid empirical information on either the volume or severity of data errors.

Reusable Human Interfaces

For the first 25 years of the software era, say from 1960 until about 1985, the way software applications interacted with their human users could be described as random and quirky. Those who moved about from Word Star to WordPerfect to Microsoft Word can well remember how differently each product looked and how arcane some of the commands were for basic and common functions such as setting tabs or justifying right margins.

Of course the Apple Macintosh domain established an early advantage in terms of ease of use by developing and enforcing a set of standard interface concepts that worked identically across all applications.

In the 1990s the situation started to improve somewhat for the IBM side of the personal computer world, and also for mainframe software. Through trial and error methods, and imitation of the well-known Apple conventions, software applications began to deal with human interface issues more or less in a similar manner. At least the left mouse button began to have similar effects across many software packages, while pressing the F1 key often invoked a "help" function of some kind.

The development of Windows 3.0 accelerated this approach although it is true that Windows interfaces were somewhat more quirky than the equivalent Apple interface conventions and did not always do what users expected.

A typical pattern of human interface adoption for commercial software applications was brought about by the explosion of software companies funded by venture capital in the 1980s.

In some areas such as word processing, spreadsheets, and personal computer database products as many as 40 or 50 start-up companies were created within a year or two, all with similar products going after the same market space.

As one of these companies began to establish a larger market share, the other companies in the same business would imitate some of their features and also support identical interface techniques in an attempt to woo customers. Of course this practice received a major setback when Lotus filed its famous "look and feel" lawsuit to discourage competitors from using the Lotus interface conventions.

Another step toward standardization and reuse of interface conventions has been brought on by the concept of suites of related products by the same vendor. The early versions of suites such as Microsoft Office sometimes infuriated users by using different interfaces between applications. Therefore all of the suite vendors moved as rapidly as they could to common interfaces for at least the generic word processors, spreadsheets, graphic packages, databases, and communication utilities that made up the basic set.

A new era of human interface technology is approaching with voice recognition logic. There is also the prospect of pen-based interfaces, and there will always be a need for special interface conventions for the severely handicapped who lack limbs, or for the blind.

Truly reusable computer interfaces that are as common and ubiquitous as steering wheels and brake pedals on automobiles are perhaps approaching, but are not yet part of the software world.

Reusable Screens

In the early days of software, developing attractive and usable screens often required more effort than building the algorithms and logic that comprised the working parts of the program or system.

However, the advent of tools for building graphical user interfaces (GUI) and the marketing of commercial screen painters has been explosive. Still other tools such as JAVA and HTML have eased the construction of screens on the World Wide Web and are starting to explode for intranet applications as well as Internet applications.

As this book is written in 1996, screen design has become so easy that some applications are now coming with screens that are flamboyant beyond anything that was technically possible even 10 years ago. Indeed many of the screens even for staid applications such as accounting can utilize sound and animation if there is a need for such items.

Right now software screen design is moving into an era of unprecedented ease and versatility. Because screens of any kind using any combination of text, graphics, sound, and animation are so easy to construct it is almost premature to consider the topic of reusable screen elements.

It is probably best to let the software development world experiment with the new screen building capabilities and let trial-and-error move toward a future combination of elements that might eventually coalesce into a set of reusable screen principles.

What will probably enter the mainstream in terms of reusable screen elements for common applications will be these features:

- Standardization of icons for common features. Already the icons for "printing" and the use of a pair of scissors as a "cut" icon are ubiquitous. However, many other icons are arcane and unintelligible until the user knows what they mean.

- Standardization of the use of sounds for warnings and special signals.

- Standardization of voice commands as an alternative to mouse and keyboard commands.

- Standardization of pen-based hand-drawn symbols for at least activating some functions of software applications.

- Standardization of the use of animation as an interface technique. From the standpoint of perception and cognitive psychology, the sudden appearance of movement on an otherwise static screen tends to draw human attention immediately.

After a few years of enthusiastic experimentation, the topic of reusable screens will probably begin to coalesce but it is premature to know the final direction.

Reusable Test Plans

It is a strange phenomenon that after 50 years of testing software, the basic topic of what should go into a test plan is sometimes still treated as a novel subject. In fact, one of the surprising aspects of the ISO 9001 quality standard is that rather than present the standard contents of an effective generic test plan, it asks instead that each software project create a more or less unique test plan.

The testing of all software applications requires certain basic kinds of testing, and there should be no need to do anything more than minor modifications to a generic reusable test plan. For example, the following factors need to be tested for almost every software application ever created:

- The installation procedure of putting the application onto a host computer.

- Cold starting the application and initializing it when it is first run.

- The sequence of moving from screen-to-screen or module-to-module.

- Algorithms in the application and all standard application functions.

- Boundaries, ranges, and formats of all inputs to the application.

- Boundaries, ranges, and formats of all outputs from the application.

- Performance, timing, and full-load conditions.

- Error conditions that users might make.

- Errors situations in the application itself that may require redundancy.

- Recovering from a sudden shutdown or failure.

- Saving and recovering any work or files when using the application.

- Deleting information or data from the application.

- Importing information or data from other applications.

- Exporting information or data to other applications.

- Using peripheral devices such as printers, plotters, scanners, etc.

- Shutting down the application after use.

- Uninstalling the application.

Unfortunately, several aspects of the software literature are very deficient in the topic of reusable test plans. Specifically, the literature on testing itself, on quality, on the object-oriented paradigm, and even on software reuse all tend to ignore or skip over this important topic. That is to say, there are many specific examples of test plans in dozens of books, and they all resemble one another to a certain degree. What is missing is the inclusion of test plans as a standard reusable artifact.

Some of the software quality tools are starting to embed reusable test plans in the front-end of their tool suites, as do a few methodology management tools. The prognosis for greater reuse of test planning materials is improving.

A strong caution about test planning is indicated. Those who work as expert witnesses in litigation involving assertions of inadequate quality often find that test plans were either absent completely or so poorly developed as to approach levels of professional malpractice.

Reusable Test Cases

As the volume of reusable software code begins to move above 50%, it is obvious that reusable cases should also reach or approach the same plateau. Unfortunately, here too there is a shortage of both literature citations and empirical data.

As this book is written, the testing literature, quality literature, object-oriented literature, and the literature on software reuse all severely understate or ignore the topic of reusable test cases.

Of course regression test libraries have contained reusable test cases for many years. However, there is no solid data or instructions available on the construction of new test cases specifically in support of reusable source code.

Every formal reusable code library or class library should have an accompanying library of test cases for each module or method that is contained in the reusable code library. However, this seldom occurs.

There is one striking observation about reusable test cases that indicates much more research and development is necessary. While there is now a fast-growing subindustry of vendors marketing reusable software components, there is not yet any commercial marketing at all of reusable test cases at all. If test cases have not reached the level of maturity such that companies can make money selling them, then testing is still something of a mystical art rather than a science or engineering discipline.

One important aspect of reusable test cases is that they themselves must have the same high quality levels as the products being tested. This criterion is very rare. (See the sections on Bad Test Cases and Defect Origins for information on defect test cases.)

RISK-ANALYSIS PROGRAMS AND SOFTWARE QUALITY

The topic of risk-analysis programs is increasing in importance. Since poor quality is a major risk factor, formal risk-analysis tends to be a reasonably effective method for defect prevention. However, formal risk-analysis is still rare enough for a lack of solid, empirical data as of late 1996.

Among SPR's total of about 600 clients, roughly 75 tend to utilize formal or semiformal risk-analysis phases when attempting major software development projects. Some of the other 525 enterprises may do informal risk-analysis or utilize project management tools that have risk-analysis capabilities, but "risk-analysis" is not a formally identifiable activity in their software development chart of accounts.

The general topic of risk-analysis overlaps a number of other topics that are discussed in this book. In fact there are so many overlaps that it is well to highlight them by pointing out in alphabetic order what other topics have risk-analysis overtones:

- Active quality assurance

- Assessments and software quality

- Clean-room development

- Formal design and code inspections

- Joint application design (JAD)

- Outsource and contract quality levels

- Project management and software quality

- Prototyping

- Quality assurance tool capacities

- Quality function deployment (QFD)

When doing assessment and baseline studies in companies that do perform formal risk-analysis, the quality results seem to be better than similar companies without risk-analysis.

The problem with this statement is that the companies that include formal risk-analysis are usually in the industries that have much better than average quality results anyway; i.e., aerospace, computer manufacturing, defense weapons systems, telecommunication manufacturing, medical instruments, and commercial software houses that build operating systems or systems software.

One of my previous books, *Assessment and Control of Software Risks* (Prentice Hall, 1995) cited 65 kinds of risks were noted during software assessment and benchmark studies. Not all of those risks have an impact on software quality, but it is interesting to note the approximate frequency of the risk factors that can degrade quality if allowed to continue unchecked.

The following table shows the approximate percentage of projects where we have noted risks with some threat of quality degradation. The percentages are shown against the overall set of roughly 7,000 projects that we have examined.

Table 1   Frequency of Risk Factors that Can Impact Software Quality

Risk Factors Affecting Quality	Percent of Software Projects Where Factor Has Been Observed
Inaccurate quality estimating	65%
Creeping user requirements	55%
Inadequate tools and methods (project management)	55%
Inadequate tools and methods (quality assurance)	55%
Excessive schedule pressure	45%
Inaccurate metrics	35%
Inadequate configuration control	30%
Lack of specialization	30%
"Silver bullet" syndrome	30%
Poor organization structures	25%
Friction between clients and contractors	12%
Error-prone modules	10%

If the top five or six of these major quality risk factors can be reduced or avoided, software projects would be much less troublesome than they are today.

SCHEDULE PRESSURE AND SOFTWARE QUALITY

The interaction of software schedules and software quality is poorly understood by many software managers and technical personnel as well. Software projects where high quality levels are the initial target and where effective defect prevention is used in concert with formal inspections and formal testing have the highest probability of achieving on-time or early delivery dates. Such projects also have lower costs and higher user-satisfaction levels, as well as the lowest volumes of delivered defects when compared to projects that were rushed to achieve arbitrary or irrational schedules.

Schedule pressure is a very common phenomenon for software organizations. Among SPR's approximately 600 clients, schedule pressure has been reported on software projects in over 500 of the enterprises. However, the incidence among specific projects was about 3,200 out of roughly 7,000 or approximately 45%.

It is interesting to note that schedule pressure correlates strongly with the overall size of the application. Below 100 function points, schedule pressure may not occur at all, or is not often disrupting. For projects above 1,000 function points, schedule pressure is endemic and occurs perhaps 80% of the time. Above 10,000 function points, both schedule pressure and schedule slippage are almost universal.

Schedule pressure does not always have a negative impact. Indeed, both project team morale and actual schedule intervals tend to be best when there is some schedule pressure, surprisingly.

However, there is an ambiguous but critical point between what might be called "healthy schedule pressure" and "excessive schedule pressure." An analogy with athletics can perhaps clarify the difference.

Suppose an athlete was training for a track event in which he or she was planning to run a one mile race. (The current world record for the mile is about 3 minutes and 55 seconds as this is written.)

If the person's coach suggested that the athlete try and run a mile in less than 5 minutes, that person would probably not even need to train because almost any competitive runner can beat 5 minutes. The athlete would probably not think much of the coach's ability because a 5 minute mile is not a competitive mark.

If the coach said try and run a mile in less than 4 minutes, the athlete would have his or her work cut out because less than 100 people in the world have achieved this mark over the past 10 years or so. However, this goal is definitely achievable even if very few runners have yet achieved it.

If the coach said try and run a mile in less than 3 minutes, the athlete would probably get another coach. Running a mile in less than 3 minutes is not only faster than the current world record by almost 25% but it probably exceeds the theoretical capacity of the human body in terms of both the energy required and the rate at which legs can move.

Some rough rules of thumb for determining whether software schedules are lax, average, tight, or unachievable can be based on raising the function point totals of projects to various powers.

These rules of thumb are not very accurate, but provide an interesting sanity check on whether schedules are within the realm of possibility. The schedule interval for these "rules of thumb" run from start of requirements to the initial delivery of the software to the first actual user or client. The results they yield are those of calendar months.

Lax (too slow)	=	function points raised to the 0.45 power
Worse than average	=	function points raised to the 0.42 power
Approximate average	=	function points raised to the 0.40 power
Tight (but possible)	=	function points raised to the 0.36 power
Unachievable	=	function points raised to the 0.30 power

Projects where the schedules are so irrational that there is no possibility of achieving them, and where managers or clients insist on various short cuts have the highest probability of being canceled, or running late, or over running their budgets. When finally delivered, these projects also have the highest defect levels, maintenance costs, and the largest volumes of customer reported defects, as well as very low levels of user-satisfaction.

The profiles of "healthy" and "pathological" software projects have been studied for more than 30 years and are clearly understood by best in class software producers. If one skimps or compresses the front end of a software development cycle, one will stretch out the testing phase to an inordinate degree.

Unfortunately, the pathological projects give the false appearance of looking like they are ahead of schedule until testing begins. Then it is discovered that the project does not work, and a frantic cycle of testing, debugging, and late night repairs begins.

Attempts to rush software into early production by skimping on front-end design rigor exact a heavy toll later. Unfortunately, the situation is hard to rectify until too late.

A study performed by IBM in the 1970s found a surprising but strong correlation between quality levels and schedules. This was a large-scale study involving more than a hundreds of IBM's commercial software products, plus systems software such as operating systems, access methods, and the like.

The IBM projects with the highest quality upon delivery to customers had the greatest chance of being finished on time or early. This was due to the fact that they did not bog down during testing with excessive quantities of severe defects.

Conversely, IBM projects that were experiencing high defect levels in customer use (such as the early versions of the IMS database product or the JES 3 job entry subsystem) had a distressing tendency to miss their announced shipped dates because they were still hung up in testing.

Following are some preliminary data points on the quality levels associated with software projects that finished late, on-time, and early. This data is taken from my book *Patterns of Software Systems Failure and Success* (International Thomson Press, 1996).

Table 1   Software Quality Results Associated with Schedule Delays

(Defects per Function Point and Defect Removal Efficiency)

Project Outcome	Project Size Expressed in Function Points			
	< 100	100-1000	1000-5000	>5000
Late Projects				
Defect potentials	3.00	4.25	5.00	6.50
Defect removal efficiency	83%	74%	67%	63%
Delivered defects	0.51	1.11	1.65	2.40
On-Time Projects				
Defect potentials	2.80	4.00	4.70	6.00
Defect removal efficiency	96%	92%	90%	87%
Delivered defects	0.11	0.32	0.47	0.78
Early Projects				
Defect potentials	2.60	3.85	4.50	5.50
Defect removal efficiency	98%	96%	94%	92%
Delivered defects	0.05	0.15	0.27	0.44

This data has a high margin of error, but supports the thesis that "quality is free." The point at which most late projects begin to run very late is during testing, when it is first discovered that there are so many bugs that schedules must slip significantly.

(See also the section of this book on the "Good Enough" Quality Fallacy.)

SEI MATURITY LEVELS AND SOFTWARE QUALITY

The Software Engineering Institute (SEI) is located on the campus of Carnegie Mellon University in Pittsburgh, Pennsylvania. SEI is a non-profit software research organization funded primarily by the U.S. government through the Defense

Advanced Research Project Agency (DARPA). (By historical coincidence SEI and my company, Software Productivity Research, were both incorporated in 1984 and both began to perform software process assessments circa 1985.)

Because the SEI is having a global impact on many aspects of software, including quality, it is useful to review the origins of the Software Engineering Institute and some of the research programs they are involved in.

Among SPR's client set of about 600 companies and government agencies, approximately 100 have been evaluated using SEI capability maturity model (CMM) concepts, while about 500 are civilian companies who have not utilized the CMM ranking scale.

Of the approximate 100 client organizations using the SEI CMM, about 60 are in the defense industry or have at least a division that does defense work. The other 40 are civilian organizations who have heard of the SEI CMM and are using some the concepts as the basis for software process improvements.

It can be seen from this distribution that the SEI CMM approach is most widely deployed in the defense sector but has started to expand into the civilian sector as well. Also of interest, about 15 of the SEI CMM users are clients from Europe, Australia, India, or Japan. From this it can be seen that the SEI CMM is becoming known throughout much of the world.

For the approximately 100 clients who have utilized the CMM approach, the distribution of SPR's clients among the five levels is similar to the results reported by SEI itself and by other researchers, except that there is very little reporting by SEI or elsewhere on the ratio of companies that use the CMM to those that don't. Therefore, the ratio that has been observed may or may not match overall U.S. patterns.

Table 1   Distribution of SPR Client Organizations on the SEI CMM Scale

SEI CMM Level	Number	Percent
Unrated using the CMM	500	83.4%
Level 1 (Initial)	70	11.6%
Level 2 (Repeatable)	16	2.7%
Level 3 (Defined)	12	2.0%
Level 4 (Managed)	2	0.3%
Level 5 (Optimizing)	0	0.0%
TOTAL	600	100.0%

By the late 1970s, the Department of Defense recognized that the annual expenses for software and computing service contracts were a major portion of the overall defense budget and amounted to many billions of dollars. These budgets were growing annually at an alarming rate. Also, the schedules for major defense software projects were in excess of five years, and the quality and reliability of the delivered software systems was less than good in many cases.

In order to explore software issues, and especially those topics associated with defense contracts, a new software research facility was funded by the Department of Defense in 1984. This was the essential origin of the Software Engineering Institute. Consider for a moment the state-of-the-art of software development practices in 1984:

- More than half of large software systems were late in excess of 12 months.

- The average costs of large software systems was more than twice the initial budget.

- The cancellation rate of large software systems exceeded 35%.

- The quality and reliability levels of delivered software of all sizes was poor.

- Software personnel were increasing by more than 10% per year.

- Software was the largest known business expense which could not be managed.

The United States Department of Defense is the largest producer and consumer of software in the world. The overall problems of building, operating, and maintaining software systems explains why the Department of Defense is vitally interested in improving software practices.

The SEI Assessment Approach

One of the early, major, and continuing activities of the SEI was the development of a formal evaluation or assessment schema for evaluating the capabilities of defense contractors. Indeed Watts Humphrey's book on this topic, *Managing the Software Process* (Addison Wesley, 1989) became a best-seller.

The SEI assessment data is collected by means of on-site interviews using both a standard questionnaire and also observations and informal data. Once collected, the assessment data is analyzed, and used to place a software organization on one of the five plateaus of the well-known SEI "capability maturity model" or CMM as it is now called. Although the assessment and maturity level concepts can be considered separately, most people regard the two as being a linked set.

Formal SEI software assessments are performed by the SEI and by a dozen or so by licensed consulting organizations. There are also less formal "SEI-style" assessments which companies can perform on their own, or which are done by consultants that are not licensed by the SEI but who use assessment approaches derived from the published SEI materials.

The SEI approach is sometimes modified or customized for various reasons. In Europe, for example, variants such as Bootstrap and SPICE are starting to occur. (See the section in this book on European Software Quality Initiatives for additional information.)

One of the more interesting customizations in the United States is that of AT&T, who have developed a hybrid assessment approach that uses portions of the SEI capability maturity model coupled with portions of our SPR assessment approach.

Because of the importance of very large systems to the Department of Defense, the SEI assessment approach originally dealt primarily with the software processes and methodologies used by very large companies that produced very large systems.

The original SEI assessment approach was derived from the best practices used by leading corporations such as IBM and ITT which employ from 5,000 to more than 25,000 software professionals, and which could safely build systems in excess of 1,000,000 lines of code or 10,000 function points.

The SEI assessment data is collected in part using a questionnaire that contains about 150 binary questions, such as:

"Does the software quality assurance function have a management reporting channel separate from the software development project management (Yes or No)?"

Based on the patterns of answers to the SEI assessment questions, the final result of the SEI assessment process is to place the software organization on one of the levels of a five-point maturity scale. The five-plateaus on the SEI maturity level are listed in Table 2.

Table 2   Approximate Distribution of U.S. Software Enterprises Based on the SEI
Capability Maturity Model (CMM) Results

SEI Maturity Level	Meaning	Frequency of Occurrence
1 = Initial	Chaotic	75.0%
2 = Repeatable	Marginal	15.0%
3 = Defined	Adequate	8.0%
4 = Managed	Good to excellent	1.5%
5 = Optimizing	State-of-the-art	0.5%

Note that the SEI CMM scores are based on an absolute scale, rather than a scale of relative performance. The use of an absolute scale explains why the distribution of software organizations is severely skewed toward the low-end of the scale.

A similar kind of skew would occur if one were to look at the distribution of candidates selected to enter the Olympics for events such as down-hill skiing. Most ordinary citizens (more than 95%) could not qualify at all. Very few athletes could make it to the Olympic tryouts, even fewer would represent their countries, and only three athletes from around the world will win medals in each event.

In addition to evaluating the software maturity levels of organizations, the SEI also recommends "key process areas" for each of the higher levels above 1. These key process areas are technologies that organizations at each level should be assumed to have mastered.

The SEI assessment program and indeed the overall set of research programs had long been criticized for concentrating on too narrow a set of topics, and ignoring other topics such as personnel, compensation, hiring practices, and the like.

In 1995 the SEI filled a notable gap by publishing a People Capability Maturity Model or P-CMM. The lead researcher on the P-CMM was the well-known cognitive psychologist, Dr. Bill Curtis. Since Dr. Curtis had formerly headed the SEI assessment practice as well as being a psychologist, he was well qualified to lead the additional work associated with personnel issues.

The general meanings of each of the five levels of the SEI CMM, the new People CMM, and the associated key process areas are approximately the following:

Level 1 or Initial organizations are characterized by random or chaotic development methods with little formality and uninformed project management. While some smaller projects may be successful due to the capabilities of individual staff members, large systems are often failures and the overall results are marginal to poor.

In terms of the People CMM, the Level 1 organizations are asserted to be deficient in training at both the technical staff and managerial levels.

SEI does not recommend any key process areas for Level 1 organizations on the grounds that they are not sophisticated enough to deploy methods consistently and will probably botch things up if they try.

Moving from Level 1 to Level 2 is the most difficult transition point. For a large company with perhaps 1,000 software personnel, the move from Level 1 to Level 2 can take from 18 to more than 36 months.

Some executives in Level 1 organizations have set arbitrary targets, such as "moving to Level 3 in 12 months." This may occur for small companies, but so far as can be determined has never yet occurred for large corporations. Nor is it likely to do so. Companies at the far back edge of Level 1 usually have no intrinsic ability to learn new methods rapidly. Also, their infrastructures and logistical support systems are so obsolete that even purchasing new tools or bringing in consultants can take more than a year.

Level 2 or Repeatable organizations have introduced at least some rigor into project management and technical development tasks. Approaches such as formal cost estimating are noted for project management, and formal requirements gathering are often noted during development. Compared to the initial level, a higher frequency of success and a lower incidence of overruns and canceled projects can be observed.

In terms of the People CMM, the Level 2 organizations have begun to provide adequate training for managers and technical staff. Further, they have become aware of the importance of professional growth and the need for selecting and keeping capable personnel.

The key process areas which SEI recommends for Level 2 organizations include requirements management, project planning, resource tracking, quality assurance, and configuration management plus subcontract management for projects that utilize multiple contractors.

The key process areas for Level 2 of the People CMM include compensation, training, staffing, communication, and work environment.

Moving from Level 2 to Level 3 is not as difficult as the first move, since organizations have usually gotten used to the idea that change will be necessary. However, the same size organization illustrated previously with 1000 software personnel, should not expect to go from Level 2 to Level 3 in less than a year, and it may take more than 18 months.

Level 3 or Defined organizations have mastered a development process that can often lead to successful large systems. Over and above the project management and technical approaches found in Level 2 organizations, the Level 3 groups have a well-defined development process that can handle all sizes and kinds of projects.

In terms of the People CMM, the Level 3 organizations have developed skills inventories and are now capable of selecting appropriate specialists who may be needed for critical topics such as testing, quality assurance, web mastery, and the like.

The key process areas which SEI recommends for Level 3 organizations include establishing an effective organizational infrastructure, training of both managers and technical staff, inter-group coordination, and the utilization of formal design and code inspections. Level 3 organizations should also be capable of effective software reusability programs.

The key process areas for Level 3 of the People CMM include career development, competency-based practices, work force planning, and analysis of the knowledge and skills that are needed by the organization.

Organizations that achieve Level 3 sometimes rest on their laurels, since Level 3 is the minimum level needed to bid on some U.S. defense projects. However, organizations that are pursing "best in class" goals will find Level 3 to be only a way station. For these energetic groups, moving from Level 3 to Level 4 can sometimes be accomplished in less than 12 months.

Level 4 or Managed organizations have established a firm quantitative basis for project management and utilize both effective measurements and also effective cost and quality estimation.

In terms of the People CMM, the Level 4 organizations are able to not only monitor their need for specialized personnel, but are actually able to explore the productivity and quality results associated from the presence of specialists in a quantitative way. Long-range predictions of future needs are also part of the Level 4 P-CMM assertions. In addition, Level 4 organizations would make extensive use of mentoring.

The key process areas which SEI recommends for Level 4 organizations include quantification of defect levels, productivity levels, and activity-based costing. Also, Level 4 organizations should be approaching 50% levels of software reuse for both design, code, and testing materials.

The key process areas for Level 4 of the People CMM include mentoring, team building, organizational competency, and the ability to predict and measure the effect of specialists and teams in a quantitative manner.

(Note: The SEI CMM has been criticized for showing measurements as a Level 4 key process. The SEI intent is that Level 4 organizations will have mastered measurements. This does not preclude organizations from starting to measure earlier, even as early as Level 1. It is obvious that organizations do not enter a CMM level and then magically find themselves in command of the key practices. The beginnings of the key processes are often a level or two prior achieving mastery of them. This is particularly true of measurements, which can take as long as three years to master.)

Moving from Level 4 all the way to Level 5 is not easy to quantify because the actual criteria for Level 5 are somewhat abstract. However, there is no reason to assume that a transition from Level 4 to Level 5 should take more than 12 months.

Level 5 or Optimizing organizations are assumed to have mastered the current state-of-the-art of software project management and development. Therefore the Level 5 groups are expected to be the pioneers who are capable of building entirely new methods that advance the state of the art beyond current levels. Although not explicitly stated, Level 5 organizations should be approaching or exceeding a volume of about 75% of reusable design, code, and test materials.

In terms of the People CMM, the Level 5 requirements are an extension of the Level 4 capabilities and hence different more in degree than in kind. However the P-CMM stresses both coaching and rewards for innovation at Level 5.

The key process areas which SEI recommends for Level 5 include defect prevention and advancing the fundamental software engineering and management technologies, plus rapid and effective technology transfer and deployment of improvement approaches.

The key process areas for Level 5 of the People CMM include encouragement of innovation, coaching, and personal competency development.

Quantifying the SEI CMM Quality Results

When the SEI capability maturity model was first published it was asserted that both quality and productivity levels would improve at the higher levels. This is an area where SEI shares the bad habits of the rest of the software industry. The SEI assertions about quality and productivity were initially made without any kind of study or empirical evidence being collected.

In fact, even in 1997 the SEI assessment approach itself still does not include the collection of quantitative information on either productivity rates or quality levels. This is a serious flaw in the SEI assessment procedure.

Even after more than 10 years of SEI assessments, there is no large database of quantitative data that shows the average results or performance ranges of the five SEI maturity levels in terms of either productivity or quality levels, although some data is now being accumulated on both topics.

This lack also means that organizations who have utilized the SEI CMM only receive qualitative data on their software performance: no quantitative benchmark data is part of the SEI CMM approach.

The topic of the exact costs and the value of the SEI maturity levels needs a great deal more research and quantification before definite conclusions can be reached. Ideally, what would be mounted is a large-scale survey involving perhaps 50 organizations and at least 250 projects at various SEI CMM levels.

Since studies of this magnitude are routine for validating other kinds of defense systems, it is sadly typical of the software community that little effort is devoted to testing new concepts before they are deployed.

Eventually the Air Force and DARPA received so many questions about quantifying the impact of the SEI CMM that they commissioned several studies to explore this fundamental question. As data began to be collected, it became evident that there is quite a bit of overlap among the various SEI maturity levels.

For example, in terms of both quality and productivity, the best software projects from level 1 organizations can be superior to the worst developed by level 3 organizations. For smaller companies that cannot afford some of the infrastructure and special departments assumed by the SEI CMM concept, rather good results are possible even at level 1. Conversely, achieving levels 3, 4, and 5 on the SEI CMM scale do not guarantee that all software projects will be successful.

Following are the SPR observations of the quality ranges associated with the five levels of the SEI CMM. This data has a high margin of error, but as with many preliminary studies, it is hoped that publishing data that may be incorrect will spur the software community to find better data and correct the errors in the future.

Note that the defect potentials shown here include these five categories of software defects which in aggregate form the "defect potentials" for software applications:

- Requirements defects
- Design defects

- Code defects

- User documentation defects

- Bad fixes or secondary defects

The SEI data on defect removal efficiency levels refers to the cumulative percentage of bugs or defects found prior to release, contrasted to the defects reported by clients in the first year of usage. For example if developers find 90 bugs and clients find 10 bugs, then the defect removal efficiency would be 90%.

Following are the current ranges of software defect potentials and removal efficiency levels observed from among client organizations that have utilized the SEI CMM:

Level 1 Quality: The software defect potentials noted from several hundred projects in Level 1 organizations run from about 3 to more than 15 defects per function point but average about 5.0 defects per function point. Defect removal efficiency runs from less than 70% to more than 95% but only averages about 85%. Thus, the average number of delivered defects for Level 1 organizations is about 0.75 defects per function point.

Level 2 Quality: The software defect potentials noted from about 50 projects in Level 2 organizations run from about 3 to more than 12 defects per function point but average about 4.8 defects per function point. Defect removal efficiency runs from less than 70% to more than 96% but averages about 87%. Thus, the average number of delivered defects for Level 2 organizations is about 0.6 defects per function point.

Level 3 Quality: The software defect potentials noted from about 30 projects in Level 3 organizations run from about 2.5 to more than 9 defects per function point but average about 4.3 defects per function point. Defect removal efficiency runs from less than 75% to more than 97% but averages about 89%. Thus, the average number of delivered defects for Level 3 organizations is about 0.47 defects per function point.

Level 4 Quality: The software defect potentials noted from 9 projects in Level 4 organizations run from about 2.3 to more than 6 defects per function point but average about 3.8 defects per function point. Defect removal efficiency runs from less than 80% to more than 99% but averages about 94%. Thus, the average number of delivered defects for Level 4 organizations is about 0.2 defects per function point.

Level 5 Quality: The software defect potentials noted from 4 projects in a Level 5 organization ran from about 2 to 5 defects per function point but currently seem to average 3.5 defects per function point. Defect removal efficiency ran from less than

90% to more than 99% but averaged about 97%. Thus, the average number of delivered defects for a Level 5 organization is about 0.1 defects per function point although there is obviously an insufficient sample at this level.

To illustrate the overlap of quality among the five levels of the SEI CMM, the following table shows our minimum, average, and maximum numbers of delivered defects per function point for each of the five CMM levels. Note that the best results from Level 1 are actually better than the worst results from Levels 3 and 4, even though the average results improve as the CMM ladder is climbed.

Table 3   Software Delivered Defects at Each Level of the SEI CMM

(Defects expressed in terms of defects per function point)

	Minimum	Average	Maximum
SEI Level 1	0.150	0.750	4.500
SEI Level 2	0.120	0.624	3.600
SEI Level 3	0.075	0.473	2.250
SEI Level 4	0.023	0.228	1.200
SEI Level 5	0.002	0.105	0.500

Although samples are small for the higher levels, there is now evidence from studies such as the ones carried out by Quantitative Software Methods (QSM) in 1993 and Software Productivity Research (SPR) in 1994 which indicate that when organizations do move from CMM Level 1 up to the higher levels their productivity and quality levels tend to improve.

Setting Quality Targets For the Five Levels of the Capability Maturity Model

Although SEI itself does not publish quantitative targets for the 5 levels of the CMM, it seems to be a useful exercise to show companies what might be achieved at each level.

Therefore, following are some suggested quality targets for the five plateaus of the SEI capability maturity model.

At Level 1 there is no value in setting a target that is any better than average results, on the grounds that Level 1 organizations can't usually do any better than average results and often do worse.

As the levels increase, the targets become slightly better than today's observed results. There is no purpose to setting targets that are already being achieved. The targets are set to be better than today's observed performance, but not unachievable. That is, the targets are actually within the range of the best software engineering technologies.

Table 4   Software Defect Potentials and Defect Removal Efficiency Targets Associated with Each Level of the SEI CMM

(Data Expressed in Terms of Defects per Function Point)

SEI CMM Levels	Defect Potentials	Removal Efficiency	Delivered Defects
SEI CMM 1	5.00	85%	0.75
SEI CMM 2	4.00	90%	0.40
SEI CMM 3	3.00	95%	0.15
SEI CMM 4	2.00	97%	0.06
SEI CMM 5	1.00	99%	0.01

These targets are hypothetical, but from observations of organizations at various CMM levels seem to be within the range of current technology from Levels 2 through 4.

The Level 5 target, or lowering defect potentials down to 1 per function point, is the hardest target of the set, and requires a significant volume of certified reusable material of approximate zero-defect quality levels.

This particular target, or a potential defect level of only 1 per function point, is actually beyond the current state of the art for projects larger than 1,000 function points in size. The other aspect of the Level 5 target, or achieving 99% defect removal efficiency, is difficult but already been accomplished by a small but growing number of our client projects.

Moving up the SEI CMM scale brings to mind learning to play golf. For a beginning player, it can take several years before they are able to break 100, or shoot a round of golf in less than 100 strokes. In fact, most golfers never do break 100. This is somewhat equivalent to the observation that many companies who are initially assessed as being at Level 1 tend to stay at the level for a very long time. Indeed, some may never advance to the higher levels.

However, golfers that do manage to break 100 can usually break 90 in less than a year. This parallels the observation that moving up the SEI CMM ladder is quicker once the initial hurdle of moving from Level 1 to Level 2 is accomplished.

Correlating SEI and SPR Assessment Results

Although SEI and SPR both began performing assessments in 1985, we did not collaborate on methodologies and scoring methods. Ironically, both Watts Humphrey and I worked at IBM during the same years and both were engaged in internal process assessments within IBM, although Watts worked at IBM's East Coast software labs and I worked at IBM's West Coast software labs.

The basic SPR assessment questionnaire and some of the quantitative results derived from the SPR assessment method were published in 1986 in my book *Programming Productivity* (McGraw Hill).

The SPR approach does not use the kind of binary questions used by SEI, and instead makes use of sets of about 300 multiple-choice questions that cover methodologies, tools, office ergonomics, experience, and other relevant factors. SPR's stated goal is to include every factor known to influence the outcome of software projects by as much as 1%.

Of the full set of 300 topical questions about 200 are specialized and used with certain kinds of companies or certain kinds of projects. For example, SPR does not use questions about military standards with civilian groups. About 100 core questions that we use in every assessment are automated and provide the statistical basis for our overall rankings.

An example of one of the SPR core questions that deals with quality assurance overlaps the same topic as the SEI question shown on page 385, although the forms are different:

Quality Assurance Function (select one choice) _____

1) *Formal QA group with adequate resources*

2) *Formal QA group but understaffed (< 1 to 30 ratio)*

3) *QA role is assigned to development personnel*

4) *QA role is performed informally*

5) *No QA function exists for the project*

Once a sample of projects have been analyzed using the SPR question set, the answers to the questions are input directly into a tool which performs a statistical analysis of the results and shows the mean values and standard deviations of all factors.

Like the SEI approach, the SPR assessment method is also used to place software development groups, contractors, and outsource vendors on a five-plateau excellence scale. However, the SPR differs from SEI's in two respects:

1) The SPR scale runs in the opposite direction from the SEI scale.

2) The SPR scale is a relative scale.

These differences are awkward historical facts. It happens that both Watts Humphrey and I published our books with our respective scales in them and did not realize until after publication that we had both used 5-point scales that ran in opposite directions.

The distribution of results using the SPR software excellence scale is shown in the following table.

Table 5   Distribution of Assessment Results Using the SPR Software Excellence Scale

SPR Excellence Scale	Meaning	Frequency of Occurrence
1 = Excellent	State-of-the-art	2.0%
2 = Good	Superior to most companies	18.0%
3 = Average	Normal in most factors	56.0%
4 = Poor	Deficient in key factors	20.0%
5 = Very Poor	Deficient in most factors	4.0%

The SPR assessments tend to produce a more normal bell-shaped distribution of results than do the SEI assessments. This is due in part to the fact that each industry is evaluated against its own norms rather than against an absolute scale. Also, small companies with less than 50 software personnel are compared against similar companies, rather than against major corporations with thousands of software personnel.

Both SPR and SEI are often asked if our assessment results are equivalent to the SEI CMM results. SPR and SEI cover quite a few of the same topics, such as quality assurance. This is not surprising since both Watts and I were at IBM during the same years and both involved with assessments of major IBM software projects.

However, a simple inversion of the scales does not produce equivalent results, since the SPR method uses a relative scale and the SEI method uses an absolute scale. But from analysis of the distribution patterns of both SEI and SPR results it is possible to convert SPR's assessment scale into a fairly good approximation of the SEI CMM by both inverting the scale and compressing our results at the same time.

SPR has built a prototype software tool that analyzes our question set, removes questions not used by SEI assessments (i.e., questions dealing with office ergonomics, staff compensation, hiring practices, etc.), and then inverts and compresses the remaining scores to generate an equivalent SEI CMM level.

This conversion tool differs from the standard CMM scoring method in that it supports two decimal places of precision. That is, it creates scores such as 1.05 or 1.89 that can differentiate placement within the overall 5 levels of the CMM. Since SEI itself does not recommend decimal places, the scores can also be expressed only in integer value form.

The compression of our scoring method that matches (more or less) the distribution of the SEI CMM results are the following.

Table 6   Conversion of SPR Assessment Results into Equivalent SEI CMM Results

SPR Scores	Meaning	SEI Scores	Meaning	Percentage
3.00 to 5.99	Very Poor	1	Initial	75%
2.51 to 2.99	Poor	2	Repeatable	15%
2.50 to 2.50	Good	3	Defined	5%
1.01 to 2.00	Very Good	4	Managed	3%
0.01 to 0.99	State-of-the-art	5	Optimizing	2%

An interesting difference between the SEI and SPR methods is that the SPR assessment approach also collects baseline data on productivity, quality, schedules, costs, staffing levels, and other quantifiable factors.

As organizations begin to improve, it is very useful to know how bad or good they were when they started, so they can judge their progress in terms of annual improvements in costs, quality, schedules and other tangible factors.

Neither the SEI nor the SPR assessment approaches are foolproof but both include extensive interviews and on-site analysis. Both SEI and SPR assessment approaches, and many others as well, can provide useful data for exploring the capabilities of internal development, of outsource vendors, and can also assist in determining whether a company's software performance may be poor enough to make outsourcing a useful option.

Gaps in the SEI Metrics and Measurement Program

The Software Engineering Institute has started a substantial practice in the software measurement and metrics domains. Unfortunately, some of the SEI work in this area is so far behind the best civilian practices that it might be considered harmful rather than beneficial.

The worst aspect of the SEI measurement program was their recommendation that a count of "physical lines of code" be part of the core software metrics, coupled with a failure to include function points as a core metric.

The rationale for the unfortunate choice of physical lines of code by members of the SEI measurement group is that, "counting physical lines of code is easy to do and can be done consistently." While these statements are true, the SEI measurement group did not address the fact that physical lines of code does not actually measure anything useful.

Unfortunately, the SEI measurement group had not scanned the software measurement literature and was unaware of the hazards of the physical LOC metric. Of course, if SEI had been collecting quantitative data, they might have noted the problem from their own studies and empirical data.

However, like many other groups that recommend LOC metrics, the SEI did not actually use this metric in day to day benchmark studies and hence did not have enough data available to have observed the problems with this metric first hand.

The most severe problem, of course, is that both productivity and quality results move backwards when lines of code are used, and thus penalize high-level languages. Indeed, I regard the usage of lines of code for cross-language studies to be an example of professional malpractice.

Regardless of SEI's endorsement, using physical lines of code for measurement purposes is fundamentally harmful. It was proven in 1978 that counts of physical lines of source code cannot be used for serious economic or quality studies that involve multiple programming languages.

For quality measurements, physical lines of code have no relevance for these topics:

- Measuring requirements defects
- Measuring requirements creep
- Measuring design defects

- Measuring user documentation defects

- Measuring design inspection defect removal efficiency

- Measuring cumulative defect removal efficiency

- Comparing quality between different programming languages

- Measuring quality of visual languages such as Visual Basic

- Backfiring to create equivalent function point totals

See the sections in this book on Barriers to Software Quality Measurement and Function Point Metrics for examples of why usage of lines of code is harmful in either the physical line or logical statement form.

Since the DoD funds the SEI, the kinds of research which SEI performs tends to reflect topics of interest to the military services. For quite a few years, the widespread military usage of the obsolete "lines of code" metric is probably why SEI made such a serious mistake. Only recently has the SEI begun to approach the more important civilian topics of activity-based costing, or exploring the power of functional metrics.

Due to strong external criticism of their original mistake, the SEI metrics research is improving. For example SEI has joined the International Function Point Users Group (IFPUG). However, the SEI's initial endorsement of a metric known to be flawed has caused both SEI and their clients to lag the leading civilian measurement research programs.

Some of the important measurement topics that SEI should be researching, but has not yet even addressed, include the following:

- Establishing quantitative ranges for software productivity and quality levels associated with each level of the SEI CMM. For example, SEI itself has published no data on quality ranges associated with the CMM similar to that shown above in this chapter. In fact, using the SEI core metrics the data in this section could not be shown since neither function points nor defect removal efficiency are SEI core metrics, although both should have been.

- Pointing out to SEI clients the situations where physical lines of code are harmful or will produce incorrect and paradoxical results, such as comparing data between languages. The SEI failure to address this problem is professionally embarrassing, because in other fields such as medicine and pharmaceuticals, publication of hazards and counter indications is a basic requirement of endorsing a therapy. SEI has endorsed physical lines of code without providing warnings of harmful side effects.

- Counting multiple languages in the same application (COBOL and SQL for example). Since about one-third of U.S. software applications use multiple languages, and some have as many as a dozen languages, this is a major topic.

- Counting very high-level languages such as Visual Basic where some of the functionality is provided by button controls rather than lines of procedural code.

- Improving the accuracy of "backfiring" or direct conversion from lines of code to function point metrics. Although backfiring is probably the most common way military services use function points, SEI has not published any reports on this topic at all.

- Providing conversion rules for counts based on physical lines into counts based on logical statements since both methods are used in the software engineering literature with equal frequency. Since data expressed in physical lines can differ from data expressed in logical statements by several hundred percent, SEI should address the topic of conversion rules.

- Exploring data metrics and the quality of data used by applications. The Department of Defense and the military services have the largest databases in the world, and hence data quality is a major military concern. Here, too, SEI has not published any useful studies.

- Exploring value metrics for calculating return on investment in software tools and approaches.

- Exploring the differences between civilian and military development activities in order to move toward activity-based costing.

- Exploring techniques for measuring hybrid projects where software, hardware, microcode, and human tasks such as consulting are all part of the final cost. Hybrid projects constitute the most common form of weapons system and hence are of great importance to the military community.

Overall, the SEI measurement program is probably the weakest link of SEI's software research. It lags behind civilian efforts by quite a bit, and by concentrating on the wrong metric, it has made little or no contribution to important economic and quality measurement topics.

The Software Engineering Institute has become a prominent research facility and has served to make a number of issues both visible and widely discussed. The impact of the SEI is now global in scope, and SEI studies are being discussed in many countries.

In spite of the gaps and deficiencies of the SEI, many of its concepts are now widely known and generating useful discussion. SEI itself is not static nor are SEI personnel unaware of the gaps and omissions of their research programs.

Hopefully, the SEI will broaden its scope of future research, and will eliminate some of the gaps and problem areas of its past research. If so then the SEI can perhaps make tangible improvements in software practices.

SIX-SIGMA QUALITY LEVELS

The Motorola Corporation has received substantial interest in its famous "six-sigma" quality program for hardware and manufactured components. The phrase "six-sigma" refers to defect densities of 3.4 in a million.

Since the six-sigma definition is hard to visualize for software, an alternative approach would be to achieve a cumulative defect removal efficiency rate of 99.999999% prior to delivery of a product. This method is not what Motorola uses but it helps to clarify what would have to be done to achieve six-sigma results for software projects.

Since the current U.S. average for software defect removal efficiency is only about 85%, and quite a few software products are even below 70%, it may be seen that software producers have some serious catching up to do.

As it happens, there are a few software products which appear to have achieved six-sigma quality levels. In the past 30 years, I have observed four projects that achieved six-sigma results in their first year of deployment out of a total of almost 10,000 projects.

Surprisingly, the prognosis for achieving six-sigma quality levels for software is fairly good. The best of the available technologies today can approach this level if a full suite of defect prevention and defect removal operations are carried out synergistically. Indeed, for software projects where reuse of certified materials top 75% by volume, and where formal inspections are used to augment testing, six-sigma quality levels should be achieved routinely.

Because the technology for achieving six-sigma quality levels exists, that does not mean that the software industry is now ready to try. There are both sociological and technical reasons that quality is held back, such as the widespread lack of appreciation of the correlation between high quality and short schedules and the shortage of commercial reusable materials certified to zero-defect levels.

TESTING

Testing has been the basic form of defect removal since the software industry began. For a majority of software projects, it is the *only* form of defect removal utilized. Considering the importance of testing and its universal penetration of the software industry, it is surprising that so little quantitative data has been published on this topic.

Among SPR's approximately 600 client organizations, testing is the only quality control approach used by all 100% of them. However, the variety and forms of testing vary considerably. The range of testing activities performed by our clients runs from a single perfunctory unit test by the programmer who wrote the program to a coordinated series of 15 discrete testing activities, with at least 10 of them performed by professional testers or quality assurance personnel.

Surprisingly for so common an activity as testing, the exact definition of what "testing" means is somewhat ambiguous. In this book testing means, "the dynamic execution of software and the comparison of the results of that execution against a set of known, pre-determined criteria."

Under the definition of testing used here, static defect removal methods such as formal design and code inspections are not viewed as testing. However, inspections are important and very effective. Indeed, inspections have higher levels of defect removal efficiency than almost any form of testing. (See the sections of this book on Defect Removal Efficiency and on Formal Design and Code Inspections for additional information about the synergy between inspections and testing.)

The term "software" can mean any of the following:

- An individual instruction (about .001 function points).

- A small subroutine of perhaps 10 instructions in length (about .01 function points).

- A module of perhaps 100 instructions in length (about 1 function point).

- A complete program of perhaps 1,000 instructions in length (10 function points).

- A component of a system of perhaps 10,000 instructions in length (100 function points).

- An entire software system that can range from 100,000 statements (1,000 function points) to more than 10,000,000 instructions in length (100,000 function points).

Any one of these software groupings can be tested, and often tested many times, in the course of software development activities.

The term "execution" means running the software on a computer with or without any form of instrumentation or test control software being present.

The phrase "pre-determined criteria" means that what the software is supposed to do is known prior to its execution, so that what the software actually does can be compared against the anticipated results to judge whether or not the software is behaving correctly.

It is interesting to consider the forms of testing SPR's clients utilize and the approximate percent of projects in our knowledge base (out of about 7,000 projects) that have been exposed to various kinds of testing.

I have divided the forms of testing into three broad categories: general testing, specialized testing, and testing that involves the users or clients themselves.

The general forms of testing are concerned with almost any kind of software and seek to eliminate common kinds of bugs such as branching errors, looping errors, incorrect outputs, and the like.

The specialized forms of testing are more narrow in focus and seek specific kinds of errors such as problems that only occur under full load, or problems that might slow down performance.

The forms of testing involving users are aimed primarily at usability problems and ensuring that all requirements have been in fact implemented.

Table 1   Approximate Distribution of Testing Methods for U.S. Software Projects

Testing Stage	Percent of Projects Utilizing Test Stage
General Forms of Testing	
Subroutine testing	100%
Unit testing	99%
System testing of full application	95%
New function testing	90%
Regression testing	70%
Integration testing	50%
Specialized Forms of Testing	
Viral protection testing	45%
Stress or capacity testing	35%
Performance testing	30%
Security testing	15%
Platform testing	5%
Year 2000 testing	5%
Independent testing	3%
Forms of Testing Involving Users	
Customer acceptance testing	35%
Field (Beta) testing	30%
Usability testing	20%
Lab testing	1%
Clean-room statistical testing	1%

Among SPR's clients, it is interesting to note that the only form of testing that is truly universal is testing of individual subroutines as they are created. Unit testing of entire modules is almost universal, although a few projects have not utilized this method (such as those using the "clean-room" method). Testing of the entire application upon completion is also very common, although here too not every project has done so.

For the other and more specialized forms of testing, such as performance testing or security testing, only a minority of projects among SPR's clients perform such testing. Sometimes the specialized forms of testing are not needed, but sometimes they are needed and are skipped over due to schedule pressure or poor decision-making by project managers.

Black Box and White Box Testing

The software testing literature often divides testing into two major forms termed "black box" testing and "white box" testing (also known as "glass box" testing). The distinction between the two concerns the knowledge that the test-case developers have.

For "black box" testing, the inner structure or control flow of the application is not known or viewed as irrelevant for constructing test cases. The application is tested against the external specifications and/or requirements in order to ensure that a specific set of input parameters will in fact yield the correct set of output values.

For "white box" testing, the test-case developer is privy to the inner structure of the application and knows the control flow through the application, or at least knows the control flow if the software works correctly. This form is also sometimes known as "glass box" testing because the inner structure and control flow of the application are known and utilized for test-case construction.

Black box testing is useful for ensuring that the software more or less is in concordance with the written specifications and written requirements.

White box or glass box testing is useful for ensuring that all or at least most paths through the application have been executed in the course of testing.

Of the 18 forms of testing discussed in this section, seven are normally black box test methods, seven are white box test methods, and four are mixed test methods which can be either white box, black box, or both.

Table 2   Black Box, White Box, and Mixed Testing Approaches

Subroutine testing	White box
Unit testing	White box
Viral protection testing	White box
Stress or capacity testing	White box
Performance testing	White box
Security testing	White box
Year 2000 testing	White box

(continued)

Table 2   *(continued)*

System testing of full application	Black box
New function testing	Black box
Lab testing	Black box
Usability testing	Black box
Customer acceptance testing	Black box
Field (Beta) testing	Black box
Clean-room statistical testing	Black box
Independent testing	Mixed
Regression testing	Mixed
Integration testing	Mixed
Platform testing	Mixed

Both white box and black box testing methods are useful so there is no serious debate or argument in the software testing literature that one form is superior to the other. The testing literature usually agrees that both forms are desirable and necessary. However, there is some debate as to whether black box testing in the form of clean-room or statistical testing is adequate.

The General Forms of Software Testing

The general forms of software testing occur for almost any kinds of software: systems software, commercial software, military software, information systems, or anything else.

While the general forms of software testing are common and well understood, not all companies use the same vocabulary to describe them. The following brief definitions explains the general meanings of the general forms of testing discussed here:

Subroutine testing is the lowest-level form of testing noted among our clients. Recall that a "subroutine" is a small collection of code that may constitute less than 10 statements or perhaps one-tenth of a function point.

Subroutine testing is performed almost spontaneously by developers, and is very informal. Essentially this form of testing consists of executing a just completed subroutine to see if it compiles properly and performs as expected. Subroutine testing is a key line of defense against errors in algorithms in spite of its being informal and under reported in the testing literature. Subroutine testing is a "white box" form of testing.

Unit testing is the lowest-level form of testing normally discussed in the testing literature. Unit testing is the execution of a complete module or small program that will normally range from perhaps 100 to 1,000 source code statements, or roughly from 1 to perhaps 10 function points.

Although unit testing may often be performed informally, it is also the stage at which actual test planning and test-case construction begins. Unit testing is usually performed by the programmers who write the module, and hence seldom has available data on defect levels or removal efficiency. (Note that for testing under cleanroom concepts, unit testing is *not* performed by the developers so data on defect removal may be recorded in this situation.)

Even in the normal situation of unit testing being performed by developers, enough companies have used volunteers who record defects found during unit test to have at least an idea of how efficient this form of testing is. Unit testing is a "white box" form of testing. Unit testing is also often plagued by "bad test cases" which themselves contain errors. (See the sections on Bad Test Cases and Clean Room Development earlier in this book.)

New function testing is often teamed with regression testing, and both forms are commonly found when existing applications are being updated or modified. As the name implies, new function testing is aimed at validating new features that are being added to a software package.

For entirely new projects, as opposed to enhancements, this form of testing is also known as "component testing" since it test the combined work of multiple programmers whose programs in aggregate may comprise a component of a larger system.

Often new function testing is performed by testing specialists since it covers the work of a number of programmers. For example, typical size ranges of major new functions added to existing software packages can exceed 10,000 source code statements or 100 function points.

New function testing is normally supported by formal test plans, planned test cases, and occurs on software that is under full configuration control. Also defect reporting for new function testing is both common and reasonably accurate. Both "white box" and "black box" forms of new function testing have been noted, although black box testing is more common.

New function testing is a key line of defense against errors in inter-module interfaces and the movement of data from place to place through an application. New function testing also intended to verify that the new or added features work correctly.

Regression testing is the opposite of new function testing. The word "regression" means to slip back and in the context of testing regression means accidentally damaging an existing feature as an unintended byproduct of adding a new feature. Regression testing also checks to ensure that prior known bugs have not inadvertently stayed in the software after they should have been removed.

After a few years of software evolution, regression testing becomes one of the most extensive forms of testing because the library of available test cases from prior releases tends to grow continuously. Also, regression testing involves the entire base code of the application which for major systems can exceed 10,000,000 lines of code or 100,000 function points.

Regression testing can be performed by developers, professional test personnel, or software quality assurance. Regardless of who performs regression test, the application is usually under full configuration control. Both white box and black box forms of regression testing have been noted.

Regression test libraries, though often extensive, are sometimes troublesome and have both redundant test cases and test cases which themselves contain errors. See the section on Bad Test Cases for additional information.

Integration testing as the name implies, is testing on a number of modules or programs that have come together to comprise an integrated software package. Since integration testing may cover the work of dozens or even hundreds of programmers, it also deals with rather large numbers of test cases.

Integration testing often occurs in "waves" as new builds of an evolving application are created. Microsoft, for example, performs daily integration of developing software projects and hence also performs daily integration testing. Other companies may have longer intervals between builds, such as weekly or even monthly builds.

Applications undergoing integration testing are usually under formal configuration control. Integration testing normally make use of formal test plans, planned suites of test cases, and formal defect reporting procedures. Both black box and white box forms of integration testing have been noted. Integration testing can be performed by developers themselves, by professional test personnel, or by software quality assurance.

System testing of full application is usually the last form of internal testing before customers get involved with field testing (Beta testing). For large systems, a formal system test can take many months and can involve large teams of test personnel. Also, the entire set of development programmers may be needed in order to fix bugs that are found during this critical test stage.

System testing demands formal configuration control and also deserves formal defect tracking support. System testing is normally based on black box principles, although sometimes the white box testing form is used. System testing can be performed by developers, professional test personnel, or by quality assurance personnel.

For software that controls physical devices (such as telephone switching systems) the phrase "system test" may include concurrent testing of hardware components. In this case, other forms of engineers and quality assurance may also be involved such as electrical or aeronautical engineers dealing with the hardware. Microcode may also be part of system test. For complex hybrid products, system test is a key event.

System testing may sometimes overlap a specialized form of testing, termed "lab testing," where special laboratories are used to house complex new hardware/software products that will be tested by prospective clients under controlled conditions.

The Specialized Forms of Software Testing

These specialized forms of software testing occur with less frequency than the general forms. The specialized forms of testing are most common for systems software, military software, commercial software, contract software, and software with unusually tight criteria for things like high performance or ease of use.

Stress or capacity testing is a specialized form of testing aimed at judging the ability of an application to function when nearing the boundaries of its capabilities in terms of the volume of information used. For example, capacity testing of the word processor used to create this book (Microsoft Word for Windows Version 7) might entail tests against individual large documents of perhaps 200 to 300 pages to judge the upper limits that can be handled before MS Word becomes cumbersome or storage is exceeded. It might also entail dealing with even larger documents, say 2,000 pages, segmented into master documents and various sections. For a database application, capacity testing might entail loading the database with 10,000 or 100,000 or 1,000,000 records to judge how it operates when fully populated with information.

Capacity testing is usually a black box form of testing, often performed by testing specialists rather than by developers. Capacity testing may either be a separate test stage, or performed as a subset of integration or system test. Usually it cannot be performed earlier, since the full application is necessary.

Performance testing is a specialized form of testing aimed at judging whether or not an application can meet the performance goals set out for it. For many applications performance is only a minor issue, but for some kinds of applications it is critical. For example, weapons systems, aircraft flight control systems, fuel injection systems, access methods, and telephone switching systems must meet stringent performance goals or the devices the software is controlling may not work.

Performance testing is a white box form of testing, often performed by professional testers and sometimes supported by performance or tuning specialists. Some aspects of performance testing can be done at the unit test level, but the bulk of performance testing associated with integration and system testing since interfaces among the full product affect performance.

Viral protection testing is rapidly moving from a specialized form of testing to a general one, although it still has been noted on less than half of our client's projects. The introduction of software viruses by malicious hackers has been a very interesting sociological phenomena in the software world. The amount of viruses numbers in the thousands and more are being created daily.

Virus protection has now become a minor but growing subindustry of the software domain. Virus testing is a white box form of testing. Although commercial virus protection software can be run by anybody, major commercial developers of software also use special proprietary tools to ensure that master copies of software packages do not contain viruses.

Security testing is most common and most sophisticated for military software, followed by software that deals with very confidential information such as bank records, medical records, tax records, and the like.

The organizations most likely to utilize security testing include the military services, National Security Agency (NSA), Central Intelligence Agency (CIA), Federal Bureau of Investigation (FBI), and other organizations which utilize computers and software for highly sensitive purposes.

Security testing is a white box form of testing usually performed by highly trained specialized personnel. Indeed, some military projects use "penetration teams" who attempt to break the security of applications by various covert means including but not limited to hacking, theft, bribery, and even picking locks or breaking into buildings.

It has been noted that one of the easiest ways to break into secure systems involves finding disgruntled employees, so security testing may have psychological and sociological manifestations.

Platform testing is a specialized form of testing found among companies whose software operates on different hardware platforms under different operating systems. Many commercial software vendors market the same applications for Windows 95, Windows NT, OS/2, UNIX, and sometimes for other platforms as well.

While the features and functions of the application may be identical on every platform, the mechanics of getting the software to work on various platforms requires separate versions and separate test stages for each platform. Platform testing is usually a white box form of testing.

Another aspect of platform testing is to ensure that the software package correctly interfaces with any other software packages that might be related to it. For example, for when testing software cost estimating tools, this stage of testing would verify that data can be passed both ways between the estimating tool and various project management tools. For example, suppose cost estimating tool such as CHECKPOINT is intended to share data with Microsoft Project under Windows 95. This is the stage where the interfaces between the two would be verified.

Platform testing is also termed "compatibility testing" by some companies. Regardless of the nomenclature used, the essential purpose remains the same: to ensure that software which operates on multiple hardware platforms, under multiple operating systems, and interfaces with multiple can handle all varieties of interconnection.

Year 2000 testing is the most recent form of specialized testing noted among our clients. The first companies among our clients to begin serious attempts to find and fix the Year 2000 problem only started in 1994, although some companies may have started earlier. The Year 2000 problem concerns using only two digits for dates, such as 96 for 1996. Many applications will fail when 1999 becomes 2000 because the 00 will disrupt calculations.

As this book is written in 1996, no fewer than 50 commercial tools for seeking out Year 2000 hits have entered the commercial market, and several hundred consulting and outsourcing companies have started Year 2000 services. Year 2000 testing is primarily a white box form of testing, although black box testing of inputs and outputs occurs, too.

Independent testing is very common for military software, since it was required by Department of Defense standards. It can also occur for commercial software, and indeed there are several commercial testing companies who do testing on a fee basis. However, independent testing is very rare for management information systems, civilian systems software projects, and outsource or contract software. Independent testing, as the name implies, is performed by a separate company or at least a separate organization from the one that built the application. Both white box and black box forms of independent testing are noted.

A special form of independent testing may occur from time-to-time as part of litigation when a client charges that a contractor did not achieve acceptable levels of quality. The plaintiff or defendant, or both, may commission a third-party to test the software.

Another form of independent testing is found among some commercial software vendors who market software developed by subcontractors or other commercial vendors. The primary marketing company usually tests the subcontracted software to ensure that it meets their quality criteria.

The Forms of Testing Involving Users or Clients

For many software projects, the clients or users are active participants at various stages along the way including but not limited to: requirements gathering, prototyping, inspections, and several forms of testing. The testing stages where users participate are generally the following.

Usability testing is a specialized form of testing sometimes performed in usability laboratories. Usability testing involves actual clients who utilize the software under controlled and sometimes instrumented conditions so that their actions can be observed. Usability testing is common for commercial software produced by large companies such as IBM and Microsoft. Usability testing can occur with any kind of software however. Usability testing is a black box form of testing and usually occurs at about the same time as system test. Sometimes usability testing and Beta testing are concurrent, but it is more common for usability testing to precede Beta testing.

Field (Beta) testing is a common testing technique for commercial software. The word "Beta" is the second letter in the Greek alphabet. Its use in testing stems from a testing sequence used by hardware engineers that included Alpha, Beta, and Gamma testing. For software, Alpha testing more or less dropped out of the lexicon circa 1980 and Gamma testing was almost never part of the software test cycle. Thus, the word "Beta" is the only one left for software, and is used to mean an external test involving customers.

Microsoft has become famous by conducting the most massive external Beta tests in software history with more than 10,000 customers participating. High-volume Beta testing with thousands of customers is very efficient in terms of defect removal efficiency levels and can exceed 85% removal efficiency if there are more than 1,000 Beta test participants. However, if Beta test participation comprises less than a dozen clients removal efficiency is usually around 35% to 50%.

Beta testing usually occurs after system testing, and is a black box form of testing. External Beta testing and internal usability testing may occur concurrently. However Beta testing may involve special agreements with clients to avoid the risk of lawsuits should the software manifest serious problems.

Lab testing is a special form of testing found primarily with hybrid products that consist of complex physical devices that are controlled by software, such as telephone switching systems, weapons systems, and medical instruments. It is obvious that conventional field testing or Beta testing of something like a PBX switch, a cruise missile, or a CAT scan machine is infeasible due to the need for possible structural modifications to buildings, special electrical wiring, heating and cooling requirements, to say nothing of zoning permits and authorization by various boards and control bodies.

Therefore, the companies that build such devices often have laboratories where clients can test out both the hardware and the software prior to having the equipment installed on their own premises.

Lab testing with the users present is normally a black box form of testing, although if certain kinds of problems are noted, such as performance or capacity problems, white box testing can be part of the process, too.

Customer acceptance testing is commonly found for contract software and often found for management information systems, systems software, and military software. The only form of software where acceptance testing is rare or does not occur is that of high-volume commercial "shrink wrapped" software. Even here, some vendors and retail stores provide a money-back guarantee which permits a form of acceptance testing. How the customers go about acceptance testing varies considerably, but usually acceptance testing is a black box form of testing.

Clean-room statistical testing is found only in the context of clean-room development methods. The clean-room approach is unusual in that the developers do not perform unit tests, and the test cases themselves are based on statistical assertions of usage patterns. Clean-room testing is inextricably joined with formal specification methods and proofs of correctness. Clean-room testing is a black box form of testing and is always performed by testing specialists or quality assurance personnel rather than developers themselves. (See the section on Clean Room Development for additional information.)

Numbers of Testing Stages for Software Projects

Looking at the data from another vantage point, if each specific kind of testing is deemed a "testing stage" it is interesting to see how many discrete testing stages occur for software projects. The overall range of testing stages among our clients and their software projects runs from a low of 1 to a high of 16 out of the total number of testing stages of 18 discussed here.

Table 3   Approximate Distribution of Testing Stages for U.S. Software Projects

Number of Testing Stages	Percent of Projects Utilizing Test Stages
1 testing stage	2%
2 testing stages	8%
3 testing stages	12%
4 testing stages	14%
5 testing stages	16%
6 testing stages	18%
7 testing stages	5%
8 testing stages	5%
9 testing stages	7%
10 testing stages	5%
11 testing stages	3%
12 testing stages	1%
13 testing stages	1%
14 testing stages	1%
15 testing stages	1%
16 testing stages	1%
17 testing stages	0%
18 testing stages	0%
Total	100%

As can be seen from the distribution of results, the majority of software projects in the United States (70%) use six or fewer discrete testing stages, and the most common pattern of testing observed includes the following:

- Subroutine testing

- Unit testing

- New function testing

- Regression testing

- Integration testing

- System testing

These six forms of testing are very common on applications of 1,000 function points or larger. These six also happen to be generalized forms of testing that deal with broad categories of errors and issues.

Below 1,000 function points and especially below 100 function points sometimes only three testing stages are found, assuming the project in question is new and not an enhancement:

- Subroutine testing

- Unit testing

- New function testing

The other forms of testing that are less common are more specialized, such as performance testing or capacity testing, and deal with a narrow band of problems which not every application is concerned with.

Testing Pattern Variations By Industry and Type of Software

There are of course very significant variations between industries and between various kinds of software in terms of typical testing patterns utilized, as follows:

End-User software is the sparsest in terms of testing and the usual pattern includes only two test stages: subroutine testing and unit testing. Of course end-user software is almost all less than 100 function points in size.

Management information systems (MIS) software projects use from three up to perhaps eight forms of testing. A typical MIS testing stage pattern would include subroutine testing, unit testing, new function testing, regression testing, system testing, and user acceptance testing. MIS testing is usually performed by the developers themselves, so that testing by professional test personnel or by quality assurance personnel is a rarity in this domain.

Outsource vendors doing information systems are similar to their clients in terms of testing patterns. MIS outsource vendors use typical MIS patterns; systems software vendors use typical systems software patterns; and military outsource vendors use typical military test patterns. This means that the overall range of outsource testing can run from as few as three kinds of testing up to a high of 16 kinds of testing. Usually the outsource vendors utilize at least one more stage of testing than their clients. (See the section of this book on Outsource and Contract Software Quality Levels for additional information.)

Commercial software developed by major vendors such as Microsoft, IBM, and Computer Associates will typically use a 12-stage testing series: subroutine testing, unit testing, new function testing, regression testing, performance testing, stress testing, integration testing, usability testing, platform testing, system testing, viral testing, and field testing, which is often called external or Beta testing. (See the section of Microsoft's Quality Methods for an example of commercial software quality approaches.)

Small software vendors, however, who develop small applications of less than 1,000 function points may only use six testing stages: subroutine testing, unit testing, new function testing, regression testing, system testing, and Beta testing.

Major software vendors such as Microsoft and IBM utilize large departments of professional testers who take over after unit test and perform the major testing work at the higher levels such as integration test, system test, and specialized testing such as performance testing or stress testing.

Systems software is often extensively tested and may use as many as 14 different testing stages. A typical testing pattern for a software system in the 10,000 function point range would include subroutine testing, unit testing, new function testing, regression testing, performance testing, stress/capacity testing, integration testing, usability testing, system testing, viral testing, security testing, Year 2000 testing, lab testing and/or field testing, which is often called external or Beta testing.

The larger systems software companies such as AT&T, Siemens-Nixdorf, IBM, etc., typically utilize professional testing personnel after unit testing. Also, the systems software domain typically has the largest and best equipped software quality assurance groups and the only quality assurance research labs.

Some of the large systems software organizations may have three different kinds of quality-related laboratories:

- Quality research labs

- Usability labs

- Hardware/software product test labs

Indeed, the larger systems software groups are among the few kinds of organizations that actually perform research on software quality, in the classical definition of "research" as formal experiments using trial and error methods to develop improved tools and practices.

Military software uses the most extensive suite of test stages, and large weapons or logistics systems may include 16 discrete testing stages: subroutine testing, unit testing, new function testing, regression testing, performance testing, stress testing, integration testing, independent testing, usability testing, lab testing, system testing, viral testing, security testing, Year 2000 testing, and field testing, which is often called external or Beta testing, and customer-acceptance testing.

Only military projects routinely utilize "independent testing" or testing by a separate company external to the developing or contracting organization. Military projects often utilize the services of professional testing personnel and also quality assurance personnel.

However, there are several companies that perform independent testing for commercial software organizations. Often smaller software companies that lack full in-house testing capabilities will utilize such testing external organizations.

Testing Pattern Variations By Size of Application

Another interesting way of looking at the distribution of testing stages is to look at the ranges and numbers of test stages associated with the various sizes of software applications.

Table 4   Ranges of Test Stages Associated with the Size of Software Applications

Size of Application in Function Points	Number of Test Stages Performed		
	Minimum	Average	Maximum
1	0	3	4
10	1	4	5
100	2	5	8
1000	3	9	11
10000	4	10	13
100000	6	12	16

As can be seen, the larger applications tend to utilize a much more extensive set of testing stages than do the smaller applications, which is not unexpected.

It is interesting to consolidate testing variations by industry and testing variations by size of application. The following table shows the typical number of test stages observed for six size plateaus and six software classes.

Table 5   Average Number of Test Stages Observed by Application Size and Class of Software

Class of Software	(Size of Application in Function Points)						
	1	10	100	1K	10K	100K	Average
End-user	1	2	2				1.67
MIS	2	3	4	6	7	8	5.00
Outsourcers	2	3	5	7	8	9	5.67
Commercial	3	4	6	9	11	12	7.50
Systems	3	4	7	11	12	14	8.50
Military	4	5	8	11	13	16	9.50
Average	2.50	3.50	5.33	8.80	10.20	11.80	7.02

There are wide variations in testing patterns so this table has a significant margin of error. However, the data is interesting and explains why the commercial, systems, and military software domains often have higher reliability levels than other forms.

This table also illustrates that there is no single pattern of testing that is universally appropriate for all sizes of software and all classes of software. The optimal pattern of defect removal and testing stages must be matched to the nature of the application.

Testing Stages Noted in Law Suits Alleging Poor Quality

It an interesting observation that for outsource, military, and systems software that ends up in court for litigation which involves assertions of unacceptable or inadequate quality, the number of testing stages is much smaller, while formal design and code inspections were not utilized at all.

The following table shows the typical patterns of defect removal activities for software projects larger than 1000 function points in size where the client sued the developing organization for producing software with inadequate quality levels.

The table simply compares the pattern of defect removal operations observed for reliable software packages with high quality levels to the pattern noted during law suits where poor quality and low reliability was part of the litigation.

Table 6   Defect Removal and Testing Stages Noted During Litigation for Poor Quality

	Reliable Software	Software Involved in Litigation for Poor Quality
Formal design inspections	Used	Not used
Formal code inspections	Used	Not used
Subroutine testing	Used	Used
Unit testing	Used	Used
New function testing	Used	Rushed or omitted
Regression testing	Used	Rushed or omitted
Integration testing	Used	Used
System testing	Used	Rushed or omitted
Performance testing	Used	Rushed or omitted
Capacity testing	Used	Rushed or omitted

The phrase "rushed or omitted" indicates that the vendor departed from best standard practices by eliminating a stage of defect removal or by rushing it in order to meet an arbitrary finish date or commitment to the client.

It is interesting that during the depositions and testimony of the litigation, the vendor often counter charges that the short-cuts were made at the direct request of the client. Sometimes the vendors assert that the client ordered the short-cuts even in the face of warnings that the results might be hazardous.

As can be seen, software developed under contractual obligations is at some peril if quality control and testing approaches are not carefully performed. (See the section on Outsource and Contract Software Quality Levels for additional information.)

Using Function Points to Estimate Test-Case Volumes

Function point and the related feature point metrics are starting to provide some preliminary but interesting insights into test-case volumes. This is not unexpected, since the fundamental parameters of both function points and feature points all represent topics that need test coverage:

- Inputs

- Outputs

- Inquires

- Logical files

- Interfaces

- Algorithms (feature points only)

Since function points and feature points can both be derived during requirements and early design stages, this approach offers a method of predicting test-case numbers fairly early. The method is still somewhat experimental, but the approach is leading to interesting results and usage is expanding.

The following table shows preliminary data on the number of test cases that have been noted among our clients, using "test cases per function point" as the normalizing metric. This table has a high margin of error, but as with any other set of preliminary data points, it is better to publish the results in the hope of future refinements and corrections than to wait until the data is truly complete.

Table 7 Ranges of Test-Cases per Function Point for Software Projects

Testing Stage	Minimum	Average	Maximum
Clean-room testing	0.60	1.00	3.00
Regression testing	0.40	0.60	1.30
Unit testing	0.20	0.45	1.20
New function testing	0.25	0.40	0.90
Integration testing	0.20	0.40	0.75

(continued)

LIVERPOOL
JOHN MOORES UNIVERSITY
AVRIL ROBARTS LRC
TITHEBARN STREET
LIVERPOOL L2 2ER
TEL. 0151 231 4022

Table 7   *(continued)*

Testing Stage	Minimum	Average	Maximum
Subroutine testing	0.20	0.30	0.40
Independent testing	0.00	0.30	0.55
System testing	0.15	0.25	0.60
Viral testing	0.00	0.20	0.40
Performance testing	0.00	0.20	0.40
Acceptance testing	0.00	0.20	0.60
Lab testing	0.00	0.20	0.50
Field (Beta) testing	0.00	0.20	1.00
Usability testing	0.00	0.20	0.40
Platform testing	0.00	0.15	0.30
Stress testing	0.00	0.15	0.30
Security testing	0.00	0.15	0.35
Year 2000 testing	0.00	0.15	0.30
Total	2.00	5.50	13.25

The use of function point metrics also provides some rough rules of thumb for predicting the overall volumes of test cases that are likely to be created for software projects.

- Raising the function point total of the application to the 1.2 power will give an approximation of the minimum number of test cases.

- Raising the function point total to 1.3 power gives an approximation of the average number of test cases.

- Raising the function point total to the 1.4 power gives an approximation of the maximum number of test cases.

These rules of thumb are based on observations of software projects whose sizes range between about 100 function points and 100,000 function points. The rules of thumb are not accurate enough for serious business purposes such as contracts, but are useful in providing estimating "sanity checks." See the section on Function Points for additional rules of thumb involving these versatile metrics.

Because of combinatorial complexity, it is usually impossible to write and run enough test cases to fully exercise a software project larger than about 100 function points in size. The number of permutations of inputs, outputs, and control flow paths quickly become astronomical.

For really large systems that approach 100,000 function points in size, the total number of test cases needed to fully test every condition can be regarded, for practical purposes, as an infinite number. Also, the amount of computing time needed to run such a test suite would also be an infinite number, or at least a number so large that there are not enough computers in any single company to approach the capacity needed.

Therefore, the volumes of test cases shown here are based on empirical observations and the numbers assume standard reduction techniques such as testing boundary conditions rather than all intermediate values and compressing related topics into equivalency classes.

Using Function Points to Estimate the Numbers of Test Personnel

One of the newest but most interesting uses of function point metrics in a testing context is to use function points for predicting the probable number of test personnel that might be needed for each test stage, and then for the overall product.

The following table has a high margin of error, but the potential value of using function points for test staffing prediction is high enough to make publication of preliminary data useful.

Table 8   Ranges in Number of Function Points Per Software Tester

Testing Stage	Minimum	Average	Maximum
Subroutine testing	0.1	1.0	3.0
Unit testing	1.0	3.0	12.0
New function testing	100.0	350.0	1500.0
Clean-room testing	100.0	350.0	1000.0
Performance testing	150.0	400.0	1000.0
Integration testing	150.0	700.0	2500.0
Acceptance testing	250.0	750.0	1500.0
Regression testing	500.0	1500.0	7500.0
Platform testing	350.0	1500.0	5000.0
Security testing	200.0	1500.0	3500.0
Field (Beta) testing	250.0	1500.0	5000.0
Usability testing	150.0	2000.0	4500.0
Lab testing	750.0	2500.0	4000.0

(continued)

Table 8   *(continued)*

Testing Stage	Minimum	Average	Maximum
Viral testing	250.0	2500.0	5000.0
System testing	750.0	2500.0	5000.0
Independent testing	500.0	2500.0	8500.0
Capacity testing	400.0	3000.0	7500.0
Year 2000 testing	250.0	3500.0	9000.0
Average	283.4	1503.0	4000.8

This table is a bit misleading. While the average test stage might have a ratio of about 1,500 function points for every tester, the range is very broad. Also, the table does not show the ratio of testers to software for testing performed in parallel.

For example, if a common four-stage combination of test stages where professional testers or QA personnel handle the testing were done in parallel rather than sequentially, the ratio for the entire combination is in the range of one testing staff member for about every 250 function points for these test stages:

- New function test
- Regression test
- Integration test
- System test

For some of the test stages such as subroutine testing and unit testing, the normal practice is for the testing to be performed by developers. In this case, the data simply indicates the "average" sizes of subroutines and standalone programs.

Testing and Defect Removal Efficiency Levels

Most forms of testing, such as unit test by individual programmers, are less than 30% efficient in finding bugs. That is, less than one bug out of three will be detected during the test period. Sometimes a whole string of test steps (unit test, function test, integration test, and system test) will find less than 50% of the bugs in a software product. By itself, testing alone has never been sufficient to ensure really high quality levels.

Consider also the major categories of defects which affect software, i.e., errors of omission, errors of commission, errors of clarity or ambiguity, and errors of speed or capacity.

Table 9 shows the approximate defect removal efficiency level of the common forms of testing against these five error categories (with a very large margin of error).

This data is derived in part from measurements by our clients, and in part from discussion with software testing and QA personnel in a number of companies. The data is based on anecdotes rather than real statistical results because none of our clients actually record this kind of information. However the overall picture the data gives of testing is interesting and clarifies testing's main strengths and weaknesses.

This table is ranked in descending order of overall efficiency against all forms of defects, and hence is slightly misleading. Some of the specialized forms of testing such as Year 2000 testing or viral protection testing, are highly efficient but only against one narrow class of problem.

Table 9   Average Defect Removal Efficiency Levels of Software Test Stages Against Five Defect Types

	Omission	Commiss.	Clarity	Speed	Capacity	Average
Beta testing	40%	40%	35%	40%	35%	38%
Lab testing	25%	35%	30%	50%	50%	38%
System testing	20%	30%	30%	50%	50%	36%
Clean room testing	35%	40%	35%	25%	40%	35%
Usability testing	55%	50%	60%	10%	0%	35%
Acceptance testing	30%	35%	35%	35%	30%	33%
Independent testing	20%	30%	30%	35%	40%	31%
Stress testing	0%	40%	0%	25%	80%	29%
New function testing	30%	30%	30%	20%	20%	26%
Integration testing	20%	35%	20%	25%	25%	25%
Unit testing	10%	60%	10%	20%	20%	24%
Platform testing	20%	70%	0%	30%	0%	24%
Regression testing	10%	45%	20%	20%	20%	23%
Performance testing	0%	10%	0%	75%	30%	23%
Subroutine testing	10%	50%	0%	20%	15%	19%
Virus testing	0%	80%	0%	0%	0%	16%
Security testing	50%	30%	0%	0%	0%	16%
Year 2000 testing	0%	80%	0%	0%	0%	16%
Average	21%	44%	19%	27%	25%	27%

The most obvious conclusion from this table is that testing is much more effective in finding errors of commission, or things that are done wrong, than it is in finding errors of omission or things that are left out by accident.

Note that there are wide ranges of observed defect removal efficiency over and above the approximate averages shown here. Any given form of testing can achieve defect removal efficiency levels that are perhaps 15% higher than these averages, or about 10% lower. However, no known form of testing has yet exceeded 90% in defect removal efficiency, so a series of inspections plus a multi-stage series of tests is needed to achieve really high levels of defect removal efficiency such as 99.9999%.

Using Function Points to Estimate Testing Effort and Costs

Another use of the function point metric in a testing context is to estimate and later measure testing effort (and costs). A full and formal evaluation of testing requires analysis of three discrete activities:

- Test preparation
- Test execution
- Defect repairs

Test preparation involves creating test cases, validating them, and putting them into a test library.

Test execution involves running the test cases against the software and recording the results. Note that testing is an iterative process and the same test cases can be run several times if needed, or even more.

Defect repairs concerns fixing any bugs that are found via testing, validating the fix, and then rerunning the test cases that found the bugs to ensure that the bugs have been repaired and no "bad fixes" have inadvertently been introduced.

With a total of 18 different kinds of testing to consider, the actual prediction of testing effort is too complex for simplistic rules of thumb. Several commercial estimating tools such as CHECKPOINT, COCOMO II, PRICE-S, SEER, and SLIM can predict testing costs for each test stage and then aggregate overall testing effort and expenses for any kind of software project, and for any size of software project. These same tools and others within this class can also predict testing defect removal efficiency levels.

For publication in a book there are too many variables involved for a static representation in a table or graph to be really accurate. Therefore, for the purposes of this book, a major simplifying assumption will be used. The assumption is that the proportion of total software effort devoted to testing correlates exactly with the number of test stages that are utilized. This assumption has a few exceptions, but seems to work well enough to have practical value.

The percentage shown in Table 10 for testing is based on the total development budget for the software project in question.

The same table also shows the approximate defect removal efficiency correlated with number of test stages for coding defects. Here too, as the number of test stages grows larger, defect removal efficiency levels increase. The essential message is that if you want to approach zero-defect levels, be prepared to perform quite a few testing stages.

Table 10   Number of Testing Stages, Testing Effort, and Defect Removal Efficiency

Number of Testing Stages	Percent of Effort Devoted to Testing	Cumulative Defect Removal Efficiency
1 testing stage	10%	50%
2 testing stages	15%	60%
3 testing stages	20%	70%
4 testing stages	25%	75%
5 testing stages	30%	80%
6 testing stages*	33%*	85%*
7 testing stages	36%	87%
8 testing stages	39%	90%
9 testing stages	42%	92%
10 testing stages	45%	94%
11 testing stages	48%	96%
12 testing stages	52%	98%
13 testing stages	55%	99%
14 testing stages	58%	99.9%
15 testing stages	61%	99.99%
16 testing stages	64%	99.999%
17 testing stages	67%	99.9999%
18 testing stages	70%	99.99999%

*Note: Six test stages, 33% costs, and 85% removal efficiency are approximate U.S. averages for software projects ≥ 1,000 function points in size.

This simplified approach is not accurate enough for serious project planning or for contracts, but it shows overall trends well enough to make the economic picture understandable.

This table also explains why large systems have higher testing costs than small applications, and why systems and military software have higher testing costs than information systems: more testing stages are utilized.

Note however, that the table does not show the whole picture (which is why commercial estimating tools are recommended). For example, if formal pre-testing design and code inspections are also utilized they alone can approach 80% in defect removal efficiency and also raise the efficiency of testing.

Thus, projects that utilize formal inspections plus testing can top 99% in cumulative defect removal efficiency with fewer stages than shown here, since this table illustrates only testing. See the section on Formal Design and Code Inspections and Defect Removal Efficiency for additional information.

Testing by Developers or by Professional Test Personnel

One of the major questions concerning software testing is who should do it. The possible answers to this question include, A) the developers themselves; B) professional test personnel; C) professional quality assurance personnel; or D) some combination of A, B, and C.

Note that several forms of testing such as external Beta testing and customer acceptance testing are performed by clients themselves or by consultants that the clients hire to do the work.

There is no definitive answer to this question, but some empirical observations may be helpful.

- The defect removal efficiency of "black box" testing is higher when performed by test personnel or by quality assurance personnel rather than by developers themselves.

- Black box testing performed by clients (i.e., Beta test and acceptance test) varies widely, but efficiency rises with the numbers of clients involved.

- For usability problems, testing by clients themselves outranks all other forms of testing.

- The defect removal efficiency of the "white box" subroutine and unit testing stages is highest when performed by developers themselves.

- The defect removal efficiency of specialized kinds of "white box" testing such as Year 2000 testing or viral protection testing is highest when performed by professional test personnel rather than by the developers themselves.

Table 11 shows my observations of who typically performs various test stages from among our client organizations. Note that since SPR's clients include quite a few systems software, military software, and commercial software vendors we probably have a bias in our data. The systems, commercial, and military software domains are much more likely to utilize the services of professional test and quality assurance personnel than are the MIS and outsource domains.

The table is sorted in descending order of the development column. Note that this order illustrates that the early testing is most often performed by development personnel, but the later stages of testing are most often performed by testing or quality assurance specialists.

Table 11   Observations on Performance of Test Stages by Occupation Group

Testing Stage	Developers	Testers	Qual. Assur.	Clients
Subroutine testing	100%	0%	0%	0%
Unit testing	90%	10%	0%	0%
New function testing	50%	30%	20%	0%
Integration testing	50%	30%	20%	0%
Viral testing	50%	30%	20%	0%
System testing	40%	40%	20%	0%
Regression testing	30%	50%	20%	0%
Performance testing	30%	60%	10%	0%
Platform testing	30%	50%	20%	0%
Stress testing	30%	50%	20%	0%
Security testing	30%	40%	30%	0%
Year 2000 testing	20%	50%	30%	0%
Usability testing	10%	10%	30%	50%
Acceptance testing	0%	0%	0%	100%
Lab testing	0%	0%	0%	100%

(continued)

Table 11   (continued)

Testing Stage	Developers	Testers	Qual. Assur.	Clients
Field (Beta) testing	0%	0%	0%	100%
Clean-room testing	0%	50%	40%	10%
Independent testing	0%	60%	40%	0%
Average	31%	31%	18%	20%

As can be seen from this table, among SPR's clients, testing by developers and testing by professional test personnel are equal in frequency and are followed by testing involving software quality assurance and finally testing by customers or their designated testers.

Testing by development personnel is much more common for the smaller forms of testing such as subroutine and unit testing. For the larger forms (i.e., system test) and for the specialized forms (i.e., performance, Year 2000, etc.) testing by professional test personnel or by quality assurance personnel become more common.

Testing should be part of a synergistic and integrated suite of defect prevention and defect removal operations that may include prototyping, quality assurance reviews, pre-test inspections, formal test planning, multi-stage testing, and measurement of defect levels and severities.

For those who have no empirical data on quality, the low average defect removal efficiency levels of most forms of testing will be something of a surprise. However, it is because each testing step is less than 100% efficient that causes multiple test stages to be necessary in the first place.

Testing is an important technology for software. For many years, progress in testing primarily occurred within the laboratories of major corporations who built systems software. However, in recent years a new subindustry has appeared of commercial test tool and support companies. This new subindustry is gradually improving software test capabilities as the commercial vendors of testing tools and methodologies compete within a fast-growing market for test-support products and services.

TOTAL QUALITY MANAGEMENT (TQM) FOR SOFTWARE

Among our clients, about 70 enterprises out of roughly 600 have utilized some form of total quality management (TQM). Of these, about half of the total quality management experiments were successful and improved quality, and the other half were failures in terms of quantified benefits.

The successful use of TQM correlates strongly with the seriousness of the commitment and the depth of understanding by executives and management.

TQM only works if it is really used. Giving the TQM concepts lip service but not really implementing the philosophy only leads to frustration.

The TQM concept is not a replacement for more traditional software quality approaches. Indeed, TQM works best for organizations that are also leaders in traditional quality approaches.

Specifically, some of the attributes of companies which are successful in their TQM programs include the following:

1) They also have effective software quality measurement programs which identify defect origins, severities, and removal efficiency rates.

2) They utilize formal reviews and inspections before testing begins.

3) Their software quality control was good or excellent even before the TQM approach was begun.

Conversely, enterprises which lack quality metrics, which fail to utilize pre-test defect prevention and removal operations, and which lag their competitors in current software quality control approaches tend to gain only marginal benefits, if any, from the adoption of the TQM method. Such enterprises are very likely to use TQM as a slogan, but not to implement the fundamental concepts.

The operative word for Total Quality Management is *total*. Concentrating on only coding defects, measuring only testing, and using the older KLOC metric, violates the basic philosophy of Total Quality Management. These approaches ignore the entire front-end of the lifecycle, and have no utility for requirements problems, design problems, documentation problems, or any of the other sources of trouble which lie outside of source code.

It is obvious that there are three sets of factors which must be deployed in order for Total Quality Management (TQM) to be successful with software:

1) Adopting a culture of high quality from the top to the bottom of an enterprise.

2) Using defect prevention methods to lower defect potentials.

3) Using defect removal methods to raise pre-release efficiencies.

If a company is serious about total quality management for software, then it needs to move vigorously to introduce synergistic combinations of defect prevention methods that can reduce defect potentials by more than 50% across the board. For example, joint application design (JAD) and quality function deployment (QFD) are both synergistic with TQM concepts.

The company's management will also need to examine and perhaps improve the company's set of defect removal methods to include such things as formal design and code inspections, assessments, and a multi-tier suite of testing stages.

However, to bring TQM to full power in an organization, the culture of the management community must be brought up to speed on what TQM means and how to go about it. Putting up wall posters and announcing that you are a TQM company will not, by itself, make any difference.

USABILITY LABORATORIES

The concept of a usability laboratory is a controlled environment where users can experiment with software packages and record both subjective feelings about ease of use, bugs, and other significant factors. The more sophisticated usability laboratories are fully instrumented for recording useful information, and some even have video and audio set ups so that users can be filmed in action while using software products. Most usability labs have one-way mirrors so that external observers can watch users without intruding on their activities, although the fact that the users know they are being observed is still a topic that can affect results.

Among SPR's clients, only 15 out of about 600 have usability labs. The total number of projects that have gone through these labs and then been measured during our assessment and benchmark studies is less than 100, so the data on this topic is sparse.

It is an interesting question as to exactly how many usability labs exist in the United States. The exact answer is not known, but I suspect that the total number of software usability labs in the U.S. is about 75. The Western European total should be about the same, while Japan and the Pacific Rim, Eastern Europe, and South America probably have another 75 or so. The world total is probably somewhere between 200 and 300 usability labs, although this is speculation.

Many large software producers such as Apple, IBM, and Microsoft have usability laboratories. Also, a few very large producers of in-house software have usability labs. For example, the U.S. Department of Agriculture has a usability laboratory as does CIGNA.

The concept of usability laboratories is now more than 30 years old, but few books or even many journal articles have been published on this topic. From performing consulting studies in organizations which have usability laboratories, the overall results appear favorable. Software packages that have been evaluated in usability laboratories generally have shorter learning curves and more satisfied users than those which have not been so evaluated.

However, the costs of a full-scale usability laboratory are high enough so that the concept is not likely to spread among small software producers unless they were able to share such a facility or commercial software usability labs become a viable business.

USER-SATISFACTION

There are at least 50 trade books on various aspects of software testing, quality assurance, inspections, and other forms of quality control dealing with quality in the sense of defect elimination. However, I am aware of only a few commercial or trade books which address the topic of measuring, raising, or evaluating user-satisfaction levels with software projects.

Further, there are a host of commercial tools available to support defect estimation, defect tracking, and various aspects of measuring quality in the sense of defects. However, I am not aware of any commercial tools that can either predict user-satisfaction early, or measure user-satisfaction after the fact other than some general-purpose tools for building and scoring surveys of various kinds.

Among SPR's 600 or so client organizations, about 200 have some form of measurement that collects at least pieces of quality data. The most common measures associated with quality are defect tracking of bugs reported by users after release of software (about 150 clients), which is sometimes augmented by defect tracking during testing (50 clients), or inspections (20 clients).

The rarest form of quality measurements among our clients are measures of user-satisfaction. Here only about 35 companies have any kind of formal user-satisfaction measurements, and 20 of these are commercial software vendors who have developed or commissioned user-satisfaction surveys.

Of course, even for companies that lack formal user-satisfaction surveys major user complaints will become known. The major gap due to lack of formal surveys is information about what users like and appreciate. Information on the good aspects of software is not as visible as information on things that don't work very well.

Because there is a shortage of solid data on the factors that influence user-satisfaction, it seems appropriate to show some of the topics that we have included in our SPR user-satisfaction survey questionnaire.

The purpose of the survey is to gain an understanding of how typical users utilize software, what benefits they perceive from using the software, and what problems (if any) they would like to have eliminated. The actual questionnaire uses a multiple-choice format and can be scored via a computer program. This set of examples merely shows some of the topics that are included.

Table 1   Selected Topics from the SPR User-Satisfaction Survey Questionnaire

---

Importance of the Software Product

How important is the software product to your job function?

How often do you use the software product?

How were your job functions performed prior to using the software package?

What are the primary benefits from using the software package?

What are the primary drawbacks from using the software package?

What is the value of the software package to you personally?

Product Evaluation and Selection

How many similar products were evaluated before selection the product?

What was the nature of the product evaluation method?

(continued)

Table 1   *(continued)*

Did you discuss this product with users prior to acquisition?

Are you a member of a user association for this product?

Did you find any reviews or critiques of this product to be helpful?

Product Modification and Customization

Did the product have to be modified for your use?

Who performed the modifications?

Did the modifications require changing the source code?

Did the modifications require changing the user instructions?

Were the modifications satisfactory?

Ease of Learning and Ease of Use

How easy was the software product to install?

How easy was the software product to learn before using it?

How easy is it to log on the product and start using it now?

Describe any tasks that are very intuitive or easy to perform?

Describe any tasks that are complex or difficult to perform?

If you make mistakes, does the product react helpfully or unhelpfully?

Is the performance of the product good, acceptable, or deficient?

Are the storage needs of the product acceptable or excessive?

How compatible is the product with other products that you use?

How easy is the product to shutdown when your session end?

How easy is the product to uninstall if necessary?

Product Quality and Service

How do you regard the quality of the product in terms of defect levels?

How do you regard the quality of the product in terms of reliability intervals?

How do you regard the quality of the product compared to others that you use?

How do you regard the quality of the training materials?

How do you regard the quality of the HELP screens and materials?

How do you regard the quality of the user manuals?

How do you regard the quality of the screen prompts and commands?

How do you regard the quality of the outputs from the product?

(continued)

Table 1   *(continued)*

Features and Functionality of Product

Are there features missing from the product that you would like to have added?

Are there features in the product that are extraneous and unnecessary?

How do the features that are present in the product compare to competitors?

Does the product have convenient interfaces to related products?

Which other products are most likely to be used in tandem with this product?

What are the five best features of the product?

What are the five worst features of the product?

Are there five improvements you would like to see in the product?

Vendor Support of Product

How often do new releases of the product occur?

Does the vendor provide a warranty for the product?

How do you report bugs or defects to the vendor?

Does the vendor provide a toll-free number for service calls?

Is it easy or difficult to contact the vendor by phone?

Does the vendor provide a fax number for service?

Does the vendor provide Internet or Web access for service?

Does the vendor have forums on any information utilities?

Does the vendor have an online bulletin board?

How does the vendor contact you about upgrades or repairs?

Are your defect reports handled promptly?

Are your reported defects usually repaired?

As can be seen from the number and diversity of topics, exploring software user-satisfaction is not a trivial task. Indeed, care must be used to develop a user-satisfaction survey instrument that is not so complicated and burdensome that it aggravates the users who are asked to answer it.

One recent change in user-satisfaction monitoring is the availability of World Wide Web sites, user forums on major information utilities, and other forms of direct computer to computer contact between clients and vendors of software packages. Used carefully, online information can give vendors up-to-the-minute data on important topics such as major bugs, repair speed, warranty needs, and a host of others.

YEAR 2000 SOFTWARE PROBLEM

The Year 2000 software problem is interesting from both a technical and sociological vantage point. This problem offers a strong lesson to the software quality community that quality needs to include long-range vision of future consequences.

Among SPR's clients, essentially all of the 600 or so enterprises will have Year 2000 repairs in greater or lesser degree. Some clients are well along in their Year 2000 effort, but many are still in early fact-finding mode. About 450 clients are still in fact finding mode; about 125 have started their Year 2000 repairs, and perhaps 25 are nearing the end of the Year 2000 upgrade cycle.

This pattern seems to replicate the global response to the Year 2000 issue, since most companies started a year or two later than the optimal period of 1994 and hence will have a great deal of frantic rush work between now and the end of the century.

A host of consulting companies and tool vendors have rushed to fill the Year 2000 needs, so a great deal of external assistance is available. Although not cheap, the better Year 2000 service companies now have the experience to find and repair Year 2000 updates at a fairly rapid rate.

Those with automated tools for seeking out Year 2000 instances can sometimes top 75 function points per staff month for finding, fixing, and testing Year 2000 hits in applications written in COBOL or other common languages. By contrast, a manual search for Year 2000 hits by novices in the Year 2000 area seldom top 15 function points per staff month. (See the section on Outsource and Contract Software Quality Levels for some additional information.)

At a practical level the Year 2000 problem also teaches us that the aphorism that "quality means conformance to requirements" is a sometimes a dangerous mistake. This is because the use of two-digit date fields has been a standard requirement for software projects for almost 25 years in spite of the fact that the eventual failure of applications adhering to this requirement could easily be predicted.

Many articles have been written on why the Year 2000 problem will occur, so it is only necessary to include a short background discussion here. The root cause can be traced back to the early days of computers, when information was stored on punched cards. Data storage was so limited and so expensive that any method that could save storage was readily adopted. Since no one in the 1950s or 1960s had any idea how long software would last, it seemed natural to store dates in two-digit form; i.e., 1965 would be stored simply as 65. This method was convenient and seemingly effective.

When magnetic storage was first introduced the cost of data storage declined slightly, but the early tape and disk based systems still were limited in capacity. Also, many card-based systems were transferred to tape or disk. But the original versions of the source code and the two-digit date logic continued to be used since there was no immediate reason to change it.

By the late 1970s and early 1980s it started to be noted that software applications were sometimes having remarkably long lives. For example, IBM's MVS operating system was approaching 20 years of age, as were a number of other widely used applications. Some tremors of alarm about date limits began to show up, but there was still no immediate serious alarm since the end of the century was 20 years away.

It was not until the early 1990s and the advent of optical storage that data storage costs declined to such a level as to be almost irrelevant. The early 1990s would have been the best time for addressing the Year 2000 problem, but for sociological reasons the human species is not very effective in disaster prevention.

Also, by the 1990s quite a significant amount of the damage had long been done. Millions of applications with two-digit date fields had already been written and many of them were in daily use throughout the world.

Hazardous Implications of the Year 2000 Problem

Here too, quite a bit has already been written about the kinds of applications that are going to be affected by the Year 2000 problem. Suffice it to say the problem is not restricted to aging legacy applications. The Year 2000 problem is also common in modern personal computer applications, and even embedded in the hardware of both mainframes and personal computers themselves.

Any software package that uses dates or has calendar routines as embedded functions is likely to be affected by the Year 2000 problem. Some common applications that will have to be modified include:

- Software with long-range calculations such as mortgages, life insurance premiums, interest compounding, pension payments, and social security benefit calculations.

- Software calendar utility functions in commercial spreadsheets such as Lotus, Excel, Quattro, and many others.

- Calendar applications embedded in personal information managers (PIM) and hand-held devices as well as those in personal computers.

- Software on-board commercial and military aircraft, weapons systems, and also software on-board satellites.

The most serious implications are the litigation consequences of the failure of calendar routines. Many important financial applications will be affected. Worse, some of the consequences may even threaten human lives and safety.

At least six kinds of potential litigation can be envisioned as a byproduct of the Year 2000 problem:

1) Litigation filed by clients whose finances or investments have been damaged.

2) Litigation filed by shareholders of companies whose software does not safely make the Year 2000 transition.

3) Litigation associated with any deaths or injuries derived from the Year 2000 problem.

4) Class-action litigation filed by various affected customers of computers or software packages.

5) Litigation filed by companies who utilized outsource vendors, contractors, consultants, or commercial Year 2000 tools but where Year 2000 problems still slipped through and caused damage.

6) Litigation against hardware manufacturers such as computer companies and defense contractors if the Year 2000 problem resides in hardware or embedded microcode as well as software.

The end of the 20th century is likely to be a very hazardous time for many executives, and for almost all software executives. Any executive who is in a position of fiduciary responsibility should by now be taking energetic actions to solve the Year 2000 problem. These same executives should also be in discussion with their legal counsels regarding the probable liabilities that they and their companies will be facing over the next 48 months and on into the 21st century.

Governments are not immune from the Year 2000 problem. All government agencies associated with revenues such as state and federal tax agencies are probably going to have major Year 2000 problems. This is also true of agencies such as social security that deal with benefits.

Although the military implications of the Year 2000 problem are not widely discussed in the software press, the on-board computers in many weapons systems, ships, tanks, and military aircraft are going to be affected by the Year 2000 problem. Logistics systems and various command and control systems will also be affected. Since the U.S. military services are far and away the most automated and computerized armed forces in the world, the United States Department of Defense will be facing one of the largest military expenses in human history.

No matter how things turn out, it is certain that the software industry in every country will be undergoing a major transformation between the years 1996 and 2005 in reaction to the Year 2000 problem.

One of the problems faced by the software industry is sociological. This industry has not been regarded by those in the older professions, such as electrical and mechanical engineers, as being true engineers or even true professionals. The fact that the software industry, collectively, has brought about one of the most expensive and hazardous problems in human history when it could easily have been avoided is going to lower our status even more.

Not only is the Year 2000 problem one of the most expensive problems in human history, it is also one of the most embarrassing. This problem has been theoretically discussed for more than 25 years, and its significance has been hypothesized with increasing alarm for more than 10 years. It is not a credit to the human race nor to the software industry that such an obvious problem with such a straight-forward technical solution should have reached the magnitude that is likely to occur.

On the other hand, the Year 2000 problem is symptomatic of a general human tendency to avoid trying to solve problems until the evidence is overwhelming. The historical difficulties which medical researchers such as Lister and Semmelweis had in introducing sterile surgical procedures, and the earlier resistance to Jenner's concept of vaccination illustrates that software is not the only learned profession that does not move swiftly to minimize potential risks.

Effort Required to Repair the Year 2000 Problem

The technical work associated with finding and fixing the Year 2000 problem can be broken down into four discrete activities:

1) Finding and isolating the Year 2000 sections of applications

2) Modifying the applications to repair the problem

3) Testing the repairs to ensure that they work

4) Regression testing the application to ensure no secondary damage has occurred

However, from preliminary observations of companies that have already begun their Year 2000 work, steps 3 and 4 (testing and regression testing) are sometimes performed in a very careless fashion. Carelessness in regression testing and validating Year 2000 repairs will have three damaging impacts later that can run well into the 21st century:

- Missed Year 2000 instances will be plentiful and troublesome.

- Bad fixes or fresh bugs accidentally injected will be common and troublesome.

- The performance or execution speeds of applications will be seriously degraded.

The approximate distribution of effort over the four aspects of the Year 2000 problem will vary significantly by language, due to the presence or absence of available tools:

Finding and isolating the Year 2000 problem should be easiest for object-oriented languages (i.e., Objective C, SMALLTALK, etc.) where dates are handled in well-formed class libraries. Next would be COBOL, since there are several specialized tools that can seek out date references in COBOL applications. Such tools also exist for other common languages such as C and FORTRAN. The toughest language will probably be Assembly, followed by languages that have tool shortages such as PL/I, LISP, FORTH and the like.

Table 1   Effort Ranges for Major Year 2000 Repair Activities

Year 2000 Activities		Percent Range of Total Costs
• Finding the Year 2000 instances	=	10% to 50%
• Fixing the Year 2000 instances	=	15% to 30%
• Testing the Year 2000 repairs	=	10% to 30%
• Regression testing the portfolio	=	20% to 50%

Because the distribution of effort varies with language, the following table shows typical ranges for languages where Year 2000 repairs will range from easy (SMALLTALK) to difficult (Assembly language). Table 2 assumes a burdened salary rate of $8400 per staff month.

Table 2   Distribution of Year 2000 Expense by Programming Language
(Results shown in terms of Cost per Function Point)

Language	Finding Year 2000 Instances	Repairing Year 2000 Instances	Testing Year 2000 Instances	Portfolio Regression Test	TOTAL
Assembly	$25	$20	$20	$15	$80
PL/I	$25	$10	$15	$15	$65
Jovial	$20	$12	$13	$15	$60
CMS2	$20	$12	$13	$15	$60
CHILL	$20	$15	$15	$10	$60
Algol	$15	$12	$13	$10	$50
Database	$7	$13	$15	$10	$45
Query	$10	$12	$12	$6	$40
PASCAL	$5	$10	$15	$10	$40
C++	$8	$6	$13	$8	$35
Spreadsheets	$5	$7	$20	$3	$35
C	$15	$7	$5	$8	$35
Ada83	$5	$7	$8	$15	$35
FORTRAN	$5	$7	$13	$10	$35
4-GLs	$5	$10	$10	$10	$35
V-Basic	$5	$5	$15	$5	$30
COBOL	$5	$6	$7	$10	$28
SMALLTALK	$3	$3	$5	$7	$18
Average	*$11*	*$10*	*$13*	*$10*	*$44*

Note that for older low-level languages such as Assembly, just finding the Year 2000 segments is a major cost all by itself, to say nothing of fixing and testing the problem areas.

For more modern languages and for strongly typed languages, finding the Year 2000 hits will not be so difficult, but testing them and the portfolio of applications will still require extensive effort.

The next aspect of the study of the Year 2000 problem is to consider the approximate amount of effort for the overall repairs that must be performed. There is quite a bit of uncertainty here, since there are large variances by industry and even larger variances by country.

The Year 2000 problem is global in scope. However, this problem is interesting because it affects industrialized countries much more severely than countries that are not fully automated in their business, government, and military operations.

The following table show the approximate per capita effort in staff months that may be needed to repair the Year 2000 problem for 30 countries. The effort is the total amount of effort needed to find instances of the Year 2000 problem, fix the problem, test the software, and then redeploy it. There is a high margin of error, but the Year 2000 problem is not a trivial one.

The effort is aggregated over the total software population of the country. That it, the months shown are the per capita amounts that are likely to be spent by every professional programmer in each country.

Table 3   Staff Months of Effort for Year 2000 Repairs in 30 Software-Intensive Countries

Country	Staff Months
Japan	4.87
United States	4.86
Germany	4.75
United Kingdom	4.75
France	4.75
Canada	4.63
Italy	4.60
Australia	4.60

(continued)

Table 3   *(continued)*

Country	Staff Months
Netherlands	4.60
Belgium	4.60
Ukraine	4.45
Taiwan	4.45
South Africa	4.45
Sweden	4.45
Spain	4.30
Russia	4.16
South Korea	4.16
Argentina	4.16
Portugal	4.16
Turkey	4.01
Brazil	3.86
Mexico	3.86
Thailand	3.56
Poland	3.27
Egypt	2.82
Philippines	2.73
Indonesia	2.52
Pakistan	2.52
China	1.78
India	1.78
Average	*3.95*

This data in this section is taken from my study of the Year 2000 software problem entitled *The Global Impact of the Year 2000 Software Problem,* Software Productivity Research, Inc., 1996.

By interesting coincidence, each reference to a Year 2000 date item seems to take about one function point for a wide variety of programming languages. Of course, each language can take quite a different number of lines of code to deal with dates. Assembly language, for example, can take as many as 100 statements while other languages with built-in date utility functions may only need a few or even one.

Table 4 shows the approximate effort and costs per function point for fixing Year 2000 instances for organizations with various numbers of software personnel.

Table 4   Effort and Costs of the Year 2000 Problem by Size of Staff

Software Staff	Number of Sites	Portfolio Size in FP	Effort in Months	Total Costs	Cost per FP
5	1	6,000	23	$195,588	$33
10	1	11,500	45	$374,877	$33
25	1	27,500	107	$896,446	$33
50	1	50,000	194	$1,629,902	$33
100	1	95,000	416	$3,483,915	$37
500	2	450,000	1,969	$16,502,757	$37
1000	3	900,000	4,200	$35,205,882	$39
5000	5	4,500,000	21,000	$176,029,412	$39
10000	10	9,000,000	42,000	$352,058,824	$39
20000	15	18,000,000	84,000	$704,117,647	$39

Table 4 assumes that companies will be doing their own Year 2000 repairs using minimal automation. Hence, this data has a high margin of error, but since all Year 2000 studies have a high margin of error the results are probably no further from reality than other reports. If specialized Year 2000 search tools are available, and if specialized Year 2000 contract personnel are used, the data in Table 4 would have to be adjusted.

Applying principles of game theory to the Year 2000 problem leads to the conclusion that a rapid and energetic attack is the minimax solution that will have the greatest return for the lowest investment.

Since the problem won't go away by itself, delays in seeking out and finding Year 2000 hits will lower the probability of finding all of them in time. Also rushing repairs and skimping on testing will damage performance and raise the probability of "bad fixes" or the introduction of fresh bugs as an accidental byproduct of fixing the Year 2000 references.

Finally, failure to repair Year 2000 problems prior to their actually doing damage may lead to the most expensive burst of litigation in human history. The end of the 20th century is going to be a very troublesome time for software executives, and a hazardous time for all industries where computers and software are used for financial, manufacturing, logistical, and military purposes.

SUMMARY AND CONCLUSIONS

Software quality has been a concern for the entire 50-year history of software production. Software quality has also been a topic of research and investigation for more than 30 years.

The current survey supports a number of observations which have been made by other researchers and by other studies:

1) There is no "silver bullet." Multiple approaches are necessary to achieve high software quality levels. There is a strong synergy between defect prevention and defect removal, and both are needed.

2) Software quality measurement is the primary key to effective quality control. Measures of both defects and user-satisfaction are needed.

3) Formal reviews and inspections before testing begins augment testing itself, and are necessary in order to achieve cumulative defect removal efficiency levels higher than 95%. Fortunately, these reviews and inspections are cost effective and can shorten schedules as well as improve quality.

4) The culture of software quality must permeate an enterprise from top to bottom to be successful. Executives, management, and technical staff must all contribute to the vision of high quality.

5) Beware of short-cuts and methods that lack solid, empirical data in support. There are many false claims and a lot of misinformation about both quality, costs, and schedules.

6) Do not depend upon a single approach such as ISO 9001 certification or moving up to Level 3 on the SEI CMM. Both approaches have benefits to offer, but neither approach deals with all of the key factors which influence software quality.

The "best in class" software producers now have defect potentials in the range of about 1.0 to 3.0 errors per function point, coupled with defect removal efficiencies that range from 95% to more than 99% for mission-critical software. This combination yields delivered defect totals of only 0.01 to 0.15 defects per function point, or roughly an order of magnitude better than current U.S. norms where defect potentials of about 5 per function point are coupled with an approximate 85% removal efficiency, which results in about 0.75 delivered bugs per function point.

Finally, quality is important for a variety of reasons. High quality software benefits market shares, development schedules, development costs, maintenance costs, user-satisfaction levels, and even staff morale. Conversely, low quality damages competitiveness, lengthens schedules, raises costs, and does not create a team of well motivated professionals with good morale levels.

ANNOTATED BIBLIOGRAPHY OF SOFTWARE QUALITY BOOKS AND RELATED TOPICS

Achieving acceptable levels of software quality is a taxing job that requires a great deal of specialized information in order to perform the work well. Fortunately there is a growing body of solid information about software quality topics, such as software quality estimating, project planning for optimal quality, measurement of quality, and many other relevant topics.

Because new books are published at monthly intervals, and the total volume of books available that covers software quality topics is approaching 200 and will continue to grow. Hence, this bibliography is of necessity a partial one. The contents reflect the books which the author found helpful in preparing this book. Also, the author and his colleagues tend to use these books as background materials in their quality consulting work.

This bibliography is organized using the same set of 10 topical headings discussed in the first section of the book, "Achieving High Levels of Software Quality" as follows:

1) Enterprise-wide Quality Programs

2) Quality Awareness and Training Programs

3) Quality Standards and Guidelines

4) Quality Analysis Methods

5) Quality Measurement Methods

6) Defect Prevention Methods

7) Non-Test Defect Removal Methods

8) Testing Methods

9) User-Satisfaction Methods

10) Post-Release Quality Control

While this organization is reasonably effective, it tends to break down for books which cover more than one of these major topics. In this case, I have made a personal selection as to which section is the best fit for the book in question.

Section 1: Enterprise-wide Quality Programs

This section of the bibliography discusses books that cover topics affecting the entire corporation or enterprise.

Andrews, Dorine C. and Stalick, Susan K.: *Business Reengineering—The Survival Guide;* Prentice Hall, Englewood Cliffs, NJ; ISBN 0-13-014853-9; 1994; 300 pages.

Business process reengineering (BPR) has become a cult of the 1990s. When BPR is used to provide better customer service, it is often successful. However, BPR has become synonymous with massive layoffs and cutbacks, and is sometimes a step to corporate disaster. This book covers the pros and cons of the topic from the point of view of someone who may have to live through a major BPR analysis.

There have now been enough BPR studies to begin to evaluate the overall impact of the BPR concept on corporate operations. Like many cults, the results seem to be harmful as often as they are beneficial, and harmful to quality more often than not.

Although BPR is not intentionally harmful to software quality, software quality is sometimes damaged as an accidental byproduct of BPR since the resulting "downsizing" had a distressing tendency to wipe out quality assurance groups.

Boone, Mary; *Leadership and the Computer;* Prima Publishing; Rocklin, CA; 1991; ISBN 1-559858-080-1; 397 pages.

It is always interesting to read case studies that deal with real companies and real people. This is a book by a well-known researcher into organization effectiveness, Mary Boone. Her book is based on interviews with senior executives and CEO's about how they personally use computers and interact with them. Some of the interviewees include Senator Gordon Humphries (R-NH), Burnell Roberts of Mead, William Esprey of US Sprint, and Michael Jordan of Pepsico. Many others are interviewed as well.

Since computer literacy on the part of top executives leads to a better understanding of quality issues, it is thought-provoking to see how top executives use computers, and why. Also, top executives set the tone for the enterprises they manage, and this book gives some interesting although incidental insights into how quality is viewed at the CEO level.

Crosby, Philip B.; *Quality is Free;* Mentor Books, New York, NY; 1979; 270 pages.

Phil Crosby was the ITT Vice President of Quality during the era of Harold Geneen, when the company grew from a mid-sized telecommunication company to become a large and highly diverse conglomerate. Crosby was responsible for a lot of the emphasis on quality that has subsequently entered U.S. businesses. This book has been a best-seller for many years, and has served to alert a whole generation of business executives to the importance of quality. Well known concepts such as the famous "Cost of Quality" breakdown were first made popular in this book.

Crosby's book is not about software quality, but rather about the importance of quality to every aspect of corporate operations. This book also has had a more recent influence: The five-level "Quality Maturity Grid" was picked up by Watts Humphrey of the Software Engineering Institute (SEI) and is the basis for the five-level SEI capability maturity model (CMM). Crosby's original maturity model is actually clearer and easier to understand than the SEI version. The five levels of the Crosby model are:

Stage 1 - Uncertainty
Stage 2 - Awakening
Stage 3 - Enlightenment
Stage 4 - Wisdom
Stage 5 - Certainty

Possibly by coincidence, both the Crosby and Humphrey maturity models resemble a maturity model developed circa 500 BC by Buddhist scholars as a kind of map for showing the stages on the path to religious enlightenment. Crosby's stages are direct borrowing from the earlier Buddhist path to enlightenment, but Humphrey's is a major modification in terminology, although the fundamental concepts of spiritual growth through constant effort remain.

Hart, Christopher and Bogan, Christopher; *The Baldrige;* McGraw Hill, New York; 1992; ISBN 0-07-026912-2; 281 pages.

The Baldrige Award, named after Malcom Baldrige a former Secretary of Commerce, is an annual award for quality. The Baldrige is not directly aimed at software, but among the author's consulting clients those who have won a Baldrige Award tend to produce higher-quality software than those who have not. This is an interesting tutorial on an important business topic.

Jones, Capers; *The Global Economic Impact of the Year 2000 Software Problem;* Software Productivity Research, Burlington, MA; 1996; 65 pages.

This is an evolving monograph rather than a full-length book. It attempts to quantify the costs of the on-rushing Year 2000 problem by country, by industry, by company, by programming language, and by size of software portfolios. The costs explored include direct costs of the Year 2000 upgrades, and also the probable costs of litigation for Year 2000 hits that do not get fixed in time. The monograph also discusses hardware upgrade expenses and the expenses of repairing databases. The data in this monograph is often cited by other Year 2000 books. This monograph is also available on a number of World Wide Web sites that deal with Year 2000 issues.

Juran, J.M. (editor); *A History of Managing for Quality;* ASQC Press, Milwaukee, WI; 1995; ISBN 0-87389-341-7; 688 pages.

To those who like to take a long view, this book is a fascinating compendium of the importance of quality through the ages. Juran's book weaves a fascinating tapestry of quality from ancient China through today, with very interesting historical segments on quality control of in shipbuilding, weapons manufacturing, the construction of cathedrals, and quality control of clock making. The sociological aspects of quality are discussed too, with interesting sections on the development of craft guilds in the middle ages. J.M. Juran together with W. Edwards Deming, introduced many of the concepts of statistical quality control to Japanese industry after World War II and the two are among the most respected pioneers of global quality research.

Kelada, Joseph N.; *Integrating Reengineering With Total Quality;* ASQC Press, Milwaukee, WI; 1996; ISBN 0-87389-339; 481 pages.

Usually the business "cults" that sweep through America have a lofty disregard for rival cults and books on one approach seldom even mention other approaches. This new book is a comparatively rare treatment that seeks to merge the concepts of two of the recent cults that have been moving through the U.S. business community: business process reengineering (BPR) and total quality management (TQM). In theory the two approaches should be complementary. In practice, the newer BPR method tends to overpower and sometimes eliminate the older TQM concept. However, this book attempts to preserve the essence of TQM in a world where BPR is now a major business activity.

Lacity, Mary C. and Hirschheim, Rudy; *Information System Outsourcing;* John Wiley & Sons, New York, NY; 1993; 273 pages.

The outsourcing phenomenon is emerging as an important topic in the software world. Mary Lacity and Rudy Hirschheim have written a very good survey of the principles and practices for selecting an outsourcer. An interesting observation about outsourcing was mentioned by Dr. Hirschheim over a lunch: "Outsourcing is a bit like getting married. If you are not happy during the courtship, you certainly won't be happy once the ceremony takes place." This is a book that will probably grow in importance as we move toward the 21st century. One of the major reasons for outsourcing is executive dissatisfaction with quality, productivity, and schedules.

Murray, Jerome T. and Murray, Marilyn J.; *The Year 2000 Computing Crisis;* McGraw Hill, New York, NY; ISBN 0-07-912945-5; 1995; 416 pages.

At midnight on December 31, 1999 many software applications may fail or start producing erratic output because they have not been set up to deal with date conversion from 1999 to 2000 AD. Essentially every software manager in the world is facing this problem, and it is not too soon to pay serious attention to the implications. This book also contains a disk with sample source code in COBOL, RPG, and Assembly language that fixes the problem. This particular book is aimed at MIS applications.

Poirier, Charles C. and Tokarz, Steven J.; *Avoiding the Pitfalls of Total Quality;* ASQC Press, Milwaukee, WI; ISBN 0-87389-355; 1996; 244 pages.

As mentioned earlier in this book, Total Quality Management fails about as often as it succeeds in the United States. This is a thoughtful book about how to avoid the situations which lead the TQM method into becoming a waste of everybody's time and money and not accomplishing anything useful.

Ragland, Bryce; *The Year 2000 Problem—A Five-Step Solution;* McGraw Hill, New York, NY, 1997.

This new book will be published in 1997. The author works for the Air Force Software Technology Support Center, so the perspective of this book is how the Year 2000 crisis will affect very large systems, including defense software systems. This is a solid book and covers many kinds of software besides management information systems.

Schulmeyer, G. and McManus, J.I.; *Total Quality Management for Software;* International Thomson Computer Press, Boston, MA; ISBN 1-85032-836-6; 550 pages.

The topic of Total Quality Management or TQM is much broader than software. That fact has been troublesome, since how TQM will work for software is often left out when companies adopt the TQM philosophy. Schulmeyer and McManus have created a very readable treatment of how TQM and be applied to software.

Shiba, Shoji; Graham, Alan; and Walden, David; *A New American TQM;* Productivity Press, Portland, OR; ISBN 1-56327-032-2; 1993; 574 pages.

The authors of this interesting book are part of the Center for Quality Management at MIT. This book is not just about software, but it deserves reading by software managers and professionals as well as any other kind of business executive or technical worker. The book traces the origin and evolution of total quality management (TQM) and then presents a form of TQM that should be comfortable in an American business environment.

Strassman, Paul A.; *The Business Value of Computers—An Executive's Guide;* The Information Economics Press; New Canaan, CT; 1990.

Paul Strassman became well-known when he was at the Department of Defense and sponsored a number of military software improvement initiatives. As a civilian author and researcher, Strassman has moved into the topic of the business value of computers, software, "best practices," quality, and other topics that have relevance to how major organizations utilize computers, software, and information. Strassman's general view is that software and computer decisions are often made from insufficient data and hence the results can be harmful about as often as they are helpful. The point of view of this book is what a very senior executive should know about computers and software to ensure that they don't damage his or her enterprise.

Walton, Mary; *Deming Management at Work;* G.P. Putnam's Sons, New York, NY; 1990; ISBN 0-399-13557-X; 290 pages.

W. Edwards Deming was one of the great business pioneers of the world. Deming, together with J.W. Duran, introduced many concepts of statistical quality control to Japanese manufacturing companies after World War II. The Japanese Deming Prize for quality was created in his honor. This book, by one of Deming's colleagues, is an excellent overview of his views and his approach to quality improvement.

Section 2: Quality Awareness and Training

This section contains a mixed bag of books whose unifying theme is that they can alert managers and executives to the importance of quality.

Brooks, Fred; *The Mythical Man-Month;* Addison Wesley, Reading, MA; 1995; 295 pages.

This is the 20th anniversary edition of a software classic. Fred Brooks was manager of IBM's OS/360 operating system. This was one of the first software systems to exceed 1,000,000 LOC in its first release. It was also the first IBM software system to be significantly late on its announced delivery date. Fred Brooks wrote a thoughtful historical analysis of why the software was late, initially published in 1975. This 20th anniversary edition adds new material, and gives Dr. Brooks a chance to discuss recent changes in software technologies. The fact that Microsoft's Windows 95 product was also late, 20 years after Fred Brook's first warning, is a sign that many of the problems discussed are still current and highly relevant. This book has been one of the best-sellers in the software world for 20 years.

Cusumano, Michael A. and Selby, Richard W.; *The Microsoft Secrets;* The Free Press (Simon & Schuster), New York, NY; ISBN 0-02-874048-3; 1995; 512 pages.

Because of the extraordinary financial and business success of Microsoft, essentially every software producer in the world would like to find out how Microsoft does it. (Literally dozens of SPR clients have asked to have their operations benchmarked against Microsoft's.) Michael Cusumano and Richard Selby are academics whose research topics deal with how software engineering companies go about their business. For example, Cusumano has also done major research on Japanese software engineering methods. This best-selling book on Microsoft does not have much quantitative data on Microsoft's quality and productivity levels, but it does have a fairly solid description of the Microsoft culture and software development processes. Curiosity alone is sufficient to make this a best-seller. The fact that it is an easy read is also useful.

Dunn, Robert and Ullman, Richard; *Quality Assurance for Computer Software;* McGraw Hill, New York, NY; ISBN 0-07-018312-0; 1982; 351 pages.

The authors, Dunn and Ullman, both worked in quality assurance for the ITT Corporation at the time this book was written. Dunn worked at the well-known ITT Programming Technology Center in Stratford, Massachusetts while Ullman was at the Defense Communication Division in New Jersey. This book discusses software quality assurance principles and practices in the same corporation where Phil Crosby made his start as a QA guru. Even though this book was published in 1982, it still contains good information on how major corporations go about serious software quality control. Unlike many books which only give opinions, this one also includes data.

Dunn and Ullman have since written several other books on similar themes, and all are recommended.

DeMarco, Tom and Lister, Tim; *Peopleware;* Dorset House, New York, NY; ISBN 0-932633-05-6; 1987; 200 pages.

This book has become yet another "classic" with a very large sale in the software community. This was one of the pioneering books to deal with social and even ergonomic topics that affect the outcomes of software projects. In particular, this book has become famous for its exploration of the impact of office space on software productivity. The research noted that programmers in the high-quartile of performance tended to have private offices of more than about 80 square feet in size. Conversely programmers in the low-quartile tended to occupy less than about 45 square feet, or to be crammed into multi-person cubicles or in noisy open-office environments. DeMarco was among the first to emphasize that software is built by people, so that the quality of the people affects the quality of the results.

Fenton, Norman; *Software Quality Assurance and Measurement—A Worldwide Perspective;* International Thomson Computer Press, Boston, MA; ISBN 1-852032-17; 304 pages.

This book, by a British author, discusses software quality primarily from a European perspective, and makes some interesting comparisons between U.S. and European approaches to the same problems. Fenton is an academic, and the book has a more academic than commercial flavor.

Howard, Phil; *Guide to Software Productivity Aids;* Applied Computer Research, Scottsdale, AZ; ISBN 0740-8374; published quarterly.

This is not a true book in the sense that most other citations are books. This is a quarterly catalog of software tools marketed in the United States. The catalog is larger than many books, and typically runs to perhaps 500 pages. The text of the tool descriptions are provided by the tool vendors, and hence may exaggerate features and functions. However, this book is useful because it has contact information for hundreds of vendors and descriptions of thousands of tools.

The reason that a catalog is included in an annotated bibliography of quality books is because this catalog is one of the most complete listings of configuration control, testing, defect tracking, and other quality-related tools in print. Here you can find out about quality estimating tools, test library management tools, methodology management tools, and hosts of other tools of interest to the software quality community. Indeed many software quality consultants (including the author) tend to use this book prior to starting an engagement since a knowledge of current tools can make us look wiser than we really are. As the 1996 edition of this bibliography is prepared, Phil Howard who is the catalog editor, reports that after January of 1996 the catalog has grown so large that it will segmented into separate topical catalogs in the future.

Humphrey, Watts; *Managing the Software Process,* Addison-Wesley, Reading, MA; 1990.

Watts Humphrey is a retired IBM software executive who was the first director of the Software Engineering Institute's (SEI) software assessment program. This book introduced many of the pivotal concepts of the Software Engineering Institute's capability maturity model. The book has become a best-seller, and is now widely quoted throughout the software world. This book also started the SEI capability maturity model (CMM) on its explosive growth in popularity.

Humphrey, Watts; *A Discipline of Software Engineering;* Addison-Wesley, Reading, MA; 1995; 785 pages.

This new book contains Watts view of how each individual programmer can achieve software excellence. It differs from his previous book in that it is aimed at single practitioners rather than entire corporations. Although the book contains many interesting insights, it is seriously flawed by Watts' dedication to the flawed and invalid "lines of code" or LOC metric. Unfortunately, Watts does not address the 35% or so of ancillary software professionals such as technical writers, database administrators, or quality assurance whose work and contributions cannot be measured using LOC metrics. Watts is strongly aware that quality is on the critical path to software success.

Marciniak, John J. (Editor); *Encyclopedia of Software Engineering;* John Wiley & Sons, New York, NY; 1994; ISBN 0-471-54002; in two volumes.

This is a massive compilation of information in two large volumes that total to about 1,500 pages. Although most of the topics relate to software engineering, there are also many topics of interest to software quality and testing managers as well. For example, there are topics on software quality and cost estimating, software quality measurements, function point metrics, and many other subjects that appeal to the software quality community. As usual with encyclopedias, there are hundreds of articles written by hundreds of authors. The value of the contributions vary from marginally adequate up to truly excellent. However, the overall average of the contributions is rather good and this encyclopedia is a welcome addition to the bookshelf of either a quality manager or a software quality engineer. Very few other sources of software information are so conveniently organized and so complete in terms of coverage.

Pirsig, Robert M.; *Zen and the Art of Motorcycle Maintenance;* Bantam New Age Books, New York, NY; ISBN 0-553-27747-2; 1975; 380 pages.

Although this best-selling book is a book of fiction and has nothing to do with software at all, it deserves inclusion in a management bibliography because it is one of the best books on quality ever written. The surface of the book is nominally about a cross-country journey by Robert Pirsig and his son on a motorcycle. While traveling, the author ruminates about the meaning of quality in various contexts. The book is thought provoking and exciting and is often used in quality training by major corporations such as IBM.

There is a long string of books whose titles begin "Zen and the Art of ...." Most of them have nothing to do with Zen itself, although Pirsig seems to know quite a bit about that topic. It may be of interest that the first book in this string, and the one that originated all the rest, was a book called *Zen and the Art of Archery* by Eugen Herrigel which was translated from the original German into English in 1953. The original book was really about the impact of Zen on the way Japanese practice archery. The Zen Buddhist philosophy is strongly intertwined with martial arts and self discipline, and so Zen is a good precursor for any discipline where knowing yourself and your own strengths and weaknesses is part of mastering the art itself.

Thayer, Richard H. and McGettrick, Andrew D. (Editors); *Software Engineering—A European Perspective;* IEEE Computer Society Press; ISBN 0-8186-9117-4; Catalog number BP02117; 1993; 691 pages.

The software engineering community in Europe is larger than the software Engineering community in the United States, and in some ways is advancing more rapidly than the U.S. In addition, a number of European software initiatives such as ESPRIT, BOOTSTRAP, and SPICE have aspects that are worthy of study anywhere in the world. This useful book collects a wide variety of information about software practices in Europe.

Weigers, Karl N; *Creating a Software Engineering Culture,* Dorset House Press, New York, NY; ISBN 0-932633-33-1; 1996; 341 pages.

This new book discusses a large-scale case study: how Kodak built its software engineering function and developed their in-house quality approaches. This is a very well-done book that is likely to attract a wide audience. What sets this book apart from many others is that it deals with how real people in a real company react to things like quality goals, process improvements, and technology transfer. Not everything happens smoothly and automatically, and sometimes progress is negative rather than positive.

Weinberg, Dr. Gerald; *Quality Software Management;* (in Multiple Volumes); Dorset House, New York, NY; 1992; ISBN 0-932633-22-6.

This bibliographic entry is really for a connected series of books by Jerry Weinberg on software quality. As this entry is prepared in 1996, three volumes are ready and more may appear in the future. All are excellent and each covers a topic in substantial depth, but with the ease and elegant prose style that has made Dr. Weinberg's books best sellers. Some of the topics include systems thinking, quality measurement, and establishing a culture of quality.

Yourdon, Ed; *Decline and Fall of the American Programmer;* Yourdon Press–Prentice Hall, Englewood Cliffs, NJ; ISBN 0-13-203670-3; 1992; 352 pages.

Ed Yourdon is also a prolific writer, and a very good prose stylist. This book deals with the growth of international competition in the software world. The thesis is that unless U.S. software professional stay competitive in terms of both quality and costs, there are plenty of hungry competitors in India, Europe, South America, and the Pacific Rim that would love to dominate the software business. This is a thought-provoking book.

Yourdon, Ed; *Rise and Resurrection of the American Programmer,* Yourdon Press–Prentice Hall, Englewood Cliffs, NJ.

This sequel to Ed Yourdon's original book on the decline and fall is a much better book than its predecessor. Ed always writes clearly and well, but in the original book he started with an interesting idea and then plugged in a lot of generic concepts that had no particular relevance to the theme of decline and fall.

Since the first book was published, Ed Yourdon and Howard Rubin were commissioned by the Canadian government to explore international software competitiveness. Ed was also an intermittent attendee at the U.S. Navy conferences on software process improvement. The bottom line is that Ed knows a lot more about the global situation now than he did a few years ago, and this book reflects a great deal of solid, empirical data that was missing from the prior work.

Ed Yourdon has popularized the concept of "Good Enough" quality, which is a dangerous phenomenon that is easy to misapply.

Section 3: Quality Standards and Guidelines

This section deals with books that concern international or national standards, plus guidelines that may be enroute to becoming standards.

Brown, Norm (Editor); *The Program Manager's Guide to Software Acquisition Best Practices;* Version 1.0; July 1995; U.S. Department of Defense, Washington, DC; 142 pages.

This small volume of guidelines was produced under the auspices of the U.S. Department of Defense's *Software Acquisition Best Practices Initiative.* The editor and coordinator, Dr. Norm Brown, is with the U.S. Navy Department. In 1994 and 1995 Secretary of Defense William Perry exhorted the DoD community to adopt civilian best practices. In order to follow this directive for software, the DoD assembled a group of well-known civilian gurus to discuss exactly what the phrase "best practices" seemed to mean. Some of the well-known participants in this group included Victor Basili, Grady Booch, Tom DeMarco, Tom McCabe, Larry Putnam, and Ed Yourdon.

The combined results of at least half a dozen meetings and dozens of participants are consolidated into this interesting volume. Some of the topics include best practices for development, quality control, measurement, maintenance, and a host of other software issues. Although the book is clearly aimed at the DoD program managers, the fact that it discusses civilian best quality practices gives the material a wide relevance.

Department of the Air Force; *Guidelines for Successful Acquisition and Management of Software Intensive Systems;* Volumes 1 and 2; Software Technology Support Center, Hill Air Force Base, UT; 1994.

The U.S. military is by far the world's largest consumer of software, and also the largest producer of custom software. The U.S. military also produces the largest software systems ever created in world history. This book does not identify specific authors, but is produced in part by the editorial staff of *Crosstalk* magazine, which is an excellent journal of defense software. Also identified as coordinators and contributors are Maj. Mike McPherson and Professor Daniel Ferens. The two volumes of this huge set of guidelines total to almost 2,000 pages in size. Although the book is obviously aimed at the defense community, there is enough useful information to recommend it to civilian software managers too. This recommendation is an easy one, because the books are distributed without charge. To receive copies, contact the Software Technology Support Center at 7278 Fourth Street, Hill AFB, Utah 84056-5205 or call 801 775-2054. What makes the volumes useful is the enormous number of references to the software literature, and a surprising amount of quantitative data from both the civilian and military software domains.

IEEE Press; *Software Engineering Standards Collection;* 1994 edition; IEEE Press, Los Alamitas, CA; ISBN 1-55937-442; 1994.

The IEEE is the publisher of more standards on engineering topics than any other known organization. While the standards can be ordered separately, this book is a useful compendium of all relevant software engineering standards. It is dry reading, but a valuable benchmark for what members of a major engineering society regard as important.

Ince, Darrel; *ISO 9001 and Software Quality;* McGraw Hill, New York,NY; 1994; 192 pages.

The ISO 9000-9004 quality standards became operational across most of the European community in 1992. ISO 9001 is the standard most often applied to software projects, and hence a very important topic for commercial software vendors who wish to market in Europe. Unfortunately, the ISO standards are not particularly modern in scope and outlook. Indeed, SPR has been unable to find any solid empirical data that demonstrates that the ISO standards, including ISO 9001, actually improve quality in any tangible way. There is substantial evidence that they raise costs, and do so primarily by causing a notable increase in the volume of paper descriptions of various quality-related topics. In spite of the fact that the ISO standards are incomplete and inadequate, they are important. This book is a good introduction to the topic.

Paulk, Mark, Curtis, Bill, et al; *The Capability Maturity Model;* Addison Wesley, Reading, MA; ISBN 0-201 54664-7; 1995; 441 pages.

Achieving Level 3 on the SEI capability maturity model is now a de facto standard for successful bidding on many defense contracts, so an understanding of the SEI CMM is an important topic. The Software Engineering Institute (SEI) was incorporated in 1985, so this book marks the 10th anniversary. It is a very readable and useful overview of a topic that is sometimes arcane and misunderstood. The capability maturity model (CMM) is a way of assessing the "maturity" of software production. The CMM creates a five-level excellence scale:

1 = Initial   (Chaotic and unstructured)
2 = Repeatable   (Beginning to achieve discipline)
3 = Defined   (Capable of successful results in most situations)
4 = Managed   (Very disciplined, with full reusability)
5 = Optimizing   (State of the art; highly advanced)

This book is a group effort by almost a score of SEI personnel and consultants. It serves as a very good general introduction to the overall concepts of the CMM. Of course, the book does not deal at all with the many gaps and omissions of the CMM. For example, the SEI assessment approach only covers about half of the factors that can influence the outcomes of software projects. The CMM does not collect any quantitative data at all, so there is no easy way to determine if the SEI claims of "higher productivity and quality" associated with CMM Levels 3, 4, and 5 are true or merely fanciful assertions.

Section 4: Quality Analysis Methods

Quality analysis concerns formal methodologies for exploring quality, or its lack. Some of the key topics associated with quality analysis are root-cause analysis, visualization of data, and the related topic of risk analysis.

Charette, Robert N.; *Software Engineering Risk Analysis and Management,* McGraw Hill, New York, NY; 1989; ISBN 0-07-010719-X; 325 pages.

Robert Charette is one of the pioneers in the exploration of software risk management, and all of his books are useful. This is a very good introduction to the overall topic of software risk analysis. Since many of the more critical risks relate directly to quality or the lack of quality, this book is highly relevant.

Charette, Robert N.; *Applications Strategies for Risk Analysis,* McGraw Hill, New York, NY; 1990; ISBN 0-07-010888-9; 570 pages.

This large book is a more complete coverage of risk-related topics than the other book cited here. Both are useful for software project managers, and recommended. The importance of software risk analysis and risk management is finally dawning on the industry, so books by Bob Charette are beginning to grow in importance as the 20th century winds down.

Grey, Stephen; *Practical Risk Assessment for Project Management;* John Wiley & Sons, New York, NY; 1995; 140 pages.

Managers don't always have the time or inclination to get involved with the full-scale risk literature such as Charette's or Jones' books in the 500 to 700 page range. This small 140 page book is an interesting introduction to the topic of risk analysis. It does not cover the topic exhaustively like some of the large books, but it is small enough to carry around easily and provides a basic framework.

Jones, Capers; *Assessment and Control of Software Risks;* Prentice Hall, 1994; ISBN 0-13-741406-4; 711 pages.

This book discusses some 65 technical and sociological risk factors associated with software development and maintenance operations. The data has been collected during the course of SPR's software process assessment activities. Among the technical risks are those of inadequate tools, inadequate methodologies, and inadequate support for quality assurance.

Among the social risks are those of excessive schedule pressure, the low status of the software community within many corporations, and the high risks of litigation. Other risks include the tendency of vendors to make false claims about quality and productivity, and the tendency of software managers and staff to believe those claims without requiring proof. Several large companies are using this book as a guide for improving their software processes, and upgrading their software curricula for both management and staff. A somewhat controversial section of this book discusses the deficiencies and gaps in the SEI assessment program. The book includes quantitative data on "best in class" quality and productivity results derived from the top 10% of SPR's clients. A Japanese translation was published in August of 1995. This book is also available on CD-ROM.

Jones, Capers; *Patterns of Software System Failure and Success;* International Thomson Computer Press, Boston, MA; December 1995; 250 pages; ISBN 1-850-32804-8; 292 pages.

This new book was published in December of 1995. The contents are based on large-scale studies of failed projects (i.e., projects that were either terminated prior to completion or had severe cost and schedule overruns or massive quality problems) and successful projects (i.e., projects that achieved new records for high quality, low costs, short schedules, and high customer-satisfaction).

On the whole, management problems appear to outweigh technical problems in both successes and failures. Other factors discussed include the use of planning and estimating tools, quality control approaches, experience levels of managers, staff, and clients, and stability of requirements. Also discussed are intermittent and extrinsic factors such as bankruptcy, layoffs, downsizings, litigation and other business problems that can affect software projects. It is possible to minimize the probability of failure and maximize the probability of success, but both technical and sociological changes must occur to achieve significant improvements.

Musa, John; Iannino, A. and Okumoto, K.; *Software Reliability—Measurement, Prediction, Application;* McGraw Hill, New York, NY; ISBN 0-07-044093-X; 1987; 619 pages.

John Musa and his colleagues from AT&T Bell Labs are among the top writers in the field of reliability modeling and measurement. For historical reasons, the quality literature and the reliability literature tend to "talk past" each other. This is unfortunate. Musa takes a more philosophic view that quality and reliability are related, but that the relationship is often tenuous because of the difficulty of collecting both quality data and reliability data on the same projects. Musa and his colleagues cover a difficult topic in a readable manner.

Perry, William E.; *Handbook of Diagnosing and Solving Computer Problems;* TAB Books, Blue Ridge Summit, PA; ISBN 0-8306-9233-9; 1989; 255 pages.

Bill Perry is the chairman and CEO of the well-known Quality Assurance Institute (QAI) in Orlando, Florida. Bill has dedicated his professional life to advancing software quality, and ranks as one of the top U.S. experts in this area. Bill is both an excellent speaker and a very clear writer. This book discusses a series of real-world problems that software managers are likely to encounter, such as cost overruns, schedule overruns, organizational disputes, etc. Then the book suggests some possible solutions. Although the book was published in 1989, many of the problems are still current and the advice is still valid.

Wilson, Paul F.; Dell, Larry; and Anderson, Gaylord; *Root Cause Analysis—A Tool for Total Quality Management;* ASQC Press, Milwaukee, WI, PA; ISBN 0-87389-163-5; 1993; 216 pages.

Root-cause analysis has become a staple of software quality control within the larger high-technology corporations. This interesting book is a good background on how to go about root-cause analysis and what the method is typically used for. There is also a companion workbook.

Section 5: Quality Measurement

This section includes a rather large number of books that deal with quality measurements and metrics, among other topics.

Boehm, Barry Dr.; *Software Engineering Economics;* Prentice Hall, Englewood Cliffs, NJ; 1981; 900 pages.

This book has become a classic in the field, and is still selling well even after 15 years (Dr. Boehm is reportedly working on a revision, but Prentice Hall does not have any date scheduled for it.) This book discusses the algorithms of the "constructive cost model" which is now widely known by the acronym COCOMO. This book discusses various aspects of measuring and estimating software projects, and has a large set of references, examples, case studies, and useful additional information.

On the down side, this book was published shortly after the function point metric began its explosive growth through the software industry. Unfortunately, there is no useful information on function points. The book assumes a traditional "waterfall" development model, and it assumes using lines of code (LOC) as the basic normalizing metric. These are serious flaws, but the book is readable and useful even with these major defects.

In spite of age and a few flaws, Boehm's book is a classic and should be on every software manager's and quality assurance manager's shelf. Boehm was among the first authors to attempt to place quality in context with other topics that affect software engineering economics.

Bogan, Christopher E. and English, Michael J.; *Benchmarking for Best Practices;* McGraw Hill, New York, NY; ISBN 0-07-006375-3; 1994; 312 pages.

Benchmarking, or comparing practices between one company and another, is becoming one of the hottest topics of the last five years of the 20th century. The authors are not dealing specifically with software benchmarking, but they know a lot about the overall topic of how to compare two organizations and achieve meaningful results. This book can be recommended as a useful precursor to carrying out any kind of benchmark, including software quality.

Card, David and Glass, Robert L.; *Measuring Software Design Quality;* Prentice Hall, Englewood Cliffs, NJ; 1990; 129 pages.

This is an interesting short book that approaches an important topic—errors in the front-end of the software lifecycle. Errors in design (and requirements) are often more pervasive and more serious than coding errors. Card and Glass are experienced software professionals, and very good writers. The only problem with this book is that it ignores the usage of function point metrics, which have become the industry standard for measuring and normalizing defects in requirements, specifications, user manuals, and many other sources of error that could not be measured easily using the older "lines of code" metric.

DeMarco, Tom; *Controlling Software Projects;* Yourdon Press, New York, NY; 1982; ISBN 0-917072-32-4; 284 pages.

This book together, with Barry Boehm's *Software Engineering Economics* is among the first to deal seriously with the quantitative aspects of software management; i.e., measurement, metrics, cost estimating, and tracking. Although the book was first published in 1982, Tom DeMarco's excellent prose style and clear thinking still make the book a useful addition to a manager's bookshelf. In addition, historians of software management will note that DeMarco invented a kind of function point metric at about the same time as Allan Albrecht invented his function point metric. In a sense, DeMarco and Albrecht are the Darwin and Wallace of the software metrics world, with DeMarco playing the part of Wallace since Albrecht published his metric in 1978 while DeMarco's was not published until 1982 in this book. As with Darwin and Wallace, both DeMarco worked independently and neither was aware of each other's work until after both had published their initial results.

DeMarco, Tom; *Why Does Software Cost So Much?;* Dorset House, New York, NY; ISBN 0-932633-34-X; 1995; 237 pages.

This book is a collection of about two dozen essays by Tom DeMarco and some his colleagues. Both the title and the first essay deal with the costs of software, and as usual with Tom's writings the discussion is interesting and unusual. Tom makes the point that few other human constructs have made as much change in the world as software, and hence the value of the results are probably worth the costs. Tom is a gifted writer, and often clarifies points about software by drawing from other domains. His essay on "Mad About Metrics" has an amusing anecdote about a Russian nail factory which went from making small brads to railroad spikes when their performance was judged on the weight of nails they produced rather than the number of nails.

Dreger, Brian; *Function Point Analysis;* Prentice Hall, Englewood Cliffs, NJ; 1989; 225 pages.

This was the first college primer intended to teach function points to those without any prior knowledge of the metric. This book is a very readable introduction to an important topic. It even manages to add a few items of humor to lighten up what might otherwise be a very dry topic. The only caveat about this book is that it was published in 1989, and the rules for counting function points underwent a minor revision in 1993 and a major revision in 1994. To learn the rudiments of function point counting the book is still useful, but to learn the most current rules and practices, the book is unfortunately out of date. As of 1996, this book will be available in a CD-ROM edition under license to Miller Freeman publishers.

Garmus, David and Herron, David; *Measuring the Software Process: A Practical Guide to Functional Measurement;* Prentice Hall, Englewood Cliffs, NJ; November 1995.

Function point metrics are expanding rapidly throughout the world. David Garmus is a member of the counting practices committee of the International Function Point Users Group (IFPUG). David Herron is a former member of the same committee, and the two authors have formed a consulting company specializing in function point metrics. This is a new primer aimed at introducing function point metrics to a wide audience. The book covers the new Version 4.0 counting practices revision and hence is current through 1995 in terms of IFPUG counting rules.

The book attempts to discuss other topics such as benchmarking and estimating, but the authors are not recognized experts in these topics and the discussions are slight and sometimes at odds with best current practices. Surprisingly, given that the title of the book is *Measuring the Software Process* the authors do not even discuss process or activity-level measurements. Their view seems to stop at entire projects, which is not granular enough for serious process analysis.

Grady, Robert B. and Caswell, Deborah L.; *Software Metrics: Establishing a Company-Wide Program;* Prentice Hall, Englewood Cliffs, NJ; ISBN 0-13-821844-7; 1987; 288 pages.

Bob Grady and Deborah Caswell work for Hewlett Packard. It is always interesting to see first-hand case studies of how real companies go about things. This book discusses the sequence and results of establishing HP's corporate-wide software measurement program. The book has good and bad features. The good parts deal with the social and cultural aspects of something major like measurements. The bad parts are those dealing with metrics themselves. Unfortunately, neither author had enough data when the book was published to understand the serious problems with "lines of code" metrics and the economic advantages of function point metrics. Except for this problem, the book is very readable.

Grady, Robert B.; *Practical Software Metrics for Project Management and Process Improvement;* Prentice Hall, Englewood Cliffs, NJ; ISBN 0-13-720384-5; 1992; 270 pages.

Bob Grady has a very clear writing style, and he writes pragmatically about the real-world measurements actually used for software within Hewlett Packard. This is an excellent book for learning about how real companies go about measurement work. The book is flawed, however, in that Grady does not deal with the well-known problems of the "lines of code" metric such as their tendency to penalize high-level languages. Once you get past the surprise that such a major topic is ignored, the book contains many useful illustrations of measurement practices.

Jones, Capers; *Programming Productivity;* McGraw Hill, New York, NY; 1986; ISBN 0-070032811-0; 282 pages.

This book introduced the topic of function points to a wide audience, and was the first to include a side by side comparison of function points with lines of code metrics. This was the first book to include a discussion of "backfiring" or direct mathematical conversion from LOC to function point metrics, which is now one of the most widely used measurement techniques in the industry. (The 30 programming languages illustrated in this book have now expanded to almost 500 programming languages as of 1995). This book dissected the factors that influenced software productivity, and included discussions of staff experience, tools, methods, quality control, and many other factors. The book has been translated into Japanese, German, French, and Portuguese editions.

Jones, Capers; *Applied Software Measurement;* McGraw Hill, New York, NY; 1996; ISBN 0-07-032826-9; 618 pages. (Revised second edition.)

This book has become a standard reference volume in many companies, and in some university software management curricula as well. The 2nd edition of the book includes U.S. national averages for software productivity and quality derived from more than 6700 projects using the function point metric for normalizing the data. It also included comparative data on productivity from 50 industries, including banking, insurance, telecommunications, computer manufacturers, government, etc.

A major revision came out in late 1996 that included data on about 2,000 new software projects, and discussed the emerging results of various new technologies such as object-oriented approaches, client/server applications, ISO 9000 certification, and the Software Engineering Institute (SEI) approach. The new edition shows data for six subindustries (system software, military software, commercial software, information systems software, contract and outsourced software, and end-user software). National averages are then derived from the overall results of these six domains.

Jones, Capers; *Critical Problems in Software Measurement;* Information Systems Management Group, 1993; ISBN 1-56909-000-9; 195 pages.

This book discusses some of the practical issues of establishing a large multinational, multi-industry of software productivity and quality data. The book includes chapters on what kind of data should be recorded, validating the data, and ensuring the confidentiality of clients organizations that provide the data. This book is somewhat controversial in that it asserted that the traditional "lines of code" metric should be considered to be professional malpractice if it continued to be used after 1995.

Jones, Capers; *Software Productivity and Quality Today—The Worldwide Perspective;* Information Systems Management Group, 1993; ISBN 1-56909-001-7; 200 pages.

This book is the first to attempt to quantify software productivity and quality levels on a global basis. Demographic information is included on the software populations of more than 90 countries and 250 global cities. Productivity data is ranked for systems software, information systems, military software, and other categories. This book is comparatively unique in that it uses the SPR Feature Point metric, rather than the more common function point metric. The book also discusses international variations in software effectiveness, quality control, and research programs. Excerpts from this book were published in the British journal *The Economist* and attracted considerable attention from the fact that the United States was lagging in several critical software areas.

Kan, Stephen H.; *Metrics and Models in Software Quality Engineering;* Addison Wesley, Reading, MA; ISBN 0-201-63339-6; 1995; 344 pages.

This is a thoughtful overview of a number of metrics in the software quality domain. The book also covers topics of great importance to the software management community, such as the Baldrige Award, the ISO 9000-9004 standards, the Software Engineering Institute (SEI) capability maturity model (CMM), and total quality management (TQM). The chapters and sections are fairly complete, and give context and background information. A full reading of this book will transfer a considerable amount of useful information to the readers, and it covers many topics well enough to give fresh insights.

Love, Tom; *Object Lessons;* SIGS Books, New York, NY; ISBN 0-9627477 3-4; 1993; 266 pages.

Dr. Tom Love, now with the World Street Journal, is the former chairman of Stepstone, the company that developed the Objective C language. He is also a former

IBM vice president, responsible for object-oriented consulting and building IBM's business in the OO domain. This is one of the few books that actually discusses the empirical evidence associated with OO projects. It is a useful book for project managers and developers too. This is a rare OO book that includes quantified data on OO productivity and quality, as opposed to just making broad and sweeping claims. Interestingly, the book uses function points as the metric for measuring OO results. Unfortunately, the results are only presented at the level of complete projects, as opposed to getting down to the level of activity-based costs. Thus it is difficult to replicate the author's data. In spite of this flaw, the book is moving in a useful direction and is one of the best managerial introductions to the OO paradigm.

Muller, Monika and Abram, Alain (editors); *Metrics in Software Evolution;* R. Oldenbourg Vertag GmbH, Munich, Germany; ISBN 3-486-23589-3; 1995.

This is an interesting book and also represents an interesting research collaboration between Canada and Germany. The German National Center for Information Technology (GMD) and the Computer Research Institute of Montreal (CRIM) have collected a number of essays by various authors, and assembled them into a significant book on both measurement and the usage of function points in a business and industrial context. What sets this book apart from the usual academic mode of theory without empirical data is the inclusion of a number of case studies from industry, such as one from Volkswagen from the German side and the Trillium project of Bell Canada on the Canadian side. Since metrics research is now a global topic, it is very useful to U.S. software project managers to gain a perspective of how their colleagues in Canada and Europe are using metrics and function points.

Multiple authors; *Rethinking the Software Process;* (CD-ROM); Miller Freeman, Lawrence, KS; 1996.

This is a new CD-ROM book collection jointly produced by the book publisher, Prentice Hall, and the journal publisher, Miller Freeman. This CD-ROM disk contains the full text and illustrations of five Prentice Hall books: *Assessment and Control of Software Risks* by Capers Jones; *Controlling Software Projects* by Tom DeMarco; *Function Point Analysis* by Brian Dreger; *Measures for Excellence* by Larry Putnam and Ware Myers; and *Object-Oriented Software Metrics* by Mark Lorenz and Jeff Kidd. In addition, the CD-ROM contains more than 30 articles from *Software Development* magazine. As the 1996 version of this bibliography is being prepared, the CD-ROM has been announced but is not yet available. The advertised price of $59.50 for five complete books and a large set of journal articles is quite attractive. The hard-cover versions of the books alone would total almost $200.

Putnam, Lawrence H.; *Measures for Excellence—Reliable Software On Time, Within Budget;* Yourdon Press–Prentice Hall, Englewood Cliffs, NJ; ISBN 0-13-567694-0; 1992; 336 pages.

Larry Putnam is the originator of the well-known SLIM software cost estimating tool. He is also a respected management consultant and the chairman of Quantitative Software Management (QSM). This book covers Larry's view of software metrics, with some interesting examples of the Rayleigh curve as it applies to software. Lord Rayleigh, a pioneering British physicist of the early part of the century, derived an interesting curve that approximates the growth patterns of many natural phenomena. Larry Putnam found that Rayleigh curves could also be applied to software projects. The most notable aspect of Rayleigh curves for software is the imbalance between effort and schedules. Attempts to compress schedules tend to drive up the effort to sometimes unmanageable levels.

Rubin, Howard; *Software Benchmark Studies For 1995;* Howard Rubin Associates, Pound Ridge, NY; 1995.

Dr. Howard Rubin received a contract from the Canadian government to compare their software costs and quality against other countries. Ed Yourdon, the well-known author and consultant, also participated in this study since he has traveled to more than 40 countries and has contacts all over the world. This is one of the few international surveys to include empirical productivity and quality data using function points. It overlaps an earlier 1993 study by Jones cited elsewhere in this bibliography: *Software Quality and Productivity Today—The Worldwide Perspective* (IS Management Group). It is exciting that enough data now exists so that international studies can be attempted, even if the results are preliminary rather than definitive. Now that this form of research has started, it can be expected to continue and expand in the future.

Software Productivity Consortium; *The Software Measurement Guidebook;* International Thomson Computer Press, Boston, MA; ISBN 1-850-32195-7; 1995; 308 pages.

This book has a large collection of authors and contributors, and hence tends to be varied in tone and content from chapter to chapter. The overall sponsor is the Software Productivity Consortium, which originated about 10 years ago as an early attempt to improve the software performance of the military and defense community. Hence, the Consortium is located in Herndon, Virginia, in the heart of the United States government and military world. It is important to remember the military emphasis of the Consortium, because some of the approaches and methods discussed in this book are seldom encountered in the civilian sector. For example, the discussion on software cost estimating mentions only a small sample of tools aimed at military projects such as COCOMO and SLIM, while totally ignoring 40 or so commercial software estimating tools used by civilians such as Bridge, BYL, CHECKPOINT, CA Estimacs, and dozens more.

While this book will probably be of interest to military and defense software managers, it is a bit too narrow and slanted to appeal to software managers in the civilian world, such as those in banking, insurance, commercial software, or most other non-military domains. Books with civilian coverage such as Kan's *Metrics and Models in Software Engineering* (Addison Wesley, 1995) or Jones' *Applied Software Measurement* (McGraw Hill, 1991) might have more appeal to the civilian sector. However, the Software Productivity Consortium does discuss function point metrics, and that has a very broad appeal to all software domains.

Symons, Charles R.; *Software Sizing and Estimating—Mk II FPA;* John Wiley & Sons, Chichester, England; ISBN 0-471-92985-9; 1991; 200 pages.

Charles Symons is a well-known British management consultant and a partner in the consulting company of Nolan & Norton. Charles was an early pioneer in the usage of function point metrics, but was dissatisfied with some of the results he achieved with the original Albrecht and IBM version. Therefore Symons developed an alternative form of function point metric which he termed "Mark II function points." The Mark II method includes counts of entities and relationships, and differs in other respects as well from the U.S. form of function point. Usage of the Mark II method is concentrated in the United Kingdom, but is also found in Canada, Hong Kong, and other countries as well. By interesting coincidence, U.S. function points and British Mark II function points tend to produce results that differ by approximately the same amount as the difference between U.S. gallons and Imperial gallons.

Section 6: Defect Prevention

The topic of defect prevention is not as well covered in the quality literature as defect removal, testing, tools, etc. Among the most powerful forms of defect prevention is that of software reusability.

Gause, Donald C. and Weinberg, Gerald M.; *Exploring Requirements—Quality Before Design;* Dorset House, New York, NY; ISBN 0-932633-13-7; 1989; 320 pages.

Don Gause and Jerry Weinberg have tackled one of the tough defect prevention topics head-on, and done a very good job too. Software requirements are often ambiguous and can change more than 3% every month! This book deals with a number of quality approaches to minimizing the risk of requirements destroying the project.

Maguire, Steve; *Debugging the Development Process;* Microsoft Press, Redmond, WA; 1994; 225 pages.

It is always interesting to read books that deal with how real companies do things. Steve Maguire works for Microsoft, and has written a number of books that describe various aspects of Microsoft's development methods. This book deals with Microsoft's quality assurance, defect prevention, and testing approaches.

Morrison, Paul; *Flow Based Programming;* Van Nostrand Reinhold, New York, NY; ISBN 0-442-1771-5; 1994; 316 pages.

Quality managers are urged not to be thrown off by the title. This is an excellent book on the foundations of software reusability, which has the greatest potential for preventing software defects of any known technology. Paul Morrison worked at IBM's Toronto research lab, and is one of the pioneers in software reuse. Although the object-oriented (OO) paradigm is currently getting the most publicity about software reuse, the OO approach was not the first and may not be the last software engineering method to deal with reusable software artifacts. Morrison deals with the fundamental underpinnings of reuse, and then shows how various approaches such as the OO approach have utilized a few or many of these underpinnings. This is a thoughtful book on an important topic.

Wood, Jane and Silver, Denise; *Joint Application Design; (2nd edition);* IEEE Press, Los Alamitos, CA; 1995; ISBN 0-471-04299-4; 416 pages.

Canada has been the origin of a number of interesting software quality approaches, such as joint application design (JAD) and flow-based programming, both of which originated at IBM's Toronto software laboratory. This is a useful primer to the JAD approach, which has developed into one of the most pervasive and effective ways of gathering software user requirements. This is a useful book on an important aspect of defect prevention.

Section 7: Non-Test Defect Removal

This section includes books on design reviews, code inspections, and other forms of static defect removal that are performed prior to testing, or on materials (such as manuals) where machine-based testing is infeasible. Since formal inspections have the highest defect removal efficiency of any known category of defect removal, this is a major topic.

Gilb, Tom, and Graham, Dorothy; *Software Inspections;* Addison Wesley, Reading, MA; 1993; 471 pages.

Although formal software inspections were invented in the 1960s by Michael Fagan and colleagues at IBM's programming laboratory in Kingston, NY, Tom Gilb has become one of the most enthusiastic supporters of the concept. Tom has a global consulting practice centering on his home office in Norway, but spanning the entire software world. Tom is a popular speaker and author, and his book on inspections is an excellent introduction to an important quality topic. Formal inspections remain among the most efficient and effective forms of quality control even after more than 35 years of usage.

Weinberg, Dr. Gerald, and Friedman, Daniel; *Handbook of Walkthroughs, Inspections, and Technical Reviews;* Dorset House Press, New York, NY; 1990; 450 pages.

Software design reviews and code inspections are two of the most efficient and effective defect removal operations in the entire software world. This useful primer by Jerry Weinberg and Daniel Friedman is a good introduction to the topics. The book is written in a question and answer format, and covers many practical aspects of software reviews and inspections.

Wheeler David A.; Brylcznski, Bill; and Meeson, Reginald; *Software Inspection—An Industry Best Practice;* IEEE Computer Society Press, Los Alamitos, CA; 1996; ISBN 0-8186-7430-0; 325 pages.

Software design and code inspections are finally starting to be recognized as "best practices" in the most favorable sense of the phrase; i.e., they really work based on solid empirical data. This new book is a useful addition to the software quality literature since it provides additional tutorial information and some background data that can be used to justify the use of inspections.

Section 8: Testing Methods

This section contains discussions of a number of books on software testing. It is interesting that so important a topic is actually rather sparsely represented in the software literature, although some of the books that are available are very good indeed.

Beizer, Boris, *Black Box Testing,* IEEE Computer Society Press, Los Alamitos, CA; 1995; ISBN 0-471-12094-4; 320 pages.

Boris Beizer is a prolific author and speaker on software testing topics. His background is in the domain of large and complex real-time systems, so his books on testing are usually "industrial strength" books aimed at serious testing by professional test personnel. This new book deals with a topic that has been under reported: black box testing, or deriving test cases from the external requirements and specifications of a software product.

Beizer, Boris, *Software Testing Techniques,* International Thomson Computer Press, Boston, MA.

Testing books come in various "flavors" based on the industrial background of the authors. Beizer's background includes systems and military software and the testing of very large systems in the 100,000 function point range. It is hard to find a book on testing of large systems that is more complete than Beizer's. Any test or quality assurance personnel dealing with large systems will find Beizer's books a welcome and practical addition to their libraries.

Dyer, Michael, *The Cleanroom Approach to Quality Software Development Techniques,* John Wiley & Sons, New York, NY; 1992.

The clean-room approach was developed by the late Dr. Harlan Mills and his colleagues at IBM Gaithersburg. It was originally used for large-scale systems software, where it apparently gave excellent results. As discussed earlier in my book, the clean-room approach is uncertain for applications with highly volatile requirements such as management information systems. Also, other authors have challenged some of the fundamental assumptions. Readers are urged to explore the clean-room concept for themselves, and Dyer's book is a solid introduction to an interesting if controversial topic. Testing books come in various "flavors" and the clean-room flavor is quite unlike most other testing methods since it uses statistical-based testing to emulate usage patterns.

Kaner, C., Falk, J., and Nguyen, HG; *Testing Computer Software;* International Thomson Computer Press; Boston, MA; ISBN 0-442-01361-2.

As already discussed, testing books come in various "flavors." The flavor of this book is how small commercial software companies with less than 100 people go about testing software. It is interesting to compare books by testers from various industries and see how differently the same topic is discussed. This book concentrates on testing of software that is less than 2,500 function points in size.

Mosley, Daniel J.; *The Handbook of MIS Application Software Testing;* Yourdon Press–Prentice Hall; Englewood Cliffs, NJ; ISBN 0-13-907007-9; 1993; 354 pages.

The testing "flavor" of this book is internal information systems which companies build for their own usage. Mosley is both a good writer and an experienced tester, and also a former academic. This book is a useful compendium of MIS testing approaches. However, when reading books on testing that represent different kinds of software and different industries, it is fascinating to see how differently they approach common problems.

Myers, Glenford; *The Art of Software Testing;* Wiley Interscience, New York, NY; 1979.

Glen Myers is something of a polymath who has made contributions in a number of diverse technical fields. For software, he was one of the original developers of the structured design and development methods, and the author of one of the classic books on software testing. Although Myers' book on the art of testing is probably the oldest book on the subject, it remains the most widely cited reference in the modern testing literature. Almost every other author on testing includes a comparison of how his or her approach is congruent or divergent from the patterns first put forth by Glen Myers. The "flavor" of Myers concept is how to test large and complex software systems such as IBM's operating systems and systems software.

Section 9: User-Satisfaction Methods

This section discusses methods for exploring and evaluating user-satisfaction. Of all software quality topics, this one and the next (post-release quality control) have the fewest books available.

Lindgaard, G.; *Usability Testing and System Evaluation;* International Thomson Computer Press, Boston, MA; ISBN 0-412-46100-5; 416 pages.

There are comparatively few books available on testing from the point of view of how clients use software. This book, by an Australian author, deals with how human beings interact with software, and how to judge the effectiveness of the interface approaches.

Naumann, Earl and Giel, Kathleen; *Customer Satisfaction Measurement and Management;* ASQC Press, Milwaukee, WI; 1995; ISBN 0-538-84439; 457 pages.

There are comparatively few books available on measuring customer satisfaction, so this one is useful even though it does not deal specifically with software. The book is something of a mix of a primer and a methodology manual, and it includes some supporting software tools for evaluating customer satisfaction survey forms.

Pardee, William J.; *To Satisfy and Delight Your Customer;* Dorset House, New York, NY; ISBN 0-932633-35-8; 1996; 304 pages.

This is an interesting book about customer satisfaction, but it is not about software customer satisfaction specifically. Pardee has developed some general guidelines for exploring and measuring user-satisfaction that can be applied to software, hardware, or even to the construction of golf courses! The fact that a leading software publisher has included this volume is a sign that some of the topics are relevant to the software community. The book is interesting and thought-provoking.

Section 10: Post-Release Quality Control

This section discusses books that deal with quality after a software application is released to customers. This topic is severely under reported in the software quality literature, and indeed maintenance has long been a neglected topic for software engineering in general.

Arthur, Jay; *Software Evolution—The Software Maintenance Challenge;* John Wiley & Sons, New York, NY; 1988; ISBN 0-471-62871-9; 254 pages.

Jay Arthur points out that the word "maintenance" is distasteful to many software managers, so he used the word "evolution" to encompass all of the forms of change which occur to software projects once they are initially released. This is a useful broad-band book that deals with the major sources of post-release software changes; i.e., corrective maintenance or fixing bugs; adaptive maintenance or moving to new platforms; perfective maintenance or adding new features, and so on. As might be expected, the quality of aging software becomes more and more important, and Arthur discusses this topic in some depth. This book is broad rather than deep, but provides a useful introduction to many key topics.

Martin, James and McClure, Carma; *Software Maintenance: The Problem and Its Solutions;* Prentice Hall, Englewood Cliffs, NJ; ISBN 0-13-822361-0; 1983; 512 pages.

James Martin and Carma McClure are both excellent writers and speakers, whose work has done a great deal to popularize software topics. In this book they address the problems of maintenance, including post-release quality. As with all of their books, the prose style is easy and the coverage is broad.

Zvegintzov, Nicholas; *Software Management Technology Reference Guide;* Dorset House, New York, NY; ISBN 1-884521-01-0; 1994; 240 pages.

Nicholas Zvegintzov has been a pioneer in a number of topics. He was among the first to recognize that software maintenance would grow almost uncontrollably. He is also among the first to realize that software project management is a critical topic, perhaps even more critical than software engineering itself, and that quality was a key management responsibility. This book is an attempt to consolidate information on some of the tools and approaches that impact software management and also quality. Nicholas is an excellent writer, although sometimes acidic in his side comments. This book contains a considerable amount of useful information for the software management and quality communities by an author who is a world expert in post-release maintenance and quality control.

SOFTWARE PUBLISHING AND DATA SOURCE CONTACTS

One of the frequently asked questions (FAQ) which the author receives from clients is "Where can I buy ... book." This listing contains contact information for major software publishing companies.

However, since bookstores rather than publishers usually sell books to individuals, this listing also includes a small sample of retail book stores that specialize in software books: Computer Literacy, Single Source, and SoftPro. There are hundreds of other book stores, but these three usually carry software project management books including those by the author (Capers Jones); they have extensive catalogs of software titles; and they also have international mail services so they can ship books essentially anywhere. Both Computer Literacy and SoftPro have stores in more than one city. However, only the main or headquarters location is listed here.

Since software project managers use information that comes from reports and consulting studies as well as information in book form, this listing also includes contact information for software information providers such as Gartner Group and Meta Group.

As more and more companies begin to use World Wide Web home pages on the Internet, any listing of contact information now needs to include Web addresses. This bibliography includes the Web address of those organizations that are known to have them. However, hundreds of companies are migrating to the Web every week.

Addison Wesley 1 Jacob Way Reading, MA 01867	Phone 617-944-3700
Applied Computer Research (ACR) P.O. Box 82266 Phoenix, AZ 85071-2266	Phone 602-995-5929
American Society of Quality Control (ASQC) 611 East Wisconsin Avenue P.O. Box 3005 Milwaukee, WI 53201-3005	Phone 414-272-8575
Artech House 685 Canton Street Norwood, MA 02062	Phone 617-769-9750
Auerbach Press One Penn Plaza New York, NY 10119	Phone 212-971-5000
Cahners Publishing Company 275 Washington Street Newton, MA 02158-1630	Phone 617-630-3900
Computer Literacy Bookshops 2590 North First Street San Jose, CA 95131	Phone 408-435-0744
Culpepper 7000 Peachtree Dunwoody Road Building 10 Atlanta, GA 30328	Phone 404-668-0616

Cutter Information Corp.   Phone 617-648-8702
37 Broadway, Suite 1
Arlington, MA 02174-5552

Dorset House   Phone 212-620-4053
353 W. 12th Street
New York, NY 10014

Gartner Group   Phone 203-964-0096
56 Top Gallan Road
P.O. Box 10212
Stamford, CT 06904-2212

G.P. Putnam's Sons
200 Madison Avenue
New York, NY 10016

IEEE Press   Phone 908-562-3969
445 Hoes Lane
P.O. Box 1331
Piscataway, NJ 08855-1331

IEEE Computer Society Press   Phone 714-821-8380
10662 Los Vaqueros Circle
P.O. Box 3014
Los Alamitos, CA 90720

Information Systems Management Group   Phone 800-748-6679
5841 Edison Place
Carlsbad, CA 92008

International Function Point Users Group   Phone 614-895-7130
(IFPUG)
Blendonview Office Park
5008-28 Pine Creek Drive
Westerville, OH 43081-4899

International Society of Paramteric Analysis   Phone 301-353-1840
(ISPA)
P.O. Box 1056
Germantown, MD 20875

International Standards Organization (ISO)   Phone +44 22 749 01 11
ISO Central Secretariat,
1, rue de Varembe
Case postale 56,
CH-1211 Geneve
Switzerland

International Thomson Computer Press   Phone 617-695-1419
20 Park Plaza, 13th Floor
Boston, MA 02116

John Wiley & Sons   Phone 212-850-6000
605 Third Avenue
New York, NY 10158-6000

McGraw Hill   Phone 212-337-4096
Professional and Reference Division   http://mcgraw.infor.com:5000
11 West 19th
New York, NY 10011

Meta Group   Phone 203-973-6700
208 Harbor Drive (P.O. Box 120061)
Stamford, CT 06912-0061

Microsoft Press   Phone 206-882-8080
One Microsoft Way
Redmond, WA 98052-6399

Ovum Ltd.   Phone 071 255 2670
7 Rathbone Street
London W1P 1AF
England

Prentice Hall   Phone 201-592-2498
113 Sylvan Avenue   http://www.prenhall.com
Englewood Cliffs, NJ 07632

Prima Publishing   Phone 916-624-5718
P.O. Box 1260MB
Rocklin, CA 95677

Productivity Press   Phone 503-235-0600
P.O. Box 13390
Portland, OR 97213-0390

Project Management Institute   Phone 610-734-3330
130 South State Road
Upper Darby, PA 19082

QED Information Systems   Phone 617-237-5656
P.O. Box 82-181
Wellsley, MA 02181

SIGS Books, Inc.   Phone 212-242-7447
71 West 23rd, Third Floor   http://www.sigs.com
New York, NY 10010

SingleSource   Phone 904-268-8639
3000-2 Hartley Road
Jacksonville, FL 32257

Software Engineering Institute (SEI)   Phone 412-268-7700
Carnegie Mellon University   http://www.sei.cmu.edu
Pittsburgh, PA 15213-3890

Software Productivity Research, Inc.   Phone 617-273-0140
One New England Executive Park   http://www.spr.com
Burlington, MA 01803

Software Technology Support Center   Phone 801-775-2054
United States Air Force
7278 Fourth Street
Hill AFB, Utah 84056-5205

SoftPro Bookstore   Phone 617-273-2499
112 Mall Road   http://www.softproeast.com/softpro
Burlington, MA 01803-5300

Van Nostrand Reinhold   Phone 212-254-3232
115 Fifth Avenue
New York, NY 10003

INDEX

Index   491